TWENTY-FIRST CENTURY GRAIL
THE QUEST FOR A LEGEND

Andrew Collins

First published in 2004 by

Virgin Books
Thames Wharf Studios
Rainville Road
London W6 9HA

ISBN 1 85227 1396
Typeset by TW Typesetting, Plymouth, Devon
Printed and bound by CPD Wales

CONTENTS

LIST OF PLATES

27. Graham Phillips inside the caves at Hawkstone Park in Shropshire.
28. Illustration from the manuscript *Aleph,* dated 1802 and written by Archarion, a German Rosicrucian.
29. Sue Collins and Richard Ward standing by St Frideswide's shrine in Christchurch Cathedral, Oxford.
30. Antique key with magical sigils unearthed close to St Margaret's Well, Binsey.
31. Heraldic shield showing three crowned female heads above an ox crossing a ford, as found on the pulpit in Binsey's church.

Plate 1 reproduced by kind permission of the OTO.

Plates 2, 5, 6, 8, 13, 17, 18, 19, 20, 23, 25, 26, 27, 29, 30, 31, 32 copyright © Andrew Collins

Plates 4, 7 and 22 reproduced by kind permission of the Bridgeman Art Library, London

Author photograph, inside flap of rear cover © Sue Collins.

In some cases it has not been posssible to establish the copyright ownership of illustrations. Holders of copyright pictures used without permission should contact the publishers.

LIST OF FIGURES

Figures 3, 6, 8, 9 with thanks to Rodney Hale.

Figure 4, with thanks to the OTO.

*This book is dedicated to Graham Phillips,
friend to the Cosmic Joker.*

ACKNOWLEDGMENTS

My greatest thanks and love go out to my wife Sue, for her invaluable help and support in the preparation of this book. I would also like to thank Graham Phillips and Richard Ward, without whom this book would not have been written; Lynn Picknett and Clive Prince, who have supplied me with help and support with various areas of research; SheerFaith, for the extraordinary cover image; Yuri Leitch, for his research on the Franks Casket and our heated debates on the origins of the Grail; David Southwell, for his continued inspiration and ideas; Rodney Hale, for his help with the maps and illustrations; Catherine Hale, for her research and translation work on my behalf; Graham and Jodi Russell, for permission to quote lyrics for '22 Years of Nothing'; Paul Weston, for creating the Avalonian aeon in Glastonbury; Kenneth Grant, for his valuable time, patience and encouragement; John Michell, for his wonderful work on sacred places; Laurence Gardner, for his continued help on awkward questions; Nigel Foster, for his never-failing wit; Niven Sinclair, for his continued networking and support; Kerri Sharp, for her support of my work; and Jonathan Harris, for believing in me.

In addition to this I would like to thank the following people: Rosemary Arscott, for her archaeological help; Andrew Baker, for his help on Shugborough and Thomas Wright of Durham; Leslie Daniels, for his notes on the history of Headcorn; David Mycoff, for his help on the Magdalene in France; Ken Tullett, for his research papers on Stephen de Staplebridge; Geoff Wilson, for welcoming us into his home at Templecombe; Eddie Lark, for the English translation of the Statutes of Roncelin and commentaries on the same; Ian Lawton, Michael Carmichael, Chris Ogilvie-Herald, Crichton Miller, Nigel Skinner-Simpson, Marcus Williamson and the rest of the No-Namers, for their continued help and friendship; also for the manuscript readers Michael Staley, Caroline Wise, Liz and John Treadwell, Amber McCauley, Rodney Hale and Catherine Hale, for spotting mistakes and making suggestions. Finally, can I thank Matt and Lisa Adams, Michael Baigent, Ian Campbell, Simon and Kerry Dar, Jean Pierre Hortoland, Guy Patton, Gordon Service, Ann Smith, Colin and Kathy Stallard, Clive Harper and Bill Breeze and all the staff at Virgin Books.

Andrew Collins
Leigh-on-Sea
22 July 2004

You say you long for the Gral?
You foolish man – this I must deplore!
For no man can win the Gral.
Other than one who is acknowledged in heaven as destined for it.
This much I have to say about the Gral,
for I know it and have seen it with my own eyes.

– Wolfram von Eschenbach, *Parzival*

INTRODUCTION

Twenty-first Century Grail is not written like any ordinary book. Although it does contain copious amounts of historical fact, drawn from my extensive research into the origins of the Grail legend in medieval and early-Christian tradition, its first-hand narrative includes a whole range of personal experiences that led me, and those around me, to explore new clues and avenues of investigation by psychic means. As bizarre as it might seem, this involved the interpretation of many colourful dreams, the experiencing of waking visions, many seen through the imagination of the mind's eye, and the induction of trancelike occurrences in which two-way communication was obtained with alleged spirit entities, such as the notorious occultist Aleister Crowley.

I have no qualms about the validity of such supernatural experiences, and use them as tools to find answers that otherwise might never have been achieved through more mundane channels. Whereas nocturnal experiences, many the product of hypnagogic hallucinations, are not rare, and have been recorded by medical science, I have tried to advance this process and propose that the more mystically inspired dreams are the result of the deep subconscious mind, or even external influences, wishing to convey 'direct information' to the conscious brain. This is a matter of debate, and one to which there is no unanimous answer. People believe what they want or need to believe, and no matter how much proof is given one way or another, they are unlikely to change their view of such matters. The existence of paranormal experiences like those suggested by this book is something that can only be accepted by faith and/or experience.

The style in which the book is written insists on the unseen reality of such occurrences. As unscientific as this might sound, it is a fact that very similar dreams and visions have inspired humanity to make personal discoveries of immense significance on many occasions in the past. Indeed, the search for the Holy Grail is itself the most obvious symbol of the mystical quest.

In the works of ancient Greece and Rome, there exist accounts of heroes being guided by the voices of gods to find the armour and weapons of their great ancestors, which they must use in battle to ensure success. In Christian tradition, we read how gifted holy men were led by blinding visions to find sacred relics, most often the bones of saints and martyrs. The Maid of Orleans, Joan of Arc, that thorn in the side of the English during the medieval wars with France, was said to have been led by the saints to discover the whereabouts of a sword belonging to Charles Martel, the French warrior hero who saved his country from Moorish occupation several centuries beforehand. In Elizabethan times, it was the role of the magus or necromancer to find buried treasure through the invocation of helpful demons, which would be commanded to reveal its whereabouts – Queen Elizabeth's personal adviser Dr John Dee and his sidekick Edward Kelly are the most obvious individuals who come to mind.

In more recent times, so-called psychic archaeology has been responsible for the discovery of previously unknown sites of human occupation – the case of architect and historian Frederick Bligh Bond being the most classic example. In the 1890s he was invited by the Somerset Archaeological and Natural History Society to become the Director of Excavations at Glastonbury Abbey in southwest England. They were amazed at how quickly he was able to uncover the site of previously 'lost' chapels of this great medieval edifice, until they discovered that he was being guided in his work by automatic writing received via his friend, the medium John Alleyne, who claimed it derived from the long-dead monks of the abbey.

The use of remote viewing to obtain information unavailable through more orthodox processes is a subject that was seriously considered during the 1970s and 1980s by the United States Government, most obviously for possible military applications, such as surveillance in hostile territories. This is no secret, nor was it part of some 'black operation' project, and the success rate of those receivers employed for these purposes was generally very high.

Yet by far the most significant belief in the power of the mind to achieve physical results, including the retrieval of hidden objects, was to be found until comparatively recently in former Tibet. Particularly among the *nyingma-pa* monastic sect, and the followers of the secret doctrine known as *dzogchen*, there existed a complete magical system whereby talented, and often 'wild', monks received mystical dreams and visions in which they would find themselves in contact with *dakinis*. These are helpful spirits who provide instructions on how to obtain *termas*, 'hidden treasure', thought to have been concealed when Buddhism first entered Tibet some 1,300 years ago. Such 'treasure' takes two forms: mind *termas*, sacred scripts which appear in vision and are written down by conventional means; and physical *termas*, which are a whole different ball game. Here instructions would be given to the prospective *terton*, or 'treasure finder', in order that he might embark on an often lengthy journey in which he would be guided to a specific location. Having found it, he would be required to confront and win over a so-called *naga* spirit, the guardian of the *terma* in question, who usually took the form of a serpent-woman. If all went well, he would be allowed to dig up the treasure, which might take the form of either a religious scroll, conveying lost teachings of early Buddhism, or a holy relic, usually a dagger, a meditative tool or a statue of a deity. Such holy objects were both revered in the monasteries and used for religious practices.

The *terma* tradition of Tibet is at least a thousand years old. Whole books have been written by monks and lamas on the different methods used by *tertons* to retrieve hidden artefacts, and although these practices were relatively unknown in the West until fairly recently, they match exactly many of the thought processes employed by the people featured in this book to achieve similar results. These, as you will see, include the discovery of objects, concealed by persons unknown, and located, described and retrieved through apparent paranormal experiences. It is a subject I have referred to as 'psychic questing' – a term I coined after the discovery through psychic means in 1979 of an antique sword in the Midlands of England.

This approach to the mysteries of life is entirely alien to conventional science, for it accepts without question the existence of other worlds, occupied by supernatural denizens available for communication through dreams, meditations and ritual practices. Even though such unorthodox activities might seem like the actions of deluded optimists, it certainly makes for an exciting lifestyle and entertaining reading. I can honestly say that as a much-respected alternative historian, who is the author of several acclaimed books, I have achieved incredible results through psychic questing. Nothing more can be said to the reader other than to suspend disbelief for the duration of the book in order to absorb a world which, although appearing at times to be pure fantasy, is a true account of very real events which occurred in England during our own time.

Those wishing to learn more about psychic questing should go to www.andrewcollins.com or write to Andrew Collins, PO Box 189, Leigh-on-Sea, Essex SS9 1NF, UK.

1. PERDURABO CALLS

On **Thursday, 21 November 2001**, Richard Ward, 37, an assistant manager of a branch of a well-known builders' merchant in the southeast of England, had a dream that was to change the course of his life. He was being yanked out of his body by an unseen force and thrust through a swirling rush of darkness from this world into the next. The blackness opened like an iris in a camera to reveal the occasional flicker of orange light coming from burning torches mounted in small, soot-stained niches cut out of the cold, damp walls. He was deep inside a cave, moving purposefully along a corridor hewn out of solid rock by ancient hands, navigating bends and avoiding side chambers that were of no concern to him.

Richard had been brought here to witness one thing, and one thing alone – a life-sized statue of a seated figure that now loomed out of the shadows before him. Its chiselled face was sullen, and on its head were tiny horns giving it the appearance of being a crudely fashioned devil. Yet the way it sat, with hands cupped on its bent knees, like some enthroned Japanese Mikado, suggested it had another identity altogether.

His gaze now focused on the hewn-out alcove behind the statue that began to evaporate, exposing a concealed tunnel from which emerged a very tall man. He carried a long, slim sword and was dressed in close-fitting leather armour over a red singlet like that of a soldier. His short curly hair was red also, as were the ruddy cheeks that seemed to hide his pale complexion. Yet all about him was an intense golden aura that gave away his identity, for somehow Richard knew that this was Bartzabel, angel of Mars.

Without any introduction, Bartzabel raised his sword and exclaimed: 'Behold, Baphomet, the Baptiser of Wisdom,' referring to the great stone statue beside him. It was accompanied by a growing sense that some kind of force was to be conferred on him through the power of baptism; yet not by water, *but by fire*. Suddenly, the angel's sword was being pushed hard against his chest, as if prompting him to swear an oath of allegiance, as in a Masonic ritual. But the experience simply left him dizzy and disorientated, as the whole scene collapsed in on itself. When the horned statue started to transform into God knows what, all the angel would say was: 'Perdurabo's spirit has called you.'

Regaining consciousness in the warm comfort of his bed, Richard could still not entirely escape from the subterranean realm in which he had found himself. His head was spinning as he attempted to sling back the duvet cover and get out of bed, retching as if he was about to be sick. These dreams were doing him no good whatsoever. Yet it was the unfortunate price he paid for being psychic, able to merge with the world of the unknown on a frighteningly regular basis. He reminded himself of this, as he tried to regain his senses and became aware of his partner Pandora sleeping peacefully next to him.

Richard thought about the caves, and the horned statue, which were strangely familiar. He had been there before, he was sure, and it took a few moments to recall where they were and why he had gone there. Then he remembered. Yes, of course, they were the caves at Hastings in Sussex, visited with friends some years back. He had noticed the statue then, and registered how odd it looked. Yet he had not thought about the place since that time, and had no reason to dream about it now. Indeed, the impression left in his mind was that he had witnessed the caves as they must have looked in the past, when the place was perhaps used for ritualistic purposes by some Templar-linked group. Baphomet was the name given to the idol worshipped by the medieval order of fighting monks known as the Knights Templar. Yet what had they to do with the horned statue in Hastings Caves?

What seemed infinitely more important was the appearance in the dream of Bartzabel, an angel that governed the astrological influence of the planet Mars. He had referred to the statue as Baphomet and stated that 'Perdurabo's spirit' had called him. Perdurabo was the name adopted by notorious English occultist Aleister Crowley (1875–1947) on entering the London temple of the Hermetic Order of the Golden Dawn, a magical society founded in 1888. Following his chequered career, during which time he excelled as a mountaineer, poet, author, philosopher, Freemason, great magus, chess master and drug fiend, Crowley retired to Hastings and spent his final two years in a boarding house just outside the popular seaside town. Since the caves must have been open to the public then, as they are today, maybe he had visited them and seen the statue for himself.

Richard now began to rationalise everything he had imagined in the powerful dream that was already fading from his thoughts. He knew about the caves. He knew about the statue, and he knew about Baphomet. Thus there was every reason to dismiss any significance in the experience, since it contained themes already familiar to him. But a nagging doubt suggested otherwise. Over the past week or so he had been glimpsing flashes in his mind of a cave opening on a wooded hillside, and a figure in red emerging from its interior holding a sword.

In the popular Hebrew system of numerology known as gematria, Bartzabel was associated with the number 325, an auspicious coincidence since 21 November, that day, was the 325th day of the year. More significantly, on 9 May 1910 Crowley had conducted a ritual to invoke Bartzabel in the company of his lover Leila Waddell and his friend, the poet Victor Neuberg, at the Dorset home of Commander G M Marston RN. So successful was this magical operation that Marston had recommended that Crowley perform the whole thing commercially on stage. It resulted in public performances later that same year of the so-called 'Rites of Eleusis' – invocations of each of the seven planets of the ancient world – on consecutive Wednesday evenings at London's Caxton Hall, but whether any of this was relevant to what was happening now was quite another thing.

* * *

Friday, 22 November. Placing down the receiver after speaking to Richard, I looked at my hasty notes on the screen of the laptop and began forming them into sentences for an entry in the diary I kept on a more-or-less daily basis. The reference to Crowley's Rites of Eleusis was intriguing, for my partner Sue (now my wife) had dreamed she was on stage during a performance of Crowley's Rites of Eleusis only very recently. Thereafter she had begun experiencing other dreams and nocturnal visitations in which Crowley had seemed to make his presence known.

Richard is one of the most talented direct-information psychics I had ever had the privilege to work with. I had known him for over ten years and, during that time, we had become close friends, working together on various historical quests. Indeed, he is credited on the title page of my 1996 book *From the Ashes of Angels* for the 'additional research' he supplied during its writing.

The biggest question concerning Richard's nocturnal encounter was where any of this was leading. Was the statue in Hastings Caves really Baphomet, the idol adored by the medieval Knights Templar? Was it the product of some much more recent Templar rite attached to Freemasonry, or had it simply been carved on a whim for purely decorative purposes by some past owner of the caves?

THE KNIGHTS TEMPLAR

The Knights Templar had their beginnings in the year 1119 when nine knights, mostly French nobility from Champagne and Burgundy, made the decision to leave behind their wealth and riches and travel to Jerusalem. Their aim was to guard the pilgrim routes in and out of the ancient city against Saracen attack. As noble a venture as this might have seemed, it is a fact that these pious individuals spent the next nine years in seclusion, possibly even conducting excavations on the site of what was once considered to be King Solomon's Stables, close to what is today the al-Aqsa Mosque, near the Dome of the Rock. Afterwards, they returned to Europe and announced the foundation of a military order that was to become known as the Order of the Poor Fellow-Soldiers of Christ and the Temple of Solomon – the Knights Templar. Bernard of Clairvaux, the great ecclesiastical figure of his age, took the brotherhood under his wing, writing their rules, which he based on those of the Cistercian order. Finally, at the Council of Troyes in 1128/9 the Templars were officially recognised by the Pope. Norman lords from all over Europe flocked to join their ranks, giving up their wealth and estates to do so. Soon their duties were extended to include leading Christian Crusaders on the battlefield against the Islamic 'infidel'. They became the stuff of legend, riding two men on one horse where necessary, and vowing never to retreat unless the odds were more than three to one against. The Knights Templar were unique, becoming on the one hand fearless warriors protecting the roads of Christendom for pilgrims and, on the other, devout monks spending long hours each day in prayer and contemplation of God.

The Order established headquarters, known as preceptories or commandaries, throughout Europe and were granted properties, tithes and churches by thousands of wealthy landowners, including the Church of Rome. Over a period of nearly 200 years, the Templars grew to become the most powerful fighting force in Christendom, owing allegiance to no one but the Pope. Yet at dawn on Friday, 13 October 1307, the Templars in France, arguably their main centre of operation, were arrested unexpectedly at the command of the French king Philip the Fair, following secret negotiations with the Pope, Clement V, and accused of religious heresy and other trumped-up charges. In due course, their brothers in other countries were likewise arrested and questioned like their French counterparts.

Under torture, many of the knights confessed to vile crimes against Christianity, including spitting and trampling on the cross and denying the divinity of Christ. Some even admitted worshipping strange idols including a demon in the form of a cat,[1] and keeping a bearded head that spoke to them and mysteriously 'had the power of making them rich, and of causing the trees to flourish, and the earth to become fruitful'.[2] Some condemned Templars even dared speak its name – BAPHOMET – which scholars believed was a corruption of Mohammed, or Mahomet, due to the knights' clandestine interest in certain aspects of the Muslim faith. However, in the early nineteenth century an Austrian Orientalist named Baron Joseph von Hammer-Pürgstall (1776–1856) proposed that Baphomet derived its name from the Greek *bapho metis*, meaning 'baptiser of wisdom', a theory that has grown with popularity ever since that time. 'Baptiser of Wisdom' was the expression used by Bartzabel in Richard's dream, with the implication that Baphomet wished to confer on him some form of baptism through fire, presumably in readiness for something that lay ahead. What this meant, however, was uncertain, although more certain was Baphomet's association with the life of Aleister Crowley.

THE OTO

In 1910, the same year that he performed the invocation of Bartzabel, Crowley was initiated into a modern-day Templar organisation, founded in Germany at the beginning of the twentieth century. Known variously as the *Ordo Templi Orientis*, the Order of the Templars of the East, or the Order of the Oriental Templars, it is generally referred to by its acronym, the OTO. Although it was not strictly a Masonic organisation, its founders were mostly Freemasons who had received initiation into existing Templar rites. The Order was the creation of Dr Karl Kellner (1851–1905), an Austrian mystic who conceived of bringing together Indian Tantric sex practices and Arab Sufi teachings with Western-style Freemasonry, following a tour of the East where he had been inducted into many of its secret societies. Crowley had likewise spent time in the Orient, where he too studied yoga and Tantric sex magic, both of which were employed in his own occult rituals, described in veiled terms within his published works.

Crowley – who used to style himself the 'Beast 666', most probably to instil horror in the prudish Edwardian society in which he moved – was thus surprised when in 1913 he was paid a visit by Theodore Reuss, the then head of the OTO, who had initiated him into the Order three years beforehand. He turned up at his London residence requesting an audience. On gaining admittance, Reuss immediately began accusing Crowley of revealing the innermost secrets of the Order. Crowley denied any knowledge of the rituals practiced in its higher grades, a brushoff which resulted in a heated exchange where the two men nearly came to blows. Eventually cooler heads prevailed as Reuss, finally accepting Crowley's word, pleaded with him not to profane any more of the Order's secrets. This the occultist agreed to do, and the two men eventually conceived of the establishment of a British branch of the OTO to be called *Mysteria Mystica Maxima* (MMM), with Crowley at its head. At his subsequent investiture in Berlin, Crowley took the title Supreme and Holy King of Ireland, Iona and all the Britains and adopted the magical name 'Baphomet'.[3]

Crowley retained his distinguished role in the OTO throughout his life, rewriting many of its rituals to include themes borrowed from his own magical system, outlined in *Liber Al*, or 'The Book of the Law', a channelled work penned by him during psychic communications with his 'holy guardian angel' in Cairo during the spring of 1904.

Like other Templar rites of the eighteenth and nineteenth centuries, initiates of the OTO venerated Baphomet as a horned deity – part human, part goat – an amalgam best conjured in an invocative drawing executed by nineteenth-century French occultist Eliphas Levi (see fig. 1). Here an androgynous figure, with the head and legs of a goat, sits on a globe with one hand pointing upwards to an eclipsed sun and the other pointing downwards towards the crescent moon. Certainly, there was a similarity between the manner in which Baphomet was portrayed by neo-Templar organisations and the statue known to exist in the caves at Hastings. Yet would Crowley have been aware of its existence and, even if he was, why would Richard's mind have been drawn to the scene?

In the days that followed, I researched the history of Hastings Caves, which are also known as St Clement's Caves. Local historians believe they started out as natural fissures in the sandstone rock, which were later enlarged through excavation for the purpose of using the soft sandstone in glass manufacture. The caves receive their first published mention in 1786 within a letter to the *Gentleman's Magazine* from one Matthew Skinner, a visitor to the town. He proposed that they might once have been a hermitage or oratory, since a deeply incised, equal-armed cross was to be seen just inside the entrance doorway (it has since been destroyed).[4]

The entrance to the caves was blocked up sometime around 1811 by Edward Milward, the owner. Thirteen years later a man named John Scott gained permission from Mr Milward to enlarge its series of labyrinthine passages and cut a new entrance to the 'upper cavern'. They were finally opened to the public in July 1827 with full pomp and ceremony, amid a candlelit procession. After Mr Scott left Hastings, another local man, Joseph Golding, extended the existing caves and created the 43-metre-long 'Monks' Walk', which contains 23 pairs of pillared niches for candles. It was also around this time that two or three crude statues are said to have been carved from the soft sandstone,[5] one of which is identified as Napoleon.[6]

Dinner functions and society events became a regular occurrence in Hastings' fashionable subterranean world, which stretches beneath the sandstone cliffs for a distance of around 400 metres. Some say the caves were used as a military hospital for Wellington's troops during the Napoleonic Wars, although more likely is that they acted as an air-raid shelter during the Second World War. In 1946, when Crowley was in residence at Hastings, St Clement's Caves were converted for use as a dance hall and waxworks, and as late as 1975 a number of ships' figureheads were found hidden deep inside one of the caves' many side chambers, where they had been left some one hundred years beforehand.

Beyond the stark reality of the caves' known history, rumours persist that they were once used for 'devil worship'. Where such an idea originated is unclear, although it is likely to be connected with the presence of the horned statue in the so-called Chapel, an area of the caves said to be colder than anywhere else. Set in a niche between various corridors, it is difficult to understand its purpose or meaning. Yet what seems clear from the earliest town guides is that (a) it predates the other 'rude efforts of sculpture' present in the caves,[7] and (b) it has been identified as St Clement since at least 1833.[8] This suggested that there was a relationship between the statue and the caves' dedication to St Clement.

So how did the statue become associated with St Clement, Peter's third successor as Bishop of Rome who lived at the end of the first century? The easy answer is to assume that the caves are named after Hastings' Norman church of St Clement, the patron saint of sailors; the horned statue gaining its appellation from some confusion arising from its assumed role as guardian of the caves. But how did this confusion arise, especially as St Clement's only known symbol is the anchor? Was it simply because the original exit to the caves (now blocked up) was in the Old Town, close to St Clement's church?

I made further enquiries and established that as well as being the patron saint of sailors, St Clement was the saint of choice adopted by the Templar fleet. It also became clear that knights of the Order were stationed at Hastings' famous castle, founded immediately after the Battle of Hastings in 1066 by William the Conqueror, and located just a few hundred metres uphill from St Clement's Caves. Moreover, Knights Templar responsible for the foundation of a medieval round church dedicated to St Clement, close to the Essex Thameside town of Grays Thurrock, were closely linked with Hastings Castle, a realisation which convinced me that they were probably behind the dedication of St Clement's church, Hastings. If so, was the order responsible for the conversion of Hastings Caves into an 'oratory', dedicated to St Clement and used for religious purposes? Even if this were true, though, there was no reason to assume that the 'Baphomet' statue was fashioned by them, or that it explained why Richard was being drawn to the caves. For the moment, all we could do was wait and see what might happen next.

Fig. 1. Nineteenth-century French occultist Eliphas Levi's haunting impression of the androgynous Baphomet, idol of the Knights Templar.

2. THE CUP OF BABALON

In sleep, Richard again found himself drawn uncontrollably to the caves at Hastings, which he entered through an open mouth on a steep wooded hillside. Darkened walls rushed past as he was led before the seated figure of Baphomet, illuminated by the dull orange glow cast by flaming torches. The air was stifling, and the place reeked of dampness.

This time there was no angel of Mars emerging from the solid rock beyond the vibrant stone-carved figure, simply the occultist Aleister Crowley walking into view out of nowhere. Richard recognised his stern-looking features and rather hypnotic eyes. Appearing to be around sixty years of age, Crowley sported a shirt and bow tie with a tweed jacket and matching trousers. This was no chance meeting, for Crowley seemed to be expecting him, even though the man simply stood there in silence waiting for Richard to react to the forced situation.

'Why here?' Richard found himself asking at last. 'Why bring me here?' He needed to know what was so important about this place.

Crowley smiled knowingly. 'You want to know why you have been brought here?' he teased. 'I'll tell you why. It is the legend of the Holy Grail, my own Cup of Babalon.'

The Holy Grail? What had that to do with Hastings? Richard was confused.

No words came. Just the overwhelming feeling of the presence here in the distant past of Knights Templar, and a passionate concern for a holy relic linked directly with the Grail, which Crowley wanted him to find. Yet Richard's thoughts now lingered on Crowley's identification of this sacred vessel as the Cup of Babalon. Babalon he knew was Crowley's take on the Whore of Babylon, the woman of St John's book of Revelation, who rides the seven-headed beast of the Apocalypse and holds a cup containing the blood of the saints and martyrs. Crowley perceived her to be not only a rather debauched personification of Venus, the Roman goddess of sex and love, but also the embodiment of everything pertaining to female sexual liberation. She was a modern goddess for a modern age, and to Crowley Babalon was the consort of Baphomet within the unique magical system he developed for the OTO, the cup her vulva and the wand of the magician his phallus to be brought together in rites of celebration. Crowley designed his own unique Tarot pack, and one card, 'Lust', shows Babalon astride the seven-headed beast holding aloft the golden chalice. For Crowley, she was the only denizen of the subconscious realms that could control this powerful force, which he saw as one aspect of Choronzon, the guardian of the abyss, the great void of inner space. This might be so, but why was Crowley implying that Hastings Caves were connected with the Holy Grail, his Cup of Babalon?

'It is for you to work out,' he responded, creating even more confusion in the psychic's inquisitive mind. 'Take the Baptism of Wisdom, and learn the *truth*.'

Richard then saw a female hand reaching down into the earth, her fingers searching and feeling until they made contact with the metal surface of a small silver-plated chalice. As she held it, something glistening oozed out of the cup – a snakelike line of blood that crept over the edge of the bowl and began slowly to flow down its outer surface, following the curves of a crudely drawn serpent. As more of the scene was revealed, he saw that the hand was that of a woman with red hair who, although he had never met her, he knew to be the psychic Helen Laurens. In 1979 she experienced a series of strange dreams about occult matters, and just a few months later had found herself in mental and visual communication with a spirit form that answered to the name Aleister Crowley.[9] As a consequence, she and Andrew Collins worked together for a short while before she disappeared from the scene, only to return again in 1989.[10] It was at Easter in that year that the two of them were led by psychic means to a secluded area in the churchyard at Ide Hill, near Sevenoaks in Kent, and here she recovered the chalice in question. It bore crudely scratched marks suggestive of a snake rising out of the liquid it might have contained, which then curled over the rim of the vessel. But why show Richard all this now? What possible significance might it have to Hastings Caves, Baphomet, or some search for the Holy Grail?

He needed to know more if he was to understand what was going on. Had Aleister Crowley ever written anything on this matter that might help him in his quest?

Crowley now held up a golden star of seven points, like some kind of visual aid a science teacher might use to explain the design of an atomic structure. It was utilised by Crowley as an abstract symbol for his concept of Babalon. Within its centre would be drawn two conjoining arcs representing the vulva, emphasising its female character.

What did this mean? Why show him this symbol?

Frater Perdurabo was not amused. With his powerful eyes fixed firmly on Richard, he began to huff and blow, as if becoming frustrated by the imbecility of this young mind. No matter how much Richard pleaded to know more, the long-dead occultist would not, or could not, say anything, forcing the psychic to lose his fragile grip of the situation. Very quickly Richard felt himself regaining a state of semiconsciousness as he eased out of his slumber, a miasma of imagery still whirling about in his busy mind, and the name of a book being repeated again and again: *Liber CLVI* ('Book 156').

Throwing back the bed covers, Richard noticed the time on the LCD display of the alarm clock. It was 04.20, two hours before he would have to get up and go to work. He thought about what had happened. Crowley appeared to be charging him – and by virtue of this Andrew and Sue also – with a search to find some sort of cup linked with the Holy Grail, seen in terms of his 'Cup of Babalon'. Even supposing that such a vessel existed, why should they be given the task of finding it? More importantly, what was Crowley doing acting as their guide? Surely, the vision of the Holy Grail as witnessed by the Knights of King

Arthur's Round Table derived from a sound Christian source, perhaps even God himself. Surely a notorious magician – once described in a celebrated legal case as 'the wickedest man in the world' – could not charge mortals like him with such a profound psychic quest. Not only did it seem particularly odd, but would they ever be able to trust his word? Would he ever tell the *truth*?

Then, as he stumbled downstairs into the kitchen and poured himself a glass of orange juice, Richard remembered that Crowley had held up the seven-pointed Star of Babalon, implying that it was some sort of clue to understanding the nature of the quest. Certainly, it was the symbol of his Lady Babalon, the Scarlet Woman, whom the occultist manifested through the licentious magical acts he performed in the company of a string of mistresses during his lifetime. Beyond this, however, Richard could not even begin to consider why the star might be important, other than to perhaps confirm Babalon's place in this story. *Liber CLVI* was most probably one of the works written by Crowley, although whether it was extant today was quite another thing. What he did know, however, is that the number 156 was attributed by Crowley to Babalon by means of the gematria system. Its letters, when changed into Hebrew, added up to this same amount. Thus *Liber CLVI* was presumably about Babalon.

THE MYSTERY OF THE GRAIL

That night I listened with genuine interest to Richard's account of his latest dream. I had no idea what to think. By far the best-known example of a visionary quest has to be the search for the Holy Grail. It is the subject of several romances written mostly in France around the end of the twelfth century and the beginning of the thirteenth century. The earliest ones[11] describe the *graal* (English 'Grail') as a wonder-working holy vessel used by Jesus to perform 'his mystery' at the Last Supper, described thus in the Gospel of Mark:

> And as they were eating, he took bread, and when he had blessed, he brake it, and gave to them, and said, 'Take ye: this is my body.' And he took a cup, and when he had given thanks, he gave to them: and they all drank of it. And he said unto them, 'This is my blood of the covenant, which is shed for many. Verily I say unto you, and I will no more drink of the fruit of the vine, until that day when I drink it new in the kingdom of God.'[12]

It was this same cup that the Grail romances tell us was afterwards removed by a Jew from the house in which the Last Supper had taken place and presented to Pontius Pilate, the Roman governor of Jerusalem. He in turn gave it to a 'soldier' named Joseph of Arimathea, a lesser-known disciple of Jesus, on the occasion that he asked for Jesus's body, who subsequently interred it in a private sepulchre. The vessel was then used by Joseph to collect drops of the *Saint Sang*, or 'Holy Blood' – that is, Jesus's blood – either as it fell from his wounds as he hung limply on the Cross, as is stated in some accounts, or as the body was being laid out in the sepulchre, as it says in others. Following the Resurrection, the Grail romances tell how Joseph was attacked by the Jews, who could not accept that Jesus was the Messiah prophesied in the scriptures. Thus they threw him in prison, where he languished without light, food or water for 42 years, until finally he was freed by the forces of the Emperor Vespasian during the sack of Jerusalem in AD 70.

Whilst in prison, Joseph survived by the power of the Grail alone, which was given to him by the ascended Christ. At this same time he was also taught the 'holy words . . . which are gentle and precious and gracious and touching [and] which are properly called the secrets of the Grail'.[13] Curiously, when this occurred, Jesus told Joseph that the vessel 'where my blood was collected from my body will be called a chalice, or cup (*calices*)', associating it with the vessel used in the Christian rite of the Eucharist (thanks-giving), the communion service or mass, which, along with baptismal initiation, has been at the heart of Christian ritual for the past 2,000 years.[14]

According to the romances, the Grail was placed on a table, mimicking that of the Last Supper, around which Joseph sat with eleven of his disciples (a twelfth place was left empty in memory of Jesus's betrayal by Judas). Alongside the chalice, a fish was placed, caught especially by Bron, or Hebron, Joseph's brother-in-law, and thereafter Joseph conducted the so-called 'service' or ceremony of the Grail. Afterwards, Bron adopted the name *Riche Pescheur*, the Rich Fisher, or Fisher King, in celebration of the fish he provided for the table of the Grail, at which time he also received into his care the holy vessel and learned the same 'holy words' that constitute the 'secrets of the Grail, imparted to him by Christ himself'. In time, Bron's wife gave birth to twelve children, one of whom, Alain, was destined to be the father of the principal Grail knight of the medieval romances, Sir Perceval. The whole party then travelled westwards, ending their journey in Britain, bringing with them the Grail, and for hundreds of years the Fisher King survived in his castle, even though he now suffered from a wound that would never heal, caused when a lance pierced his side.

During the mythical age of King Arthur – who in the medieval romances is based on folk tales from a much earlier era that became popular in France following the Norman conquest of 1066 – Britain is said to have become enchanted by a curse that caused it to become a wasteland. As a consequence, the Grail knights go in quest of the holy vessel, and one by one they each come upon the Castle of the Fisher King, where during a meal with the host they witness a procession in which the Grail is being carried by a maiden, while the lance that pierced Christ's side when on the Cross is carried by a youth. On the occasion that Sir Perceval – who, unknown to him, is the grandson/nephew of the Fisher King, depending on the version read – visits the Castle of the Grail he at first fails to ask the correct questions about the procession, which would have broken the spell imposed on the country, and cured the Fisher King of his wound. Yet on realising the consequences of his silence, he takes it upon himself to learn the mystery of the Grail, which he finally discovers is that it serves the father of the Fisher King (who is never mentioned before or afterwards in the account) each Good Friday with a single consecrated wafer, which miraculously appears within its bowl. In some of the romances,

Perceval's role is replaced by other knights such as Sir Gawain, Sir Lancelot and, eventually, the pure and perfect Sir Galahad.

The search for the Grail is the ultimate psychic quest, and so to be charged to find it was the greatest honour that could be bestowed upon any modern-day quester. Yet the age of chivalry is dead, and in its place is an era of fast living, motorway service stations and urban sprawl. No more can the mysterious appearance of cackling wise women, saintly hermits or black knights determine the course of a quest; they exist today only in our dreams and visions. Too many uncertain factors come into play, and it is these that make or break a quest, not whether the best knight in the land has rescued a damsel in distress or won the favour of God after vanquishing his opponents in open combat.

But just what if, for the sake of argument, a quester today *was* charged with the search to find the Holy Grail? If he or she accepted the challenge, what trials would they have to undertake, and where eventually would it lead them? It got me thinking. Richard's dream did seem to point towards the fact that some kind of representation of the Grail or, as Crowley called it, the Cup of Babalon, might be possible to find, so what if we were to pursue the matter? Where would it lead us?

If nothing else, it might throw new light on an ancient mystery that was still there for the taking. For although the questing knights of King Arthur's Round Table ultimately achieved custodianship of the Grail, its whereabouts today were entirely unknown. Of course, there were various claimants to being the authentic item, but by their sheer number it had to mean that others – perhaps even the original one – were still out there somewhere awaiting discovery. How great would that be – finding the Holy Grail, or at least *a* Grail.

Yet what exactly is the Holy Grail? I had to admit that my vision of what it looked like and what it signified was based more on the colourful imagery of blockbuster movies than medieval literature. A scene came to mind in which maverick archaeologist Indiana Jones in the film *Indiana Jones and the Last Crusade* is told by its knight guardian to pick the true Grail from among a multitude of jewel-bedecked chalices in gold and silver, only for him to make the right decision by choosing a simple wooden cup. I recalled also John Boorman's 1984 film epic *Excalibur* where Sir Perceval receives a vision of the Grail as he stares death in the face when drowning in a rocky stream. On a lighter note, there is the irreverent humour in the film *Monty Python and the Holy Grail* when King Arthur (Graham Chapman) asks the French knights that guard the battlements of a castle if they will join him in the quest to find the Holy Grail, only to be snubbed with the words: 'Go away, we already have one!'

I had heard stories that the Grail was variously described as a cup, a dish, a small jewel-like stone and even a head on a platter! Some scholars saw it as a relic connected with the life of Jesus, while others argued that it was really just a Christianised variation of a sacred cauldron or horn of plenty transposed from

Celtic myth and legend. Still others have proposed that it is a Christian symbol based on the communion chalice and dish in which the wine and wafer of the Eucharist, signifying the blood and body of Christ, are placed. So what is the real answer? What exactly is the Holy Grail? My curiosity had been well and truly aroused, and in the coming weeks and months hopefully we would begin to understand not just the true nature of this, the ultimate, holy vessel, but also the quest to find it.

3. THE HEAD OF GOD

Tuesday, 4 December. Richard reclined in an easy chair in our front room, his darkened form illuminated in the gentle flicker of the candle flame. The idea was to allow his mind to attune as best as it could to the source of the dreams that had recently haunted him. Very quickly Richard found himself back in Hastings Caves, gazing at the Baphomet figure illuminated by flame-lit torches.

Standing before him were two figures, both from different periods of history, with only one being aware of the other's lingering presence here. Aleister Crowley, appearing once more as a sexagenarian, was bizarrely dressed in a showman's outfit, as if a ringmaster in a Victorian circus. His words were even more mysterious: 'Roll up, roll up, come and see the infinite people of the past,' he exclaimed, with a mild sense of anguish as he gestured towards the other figure present in the caves – a medieval knight dressed in a pointed brown woollen cowl, which covered his shoulders and neck. On asking who exactly this was, Crowley replied: 'Stephen de Staplebridge – a Templar knight.' With this came the feeling that just one year after his induction into a secret chapter of the Knights Templar, de Staplebridge visited the caves for reasons relating to the Order's veneration of Baphomet and the Grail.

Crowley claimed there was a key in his initiation. 'It is recorded down,' he insisted. 'Wilkins wrote about it in his *Concilia Britanniae*.' It was said as if we should know of the book's existence, which we didn't – not at that time, anyway (see Chapter 11).

Then came flashes of something else – the fashioning with crude tools of the Baphomet figure in the caves by a strange man dressed in a leather apron, breeches, boots and a battered brown hat. His name was 'Arnold', with the year being 1692. It was simply a lingering place memory, and no more information was offered on the subject as Crowley began to talk again: 'They (the Knights Templar) will show you the key *and* the Star of Babalon. The Cup of Babalon is at the centre of the star. Are you drawing the star? Have you not grasped the inner mysteries of what I have given to you?'

I did not understand. Was he referring to his work *Liber CLVI*, which we had been told to read? And what did he mean: 'Are you drawing the star?' What star? Was he implying that we should draw the seven-spoked Star of Babalon on a map to discover the whereabouts of the Cup of Babalon? If so, then what were its fixed markers? Was one of them Hastings Caves? I presumed so, but what then were the others? Could he tell us?

'Read between the lines of my work,' he said, frustrated by our insolence. 'Draw the star, take the cup, and the mystery of all things will be revealed. Are you ready to take the mantle?'

I said we were. And the star? how could we find that?

'You can plot the star now if you try,' he exclaimed.

The setting that Richard saw then changed. Inside a stone tower connected to the thirteenth-century church of St Michael at Garway in the county of Herefordshire were seven knights in white surcoats lying in a star-shaped pattern on the stone floor. Their feet were directed towards the centre of the circle, as were their drawn broadswords, held between the knights' open legs. In their midst was a scantily-clad woman holding aloft a small cup, or chalice, while the knight seen earlier, Stephen de Staplebridge, also in chain mail and a white surcoat, stood by, seemingly officiating over what was going on. As if aware that the setting was now being observed by prying eyes from beyond time, the Templar knight turned around to reveal that he was holding a silver reliquary (a relic holder) in the shape of a two-faced bearded head at which he proclaimed: 'I bring you the Head of God.'

With this amazing sight Richard received a sudden download of knowledge: the silver reliquary represented Baphomet, the idol of the Templars, making sense of the stories about the warrior-monks worshipping a bearded head that spoke to them. Inside its beaten metal frame were pieces of a skull belonging to the patron of the order, seen by them as an incarnation of the Christ. It was a sacred relic of immense importance, treasured by the Templars of England and used by them in their secret rituals.

Speaking directly to the spectral intruders, Stephen de Staplebridge urged that 'only when the true nature of the star is realised, and you possess the cup, will this be given to you'.

By its very nature, so-called psychic information can never be one hundred per cent accurate. The best super-psychics, or direct-information psychics, I have known can only produce an accuracy factor in the region of ninety per cent tops, which means that ten per cent of everything they say is at best inaccurate, if not down right wrong. To put it another way, one statement they make in every ten turns out to be nothing more than pure imagination. Decrease the accuracy factor, and the level of intelligibility goes down even further. Stage mediums, along with psychic readers at the end of piers, and the sort of clairvoyant that you might visit in order to learn more about your life and affairs, are never any more than thirty per cent accurate. Some are as low as twenty or even ten per cent accurate, which is basically the level of psychic awareness that can be attained by anyone who chooses to do so.

I say all this because when you are presented with a plethora of psychic statements and curious imagery that appears to be beyond the normal capability of the conscious mind, it is important not to become too excited. Sift through the information as best as possible, check it out in available source books or online, assess its significance and then simply put it to one side pending further information on the same subject. What Richard had seen and experienced was beyond the norm, and I intended finding out what there was to know about its key themes. Did the Templar knight named as Stephen de Staplebridge really exist, and, if so, was he connected with Garway church in Herefordshire, and, of course, Hastings Caves? I was also intrigued by the references to some kind of star pattern on the landscape, seemingly overlaying southeast England. Was it mimicked perhaps by the seven knights lying down in a star shape inside the detached tower at Garway, which I knew to exist because Richard and I had visited the church there back in March 1997 as part of a separate psychic quest? On that occasion, a group of us had lain down on the floor of the tower in a star pattern during a Templar-style ritual, which we had conducted following psychic instructions provided to me through dreams and visions. Garway church is a fabulous place preserving strong memories of the presence thereabouts of a major Templar preceptory, which thrived before the arrest of its remaining knights in January 1308, three months after their less fortunate brethren in France. What then were we to make of the two-faced head reliquary said to represent Baphomet, the idol of the Templars, allegedly used by the Order in its secret rituals? Moreover, where did any of this fit into our quest to find the Holy Grail?

THE TEMPLECOMBE PANEL

The search began with the name de Staplebridge, or 'of Staplebridge', suggesting that Stephen either came from a town or village of this name, or that he held lands there. With a little bit of checking, I quickly realised that Staplebridge was the medieval name for a small village in the English county of Dorset known today as Stalbridge.[15] If Stephen did come from here then it was a fascinating discovery indeed, for just a few kilometres away, over the border in Somerset's Vale of Blackmore, is the village of Templecombe. This I knew to have been the site of a major preceptory of the Knights Templar from 1185 through to the arrest of the English Templars. As with most of the Templar properties in England, little is known about its activities other than what is found in existing charters and court rolls concerning the acquisition and transfer of lands and properties by the Order. In Templecombe's case, it was most probably linked with the thriving wool industry established in the West Country by the Templars, while other sources suggest that it was a regional centre, training and recruiting local men for the Crusades in the Holy Land.[16] The proximity of the estate to the old Bristol road would have meant close ties with this great medieval town and port, where the preceptory of Temple Mead was to be found. (To this day, Bristol's main railway station bears the name 'Temple Meads'.) Regularly, sailing vessels belonging to the Templar fleet would arrive at Bristol from the French ports of La Rochelle and Marseilles, loaded with arms, munitions and other produce destined for the Order's key properties in England.[17]

Even after the West Country's top archaeological experts gathered at Templecombe to film an episode of Channel Four's popular *Timeteam* television programme back in 1995, very little can be said about the presence in the village of the Knights Templar for a period of around 125 years. Certainly, Stephen de Staplebridge's name was not listed among the four brethren from the preceptory placed under arrest in 1308. However, there is one rather curious fact known about Templecombe which might help us better understand the headlike reliquary which became the idol of the Templars.

During the Second World War Templecombe became a strategic target for German bombers, due to the presence there of a major rail junction. On one fateful night a school and several houses were badly damaged by falling bombs. More tragically, nineteen people were to lose their lives. Yet amid this mayhem came an unusual discovery, which was to assume a much greater significance once it became known to the outside world. In 1945 the owner of a cottage in West Street, off the High Street, removed the ceiling of an outhouse and uncovered a painted wooden panel. Dated tentatively to 1280, when the Templars were still in residence, it depicts an extraordinary bearded male head of great serenity with shoulder-length orange-brown hair. It is set within a stylised diamond-shaped frame that further accentuates its mesmeric form. Most striking are the large gentle eyes and the mouth, which is open in a manner suggestive of the fact that the head is speaking to the observer, bringing to mind the claims made by some Templars that the bearded head they venerated actually spoke to them.

Scholars on the subject of the Knights Templar have been extremely cautious concerning the possible identity of the face painted on the Templecombe panel, as well as its likely association with the Order. Some see a remarkable similarity between the face on the panel and that displayed on the Turin Shroud, even though this precious relic of immense religious significance to the Catholic faith is almost certainly a medieval fake. Yet because of this obvious comparison, the head is generally identified as that of Jesus Christ, a conclusion that makes little sense in relation to what we know about the activities of the Templars, and the iconography associated with Jesus Christ. Firstly, why should Christ's head be shown severed, since the Gospels tell us that he ascended bodily to heaven? Admittedly, a cult grew up in medieval times around the story of what is known as Veronica's Veil, a handkerchief on which appeared an image of Christ's face after it was offered by the kindly St Veronica to the Saviour as he made his way to Calvary Mount. However, from its stylisation the diamond-shaped frame surrounding the face on the Templecombe panel is clearly not meant to represent Veronica's Veil. More likely is that the Templecombe panel shows the head of John the Baptist – the forerunner of Jesus Christ who is so intimately linked with both the Knights Templar and their latter-day descendants.

JOHN THE BAPTIST

As a prophet preaching a return to the values of the Old Testament patriarchs, John the Baptist was rivalled in his age by only Jesus himself. His story is told in the Gospels, and also in the writings of Flavius Josephus, the Jewish chronicler who wrote in the last quarter of the first century AD. The Gospel of Luke tells us that John was the son of Elisabeth, an elderly woman 'of the daughters of Aaron', and Zacharias, a temple priest in Jerusalem.[18] Even though Elisabeth was barren, the archangel Gabriel appeared to her husband when at his duties and predicted the coming to his elderly wife of a child who shall be called John. Not believing what he had been told, Zacharias was struck dumb until after the child was born.

Nothing more is given regarding John's life until the Gospels inform the reader that in the reign of Herod Antipas, tetrarch of Galilee (following the death of Herod the Great in 4 BC, the Romans split Palestine into four provinces, each to be controlled by a Roman henchman, with Herod Antipas being made ruler of Galilee), John was a fiery preacher of repentance, dressed in a camel-skin and leathern girdle, who ate only locusts and wild honey. Although his parents were from Jerusalem, John established a large following with his own disciples on the River Jordan, bordering what is today Jordan. Thousands of people from all classes of society sought him out in order to wash away their sins through full bodily immersion, or baptism. According to the Gospels, these included soldiers, publicans, temple priests and members of other Jewish religious sects such as the Pharisees.

The activities of the Baptist became widely known as his following increased. Jesus himself travelled to the River Jordan where he received baptism from John, who was said to have recognised him as the one who was to come after him, the one prophesied in the Book of Isaiah. Yet he would baptise not with water, but with the Holy Spirit and with fire, according to the Gospels,[19] reminding me of Bartzabel's insistence that we should undergo a 'baptism of fire', presumably when finally we visited Hastings Caves. The Gospel of John even tells us that John identified Jesus as 'the Lamb of God, which taketh away the sin of the world'.[20] During his baptism the Holy Spirit was said to have entered Jesus in the form of a dove, and thereafter his own ministry began in earnest, following a period of forty days spent in the wilderness 'beyond Jordan', where he was tempted by Satan himself.

Shortly after this time, John was thrown into prison by Herod. What events led to this eventuality are not made clear in the Gospels, for they say only that John objected to the tetrarch abandoning his lawful wife and marrying Herodias, his brother Philip's wife. However, the writings of Josephus record what is perhaps the true reason for his imprisonment and death. According to the Jewish historian, Herod, on learning of the extraordinary power with which the Baptist was able to persuade men to his way of thinking, feared that he might incite a revolution among the reactionary movements fighting against the Roman occupation of Palestine. He thus had him arrested and placed in chains within the fortress of Machaerus in Peraea, a Roman province bordering Arabia and Egypt, and 'separated from the other parts of Judaea by the river Jordan',[21] and thereafter he was put to death.[22] It is an extraordinary account, and one that is accepted as authentic, and thus complementary to the Gospels, by all but the most ardent sceptics of the Bible.

That John's ministry was real, and the fact that Jesus was baptised by him, should be borne in mind when considering the Gospel account of the Baptist's death. The story goes that it was Herod's birthday, and the daughter of Herodias is said to have danced 'in the midst' of the assembled audience, pleasing the tetrarch greatly, and so 'he promised with an oath to give her whatsoever she should ask. And she, being put forward by her mother, saith: "Give me here in a charger the head of John the Baptist." '[23] Although Herod was much grieved by this thought, he did as she wished and had the Baptist murdered and afterwards his head was brought to his stepdaughter on a platter, who in turn took it to her mother. Although the Gospels fail to provide the name of Herodias's daughter, Josephus does, for it was Salome.

Visions come to mind of Salome dancing the dance of the seven veils before Herod in skimpy Arabesque dress, or even of her kissing the head of John the Baptist in some kind of depraved state of ecstasy. Yet such thoughts stem from modern interpretations of this gruesome episode created by those writers or artists who have become transfixed by its obviously burlesque qualities.

Despite his death at the hands of a Jewish ruler who feared the Baptist might raise a rebellion against him and his Roman allies, the immense power possessed by his name lived on, for when shortly afterwards Herod heard reports concerning Jesus's own ministry he cried out: 'This is John the Baptist; he is risen from the dead; and therefore do these powers work in him [i.e. through Jesus now].'[24]

In the wake of John's death, Jesus withdrew temporarily from his public ministry in order to get away from the large crowds that now began seeking him out, but even then he was not left alone. They came out of the towns intent on finding him, and when he did finally return to Jerusalem he discovered that his own following had swollen immensely, necessitating the sermon in which he is said to have broken five loaves and two fishes in order to feed a multitude of 'five thousand men, besides women and children'.[25] It is likely that his flock now included many of the Baptist's followers, as well as some of his disciples, who had become convinced that Jesus intended fulfilling John's own mission of repentance through baptism. Indeed, it was believed by some of the Jews that Jesus was either John returned, or the prophet Elijah, since he is thought to have worked through the Baptist during his lifetime.[26]

Such was the power of John the Baptist, both alive and dead. Yet what became of his headless body? The Gospels tell us absolutely nothing, and Josephus does not even record the Baptist's manner of death. All we are told is that John's disciples came and took up the corpse, and buried it.[27] Slightly later traditions preserved among the early Christians asserted that his remains were carried to 'Sebaste', i.e. Sebasten, a city in Northern Palestine, where they were ceremoniously interred.[28] Thereafter John's tomb became the scene of many miracles as people flocked to venerate his supposed resting place. That was until the matter came to the attention of Flavius Claudius Julianus, Emperor of Rome (360–3), who was known as the apostate, or rebel. He had the remains disinterred, burned and then powdered into dust in order that they might be scattered like chaff on the fields; all this so as to prevent the spread of John's still influential cult.[29]

That might have been the end of the Baptist's power, were it not for a story concerning the appearance out of nowhere of certain monks from Jerusalem who had learned of what was transpiring at Sebasten. Hastily, they collected up what was left of the bones, and as much of the powder as they could gather, and bore them to Philip, 'patriarch of Jerusalem'. He dispatched them forthwith to Athanasius (296–373), Bishop of Alexandria, who in turn conveyed them to Theophilus, a later bishop of the same city (385–412). He placed them in the temple of the pagan god Serapis, which had been converted into a church dedicated in honour of John the Baptist, and there they are said to have rested in peace.

By early medieval times the saint was venerated on two separate feast days, his nativity, celebrated on 24 June at the time of midsummer, and his so-called 'decollation', or death, held on 29 August. It was also on this same day that his head was said to have been unearthed, at least according to the writings of one Jacobus de Voragine (c. 1229–98), Archbishop of Genoa. Sometime around 1267 he compiled a valuable source book on the lives of Christian saints, drawn from several earlier texts, entitled the *Golden Legend* (*Legenda aurea*). It claims that after John's head was smitten off in a fortified town in Arabia called Macheron, or Machaerus, it was taken by Herod back to Jerusalem where it was secretly buried in order that the prophet might not rise again.[30] Yet his head at least would not rest, for it was eventually disinterred, before being guarded, carried and stolen by a series of different holy figures until eventually it reached Constantinople (modern Istanbul in northwest Turkey), the capital of the eastern Roman Empire, during the reign of Flavius Valens (364–78). Here it was ceremoniously interred in a church until the reign of the French king Pepin (817–38), who is said to have carried it off to 'Poictou', or Poitou, a region and former province in western France, 'and there by his merits many dead men were raised to life'.[31]

In this way, the head of John the Baptist entered popular consciousness in France, the place of origin of the Knights Templar in the first quarter of the twelfth century. Some sources suggest it was for ages venerated at the cathedral in Poitiers, the capital of Poitou, while others speak of the skull being broken into three pieces, with the back of the cranium going to Constantinople, the jaws to Genoa and the chin to Rome.[32] More confusing still is the fact that by medieval times no less than ten churches in Christendom claimed to preserve the sacred relic, including the cathedral at Amiens in France, making it impossible to determine its true fate. Then, of course, there are the claims of the Knights Templar, whose persecuted brethren spoke of venerating a sacred head, and the fact that their latter-day descendants in the eighteenth and nineteenth centuries insist that the patron of the order was St John the Baptist, and not Jesus Christ.

No one knows whether the Templars ever possessed the head of the Baptist, for those heads allegedly in their possession were never named as such. Moreover, they are said to have come in all shapes and sizes – single-faced, double-faced and even triple-faced – suggesting that they were either saint relics or deliberately created showpieces designed for ritual purposes. Yet certain pieces of evidence demonstrate that the Templars were at least interested in the head of John the Baptist. Firstly, some Templar seals from the mid-thirteenth century bear impressions depicting a bearded head with long scraggly hair, like that which the Baptist might have been expected to possess. Most significantly, one of these seals even shows a bearded head with long messy hair *on a platter*, which has to be a representation of the Baptist's severed head.[33] Furthermore, the church of St John the Baptist at Angeghem in Flanders once belonged to the military order, a significant point, for it is recorded that builders here unearthed a bearded wooden head reliquary of medieval origin which, when opened, was found to contain a skull thought by local people to be that of the saint.[34] This, along with further claims concerning the modern-day existence of head reliquaries said to have once belonged to the Knights Templar, is enough to demonstrate their close association with both the Baptist and the cult of the head in general. What it did not do, however, was explain why head-related imagery and information, or indeed the subject of the Knights Templar, should come up with respect to our search to understand the Holy Grail, matters that would have to be addressed before we progressed with our own search for this sacred relic.

4. THE FRENCH CONNECTION

Tuesday, 11 December. Around seven o'clock Richard arrived at our home, and in order that we might commence the evening on a full belly he accompanied Sue and me to a local curry house. Waiting to order our meals, he went over various ideas that had been invading his consciousness over the past few days. Previously, he had seen a silver head reliquary in the hands of a Templar knight named Stephen de Staplebridge. The imagery showed him present at some kind of unorthodox ceremony in a stone tower at Garway, the site of the Order's main preceptory in Herefordshire. Why exactly he was unsure, but something told him that this precious holy relic had been in their possession before it was transferred elsewhere.

It was a powerful thought, and one that made sense of the events as they unfolded in England after the fall of the Templars. Following the issue of a papal bull calling for the arrest of the Templars of England in December 1307, the king, Edward II, reluctantly complied with its wishes, even though many of the knights were allowed to remain in their preceptories, an ideal opportunity to spirit away any holy relics still in their care. More curiously, I discovered that there exists an account of a secret initiation at Garway that shows that the preceptory was of extreme importance to the Order.

JOHN DE STOKE'S RECEPTION

It concerns the confession of one John de Stoke, not a Templar knight but a Templar priest, who would attend to the spiritual needs of the brother knights and perform mass each day. On 1 July 1311 he made a formal statement concerning his two separate receptions into the Order. The first of them had taken place eighteen years previously, and was orthodox in nature. Yet a year later, thus 1294, he underwent a second, more secretive initiation at the preceptory of 'Garewy', in the diocese of Hereford, presided over by the head of the Order, Jacques de Molay (c. 1244–1314), Master of the Temple. John de Stoke claimed that, during this ceremony, a crucifix was placed down before him and he was asked by de Molay what it signified, to which he responded: 'Jesus Christ who had suffered for the redemption of the human race.'[35] Not the answer that the Master of the Temple had expected, for he responded with the following words: 'You speak badly, and you are in error; for he was the son of a certain woman, and since he said that he was the Son of God, he was crucified.'[36]

Jacques de Molay next asked de Stoke to deny Christ, and when he did not, the priest was allegedly threatened with prison. It was apparently no idle threat either, for as this was taking place two brother knights held their swords menacingly towards de Stoke, forcing him to make the denial. On enquiring as to whom he should honour his devotions if not Christ, de Stoke was told by de Molay, to rejoice 'in the great omnipotent God, who created heaven and earth, and not in the Crucifixion'.[37]

John de Stoke could easily have made his confession under extreme torture, or with an assurance that if he confessed then he would be absolved of his sins and released from captivity (which he was just two days later). Thus, his confession should be treated with a certain amount of caution. Yet what he had to say seems of extraordinary significance, and has an air of truth about it.

Why such a high-ranking Templar might have been at Garway, close to the border with the ever-hostile Welsh territories, is difficult to explain, especially as he had become the 23rd Master of the Temple the previous year, and was now based in Cyprus, where the Order had its headquarters. Presumably, it was unusual for de Molay to visit an English preceptory. Moreover, when he did so, he would surely have been accompanied by a retinue of foreign knights and servants, making secret visits virtually impossible. Could the association of Jacques de Molay with Garway just thirteen years before the arrest of the French Templars signal some kind of hitherto unrecorded significance to the place? Might it be linked with the idea that it contained a holy relic of immense importance to the Order, possibly a head reliquary? A recent article in *The Temple* magazine, on Garway's church of St Michael and Jacques de Molay's presence there at the reception into the second order of John de Stoke, makes some interesting observations about the place:

> Surrounded by tall trees, hidden away, veiled in mystery, it gives a feeling that it is hiding something . . . Its importance can be understood because we know that the last Grand Master of the Templars, Jacques de Molay, visited Garway preceptory in 1294. One of the few preceptories in England to receive the honour.[38]

IDOLS IN ENGLAND

Adding weight to the argument that Garway might have possessed a head reliquary is the fact that during the trials of the English Templars, a Minorite friar came forward to affirm that there *were* idols worshipped by his brethren. Four of them were in the possession of preceptories in this country, 'one in the sacristy of the Temple in London, another at Bristelham, a third at Brueria, and a fourth at some place beyond the Humber.'[39]

Such idols were unquestionably head reliquaries, or skulls, for it is recorded that they were worshipped in the Order's chapters and congregations, and that each different province possessed one.[40] In this instance, they were to be found at New Temple, London; Temple Bruer ('Brueria'), a major preceptory in Lincolnshire, as well as at an unnamed preceptory in Yorkshire, where the Templars built several strategically important bases, and at 'Bristelham', which can only be a reference to Bristol. Was it possible that one of these idols, presumably the one held in Bristol, found its way to Garway? It was an exciting prospect, although there was no indication of what exactly any of these idols in the English preceptories actually looked like. According to our reckoning, the one to be found at Garway was silver, twin-faced, with a beard on one face at least. Strangely enough, this description matches the report of a head witnessed by Guillaume de Arrablay, the French king's almoner, when he received admission into the Order, presumably at the Paris temple. It was carried before him and placed on the high altar, at which he was able to see that it was made of silver with 'two faces, a terrible look, and a silver beard'.[41] Other knights described seeing very similar heads, some with single faces, others even with three faces,[42] although whether they were moved around from preceptory to preceptory is not made clear.

'I feel that the head used at Garway for the star ritual involving the seven knights was important to the whole Order,' Richard interjected, 'not just in England, but also in France.'

So what became of it? Presumably the head never fell into the possession of Edward II or it would have been recorded in history. Perhaps the Inquisition got hold of it, and spirited it away to Rome?

Richard shook his head. 'Don't ask me why I say this, but I feel that it remained in this country for a few years after the arrest of the English Templars, and was then taken out of the country under a cloak of secrecy, very possibly with the help of Stephen de Staplebridge.'

So where did it end up?

He hesitated in his reply. 'As ridiculous as this might seem, I think it ended up at or very close to Rennes-le-Château.'

THE MYSTERY OF RENNES-LE-CHÂTEAU

Rennes-le-Château, on the northern edge of the Pyrenees, is a small, mountaintop village that overlooks the Aude valley in the Corbières region of the French Languedoc. Here, in the last decade of the nineteenth century, a Catholic priest named Berenger Saunière became unbelievably wealthy virtually overnight, seemingly after discovering something of immense value or significance in his church (even though sceptics of the mystery explain away his riches as the profits of illicit masses he is known to have performed for those who required them). Saunière is said to have spent lavishly redesigning the tiny hilltop structure, building a strange belvedere tower as his library called Tour Magdala and constructing a guest house known as Villa Bethania. He is also reported to have started acting oddly, erasing inscriptions on tombstones, carrying out nocturnal excavations in both the church and churchyard, and receiving visitors totally beyond his standing as a simple curé in a remote part of southern France.

No one knows exactly what Saunière might have stumbled upon, but it was either a commodity, such as gold or treasure (many rumours existed in the area concerning lost treasure), or a great secret which he was handsomely paid to keep quiet about by an unknown paymaster. Another strong rumour preserved locally indicates that shortly after he made his discovery he travelled to Paris, where he met various individuals including priests of the seminary of Saint

Sulpice, who directed him to obtain copies of paintings hanging in the Louvre. One of these was a masterpiece by French artist Nicholas Poussin (1594–1665) entitled *Les Bergers d'Arcadie* ('The Shepherds of Arcadia'), painted around 1640, which shows three shepherds and a shepherdess examining a stone sarcophagus standing on the edge of a rocky precipice (see plate 7). Their eyes gaze in bewilderment at a Latin inscription carved upon its face which reads *ET IN ARCADIA EGO* ('Also in Arcadia I', or 'I too am in Arcadia'), interpreted by art historians as meaning that even in Arcadia, the earthly paradise where dwells the great god Pan, death is to be found.

The strange thing is that a stone tomb matching the description of the one in Poussin's painting was, until its destruction in the late 1980s, to be seen perched on a rocky outcrop overlooking the mountainous Aude valley, at a site called Les Pontils, close to the town of Arques, some 7 kilometres (4 miles) east-northeast of Rennes-le-Château. Obviously, this has suggested to the inquisitive that Poussin might have visited the area on his travels and decided to paint the view, using the tomb as a central focus. Unfortunately, however, the tomb in question dated back only to the beginning of the twentieth century, yet local tradition asserts that it replaced an earlier example on the same spot.[43] Moreover, Poussin is not known to have visited the Corbières region of southern France, thus any similarities between the painting and the Tomb of Arques – or Poussin's Tomb, as it was known – should be purely coincidental.[44] Yet strangely, the line of hills shown in the background of the painting feature three prominent local landmarks as viewed from the real tomb's elevated position – a peak called Pech Cardou, a promontory with a ruined tower named Blanchefort, and, on the right-hand edge of the picture, the hill on which Rennes-le-Château stands. Was a clue to the mystery of Rennes-le-Château being offered by Poussin's painting, and was Saunière aware of some hidden tradition that revealed an occult secret of immense importance?

THE TEMPLARS OF ROUSSILLON-ARAGON

What is the likelihood that one of the idols of the Knights Templar, a head reliquary referred to as the 'Head of God', left England shortly after the arrest of the Templars of England and eventually found its way to this region of the globe? Well, every likelihood, actually, for after its official endorsement at the Council of Troyes in 1128/9, the Order shifted its power base from Champagne to the Languedoc-Roussillon region of what is today southern France. From 1132 the region's principal preceptory at Mas Déu served as the order's nerve centre, although not under the jurisdiction of the Templars of France, but under the protection of the Spanish kingdom of Aragon. Extensive properties and lands including numerous châteaux, farms, mills and vineyards were given to the Templars of Roussillon and Aragon by very rich benefactors, including the Count of Barcelona. The purpose of this mass accumulation of wealth was apparently in order for the Templars to carve out their own independent state, a plan conceived as early as 1143. As one commentator on the subject has written:

From then on, the Templars conceived a great project: that of creating a vast independent state in the Midi [i.e. the south]. This project they never abandoned [for it was pursued by] . . . the Templars of the Roussillon and Aragon. This extraordinary and secret enterprise was directed at the end of the 13th century by the commandery of Mas-Déu. [45]

Being so far away from Paris, the seat of the French king, the Templars of Rousillon-Aragon rarely came under any kind of official scrutiny and were virtually a law unto themselves. In fact, the preceptor of Mas Déu became so powerful that he acknowledged both the King of Aragon and the sovereign Count of Roussillon as equals. Indeed, under Jacques I, King of Aragon, the Templars were to carve out a territory extending from Montpelier in the north to Barcelona in the south, and this included extensive lands and properties on the Balearic island of Majorca, which was also under the sovereignty of Aragon.

In the middle of the thirteenth century the Knights Templar of Roussillon-Aragon, under the authority of Mas Déu, sought out and gained possession of lands and properties at Le Bézu, 6 kilometres (4 miles) south-southeast of Rennes-le-Château. Here in a valley beneath a hilltop castle they established a preceptory, marked on the maps today as a farm called Les Tipliés, known also as the 'Château des Templiers'. This is a strange fact, for there was already a Templar presence in the area, at Campagne-sur-Aude, although this came under the control not of Mas Déu and the Templars of Roussillon-Aragon, but the French *commanderie* of Douzens, located close to the fortified city of Carcassonne. This fact has led some historians to question why the Templars of the south should have wanted to found a new preceptory at Le Bézu, so close to Campagne-sur-Aude. According to one book on the mystery of Rennes-le-Château, which speaks of several treasures hidden locally:

> The prevailing and enduring tradition among the locals was that the Templars had discovered and wanted either to exploit a hidden treasure, or to bury one of their own . . . what better place to hide the enormous Templar treasure away from the clutches of King Philippe than in the heart of the Templars' own intended kingdom. Unlike Douzens, Mas Dieu was of course not within the realm of the King of France. It is thus logical that the isolated valleys of the Corbières . . . [were] thus . . . chosen as the last hiding place of the treasure of the Knights Templar. [46]

Powerful stuff, and of equal interest was the knowledge that, unlike their French brethren, the Templars of Roussillon-Aragon were not arrested prior to the dissolution of the order in 1312. It made sense of why any major Templar relic might have been shipped back to this region, where it would remain safe in the hands of these knights, who were now under the exclusive protection of the King of Aragon. Was this, then, what happened to Richard's two-faced head reliquary, which apparently started its journey at Garway, England, and ended up in the French Languedoc?

* * *

'I would even go so far as to say that the head was in some way responsible for the mystery of Rennes-le-Château,' Richard went on to say, 'and that Saunière was aware of its existence. He thought he knew where it was hidden, and somehow this brought him into conflict with some organisation, most probably the Vatican. They ensured that he lived a healthy and prosperous life on the condition that he kept quiet about the whole matter, since there were elements of it which would have undermined the foundations of the Catholic faith.'

This conversation was getting more bizarre by the minute. Yet I let Richard carry on, knowing that in his mind what he was saying did not stem from some crazy story he had concocted overnight, but was the product of deep emotional feelings, which he believed came from his subconscious mind. The motto of psychic questing is simply to go with the flow, and see where it leads you. Do not believe, and do not disbelieve.

'You know, it's strange,' he continued, with our meals now ordered. 'I see the head as being kept inside a stone casket at some point. I reckon that the Vatican made some attempt to steal it, not from Saunière but from someone else – someone who was in on the whole secret – but they failed. Somehow, those involved were tricked into taking the wrong thing, and so the head remained safe and is still out there today. Saunière knew this and, although he was unable to reveal to anyone what was going on, he did manage to leave various clues as to its whereabouts inside the church at Rennes-le-Château.'

I was beginning to wish that I had recorded this conversation on tape. Still, we could go over everything when we got back to the house.

'There are other clues at Arques,' he added, quickly, the thought entering his mind as we spoke. 'There's a château there which is important to this story.'

In addition to its famous tomb, which resembled the one in Poussin's painting, there was certainly a major château just outside of Arques, although I knew very little about it. I next asked Richard what he thought the connection was between the search for the 'Head of God' and the quest to find the Holy Grail.

He shrugged his shoulders dismissively, a bemused look on his face. 'I'm not sure, although I get the feeling there's a relationship between the two, and that it involves the Languedoc somehow, and the beliefs of the Cathars.'

THE EMERALD CUP OF LUCIFER

The Cathars were a heretical religious sect that seriously threatened orthodox Christianity in Western Europe during the second half of the twelfth century. They spread quickly, mostly across southern France, resulting in their brutal suppression during the so-called Albigensian Crusade, sanctioned by the Pope at the beginning of the thirteenth century. The Cathars' last stand was the mountaintop fortress of Montségur, which has long been associated with a form of the Grail referred to in German romances of the thirteenth century as the *Lapsit exillis*, a Latin or pseudo-Latin name, which seems to be a corruption of 'small stone' (*lapis exilis*). This wonder-working gem was identified in the romances with a stone that fell to earth from the crown of Lucifer as the archfiend struggled with the archangel Michael during the war in heaven.[47] According to legend, this jewel, the purest emerald anyone had ever seen, was kept for a while at the Temple of Hercules in Tyre, Phoenicia, before it passed into the possession of the Queen of Sheba, who gave it to her lover King Solomon. Afterwards, it was fashioned into the likeness of a cup and used by Jesus at the Last Supper, before being handed by a Jew to Pontius Pilate. He gave it into the care of Joseph of Arimathea, who used it to collect the Holy Blood of Christ.

This account of the Emerald Cup derives from the biography of a Genoese nobleman named Guglielmo Embriaco, the discoverer of the so-called *Sacro Catino* – a hexagonal green-glass dish long associated with this legendary vessel.[48] Housed today in the Museum of San Lorenzo, Genoa, the *Sacro Catino* – once thought to have been fashioned from a single emerald – was taken as booty from a 'temple dedicated by Herod to Augustus Caesar' as the Crusaders sacked and pillaged the port city of Caesarea at the end of May 1101. Why exactly this exquisite art treasure became so important, even to the extent of being identified as both the dish (*catinus*) on which meat was served at the Last Supper, and the receptacle of the Holy Blood, remains obscure. It also begs the question, which came first – the *Sacro Catino* or the story of the Emerald Cup?

A separate tradition implies that the true Emerald Cup was spirited out of Montségur prior to its fall in March 1244, resulting in a modern-day quest by the Nazis to find it shortly before the Second World War. Even though there are claims that they did discover a 'Holy Grail' somewhere in the region,[49] there is no reason to assume that it was the Emerald Cup of legend.

Richard then hesitated, as if giving a new thought some consideration, before he turned back towards Sue and I and said: 'Who knows, with Crowley's guidance we might even find ourselves in a position to find both the cup *and* the head.'

It was a tantalising thought but, before rushing off to France, it was perhaps important to examine the apparent connections between the Grail romances, the Cathars and the Languedoc to establish whether the legendary links between them were imaginary or real. It turned out to be a lengthy though very important exercise, which would throw new light on the origins of the Grail and its relationship with both the Last Supper and John the Evangelist, traditionally the writer of the Fourth Gospel and the book of Revelation.

5. LIGHT OF THE GRAIL

The earliest literary source behind the story of the Grail was the poet and probable troubadour Chrétien de Troyes (fl. 1160–1190), who came from the Champagne region of eastern central France. Here he would seem to have become acquainted with Philip of Alsace, Count of Flanders, a patron of the arts, who often visited Champagne from his homeland in Flanders. It was from him that Chrétien claimed to have received a book on the Grail, which he used to construct his own romance called *Perceval: Le Conte de Graal* ('Perceval: The Story of the Grail'), the earliest existing work on the subject.[50] Moreover, Philip of Alsace also became a guardian of a vessel said to contain the Holy Blood of Christ after inheriting it from his father Thierry of Alsace. It is a connection that must have influenced the evolution of the Grail, which in the very first romances is described as the vessel in which the Holy Blood of Christ was collected by Joseph of Arimathea, and not as the cup or dish used at the Last Supper. For instance, what is known as the First Continuation of Chrétien's *Perceval*, written c. 1190–1200 by a French poet named Gautier de Doulens as a sequel to the original romance,[51] says that Joseph of Arimathea – cited as a relative of Jesus – 'caused [the Grail] to be made'.[52] He took it to Calvary Mount, where it was placed 'at once below His [Jesus's] feet, which were wet with blood which flowed down each foot, and collected as much as he was able in this Grail of fine gold.'[53]

Wolfram von Eschenbach, the German *minnesinger* who wrote another Grail romance entitled *Parzival* c. 1200–1210, in which the Grail becomes the wonder-working stone known as the *Lapsit exillis*, informs his audience that although Chrétien wrote of the Grail, he did not do it justice.[54] Von Eschenbach claimed that he had received the story from one Kyot of Provens, almost certainly the poet, trouvère (troubadour) and Templar apologist Guiot of Provins (1145–1208). He travelled widely among courtly circles, particularly those of Champagne, although also in Germany, before eventually retiring from the world to become a monk, initially at Clairvaux and later at Cluny. His experience of the monastic orders led him to conclude that they were mostly vile and filthy, and yet he testified to the complete integrity of the Knights Templar, praising them above all other religious orders, although he said that he himself was not strong enough to join their ranks. Why exactly Guiot supported the Order is unclear, although Provins, where Guiot lived, was at the time a major Templar stronghold, with two main houses – one dedicated to Mary Magdalene and the other to Saint John. Indeed, Hugues de Payens, the first Master of the Templars, came from Champagne, while the Order's first properties and lands were donated by bishops and noblemen from the region, including one Baillie de Provins.

Like Chrétien, Guiot's patron was Philip of Alsace, who probably commissioned both men to construct a romance featuring all they knew about the

Grail. If so, then it implies that two of the earliest forms of the Grail story came from essentially the same source. Yet if this was so, then in what part of France were these stories written?

Both Troyes, where Chrétien came from, and Provins, the home of Guiot, are located in Champagne. It is for this reason that most scholars assert that the Grail romances were written in French, the language of the North, a conclusion I cannot dispute. However, there are clear indications that some of the real names found in *Parzival* derive from the *langue d'Oc*, the language of the South, and its colloquial variation Provençal, the language spoken until the end of the Middle Ages in nearby Provence.[55] To start with, Wolfram von Eschenbach states clearly that the 'Kyot' who supplied him with the story of the Grail was of 'Provence', from where the legend derived before its entry into Germany. This is not to say this 'Kyot' was not the historical Guiot of Provins, which does makes perfect sense, only that Wolfram might have been confusing the fact that although Guiot came from Champagne, he also frequented the courts of Provence, in the south of the country, where perhaps he first heard mention of the Grail.

In addition to these facts, the word used by Wolfram to describe the guardians of the Grail in the Grail Castle at Munsalvsche, the Mount of Salvation, is *templeis*. It is a word that many commentators like to dissociate with the medieval order, whose fighting monks were known in France as *templiers*. This is because the two words are linguistically very different to each other. Yet in their work *The Krater and the Grail*, Henry and Renée Kahane demonstrate that in Aragonese Catalan, a form of the *langue d'Oc*, the Templars were known as *templés*, close enough to Wolfram's *templeis* for it to have derived from the same word. This suggested to the authors that it was 'Kyot of Provens', Wolfram's alleged source for his *Parzival*, who introduced this variation of the name 'Templars' to the story, because he was obviously associated with the *langue d'Oc*.[56] What this surmise also tells us is that, firstly, Wolfram really did believe the Templars to be guardians of the Grail, and, secondly, that some knowledge of the Grail came from the South, and not the North as has always been assumed.

With these sound linguistic arguments in mind, it seems likely that the word *graal* might not derive from the Low Latin *gradale*, meaning 'in stages', as is generally accepted by scholars today. This explanation for the origin of the name was proposed as early as 1209 by a monastic writer from northern France named Helinandus of Froidment. It led him to conclude that the vessel referred to by Chrétien and those who followed him was most probably a '*scutella aliquantum lata*', a shallow dish or pan, used to serve different courses of a meal in stages, as at a banquet. Yet more likely is that the word *graal* is a condensed form of the *langue d'Oc* word *grasal, grazal, grezal*, which in the Catalonian language of the Spanish–French border region becomes *gresal*. All of these forms of the word describe an earthenware or stone pot, jug or vase in which to put liquid,[57] and it is as variations of this spelling that the *graal* appears in at least one work written in the *South* at the beginning of the thirteenth century.[58] This means that when Chrétien first employed the use of its abbreviation *graal*, since the *s* is silent (as the *d* is in *gradale*), anyone from the North, i.e. France, might not easily have recognised this strange word in the language of the hated southerners. It is a confusion that has, I believe, resulted in the eternal problem over whether or not the Grail is in fact a cup or a serving dish – the latter being an unlikely vessel to use to catch drops of the Holy Blood as Jesus's body hung on the Cross.

So where exactly did the concept of the Grail come from? Where might Chrétien, Guiot or even Philip of Alsace have obtained their knowledge of the Grail legend? Over the past 200 years scholars have attempted to explain the symbolism behind the Grail in terms of high Catholic ritual, Orthodox Church liturgy, pagan vegetation cults of death and rebirth, and Celtic vessels such as cauldrons of regeneration or horns of plenty. Yet as the Italian Grail scholar Leonardo Olschki makes clear in his wonderful book *The Grail Castle and Its Mysteries*, to determine the influences that inspired the writing of the earliest Grail romances one must look at the situation from the perspective of the individuals who wrote them. These poets lived and composed their works at a time when religious heresy was seeping into every darkened corner of medieval society.

THE DUALIST HERESY

Among those sects that vied for the attention of the French nobility were the Cathars, who spread across extensive areas of Western Europe from the mid-twelfth century onwards. Their inspiration was the teachings of a much earlier heretical faith known as Manichaeism, founded in the third century by an enlightened figure named Mani, whose followers believed wholly in the concept of dualism, which will require some explanation. Due to the sin of Adam and Eve, and the corruption of humanity by the fallen angels, everything in the physical world was thought to be under the influence of Satan, or Lucifer, ruler of darkness, while that which was unmanifest reflected the Light of God.

Manichaeism spread its influence across Eastern and Western Europe from the early fourth century onwards, virtually coincident to the rise of orthodox Christianity as the official religion of the Roman Empire. It established churches in Gaul (modern-day France) and reached as far as Spain. Yet its rivalry with the emerging Church of Rome brought the two into conflict, and very rapidly Manichaeism was halted in its tracks and had all but disappeared from European history by the end of the fifth century. However, most heresies are never completely wiped out but simply go underground, and this is where Manichaeism remained until the eleventh century, when small pockets began re-emerging in Western Europe, particularly in Flanders, Germany and northern Italy.

In Eastern Europe neo-Manichaeism flourished from the tenth century onwards under names such as the Luciferans and Bogomils. They denied the divinity of Jesus Christ, and thus questioned the blessing of the sacrament during the Catholic mass. In the early twelfth century, Bogomil missionaries entered Western Europe, catalysing the sudden expansion of the Cathar Church, which by the middle of the century possessed a hierarchy, liturgy and various religious texts. Its first bishopric was established in 1149, and within a few years others were established at Albi in southern France and in Lombardy.

Like the Manichaeans before them, the Cathars taught that life itself was evil, and that the human soul was entrapped in the world of matter, and had therefore to be saved from perpetual darkness and ignorance – the world of Lucifer. This was achievable only through knowledge and spiritual truth, which would bring about the salvation of the soul and direct communication with the Godhead. Yet despite this rather gloomy view of the world, the Cathars (known as the Bonhommes, or 'good men', in England) were essentially good Christians, advocating celibacy, vegetarianism, equal rights for men and women and a belief in reincarnation. Indeed, some freethinkers of the twentieth century saw them as the role models for new-age Christianity.

There is no suggestion that poets such as Chrétien de Troyes and Guiot de Provins were Cathars. Yet one can imagine them employing the use of such dualist teachings in their writings in order to elevate their own ideals of spiritual perfection. Indeed, as individuals travelling among the noble courts of Champagne, and plausibly those of the South as well, it would have been the safest policy by far in order to impress possible future patrons, who were either openly or covertly sympathetic to the Cathar cause.

THE GNOSTIC LIGHT

If correct, then the Cathar influence should leave Chrétien's *Perceval* and Wolfram von Eschenbach's *Parzival* littered with suspected references to the dualistic doctrine, and this is exactly what we find. Repeatedly, the Grail is spoken of in terms of its radiance, or dazzling light, which in Chrétien's *Perceval* is so intense that the candles on the candelabra carried before the Grail by two youths during the Grail procession lose their brilliance. In *Parzival*, on the other hand, we find the hero Parzival as a child asking his mother Herzeloyde 'What is God?' – to which she replies: 'My son, He is light beyond all light, brighter than summer's day,'[59] before going on to explain the difference between the 'light and the dark'. They are words which go on to influence much of the book's story line, even down to the skin colour of Parzival's half-brother, Feirefiz, born of an infidel mother and a Christian father, for it is said to have been a mixture of black and white patches.

These blatant references to the Light of God in the early Grail romances are something that Leonardo Olschki discusses in his book, asserting that from the outset both Chrétien de Troyes and Wolfram von Eschenbach express the 'imminent antithesis between the god of light . . . and the god of darkness, who created the world and man'.[60] For Olschki, light as an expression of Godhead, and not simply as a metaphor for the divine, was a belief peculiar to the unorthodox religious communities of medieval France and Italy.[61] It was a religious view derived originally from a quite literal interpretation of the opening verses of the Gospel of St John, which speak of life being in God, 'and the life was the light of men. And the light shineth in the darkness; and the darkness apprehended it not.'[62]

A similar statement concerning the Light of God appears in the First Epistle of John, traditionally ascribed to the same author as John's Gospel (although contested by modern scholars), which reveals that:

> ... God is light, and in him is no darkness at all. If we say that we have fellowship with him, and walk in the darkness, we lie, and do not the truth: but if we walk in the light, as he is in the light, we have fellowship one with another, and the blood of Jesus his Son cleanseth us from all sin.[63]

Scholars have examined these lines and concluded that either they were written for a 'Gnostic' Christian audience, or that John was a Gnostic himself. Certainly, the works of St John were valued highly by the Gnostics of the second and third centuries AD, particularly the Valentinians, the followers of Valentinus, c. 105–65, who apparently revered a corrupt form of the Gospel of St John.[64] The term 'Gnostic' (from the Greek *gnōsis*, 'knowledge') merely describes all heterodox or unorthodox forms of Christianity that diverged from the simple truth of the Gospels, even though many of the sects classed under this name did profess to have a secret doctrine superior to that of the apostles of Jesus, which by its nature could not be communicated to outsiders.

CONSOLAMENTUM

Beyond its obvious expressions of Gnostic dualism, the First Epistle of John makes the link between the Light of God and 'the blood of Jesus his Son', through which the darkness of sin is removed, recalling Christ's 'mystery' at the Last Supper and the origins of the Eucharist ceremony. Once again this was an important aspect of the Cathar doctrine, which held that salvation came only when the soul had been purified through a special ritual known as the *consolamentum*. It took the form of a reception that candidates would have to undergo so as to purge their bodies of sin and prevent them from slipping back into the path of temptation. However, it could only be undertaken by a person ready to become pure again, and at a time when they were aware enough to comprehend what was going on.

Since the Cathars had no formal temples or churches, and did not use altars, the *consolamentum* was performed in a private house where the focus was a table on which were several pure white napkins. The only other decorations were countless candles, their light signifying the Holy Spirit that descended as tongues of fire upon the Apostles at Pentecost, which was seen by later Christians as the fulfilment of the Baptist's prophecy concerning the one who would come after him baptising not with water but with the Holy Spirit and with fire.[65] Around the table would stand those ministers ordained to receive the candidate – deacons, so-called *perfectae*, dressed in long black robes to signify their withdrawal from the world.

On a side table in the sparsely decorated room would be a wash basin, in which the ordaining minister and his two assistants would wash their hands before placing a copy of the Gospels on the head of the candidate. The three would then place their hands on his or her head, and visualise the Holy Spirit, the Light of God, descending into the person in the form of a dove. This was followed, firstly, by a recital of the Lord's Prayer and afterwards a reading of the first seventeen verses from St John's Gospel, starting with, 'In the beginning was the word . . .'[66] Thereafter he or she would receive the so-called kiss of acceptance, before being asked to choose another *perfecta* to become a constant travelling companion in their missionary work.

The description of the Cathar *consolamentum* brings to mind the service of the Grail held around the table in memory of the Last Supper, as mentioned in one form of the Grail story written c. 1200–15 by a Burgundian poet named Robert de Boron and entitled *Joseph d'Arimathie*. Here the 'holy words', or 'secrets of the Grail', are imparted by Christ only to those chosen as guardians of the sacred vessel. Were such ideas inspired by some knowledge of the *consolamentum*, and did the significance of the Grail as a vessel in which the Holy Blood was collected stem from its ability to purify the soul, as is suggested in the First Epistle of John? Was this why only those who were pure at heart could set eyes on the Grail, and why in Wolfram's *Parzival* the hero knight has to remove his rusty armour and put on a purple cloak provided by the Grail maiden, Repanse de Schoye, before he is able to witness the Grail procession? Purity, innocence and perfection are themes which connect together all the early Grail literature, and there has to be a good chance that it derives not from Catholic doctrine, but some earlier form of communion meal performed by the earliest Christians and later Gnostics, and passed on to the dualist heretics such as the Manichaeans, Luciferans, Bogomils and Cathars. Yet if this was so, then it implied a secret or Gnostic origin to the Grail story, which I had no option but to explore next.

6. THE POISON CHALICE

It is not difficult to see that certain aspects of the Grail romances reflect the written works of John the Evangelist, or at least the books and teachings ascribed to him. The Cathars revered not just his Gospel, and seemingly his First Epistle, but also a secret Gospel of St John, quite possibly a more Gnostic-influenced version of uncertain origin. As early as the second century, John's Gospel was viewed as heretical by some Christians of Asia Minor (modern Turkey), since it contained unorthodox teachings, particularly concerning the nature of the Holy Spirit.[67] Later forms were quite obviously watered down, although not enough to deter the interests of later Gnostics such as the Manichaeans and their medieval descendants. In addition to these known works of John, the Cathars prized an even more blasphemous work entitled the *Cène Secrete* ('Secret Last Supper'), also known as the *Interrogatio Iohannis* ('Interrogation of John'). Transmitted to the Cathars of Italy and the Languedoc by the Bogomils of Eastern Europe sometime around 1190, it was written in Latin and tells of the fall of Lucifer, from a being who bathes in the light to a demon in human form, and then finally how he became a serpent. In addition to this it features Lucifer's attempts to beguile St John into accepting his views on various matters of theological debate.

What was it about John the Evangelist and his works that so fascinated the Gnostics? I understood the value that dualists might have placed on John's doctrine of the Light of God and earth as the realm of darkness. However, if the righteous ideals expressed in the earliest Grail romances were inspired by the very same doctrine, then might there be a relationship between the life and works of John the Evangelist and the origins of the Holy Grail?

THE LIFE OF JOHN
As the brother of disciple James, known as 'the Great', John was the younger son of Zebedee and his wife Salome. Brought up in the town of Bethsaida in Galilee, his early years of adulthood were spent learning the family trade of fishing on the Sea of Galilee (modern Lake Tiberius). The brothers became disciples of the Lord when one day Jesus came to the shore and called out to Simon Peter (later just Peter) and his brother Andrew, who were in partnership with James and John. After entering their boat and causing their empty nets to be filled to the brim with fish, Jesus asked them all to join him in becoming 'fishers of men'. Certainly, this is the story according to the Gospels of Mark and Luke (Matthew says nothing).[68] Yet as we shall see, the manner in which Andrew and John became followers of Jesus in John's Gospel is entirely different.

John's role in his own Gospel is strikingly in contrast to that contained in the other three, the so-called 'Synoptic' Gospels, which all borrowed from one another and had their roots in a now-lost source book containing the sayings of Jesus and known to scholars as the 'Q Gospel'. John, who is thought to have written independently of the other Gospels, alludes to himself in the text only as the disciple 'whom Jesus loved',[69] or as the 'other disciple',[70] or simply 'another disciple'.[71] The anonymous, third-person stance on the part of the writer of John's Gospel has led Bible scholars to refer to this unidentified character as the 'Beloved Disciple'. Most assume him to have been John, but others argue that he was a completely separate person,[72] a view that makes little sense of the testimony presented by the Gospels.[73] More curiously, John's Gospel strangely refers to the Beloved Disciple as 'reclining in Jesus' bosom',[74] or leaning 'back on his [Jesus's] breast' during the Last Supper.[75] No explanation is ever given for this blatant overfamiliarity between John and Jesus. It could simply be the manner in which John, or the Gospel writer (if different from John), wished to convey the close bond that existed between the two men. Certainly, John would appear to have been a man of some influence in Jerusalem, for his Gospel tells us that the Beloved Disciple was 'known unto the high priest', and was perhaps of a priestly caste himself.[76] Apparently, following the arrest of Jesus in the Garden of Gethsemane, where he rested the night before the Crucifixion, John was able to gain entry into the High Priest Caiaphas's palace in order to listen to the charges being levelled against his master as Peter was forced to wait outside in the courtyard.[77]

Additional evidence that John might have been a priest comes from the testament of Polycrates of Samos, Bishop of Ephesus, who thrived in the last decade of the second century. He wrote to Pope Victor in defence of the Asiatic Church saying: 'John also, he who leaned upon the Lord's breast, who became a priest wearing the *petalon* and was a witness and a teacher, he sleeps at Ephesus.'[78] Thus he confirms that John was the Beloved Disciple, that he 'sleeps' in Ephesus, where John established his community in Asia Minor (see below), and that he wore the *petalon,* the badge of a Jewish rabbi.

A further example of John's importance is that he was the only one of the twelve disciples not to desert Jesus following his arrest, a commitment that prompted Jesus to ask him to take his mother Mary into his household as if she were his own.[79] Thereafter John stands at the base of the Cross on Calvary Mount, otherwise known as Golgotha, 'the place of the skull', watching the grim spectacle in the company of Jesus's female followers. In John's Gospel these are named as Mary, the mother of Jesus, Mary Clopas (or Cleopas), the sister of Jesus's mother (plausibly James and John's own mother Salome), and Mary Magdalene.[80] The only other males that feature in the Crucifixion and its aftermath are, according to John's Gospel, Joseph of Arimathea and Nicodemus, who both help remove the body at sundown,[81] and the Roman soldier, named in the apocryphal *Evangelium Nicodemi* ('The Gospel of Nicodemus') as Longinus, who pierces Christ's side with his spear and brings forth 'blood and water'.[82] The author of John's Gospel makes it clear that he himself had borne witness to these events, and that his word is true.[83]

After the Magdalene returns to the sepulchre in which Jesus's body had been laid to rest and finds it empty, it is John and Peter that she runs to in order to tell the disciples what has happened,[84] and it is John who, running ahead of his companion, discovers the empty tomb for himself.[85] However, he does not enter, even though he can see the linen garments left behind, but instead waits until Peter has confirmed the body is missing before entering himself. This is a very valuable statement for it hints strongly at John's priestly status, since it was against Jewish law for a rabbi to defile himself by entering a tomb containing a decomposing body.[86]

John is present also when some time after the Resurrection several of the disciples are fishing once more on the Sea of Galilee. Simon Peter is having difficulty catching fish when suddenly he and the disciples become aware of a figure on the shoreline who tells them to cast their nets over the right-hand side of the boat. In a similar scene to the one in which Simon Peter and Andrew, James and John are first called to follow Jesus, this advice results in their nets bulging with fish (indeed, exactly 153 in all!) prompting the disciple 'whom Jesus loved' to remark to Peter: 'It is the Lord'.[87]

THE JERUSALEM CHURCH

Following Jesus's Ascension, John and Peter are thought to have stayed together in order to spread the Gospel. There are even indications in Acts and the Epistle of Paul to the Galatians to suggest that, along with James 'the Less', also known as 'the Just', who is spoken of as the 'brother' of Jesus (although he was probably only a cousin), John became a leader of the earliest Christian Jews of Jerusalem.[88] They adhered strictly to the ancient laws of Moses and very quickly found themselves at loggerheads with the alternative form of Gentile, or non-Jewish, Christianity envisioned by the apostle Paul, who was formerly Saul of Tarsus. Paul's father had been a strict Pharisee, and, after leaving his home town in southeast Asia Minor, he learned to become a rabbi in Jerusalem. It is possible that he eventually joined the Sanhedrin, the supreme judicial and administrative council of the Jews, which consisted of the chief priests and elders of the people. Following the Resurrection they are said to have persecuted any known follower of Jesus, or promoter of his doctrine. However, whilst on the road to Damascus Saul purportedly underwent a miraculous conversion whereby the ascended Christ appeared to him and, having rebuked him for his sins, instructed Saul to take the Christian faith to the Gentiles. So, after receiving baptism and adopting the name Paul, he did just this, preaching the gospel of the Resurrection and the Eucharist, quite literally the 'breaking of bread', to Greek, Roman, Jew and Pharisee alike.

Very quickly Paul established an influential Gentile Church that infuriated the Christian Jews, who had by now spread across Palestine and Syria, and a bitter rift developed between the two communities. On the one hand there were James, Peter and John, who stood firm regarding the position of the Jerusalem enclave, and on the other there was Paul, who continued the process of evangelisation in towns and cities throughout the Eastern Mediterranean, and into Asia Minor. He even had the nerve to preach the resurrection of Jesus in certain synagogues, where he earned an unexpectedly warm reception. Despite a noble attempt at reconciliation between the two communities by John, and even by Paul, the rift remained and eventually the Gentile Church severed its links with the Christian Jews, many of whom were members of Jesus's extensive family. Henceforth Paul's followers were to be known as Christians, followers of the Christ, while the Jerusalem Church, as it was known, gradually lost its importance in the emergence of the faith of the resurrected Jesus. However, by AD 50 the Christian Jews had made inroads into Rome, the den of the lion, and it was this vital link which enabled Peter's name to become well known among converts in the Roman capital, and not that of Paul. According to later tradition, Peter is supposed to have visited Rome himself and become its first bishop, thus transmitting his own apostolic succession to what would become the Church of Rome. Despite the persecutions, it grew with such strength that some kind of mutual co-operation had to take place between Peter's followers and those of Paul's Gentile Church. It was an act which resulted in them being seen as the joint founders of orthodox Christianity, a proclamation which inevitably led to James the Less's role as Jesus's familial successor being conveniently forgotten.

Yet around this same time, John the Evangelist would seem to have fallen out with the Jerusalem Church and fled to Ephesus in Asia Minor, where with a dedicated band of followers he established his own unique brand of Christianity, practised by the so-called Johannine community i.e. the followers of John. Perhaps inevitably, it was a whole different animal to either the Jerusalem Church or Paul's Gentile Church. It relied more on personal enlightenment through the process of divine revelation, an ideal that would help inspire the more or less dualist doctrine expounded in the written works which bear his name. With the help of Paul, John went on to establish the Seven Churches of Asia Minor. These John addresses individually in the book of Revelation,[89] which he is also credited with having written under the slightly altered name of John the Divine (another matter seriously contested by Bible scholars).

Beyond what the New Testament tells us there are only legends concerning the later life of John the Evangelist, which were recorded by early Church Fathers such as Tertullian, and other Latin writers.[90] The most popular of these attest that during the persecution of the Christians under Titus Flavius Domitian, Emperor of Rome (AD 81–96), John was sent in fetters to Rome where next to the Latin Gate he miraculously survived an attempt to martyr him when he was immersed in a cauldron of boiling oil.[91]

Following the death of Domitian, John was released from captivity and allowed to return to his community at Ephesus, and here he is supposed to have written his gospel at the ripe old age of ninety. Initially, it was not accepted by the Roman Church, which had adopted the Gospel of Mark, written by the apostle Mark, a follower of Peter, along with its variations, the Gospels of Matthew and Luke. Yet so much influence did the Gospel of John achieve throughout Asia Minor that it was somewhat reluctantly accepted into the existing canon to become what is known as the Fourth Gospel. John himself died at the dawn of the new century (c. AD 100/101), having outlived all his former disciples and friends, and left as a legacy a body of literature that would have repercussions down the ages.

CHRISTIANITY'S FIRST PRIEST

As an apostle of Christ, John the Evangelist is portrayed in Christian art as a young, beardless and rather effeminate-looking individual, while as the elderly evangelist he is depicted as a humble old man with a beard and receding hairline, his Gospel under one arm. Alongside him is usually an eagle, the evangelical symbol attributed to John as one of the four gospel writers. More significantly, John is occasionally portrayed holding a chalice from which emerges a black snake, or serpent, something that is thought to stem from one of several different legends going back to within a century of his death. In its original form, derived most probably from the apocryphal Acts of John, it tells how the Emperor Domitian, hearing of John's teachings at Ephesus, asked for him to be brought to Rome. Here he was made to drink poison, which had no effect on him, even though the dregs managed to kill a criminal whom John immediately brought back to life. For this insolence, John was banished to the island of Patmos, where he is supposed to have written the book of Revelation.[92] Another version of the story, retold by St Isidore of Seville (c. 560–636), asserts that whilst in Rome an assailant made an attempt to kill John by filling the chalice with poison during the feast of the Eucharist.[93] Yet he was able to drink from the vessel without any ill effect, and was then able to offer it to the congregation with no personal injury to anyone, the poison having issued from the cup in the form of a serpent. Afterwards, the assailant, consumed by his own evil, dropped dead at the feet of the apostle. In still another variation of the tale, the assailant was Aristodemus, the high priest of the temple of the goddess Artemis (Roman Diana) in Ephesus.[94]

As attractive as this story might seem, it is likely that John's association with the chalice began long before he arrived at Ephesus. For instance, it has been proposed[95] that his cup symbolism derives from the words spoken by Jesus after James and John (or their mother Salome on their behalf in one version[96]) ask whether one day they might be able to sit in glory with him in heaven, one on his right side and the other on his left. In Mark's Gospel, Jesus is said to have replied: 'Ye know not what ye ask. Are ye able to drink the cup that I drink, or to be baptised with the baptism that I am baptised with?'[97] The brothers answer that they *are* able, prompting Jesus to reply: 'The cup that I drink ye shall drink; and with the baptism that I am baptised withal shall ye be baptised: but to sit on my right hand or on my left hand is not mine to give: but it is for them for whom it hath been prepared.'[98] They were words that I would return to often in the coming months, their significance growing on each occasion.

Such thoughts might help explain why sometimes in Christian art the snake seen climbing out of John's Poison Chalice, as it became known, is replaced by a consecrated host of the Eucharist,[99] and why he is occasionally shown with Jesus at the Last Supper, the wine cup of the sacrament in his hand.[100] There can be little question that this is supposed to send out a clear message that he was Jesus's first priest, especially in the knowledge that the Last Supper was seen as the point of instigation of the Christian priesthood[101] and John was, like Jesus, considered a rabbi.

Remember too that John tells us that he is the disciple 'whom Jesus loved', and that at the table of the Last Supper he was 'reclining in Jesus' bosom', or leaning 'back on his breast',[102] suggestive statements that hint at a special relationship between the two men. Some Bible scholars will point out that the overfamiliarity between Jesus and John implies that the Last Supper actually took place in the latter's house, where he would afterwards take care of the Virgin Mary. Yet separate traditions place the location of the Last Supper at the house of Simon the Leper (see Chapter 16).[103] Wherever this crucial event in the life of Jesus took place, I felt it strange that although John's Gospel provides an account of the Last Supper, the scene in which Jesus asks his disciples to partake of the wine and bread in memory of his blood and flesh is bizarrely absent. This fact will not have gone unnoticed by those Gnostic sects whose entire doctrine was influenced by this single Gospel.

THE CUP OF REVELATION

So if John's chalice is essentially the cup of the sacrament which Jesus asked whether the sons of Zebedee and Salome were able to drink from, then what exactly were the origins behind the small black serpent seen slithering out from this same cup in Christian art? Although it might plausibly signify a real poison administered to John when in Rome or Ephesus, it is more likely that it symbolises the continuance of an unorthodox form of the Eucharistic rite among the Johannine community, which might have been seen as heretical by the fledgling Church of Rome.

Fig. 2. An effeminate John the Evangelist, the 'Beloved Disciple', shown bearing the Poison Chalice out of which slithers the Gnostic serpent of wisdom (after Raphael).

To the Gnostics, the serpent was an expression of divine knowledge and otherworldly wisdom, as well as the medium by which the pure of heart could attain revelation. Among sects such as the Ophites and Naasenes – the first deriving its name from the Greek for 'snake' and the second taking its name from the Hebrew form of the same word – the serpent was venerated as a symbol of the demiurge, the ruler and creator of the physical world. Born of Sophia, the personification of female wisdom, he stole his mother's power in order to take control of the physical universe and gain the allegiance of authorities and kings. His most well-known name was Ialdabaoth, and generally he would be portrayed as a lion-headed serpent with a crown of either seven or twelve rays. Did this connection between the serpent and John's chalice thus imply that, in partaking of the goodness contained in the cup of the Eucharist, the celebrant would experience revelation?

Such thoughts brought to mind the theories of certain left-field scholars who have proposed that the Last Supper was of non-Jewish origin, and could better be described as an *agapē*, or 'love' feast, a term used by both the Early Christians and the Gnostics alike. This seems particularly so in the knowledge that the rite does not conform to any orthodox Jewish ritual associated with the Passover, such as the feast of the Unleavened Bread, at which time the events leading up to the Crucifixion are thought to have taken place. Certainly, the Jews abhorred the concept of the Last Supper, and in one extremely derogatory account of Jesus's life known as the Toledoth Jeschu, which circulated Europe from the thirteenth century onwards, at the Last Supper the disciples are said to have 'drank of the wine wherewith was mingled the Water of Forgetfulness'.[104]

Gnostic sects practised their own variations of the thanksgiving/Eucharistic rite, and some of these involved not only the breaking of bread and the passing around of the cup of wine, but also certain curious elements that throw some light on the chalice symbolism connected to John the Evangelist.

Epiphanius of Salamis (d. 403), an early Greek father and Bishop of Constantia, preserved an account of an Ophite *agapē*-love feast of the type known to have been celebrated during the third century. Those taking part, both male and female, first settled around a table on which was placed loaves of bread in a basket. A snake would then be coaxed out of a box and allowed to mingle with the bread that was afterwards broken in the manner of the Last Supper and offered up to celebrants. Once the snake had been 'charmed' by sorcery, it was likewise passed around among those present, who were then expected to kiss it on the mouth. Afterwards, the celebrants were to prostrate themselves before the creature in worship and call this the 'thanks-giving', i.e. Eucharist, 'which originates from the snake's wallowing in the bread. Then with its help they offer a hymn to the Father on high.' In such a manner they conclude their mystery feast.[105]

So in addition to partaking of the bread and wine, the necessary ingredient of the *agapē*-love feast was the serpent, bringing alive the symbolism of the chalice held in the hand of John the Evangelist in Christian art. Some scholars have gone so far as to suggest that the bread used at these love rites, which were always thought by orthodox Christians to degenerate into licentiousness, was deliberately contaminated by ergot, or mould, which possesses psychoactive properties that could have produced hallucinations among the celebrants.[106] This might have been seen as the Holy Spirit, in the form of the dove, entering the celebrant in order to induce divine revelation or illumination. Others, such as the great British archaeologist and writer John Allegro, proposed that the *agapē*-love feasts might have involved the consumption of *Amanita muscaria*, the active ingredient of the fly agaric mushroom, which possesses hallucinogenic properties and, once again, would have induced visionary experiences and possibly even feelings of otherworldly contact.[107]

Unfortunately, I had little time to enquire further into such amazing theories. Yet it seemed plausible that if certain Gnostic sects, such as the Ophites, were using psychoactive drugs in either the bread or wine of their *agapē* feasts, which took the place of the Eucharistic rite, then this would explain why the serpent, and perhaps even the communion cup, became a symbol of divine revelation. Thus it seemed difficult not to conclude that there was some profound relationship between John's Poison Chalice and the symbol given to that poison – the serpent. All this might conceivably recall some kind of *agapē*-style celebration of the mysteries practised by John, and/or his followers and/or their community, which seems to have expressed strong Gnostic tendencies and might well have had a direct influence on later medieval Gnostic sects such as the Luciferans, Bogomils and Cathars.

Even if this was so, then how was it linked with the quest to find the Holy Grail? Andrew Sinclair, the prolific historian, novelist and writer on the subject of the Grail, certainly recognises a relationship between the Holy Grail and John's Poison Chalice, which he describes as the 'Gnostic' Grail.[108] Indeed, in his opinion: 'The Grail was a Gnostic vessel, not a Christian chalice,'[109] an observation which I found difficult to dispute. Even so, this realisation brought me nowhere near comprehending what exactly the physical Grail might be, or whether it ever came into the possession of either the Knights Templar or the Cathars. Yet the idea of a serpent slithering out of the dark poison in St John's chalice did make me recall Richard's strange dream where he saw the psychic Helen Laurens unearthing a silver-plated goblet at Ide Hill in Kent in 1989. Emerging from its crimson contents had been a snakelike line of blood. Had this been some kind of cue for us to start investigating John's involvement in the Grail mystery, or was it all just coincidence?

WHY JOSEPH OF ARIMATHEA?

The bigger problem was that although John seems intimately connected with cup symbolism, which might well have given birth to the powerful vision of the Holy Grail, in the medieval romances it is Joseph of Arimathea alone who is said to have gained possession of this precious vessel. Furthermore, Joseph and his immediate family are credited with having practised an overtly Gnostic 'service' of the Grail, complete with 'secrets' imparted by Christ himself. Why was this esteemed place in the history of Christianity accredited to such a minor follower of Christ? Surely, it would have made better sense if the romances had outlined the existence of a Christian succession that rivalled St Peter's Church of Rome and stemmed not from Joseph of Arimathea but from John the Evangelist, who in Christian legend seems to have been the original bearer of the cup of the Last Supper.

It is not difficult to see how Joseph of Arimathea's name might have been substituted for that of John the Evangelist in connection with the bringing of the Grail to the West, and the clue can be found towards the end of John's Gospel. At one point, Peter turns to the resurrected Jesus and asks what he has in mind for the Beloved Disciple, i.e. John, to which the Lord replies: 'If I will that he tarry till I come [back], what is that to thee[?]'.[110] The author of the Gospel then goes on to explain that these words said by Jesus 'went forth among the brethren', implying that this 'disciple [i.e. John] should not die', when all Jesus had meant was that it was *his* business what became of the Beloved Disciple, and not Peter's.[111]

Despite John's attempt at correcting this misinterpretation of Jesus's words, it had obviously become a problem even by the time he (or whoever) came to write his Gospel, for it would seem that his followers had quite literally come to believe that he would live forever!

Even after John's death, rumours spread that he had risen again and now walked the earth. For instance, the apocryphal Acts of John says that the day after he was buried his followers dug, 'in the place [of his burial], and him we found not, but only his sandals, and the earth moving, and after that we remembered that which was spoken by the Lord unto Peter'.[112] It was a mania that persisted for hundreds of years, since the legend of John's longevity is cited also by Augustine (354–430). He records that 'on the authority of grave men' John the Evangelist, known also as 'John the Presbyter',[113] still sleeps in his tomb at Ephesus, 'where the moving earth testifies to his breathing'.[114] Yet at some early stage in the history of the Christian Church, the tradition that John still walked the earth became confused with another growing legend, this one concerning a figure who came to be known as the 'wandering Jew', a name intimately associated with that of Joseph of Arimathea.

THE LEGEND OF THE WANDERING JEW

The earliest-known reference to this story in the West is found in the *Flores Historiarum* of the Englishman Roger of Wendover, which dates from 1228, a full two generations after the emergence of the Grail romance. However, as Professor Hugh Schonfield, the noted historian and expert of Near Eastern religions, pointed out, the legend must already have been old by this time. According to Roger of Wendover, when the Archbishop of Armenia came to England to see the relics of the saints and visit its holy places, he visited St Alban's Abbey where the abbot and monks greeted him cordially before asking him about the story of Joseph of Arimathea, 'a man of whom there was much talk in the world'.[115] The archbishop answered that he had himself seen and dined with him in Armenia, and that his name was Cartaphilas (Ahasverus in other variations of the story).[116] On passing Jesus carrying the Cross this man had apparently exclaimed: 'Go on quicker', the Saviour thereupon answering: 'I go; but thou shalt wait till I come.'

It is a statement that echoes the one made by Jesus in John's Gospel with respect to the longevity of the Beloved Disciple, a fact acknowledged by the medieval historian A.S. Rappoport in his book *Medieval Legends of Christ*, published in 1934.[117] Indeed, he points out that the name Cartaphilas derives from the Greek κάρτα φίλος, the 'well-beloved', an allusion to John the Evangelist as the Beloved Disciple. He goes on to state:[118]

The religious mind of the Medieval Ages, anxious to find some justification for these passages, suggested that John might be still alive, and a belief soon arose that certain persons who had witnessed the Passion of Christ had miraculously escaped death and could testify to the truth. Their deathless life, however, was variously interpreted. Sometimes it was regarded as a mark of the highest favour, which is in accordance with the true character and teaching of Christ; in other cases, under the influence of pagan and particularly Teutonic mythology, it was interpreted as a curse and a punishment.[119]

Professor Schonfield accepted that the medieval legend of the Wandering Jew became confounded with the life of Joseph of Arimathea, who witnesses the Passion, gains possession of Christ's body, inters it in a private tomb, and then ventures into foreign lands preaching the Gospel of the Lord – the story as found in the Grail romances. He argues that this same legend might well have been the inspiration behind the medieval belief in a mysterious priest-king known as Prester John, even though it is more likely to have resulted from a continued belief among the peoples of the Orient concerning the survival of John the Presbyter, i.e. John the Evangelist.

Prester John first rears his head in the mid-twelfth century when rumours circulated Europe telling of how this mysterious priest-king – a descendent of the Wise Men, or Magi, who visited the infant Jesus in the Gospel of Matthew[120] – had defeated the Saracens in a decisive battle and established a Christian kingdom in the remotest East. There was even talk that he was ready to come to the assistance of the Christian Crusaders in the Holy Land, news of which lifted Europe's flagging morale following several defeats on the battlefield. Although nothing came of this rumour, a belief in the existence of Prester John and his Asian kingdom never died out. Additionally, he was to feature in Wolfram von Eschenbach's *Parzival* as the son of Parzival's half-brother Feirefiz and the Grail maiden Repanse de Schoye, who together establish a kingdom in 'India'. Moreover, ever since that time, we are told, the inhabitants of this distant land have called their kings 'John', a generic title once more invoking the memory of Christianity's first priest, or minister, John the Evangelist.[121] If all of this makes sense, then it seems probable that it was John the Evangelist and not Joseph of Arimathea who was the original guardian of the Grail, as well as the founder of the service of the Grail with all of its 'secrets'.

Moreover, a link between Richard's Head of God and the Grail was becoming clearer, for I discovered that before becoming a disciple of Jesus, John the Evangelist was almost certainly a follower of John the Baptist.

7. THE TWO JOHNS

According to John's Gospel alone, when John the Baptist saw Jesus and pronounced him 'the Lamb of God',[122] he who had come to redeem the sins of mankind, two of the Baptist's disciples immediately swapped allegiance to this unknown prophet, the son of Joseph and Mary. One only of the disciples is named, and he is Andrew, the brother of Simon Peter. Since we know that Andrew, like James and John, was a fisherman from Bethsaida in Galilee, who afterwards called to his brother to join him and his friend in following Jesus, Bible scholars have assumed that the unnamed follower of the Baptist was John. It is a deduction that makes perfect sense of the fact that in his own Gospel John *never* refers to himself by name, merely as the disciple 'whom Jesus loved', i.e. the Beloved Disciple.

This connection between Jesus and two of the Baptist's own disciples is intriguing, for I knew that the rivalry between the two camps was more direct than the Gospels would ever have liked us to believe. Following the Ascension, the apostles fought a fierce campaign against those who still adhered to the teachings of the Baptist, which it now saw as anathema. John's followers were dispersed widely, with most of them leaving Palestine altogether. One group led by a man named Apollos – who came from Alexandria, where the hub of the Baptist's religion would seem to have been focused after his death – is known to have established a community at Ephesus.[123] Yet when St Paul encountered them on his travels they are said to have been completely ignorant of the fact that their master had prophesied the coming of one greater than himself, i.e. Jesus Christ.[124] Since Ephesus was where John the Evangelist established his own community, might it be possible that he came into contact with the followers of the Baptist, and somehow the two groups merged together as one?

PATRON SAINTS OF FREEMASONRY

Whatever the answer, there seems to have existed some special relationship between the two Johns, something borne out in Christian art, which often shows them standing together, either on their own or in the company of Jesus. In other pictures the two Johns are shown as infants in the company of the Virgin Mary, who holds the holy child. Usually, the Evangelist is denoted by his eagle while the Baptist is shown holding a reed cross. Their unity in art might simply be because they were saints and prophets who shared the same name, but as the great nineteenth-century Christian art expert Mrs Jameson keenly observed: 'the contrast between the dark, emaciated, hairy prophet of the wilderness, and the graceful dignity of the youthful apostle, has a striking effect'.[125]

It is not only in Christian art that the two Johns appear together. It is no secret that in Freemasonry John the Baptist and John the Evangelist are the patron saints of the craft, and have been so for at least 300 years. Freemasons celebrate this fact with major functions on their feast days – 24 June in the case of John the Baptist, and 27 December in the case of John the Evangelist. It cannot be coincidence that these feast dates are almost exactly six months apart – one close to the longest day of the year, i.e. midsummer, and the other close to the shortest day of the year, i.e. midwinter. Yet it opens up a very intriguing possibility indeed, and one that throws light on the nature of the two-faced head that became the idol of the Templars. For if the sun's yearly cycle might be seen as a 360-degree clock and the two Johns can be imagined standing back-to-back at its centre, when John the Baptist gazes out towards the point of midsummer his counterpart, John the Evangelist, faces towards midwinter. Six months, and one half-turn of the clock, later John the Baptist would fix his gaze at the point of midwinter while John the Evangelist would face the sun at midsummer. Interestingly, John the Evangelist's death-day is considered to be 24 June, the feast of the nativity of John the Baptist, even further confirming the saints' dual relationship with regard to the solstices.

The purpose of this visual exercise is to demonstrate that the two Johns, ruling opposite ends of the sun's yearly cycle, are to be seen as two halves of a polelike axis which gazes out at the turning of the yearly calendar. Was this something that the Knights Templar attempted to express as a twin-faced head reliquary of the sort described in their trials, and seen by Richard in vision?

Before advancing too quickly into the role in this mystery played by the Knights Templar, it is worthwhile enquiring how Freemasons consider the two Johns came to be their patron saints. Suffice to say that the ruling body of Freemasonry, known as the Grand Lodge of England, was 'revived' on the feast of John the Baptist, 24 June 1717, and thereafter a festival was held on this day through until 1727, when it was switched to the feast of John the Evangelist. The Grand Lodge of Scotland also held their annual celebrations on the feast of John the Baptist, but this was swapped in 1737 to the feast of St Andrew, which occurs on 30 November.

THE GRAND PARALLELS

In addition to the two Johns being patron saints of Freemasonry, all Masonic buildings, or lodges, in the English craft system are dedicated to them, a fact that has baffled historians of the subject. For instance, the scholar Kenneth Mackenzie (1833–86) merely asserts in his *The Royal Masonic Cyclopaedia* that 'the dedication of these Saints did not arise from circumstances connected with the doctrines of Christianity, but from historical facts. It is most probable, however, that the custom of dedicating Lodges to these saints arose from astronomical reasons',[126] following which he observes that the festivals appear to revolve around the opposite ends of the zodiacal year. In Roman times, midsummer was seen as the moment when Sol, the sun-god, was in his majesty, while around midwinter, usually 25 December, the celebrations were reserved for the rebirth of the sun, an event adopted under Constantine the Great, Emperor of Rome (c. 324–37), as the feast of the Nativity of Jesus Christ.

Somehow, John the Baptist managed to be perceived in Gnostic terms as an incarnation of the sun-god in his guise as the Graeco-Roman Helios, while the celebrations of the rebirth of Sol Invictus, as he was known in the Roman world, came to be associated not only with Jesus but also with John the Evangelist, a strange mystery in itself. Obviously, they could not have the same festival date, and so somehow the apostle was allotted a date which has settled as 27 December.

Arthur Edward Waite (1857–1942), the noted mystic and historian, addressed the question of the dedication of Masonic lodges to the two Johns in his *A New Encyclopaedia of Freemasonry* by providing the transcript of a question-and-answer session created in order to help educate a First Degree Mason on this matter at the time of his investiture:

Q. King Solomon being a Hebrew and living long before the Christian era, to whom were they [i.e. Masonic lodges] next dedicated?
A. John the Baptist.
Q. Why to John the Baptist?
A. He being the forerunner of our Saviour, preached repentance in the wilderness, and drew the first line of the Gospel.
Q. Had St John the Baptist an equal?
A. He had St John the Evangelist.
Q. Wherein is the Evangelist equal to the Baptist?
A. He coming after the forerunner, finished by his learning what the other had begun by his zeal [an allusion preserved to this day in the Grade of Masonic Knights Templar – A. E. Waite] and thus drew a line parallel.[127]

Thus from the time of the construction of the First Temple under King Solomon (c. 1004 BC) until its destruction at the time of the Babylonian Captivity of the Jews (c. 586 BC), Masonic lodges were dedicated to Solomon himself. From the time of the Restoration, when the Second Temple was built under the new governor Zerubbabel (c. 535 BC), until the coming of Jesus, all lodges were dedicated to Zerubbabel. From then on until the destruction of the Temple of Jerusalem under Titus, the son of the Emperor Vespasian, in AD 70, lodges were dedicated to John the Baptist. Yet, we are told, 'owing to the many massacres that attended that event, Freemasonry fell much into decay, insomuch that many Lodges were broken up, and few could meet in sufficient numbers to constitute them legal ones'.[128]

It prompted a gathering of the Masonic brethren in the 'City of Benjamin', plausibly Mizpah, meaning 'watch-tower', located 6 kilometres (4 miles) from Jerusalem. Here they all agreed that in order to prevent any further decay a new patron should be chosen as Grand Master of the Craft. Therefore, 'seven brethren'[129] were dispatched to the city of Ephesus where John the Evangelist was now bishop of that city. Having sought him out, they asked whether he would accept the office of Grand Master, to which he said that he was now very old and too frail to take on such a responsibility. Yet it was then he remembered that:

. . . he had been initiated into Masonry in the early part of his life [i.e. when he was still a disciple of John the Baptist? – author], and being a lover of the Craft, he consented to take the office, and while he presided over the Fraternity, finished by his learning what the other St John had begun by his zeal, and thus drew what Freemasons term a line parallel.[130]

Masonic historians insist that this story is simply a fiction to help explain that which is unexplainable. Freemasonry, they say, was originally known as Speculative Masonry which itself evolved out of Operative Masonry, the trade of the medieval guilds and craftsmen, and thus any inference that Freemasonry is older than this era is complete nonsense. Such a conclusion might well seem appropriate, but the choice of saints as patrons of Freemasonry is strangely meaningful. Was John the Evangelist chosen as the last great patron of the Craft purely because he shared his name with Jesus's forerunner, about whom the Gospels tell us so little? Was it because St John had been a follower of the Baptist before becoming a disciple of Jesus, thus demonstrating fraternal qualities of the type recognised in Freemasons today? Or was it perhaps that the roots of Freemasonry really did involve some kind of lineage or succession passed from John the Baptist to John the Evangelist and his followers? Was it possible that, however vaguely, the Freemasons were providing support for the theory that the followers of John the Evangelist initiated some kind of Gnostic doctrine, which eventually filtered through to heretical sects such as the Cathars? Did this doctrine also influence the religious convictions of the Knights Templar, who unquestionably venerated John the Baptist and, as we shall see, would seem to have had an affinity with John the Evangelist too? Finally, was it inherited by the earliest Freemasons as descendants of the medieval Knights Templar?

THE JOHANNITES

The Templar revivalist groups of France and Italy which emerged largely during the eighteenth century liked to make it known that they were the outer manifestation of an underground strain which went back to the original Knights Templar. Some even asserted that whilst embarking on the Crusades in the Holy Land the original Templars had learned from the 'initiates of the east' a secret doctrine attributed to St John the Apostle. So profound was this teaching that they had instantly 'renounced the religion of St Peter', i.e. the Church of Rome, and became 'Johannites',[131] that is followers of John the Evangelist.

The most well-known Johannite Templars were the *Ordre du Temple* ('Order of Temple'), founded in 1804. In papers published in 1811[132] and 1831[133], the Order claimed that prior to his death, Jacques de Molay, the last official Master of the Temple, appointed one Jean-Marc Larmenius as his successor. From that time onwards an unbroken line of Grand Masters existed through until the beginning of the eighteenth century when in March 1705 the brethren gathered in Versailles, France, and elected as their new Grand Master Philip, Duke of Orleans, who was heir to the French throne. It was a role he honoured through to his death in 1723, when the title went to the first of three Princes of Bourbon who held on to the Grand Mastership until 1776. It then passed to the Duke de Cosse Brissac, who retained the title until his execution in 1782. Somehow the *Ordre du Temple* survived the French Revolution, and in 1804 one Bernard Raymond Fabré Palaprat became its new leader. Thereafter, the Order went public and quickly spread to other countries including Belgium, Germany, Switzerland and Great Britain, where it was under the leadership of the third Duke of Sussex.[134]

One document possessed by the *Ordre du Temple* and dated 1154 sets out the supposedly *real* circumstances behind the foundation of the Knights Templar. It relates how Hugues de Payens – the leader of the original band of knights to go to Jerusalem in 1119 – was initiated into the religious doctrine of 'the primitive Christian church' by Theoclet, the Sovereign Pontiff and Patriarch (whose name is not recorded elsewhere). He is said to have been the sixteenth 'John' in direct succession from St John the Apostle,[135] a claim which highlights the belief that John the Evangelist was considered the first priest of Christianity. According to this extraordinary document, Jesus received initiation into an ancient lineage that had begun with Moses the Lawgiver and his brother Aaron. This had taken place in a mystery school at Alexandria in Egypt, where Jesus was imbued with the divine spirit and attained all the degrees of the Egyptian mysteries, after which he returned to Jerusalem. Thereafter, we are told:

> Jesus conferred evangelical initiation on his apostles and disciples. He transmitted his spirit to them, divided them into several orders after the practice of John, the beloved disciple, the apostle of fraternal love, whom he had instituted Sovereign Pontiff and Patriarch.[136]

It was this apostolic succession that had been conferred on Hugues de Payens, providing the Knights Templar with guardianship of a secret doctrine practised by the Primitive Christians since the time of John the Evangelist, and before him Jesus, John the Baptist, Moses and Aaron.

In addition to these obscure documents, the *Ordre du Temple* announced that they had inherited a version of John's Gospel that was wholly different from the standard one, in that it omitted the resurrection of Jesus Christ. According to them this was the reason why Templar knights trampled on the Cross, since they refused to worship an idol, once more bringing to mind the statement made at the trials by John de Stoke, who claimed that during his second reception at Garway, Jacques de Molay asserted that Jesus was 'the son of a certain woman, and since he said that he was the Son of God, he was crucified',[137] a statement clearly denying Christ's divinity. The authenticity of the *Ordre du Temple*'s Gospel of John has been doubted by many leading Bible scholars, although several other experts who have examined it feel that it was composed during the thirteenth, or possibly the eleventh, century.[138]

Such early dates tell us that, like the Cathars, whom they often saw as allies,[139] the Knights Templar venerated the Gospel of John over and above any other gospel. Moreover, it is clear that, in addition to adopting John the Baptist as some kind of patron to the Order, they saw John the Evangelist in this dual role as well, a tradition carried into Freemasonry by the Order's latter-day followers, who according to certain historians might well have formed secret enclaves following the dissolution of the order in 1312 (see Chapter 11). Such ideas are certainly not new and have been speculated upon by the more mystically inclined historians of the Knights Templar for over 250 years. They show that a secret tradition existed among the Gnostic Christians that continued among the Manichaeans, the Luciferans, the Bogomils and the Cathars, but 'always [as] a secret society, with degrees, distinguished by signs, tokens, and words, like Freemasonry'.[140]

THE BROTHERHOOD OF ST JOHN

Much time has been dedicated in books on secret societies to the Johannite tradition within both the Knights Templar and Freemasonry, although often what is said has been little more than wishful thinking. However, once in a while a book appears that makes claims which cannot be ignored. For instance, in Bernard H. Springett's *Secret Sects of Syria and the Lebanon*, published in 1922, it states that:

> German Masonic writers trace the connection of the Manicheans with the Western Brotherhood of St John, relying on what is known as the *Cologne Record*, whose authenticity is, as would be expected, rejected by materialistic Masons, but usually accepted as genuine by the more enlightened and broad-minded Mystics. This record, which is dated 1535, states that a secret society under the name of the Brotherhood of St John existed before 1440, and since then, and up to 1535, under the title of St John's Order of Freemasonry, or Masonic Brotherhood. This record contains the following passage: 'The Brotherhood, or the Order of Freemason Brothers, bound together according to St John's holy rules, traces its origin neither from the Templars, nor from any other spiritual or temporal Knightly Order, but it is older than all similar Orders, and has existed in Palestine and Greece, as well as in various parts of the Roman Empire. Before the Crusades our Brotherhood arose, at a time when, in consequence of the strife between the sects teaching Christian morals, a small number of the initiated, entrusted with the true teaching of virtue, and the sensible exposition of the secret teaching – separated themselves from the mass.'[141]

The Grand Lodge of Germany further assumed that, in addition to the building guilds of the Middle Ages, there existed a 'substratum' in which was the 'real Christian mystery'. It had adopted as its originator and example John the Baptist, 'the forerunner of the Light of the world'. Furthermore, it was this underground stream that paved the way for what became known as St John's Masonry, which went on to form the higher degrees of the fraternity, an assumption fully affirmed by documents in its archives.[142] There can be little question that this was a general belief among the earliest Freemasons of many countries, and the fact that the *Cologne Record* of 1535 denies that the Brotherhood of St John gained its line of succession from the Knights Templar should be taken with a pinch of salt. No one in their right minds would have wanted to openly associate themselves with this hated medieval heresy for fear of being condemned in the same way.

Should it be established that the archives of the earliest Templar revivalists, or indeed the first Freemasons, preserve documents which genuinely imply that the origins of the Knights Templar stem from a line of succession which began with John the Baptist and then passed to John the Evangelist, then it would confirm everything I had surmised about the significance of the apostle who was the principal catalyst for the creation of the Gnostic teachings that inspired the writing of the first Grail romances. Even if the documents are fakes, created at the beginning of the eighteenth century, as most historians assert, then it still implies that those who chose to revive the medieval order were under the impression that an underground stream beginning with the two Johns permeated history and influenced not only the Knights Templar but all other secret organisations through to their own age.

THE TEMPLARS OF RHEDAE

Richard believed that Rennes-le-Château and its mystery might hold a key to discovering both the Templar reliquary referred to as the 'Head of God' and the Grail itself. When these ideas were first proposed, I was willing to go with the flow and take the matter further, but had not really understood the relationship, or how it might help us better understand the nature of the Grail. A greater knowledge of the Cathars, their relationship to the Languedoc, and the mounting significance of the two Johns – symbolised by the head and the cup – was now making the picture a lot clearer. Yet how exactly the village of Rennes-le-Château fitted into the story had been a little more difficult to understand, and so I began conducting a few investigations of my own.

Records show that on 16 March 1147 two brothers, Pierre de St Jean ('of St John') and Bonetus de Rhedae (Rhedae being the ancient name for Rennes-le-Château), following the advice and will of their mother Blanche, gave their entire possessions, which included vast areas of arable land, villas, farms, vineyards, gardens, lakes, water supplies and much more, to the Knights Templar.[143] Indeed, it would seem that the only property which remained in the family's possession was the citadel of Rhedae, which was donated to Bonetus's daughter Sobrobs, the Languedoc equivalent of the French name Severine.[144] In addition to this, Pierre and Bonetus donated to the Order titles and deeds to properties in Espéraza, a town which lies just northwest of Rennes-le-Château, St Jean de Brucafel near Carcassonne, and at Douzens and Campagne-sur-Aude, where major Templar *commanderies* were subsequently built.

On 21 March 1147, just five days after Pierre and Bonetus gave virtually their entire wealth to the Knights Templar, one of the brothers, Pierre de St Jean, was received into the Order. He climbed rapidly through the ranks as he gained a reputation for being the instigator of donations and the organiser of assets received, which he seemed to have a particular knack of obtaining on the Order's behalf. By 1156 he was Master at St Jean de Brucafel, a post he held until 1169.[145] In 1159 he is recorded as the 'Procurator of the Honour of Rhedez' of the Maison Seigneuriale of Rennes-le-Château.[146] From 1167 to 1169 the citadel prospered under him, for he was by this time 'Commandeur' ('preceptor') of Douzens and Brucafel, 'Preceptor and Master' of the two Honours of Carcassonne and Rhedez (Rennes-le-Château), with the title of 'Minister, magister, Comendator, Preceptor, Procurans Honoris Militaie'.[147]

There seems little doubt that the medieval charter in which these transactions are preserved confirms that there was a prominent Templar presence at Rennes-le-Château as early as 1147, a fact that has received scant attention until now. Exactly how long this presence remained is unclear, although it might well explain the former existence there of a church of St John, which was destroyed during an assault on the besieged citadel in 1361, which by that time was little more than a defensive town. Those responsible for these actions were Aragonese mercenaries loyal to a prince named Henri de Trastamare, who opposed the rule of his brother Pierre I, King of Aragon and Castille. According to tradition, the church was dismantled stone by stone as the mercenaries were 'searching for a precious deposit'[148] (the present church of Mary Magdalene where Berenger Saunière was priest from 1885 until his death in 1917 was formerly a chapel attached to the town's château[149]). This might seem like an inconsequential point, but the knowledge that Pierre's title 'de St Jean' derived from his lands and properties in St Jean de Brucafel, which were also given to the Order, makes the association with this saint even more appealing. What type of devotion did this man hold for, presumably, St John the Baptist, and was it linked with Richard's belief that the Templar head reliquary known as the Head of God was transported from England to Rennes-le-Château shortly after the arrest of the English Templars in January 1308? Was it this that the Aragonese mercenaries had been attempting to find when they dismantled the citadel's church of St John in 1361? Had knowledge of its existence come from former Knights Templar of Roussillon-Aragon loyal to the King of Aragon and Castille?

All I knew for certain was that the Knights Templar did indeed play a prominent role in preserving the Gnostic mysteries surrounding the teachings of the two Johns – the Baptist and the Evangelist – and that these saints subsequently influenced the development of speculative Masonry, what we know today as Freemasonry. Moreover, there was real evidence to suggest that the Johannites saw John the Evangelist as the first priest of Christianity and the bearer of the cup of the Last Supper, which, as the vessel used to contain the Holy Blood of Christ, played a crucial role in the emergence of the Grail legend. Whether this new-found knowledge might eventually translate into tangible results was another matter altogether. For the moment, there was little more we could do than study the background of the Holy Grail and await further communication through dreams and visions, which would not be long in coming.

8. THE WORLD TREE

Friday, 28 December. The dream began mundanely at first, with Richard dealing with clients at the front counter of the well-known hardware chain at which he worked. Yet then the imagery took on more engaging dimensions, as he found himself leaving the warehouse and descending a set of stone stairs illuminated by gaslight. At their base was the entrance to a dimly lit underground crypt of enormous size, so big in fact that it had to be beneath a large religious building, such as a cathedral or abbey. All around him were thick round pillars that bore carvings of devils and demons of the sort he would stop to examine if he were given the chance to do so.

The crypt was by no means empty. An audience sat facing a makeshift wooden stage at the far end where an entertainer – a stocky man in a checked suit, like something out of an old music hall – kept them entertained with his own brand of humour. Richard attempted to listen to what was going on – what jokes they were laughing at – but it was no good. Everything existed just beyond the realm in which he now found himself. Nervously, he decided to take a seat at the back, where the chairs were mostly empty, and here he waited in anticipation as to what might happen next.

He was not kept waiting, for at that moment he saw walking towards him a beautiful woman, tall, curvy and in her thirties. She was dressed in a knee-length black suit with a matching pillbox hat and veil, worn slightly askew, obscuring most of her heavily made-up face. Her style of dress seemed to suggest the 1940s, he told himself.

She sat down next to him, allowing Richard to see that her long dark red hair was rolled up tightly into a fat bun. Looking directly at him, she glanced around somewhat pensively before moving her head closer. 'You seek my cup, and know of its Gnostic mysteries,' she began, a note of urgency in her melodic voice. 'Then you must find the World Tree.' She then reached across and clasped one of Richard's hands, at which he saw that the woman was wearing dainty black gloves made from a soft, see-through fabric. More peculiarly, he noticed that her hands bore henna-like tattoos showing spiders' webs.

Her touch made him lose control of the setting, for instantly the whole room began to spin, making it seem as if he was drunk on her energy. Pulling away now, he leaped backwards out of his seat and began staggering towards the stage.

'What is this?' he found himself saying. 'What's going on here? Where am I?'

The laughing echo of the audience swirled around in his head. Were they laughing at him, or the entertainer? He could not tell, and did not understand. A set of wooden steps led up to the level of the wooden platform and almost involuntarily he found himself climbing them and falling down into a gilded throne on the right-hand side of the stage.

Richard now saw that the entertainer in the checked suit was in fact Aleister Crowley, who grinned inanely as he advanced holding a seven-spoked crown of gold.

'I crown you King Mithras,' laughed the Beast 666, before placing it on Richard's head. Like some powerful hallucinogen, it had the effect of plunging the dreamer on to another level – one where only fleeting images broke the eternal blackness. Before him now was the woman, who he realised was a personification of Venus as Babalon, the Scarlet Woman. In her hands was the Grail cup, and he saw that engraved around its base was a circular snake biting its own tail, a symbol of eternity. On the bowl was the letter A, stylised to look like the end of a penis, something that was used by Crowley as a bizarre abstract signature.

Then came words, from her.

'Seek the World Tree upon my star. Find this and all shall be revealed.'

A rush of vibrant colour gave way to more imagery. He could see himself in the darkness walking towards a gnarled old tree, a great oak perhaps, standing on its own, as a blustering gale raged around him. Yet there was something wrong with the way it looked, for it seemed as if a great axe had sliced the trunk down the middle, giving it the appearance of two quite separate trees. It stood on the edge of a churchyard, close to a medieval church of some distinction. Gravestones and a boundary wall or fence were to be found nearby. Somehow, the tree was an intelligence in its own right, regal in feel, almost as if its essence preserved profound secrets that reached back to the very roots of Christianity on these shores. It symbolised what was known in Norse mythology as Yggdrasil, the World Tree, standing at the centre of the universe – its roots in the underworld, its trunk in this world and its branches in heaven. Moreover, Richard felt sure that it was placed right at the centre of a huge circle containing a seven-fold starlike pattern that overlaid southeast England, each point corresponding to one of the seven degrees of initiation in the Roman cult of the god Mithras. He was not sure why. All he knew was that the tree existed somewhere out there, and that it signified the very heart of their quest, and only by unlocking its secrets could they hope to find the Grail.[150]

Saturday, 29 December. Sue and I listened carefully as Richard related the details of his dream over a drink in a quiet pub in the Kent seaside town of Margate, where we had gone that day on questing business. There seemed every reason to believe that a geometric pattern of profound importance existed somewhere in the landscape of southeast England. If we were to determine its precise location then its centre would have to be fixed, and this was now our goal. It sounded easy, and yet so far we knew of just two places on the circle's perimeter: St Clement's Caves, Hastings, and a medieval castle at Saltwood, near Hythe in Kent, which during a new psychic session Crowley had indicated would be found at its east-southeastern extremity.[151] By using this meagre information, I had managed to calculate what I believed was the circle's dead centre, which fell without any fanfare close to the parish church of Stockbury, a small village situated on the North Downs of Kent. In view of Richard's new-found belief that the cup might be located at or very close to this crucial location, I read up on Stockbury, but found nothing of any interest, other than the mention of an old yew in the churchyard.[152] Was this the gnarled old tree that Richard now felt stood at the centre of the circle? It was essential that we visited the church to find out, and this is what we intended to do on the way home later that night.

Richard's peculiar dream showed that Aleister Crowley was also still centre stage in our Grail quest. However, the presence of the beautiful woman in 1940s dress also intrigued me. As Babalon, she appeared to be a modern personification of Venus, goddess of sex and love. Instead of holding in her hands an ancient stone cup like some of her Near Eastern pagan counterparts, Babalon bore a silver chalice personalised by Crowley himself. Was it this that we could expect to find concealed within the vicinity of the ancient tree at the centre of the landscape Star of Babalon, or did it simply fit into the dream's specific time frame, which appeared to be sometime around the Second World War?

THE CULT OF MITHRAS

That Richard was crowned 'King Mithras' by Crowley was also of extreme interest. To start with, the occultist believed that Baphomet was in fact the Persian god Mithras, whose cult, which spread throughout the Roman world coincident to Christianity, did indeed have seven degrees of initiation. In addition to this, I discovered that during one of the ceremonies of initiation into the higher degrees, the candidate would be offered a crown. Apparently, the mystic, aspiring towards the title of *Miles*, would refuse to take it, proclaiming that Mithras was his only crown. Thereafter, according to Franz Cumont (1868–1947), the noted Belgian historian of the religions of antiquity, the candidate 'never wore one neither at banquets nor when it was awarded to him as a military honour, replying to the person who conferred it: "It belongs to my god," that is to say, to the invincible god.'[153]

Mithras's crown of seven rays was really a metaphor for the golden sun-disc, which he gave to his companion Helios, or Sol Invictus, who was essentially an aspect of himself. He controlled the world through the sun's yearly course from solstice to solstice, and then back again. It was Helios who, as the sun-god, was transformed into the two Johns – John the Baptist and John the Evangelist – by the Gnostics of the second and third centuries.

Another factor that intrigued me about Richard's dream was the underground crypt in which it had taken place. I recognised it as the one beneath Canterbury Cathedral where theatre productions, particularly historical re-enactments, were staged on a regular basis. Even though Richard had never been there, he was right in the fact that it did contain various carved Romanesque pillars with devils and demons on their capitals. It had to be the same place, but why Richard's mind should have selected this location as the setting for his dream was unclear.

* * *

When our cars came to a halt on the deserted approach road outside the entrance to Stockbury's secluded church, it was already past midnight. The weather was clear and dry, even though the temperature was not much above freezing point. Locking the vehicles, Richard, his partner Pandora (who had joined us after visiting a friend that afternoon in Margate), Sue and I made our way to the rear of the churchyard in search of the aforementioned old yew tree, which was nowhere to be seen. Either it did not exist any more or it was hidden out of sight beyond the dozens of other trees on the south side of the churchyard. Eventually, when the bitter cold began to bite, we retired into the darkened porch, which seemed the obvious place to huddle together, in order to conduct a brief meditation.

Closing our eyes, we tried desperately to gain any information that might help progress the quest forward, but on this occasion there seemed to be very little going on in our minds. Nothing about Stockbury captured Richard's imagination, and I was beginning to feel that we were at the wrong place. Afterwards, the four of us walked to the southern edge of the chilly churchyard and continued the search for the lost yew tree.

'It's not here,' Richard at last admitted, looking out beyond the Downs towards the flickering lights of distant villages. 'I mean the tree, it's not here, and if I get a pulling anywhere, it's to the south.'

South of here was West Malling, and the town of Maidstone, but aside from this I knew very little about the geography of Kent. I asked him if he could tell me any more about the gnarled old tree we were meant to find.

'Not much, I'm afraid,' he sighed, cupping his hands as Pandora snuggled up to keep warm. 'I just keep seeing some kind of crack down its centre, almost as if it's been split in two by a lightning strike, or something.'

Was it a yew tree?

He shrugged his shoulders. 'Maybe. I don't know, really. It could be an oak, I suppose.'

This was interesting, since there were examples in Britain and abroad of great oaks standing at the centre of ritual landscapes, symbolically acting as a cosmic axis turning the cycles of heaven, just like the Yggdrasil of Norse tradition, which is actually an ash tree. For instance, at Lillington, near Leamington Spa in Warwickshire, there was until recently an ancient oak, known as the Midland Oak, that was supposed to mark the centre of England, a claim which went back several centuries.[154] A few kilometres away is a rival claimant to the same title in the village of Meriden, where the Meriden Cross, a prominent obelisk, is said to mark the centre of the country. Was it something of the calibre of the Midland Oak that we should expect to find at the centre of the great circle of sites? It would be nice to think so, but no obvious candidate had revealed itself so far, and Richard knew that it was up to him to produce fresh information if we wanted to take this Grail quest any further.

9. THE CALL OF ARCADIA

Before him on the floor of the semi-darkened room in his London home was a large-scale map of southeast England with the seven-pointed Star of Babalon design superimposed, on which Richard now focused his mind. It took a moment to see anything, but following a sudden rush of vibrant colour created by the retina, specific images began to crystallise into a real setting. He found himself walking towards the old gnarled tree, which he could now see was definitely an ancient oak, at least several hundred years old, perhaps even older. He tried to gain some sort of fix on its location, but was instantly torn away to glimpse another place altogether.

Richard found himself travelling northwards from the verdant green landscape of Kent and Sussex to somewhere less familiar to him with woods, rolling hills and an extensive landscaped garden surrounding a large country mansion. Flashes of temples, follies and a Chinese pavilion were passed by in favour of a peculiar monument unlike anything he had ever seen before. On top of a huge Greek-style stone urn was what appeared to be a carved domestic cat, which, although innocuous-looking, he felt reflected the stories told at the trials of the Templars about a demon in the form of a cat worshipped by initiates. Elsewhere on the monument were goats, or goats' heads, that represented Baphomet in his guise as Pan, the Greek god of nature and controller of the cosmos, whose realm was Arcadia, the earthly paradise so full of myth and legend.

These clues were merely pointers to something of far greater importance, for on the plinth that supported the vase was a plaque or design that bore either an inscription or a heraldic shield or crest. As incredible as it might seem, he felt this would prove to be a major key not only in their quest to seek the Holy Grail, but also to the mystery of Rennes-le-Château – thoughts which betrayed the whereabouts of this monument. There seemed little question that he was now in the grounds of somewhere that had concealed a clue to this mystery for the past 250 years. It was Shugborough Park in Staffordshire, where the visitor can marvel at a temple-like façade known as the Shepherd's Monument, on which is a puzzling representation of Nicholas Poisson's famous painting *Les Bergers d'Arcadie* ('The Shepherds of Arcadia'). Strangely, he now sensed that this monument, which had been the focus of attention for researchers and writers on the subject for many years, was a false clue, a red herring, and that the real key was this strange urn on a plinth. Somehow, its stark feline and goat-orientated symbolism hinted at the idea that it was created by someone with a deep interest in the Knights Templar.

No words came to him on this occasion, although further flashes of inspiration did enter his mind. He again saw the château of Arques, so close to Rennes-le-Château, as well as a heavy stone casket with a carved lid that showed an androgynous figure with their arms held by chains and the sun and the moon above the left and right shoulders. He knew that line drawings of similar casket lids dating from the thirteenth century were shown in the works of nineteenth-century Austrian Orientalist Baron Joseph von Hammer-Pürgstall, who saw them as representations of Baphomet, the idol of the Templars. Some of these figures were horned, leading Templar apologists in the nineteenth century to conclude that Baphomet was goat-headed, and thus a form of the master of the witches' sabbath, exactly how he is presented in the classic illustration of the so-called 'Goat of Mendes' by French occultist Eliphas Levi. He saw Baphomet as an androgyne with the head and legs of a goat, the torso of a woman and a male member symbolising the cosmic axis.

Richard realised that his brain was fast switching into rational mode, and that it was time to come back down to earth. Opening his eyes, he emerged from the meditational state vowing to do some library research into the work of Baron von Hammer-Pürgstall and his controversial theories concerning the Gnostic origins of the Knights Templar. Beyond that there was little more he could add to the poignant imagery he had just encountered, other than to externalise a few floating thoughts still buzzing around in his head. For instance, he felt that the person responsible for creating the Cat Monument at Shugborough was someone called 'Thomas Wright', although the only Thomas Wright he knew was the nineteenth-century English antiquarian, archaeologist and author of a large number of books including *An Essay on the Worship of the Generative Powers During the Middle Ages of Western Europe*. This classic work was privately published in 1865 alongside an edition of Richard Payne Knight's *A Discourse on the Worship of Priapus and its Connection With the Mystic Theology of the Ancients*, which demonstrates the overt sexual nature of ancient worship among pagan religions. Wright's own work continued the same theme but also examined the heretical beliefs of the Knights Templar as revealed during the trials of the early fourteenth century. He also had much to say about von Hammer-Pürgstall's proposed Gnostic origins of Templarism and included several illustrations from his extremely rare books, a coincidence which Richard felt was relevant somehow. If this Thomas Wright was behind the monument at Shugborough, could it have been him who decided that it should include overt goat and feline symbolism?

The only other suggestion going around in his mind was a possible link between the designer of the Shugborough monument and the infamous eighteenth-century Englishman Sir Francis Dashwood. He was the leader of the Hellfire Club, the name given by his adversaries to the debauched revelry that went on inside his homes at West Wycombe, Buckinghamshire, and Medmenham Abbey, near Marlow, in the same county. How he might be linked with Shugborough Park was not made clear, although it was an intriguing connection nonetheless. Perhaps, he thought, Andrew could shed some light on it.[155]

* * *

I visited Shugborough back in 1980 and saw the Shepherd's Monument on that occasion, but could not recall a stone urn in the gardens with a cat on it. But then again I was not an expert on the subject, although I did know someone who knew more about the place than me. This was Storm Constantine, one of Britain's leading fantasy writers, who was also a good friend of mine. For most of her life she has lived in the town of Stafford, which is just a few kilometres down the road from the Shugborough estate.

After dialling her number, and saying our hellos, I ran through the details of Richard's dream and asked her if she knew of a stone urn there with a carved domestic cat perched on top.

'No,' she replied, after thinking for a moment. 'There is a monument with a cat at Shugborough, but I don't remember any kind of urn. I even wrote a short story about it when I was younger. But I don't think it's what you're describing.'

This was not going well.

'Trouble is that you won't be able to get in there until the house and gardens re-open in the spring,' she pointed out. 'I think it's Easter that they open. I'll check with my dad. He'll know.'

If the monument was some kind of key to understanding both the Grail quest and the' mysteries of Rennes-le-Château, then we were going to have to wait for another four months to find out why. In the meantime, I attempted to establish what I could about Shugborough and its mysteries through other means.

IN SEARCH OF SHUGBOROUGH

Situated on the edge of the wooded expanse known as Cannock Chase, the 900-acre estate (now under the joint administration of the National Trust and Staffordshire County Council) was begun at the end of the seventeenth century by William, Lord Anson, who in 1695 constructed a new, two-storey, brick-built house. He was the first of the Earls of Lichfield to live at Shugborough, which prior to this time had consisted of a manor house that acted as a residence for the Bishops of Lichfield, as well as a small country village. The estate was inherited in 1720 by his eldest son Thomas (1695–1775), whose younger brother George (1697–1762) was destined for a life on the high seas, first as a captain, then as the First Lord of the Admiralty and finally, in 1761, as Admiral and Commander-in-Chief of the Fleet.

Thomas Anson gradually bought up more and more land in Shugborough, demolishing the existing buildings in order to make way for the development of his new park and gardens. From 1745 onwards his building project was realised in full as he commissioned the reconstruction of the existing house and the landscaping of the park using money raised from the sale of Spanish treasure sequestered by his younger brother during a celebrated four-year circumnavigation of the globe (1740–4). Two years later George was awarded the title Lord Anson (presented to him purely because of his outstanding naval service to the country), and within a very short time Shugborough was transformed into a beautiful mansion and fine Rococo park complete with neo-classical monuments, such as the Arch of Hadrian and the Tower of the Winds, designed by the architect James 'Athenian' Stuart (1714–88).

Even though George became Lord Anson, he never owned Shugborough, and the development of the house and park was entirely the brainchild of his bachelor brother Thomas, who in 1747 was elected Member of Parliament for Lichfield. Along with the Earl of Sandwich, he was a founder member of the Dilettanti Society,[156] created in 1732 as a dining club for the study and promotion of Greek classical art and architecture. It was through this society that he came to know both the architect James Stuart and another of its primary members, Sir Francis Dashwood (1708–1781), the notorious name behind the Hellfire Club. Despite its reputation as a hive of devil worship, the revelry that went on at its meetings was little more than an excuse for drunken debauchery done under the name of a fake Franciscan order, complete with its own mock services. Dashwood knew Thomas Anson very well, for both of them were also founders of the short-lived Divan Club, whose members met to express their interest in all things Oriental, or Turkish, which included the obligatory wearing of turbans.

It is not thought that Thomas Anson became involved in the Hellfire Club, even though he certainly knew key individuals who were regular attendees of its pseudo-Elysian rites at Medmenham Abbey on the River Thames. Like Dashwood, Anson was also a member of the Royal Society, through which he became associated with some of the most eminent freethinkers of the day, including Erasmus Darwin and Josiah Wedgwood.

THOMAS WRIGHT OF DURHAM

Among the architects and designers brought in by Thomas Anson to help redesign Shugborough's house and park was Thomas Wright – no, not the antiquarian and writer as Richard had speculated, but the astronomer, architect and mathematician of County Byers, Durham (1711–86) – who, as I was to find out, came to Staffordshire with a very strange pedigree indeed. He was almost certainly responsible for the Shepherd's Monument, which consists of a false temple façade (with slightly later Doric pillars added either side) set within which is a bas-relief showing Poussin's *Les Bergers d'Arcadie* transposed, mirror fashion. Resting on the tomb, which bears the famous Latin legend *ET IN ARCADIA EGO*, is an arklike casket that has no obvious explanation whatsoever. Just as mysterious are a series of initials on a plaque set beneath the Poussin painting, which no one has been able to satisfactorily decipher. In two lines, they read:

O U O S V A V V

D.   M.

Thomas Wright created this puzzling monument sometime between the years 1750 and 1755,[157] although why, exactly, remains a complete mystery. As a self-taught astronomer, he was the first to propose that the Milky Way was an optical effect of seeing the galaxy as a disc side on, a theory voiced in his book *An Original Theory or New Hypothesis of the Universe*, published in 1750. He also speculated on the existence of other galaxies, each with an infinite all-active divine power at its centre.[158] These cosmological musings heavily influenced the theories of a young Immanuel Kant (1724–1804), who in his *Universal Natural History and Theory of the Heavens*, published in 1755, elaborated on Wright's ideas, which he first came across in a Hamburg periodical.

In addition to his interest in astronomy, Wright was a self-taught mathematician who was the tutor of Lady Anson's sister-in-law at Wrest Park, the home of the de Grey family at Silsoe in Bedfordshire (where curiously, in 1749 he designed a pagan altar to Mithras), which was how he came to meet Thomas Anson. Although originally from Durham, Wright had moved to London where he became acquainted with the noted antiquarian Roger Gale (1672–1744), the first vice-president of the Society of Antiquaries. With his younger brother Samuel and the Earl of Pembroke, Gale helped spearhead the revival in Druidism with their friend, the famous antiquarian, Anglican rector and scholar of sacred history William Stukeley (1687–1765), who was the first secretary of the society. Like them, Wright applied his mathematical skills to surveying and measuring prehistoric sites, usually stone circles, in Britain and Ireland, believing them to be the remnants of a lost religion with knowledge of the celestial bodies.

THE PHILADELPHIANS AND QUIETISTS

Aside from his interest in Druidism, Thomas Wright's first book, *A Theory of the Universe*,[159] published in 1734 (and written when he was just 22 years of age), reveals a profound understanding of mystical cosmology based on medieval concepts of heaven and hell, complete with archangels, seraphim, cherubs, Satan and fallen angels. It is clearly guided by the hidden teachings of the Hebrew Cabbala as well as the symbolism of Ancient Egypt, the latter of which is acknowledged in the text.[160] Commentators on Wright have sought to identify the source of his mystical cosmology with the works of Robert Fludd (1574–1637), a prominent English Rosicrucian and writer of occult philosophy, and Jacob Boehme (1575–1624), a German protestant and mystic.[161] Indeed, there is every reason to believe that Wright was heavily influenced by the religious ideals of The Philadelphian Society for the Advancement of Piety and Divine Philosophy, founded by Jane Leade (1623–1704) and John Pordage in 1670.[162]

Inspired by the works of Boehme, which had recently been translated into English, the Philadelphians believed in divine revelation through quietness and contemplation, a discipline Jane Leade acquired from another sect known as the Quietists, founded in Spain during the same century. She was the author of a large number of books, and was said to have received visions of a woman she identified only as Virgin-Wisdom. Among the greatest supporters of the Quietists was Francois Fénelon (1651–1715), a famous French writer and Archbishop of Cambrai, who expressed his own take on their mystical philosophy in his book *Maxims of the Saints*, published in 1697. He spent ten years in Paris's famous seminary of St Sulpice, much linked with the mystery of Rennes-le-Château.

One of Fénelon's greatest supporters, and another Quietist, was Andrew Michael Ramsay (1686–1743), a Scottish-born writer and philosopher, who met Fénelon in 1710, and afterwards converted to Catholicism. He spent most of his life in France, before being asked in 1724 to go to Rome to tutor the exiled Stuart princes Charles Edward and Henry, who afterwards became cardinal of York. Known also as Chevalier Ramsay, he was a prominent Freemason, who in a famous oration claimed that the Craft was descended from the knights of the Crusades. He is credited with the invention, or at least the spread, of several Templar degrees, known collectively as Ramsay's Rite, which he tried introducing to England's Grand Lodge in 1728–30. Whereas they rejected them out of hand, these degrees were incorporated eleven years after his death into the system being formulated by a French Masonic organisation known as the Emperors of the East and West, founded in Paris in 1758 (see Chapter 24).[163] How many, if any, of these connections were known to Thomas Wright, or indeed Thomas Anson, is not known.

THE SHEPHERD'S MONUMENT

Following Wright's death in 1786, masses of unpublished writings were found at his home at Byers Green, near Durham City, including the preliminaries for a Druidic cosmological romance in which a city named Heliopolis (Greek for 'city of the sun') was located at the centre of Britain. Was this what we too were attempting to establish, our own 'city of the sun' at the centre of the Star of Babalon overlaid on the landscape of southeast England?

To know that such an extraordinary character was responsible for the reconstruction of the Shugborough house and park was one thing, but to also find out that he was responsible for the Shepherd's Monument was certainly interesting, if nothing else. Apparently, the structure was designed originally as an alcove, similar to one Wright built in 1750 at Badminton Park, Gloucestershire, which incorporates a landscaped grove with a 'talisman' of trees disposed in magical numbers. Was it possible that, red herring or not, the Shepherd's Monument encoded within its design some profound mystery of the universe?

Whatever the answer, Thomas Wright could not have worked alone on this project. He probably shared his enthusiasm for the mysteries of life with Shugborough owner Thomas Anson, who must have commissioned the monument in the first place. The dining room at Shugborough Hall features the Egyptian deities Isis and Serapis, revealing Anson's passion for Ancient Egypt, whilst his time hanging out with Sir Francis Dashwood can only have enhanced his appetite for the mystery cults of the classical world. Yet why a mirror image of Poussin's *Les Bergers d'Arcadie* should have featured on the Shepherd's Monument remains unclear. The only clue is the fact that television presenter and Rennes-le-Château stalwart Henry Lincoln visited the estate in the 1980s and discovered among the archives of the Lichfield family a pencil sketch copy of an early version of Poussin's *Les Bergers d'Arcadie*, completed for the Duke of Devonshire some thirteen years before the more famous version found in the Louvre.[164]

No one knows how Shugborough came to be linked with the story of Rennes-le-Château, although Lincoln concludes that the Shepherd's Monument is tangible evidence of that connection. Its strange sequence of initials, **O U O S V A V V** and **D – M**, was interpreted by the grandmother of the current Lord Lichfield as meaning:[165]

> Out Your'n Own Sweet Vale, Alicia, Vanisheth Vanity
> 'Twixt Deity and Man thou shepherdest the way.[166]

Only the U has been altered to a Y in order to make 'Your'n', otherwise the sequence is perfect, a fact which cannot be ignored. However, there is every reason to conclude that the Countess of Lichfield invented this poetic interpretation of the initials, for it is nowhere to be found in the known history of Shugborough Park.[166] Furthermore, the letters D and M in the second line often appear in Roman funerary inscriptions and stand for *Dis manibus (sacrum)* – 'sacred to the dead' – implying that the letters on the Shugborough monument are commemorative in some way.[167]

So much for the Shepherd's Monument, which I was not convinced should be dismissed as a red herring on the Rennes-le-Château trail. All that could be said was that there was no sign anywhere of a monument at Shugborough that featured a stone urn on which languished a carving of a domestic cat. Either it was so insignificant as to be overlooked by the sources I consulted, or it never existed. Our friend Storm did refer to a cat statue in the grounds of the park, although this appeared to be quite different from the monument being described by Richard. She said she would ask her father, John Bristow, a local historian, whether he knew anything about the inner history of the Anson family. Beyond that there seemed very little we could do but wait until the house and gardens re-opened at Easter. For the moment, our greater concern was finding the old oak tree which apparently stood at the centre of the great circle of sites to be found somewhere in southeast England, for without that there was no Grail quest.

10. SECRET LAST SUPPER

Monday, 31 December. Emerging from the darkened interior of St John's church, Glastonbury, our party crossed the road and headed towards the bottom end of the High Street, dominated by new-age stores and shops selling everything from replica medieval swords to crystal balls, statues of the great goddess and books on the Holy Grail. They are a joy to visit, and each time I go to Glastonbury the atmosphere exuded by its ancient and sacred places revitalises my inner spirit. Yet at least some of the town's precious sanctity is, in my humble opinion, based on false pretences, and this should not be ignored by anyone trying to get to the truth of its ancient power, which can still be felt and experienced today.

The popular tradition that Joseph of Arimathea came here bringing the Grail, or in fact two cruets, containing the blood *and* sweat of Jesus, is based on falsifications created by the cunning abbots and monks of Glastonbury Abbey during the thirteenth century, due to their fierce rivalry with Canterbury, which was recognised as England's principal centre of pilgrimage. Before the appearance of the first Grail romances, no written evidence existed supporting the belief that Joseph reached these shores, despite the fact that Glastonbury was once seen by the ancient Britons as an island of the dead,[168] a Celtic otherworld, lying on the edge of the western sea. Yet who might have been responsible for its first Christian foundation remains a complete mystery, and after coming to Glastonbury to investigate its associations with the Grail, I had to conclude that there was no point in pursuing the matter any further, for the trail had come to an end. Yet by some strange irony what could turn out to be one of the most important developments in Grail research for a very long time had occurred in Glastonbury over the past few months.

Yuri Leitch is an artist and historian, as well as a friend and colleague, who at the time was working on the first edition of a new journal on the Knights Templar entitled *The Temple*. In its first issue he would reveal what is arguably the oldest-known pictorial representation of the Grail cup, a discovery that was already causing ripples among writers and researchers in the field.[169] It would surely be the topic of conversation when later we met at Glastonbury's only curry house, where we intended gathering together for a hearty New Year's Eve meal and a few drinks before preparing ourselves for the long walk up Glastonbury Tor for midnight.

THE FRANKS CASKET

Yuri's research centres on the Franks Casket, a box 13 centimetres (5 inches) high, 23 centimetres (9 inches) long and 19 centimetres (7.5 inches) wide, fashioned in panelled sections from a piece of whalebone sometime around AD 700–50. Each of its four sides, as well as its damaged lid, bears carved scenes taken from episodes in pagan Anglo-Saxon and classical mythology, as well as events connected with early Christianity. All are accompanied by single words and cryptic inscriptions in Northumbrian Anglo-Saxon and Latin, which are written using characters from the so-called runic alphabet. No one knows who was responsible for this priceless treasure, although some have thought it to be the work of an unknown artist monk from the monastery of Holy Island at Lindisfarne in the county of Northumbria.

The box's modern history begins in 1857 when Sir Augustus W. Franks, an English antiquarian, purchased it in pieces from a Paris antiques dealer. Almost immediately, Franks attempted to trace its provenance and found that the trail led to a Professor Mathieu of Clermont-Ferrand in Auvergne, France, who had sold it to the dealer. Mathieu in turn had come across it in a middle-class home at Auzon in the Brionde district of Haute-Loire country, where it was being used by the ladies of the farmhouse in question as a workbox in which to keep their needles and cotton! At the time it had silver mountings, but these were stripped off by one of the sons of the household and replaced by crude rings. As a consequence of this vandalism the whole thing fell to pieces, resulting in the supposed loss of one of the side panels. Satisfied by what he had found out about the exquisite piece, Franks donated it to the British Museum, where it remains on display to this day.

Only much later did it emerge that Franks was in fact misled by the Paris dealer, a M. Carrand. He had received into his possession the missing panel, which he said nothing about and bequeathed in his will to the Bargello Museum in Florence. At some point, the British Museum made a cast of the panel and thus were able to restore the casket to something close to its former glory.

Aside from panels showing scenes from episodes in the *Lay of Voland*, found in a collection of Saxon poems called the *Verse Edda*,[170] a section on one panel shows the three Wise Men of the Nativity story presenting gifts to the infant Jesus, held in his mother's arms inside a pillared shrine, representing the manger. Above the figures is a stylised Star of Bethlehem as well as the word MFXI, 'Mægi', alluding to the fact that the Wise Men were thought to be Magi from Persia. Another panel shows the classical story of Romulus and Remus, the legendary founders of Rome, who are seen being suckled by a kindly she-wolf. Yet it is the panel at the rear of the casket that had become the focus of Yuri's attention (see Plate 11).

In the centre of the panel is a stylised domed structure, fronted by two pillars, that takes up its entire height. Marching towards this building from the upper left-hand side are soldiers in pleated kilts carrying spears and swords, as smaller individuals flee on to its arched roof. A Latin inscription along the top edge of the panel in runic characters reveals that the scene shows the destruction of the Temple of Jerusalem, sacked and razed to the ground in AD 70 by Titus, the commander of the legions and future Emperor. It reads: 'Here fight Titus and the Jews. Here the inhabitants flee from Jerusalem'. The scene on the upper right-hand side of the panel shows people escaping from the city, and directly below them is a line of figures, next to which is the word *gisl*, 'hostage', referring to the fact that various Jewish dignitaries were taken as hostages in order to ensure their country's allegiance to Rome.[171] According to Flavius Josephus, the first-century Jewish historian, who witnessed the destruction of the Temple and sack of Jerusalem and then wrote about it in his *Wars of the Jews*, some 97,000 Jews were carried off as captives, while another 1,100,000 perished either through famine or by the sword.[172]

The main mystery surrounds the fourth and final scene of the panel, which appears beneath the line of Roman soldiers in the left-hand corner. A central figure is seen seated on a chair with a back rest that terminates in what appear to be shepherds' crooks. He holds a cup up to his heart, while a second, much smaller figure, seated beneath him, holds a similar cup in his outstretched right hand. To the right of the central figure are two men moving towards him, one of whom is clearly a soldier, while to the left of him are two more figures engaged in an act, the nature of which has become a matter of some dispute. Next to them is a single word in runes, which reads *dom*, 'doom', or more correctly 'judgment', something which has led at least one scholar to assume that the central figure in this scene is a judge making his deliberations.[173]

YURI'S FINDINGS

No Anglo-Saxon art historian who has studied the Franks Casket sees any special significance in the Temple of Jerusalem panel, and rarely do they make any comments on its striking symbolism. However, Yuri Leitch, a first-class student of Christian and pagan art, has come up with his own unique take on this scene, which he sees as Christian in origin. In the knowledge that the panel revolves around the destruction of the Temple, he believes that the small figure at the centre of the scene beneath the seated 'judge' is in fact Joseph of Arimathea who clutches the Holy Grail, following his release after 42 years of captivity at the hands of the Jews, a story found in the Grail romances.[174]

The significance of such a discovery would be enormous, for it would provide firm evidence that nearly 500 years before the emergence of the Grail romances, Joseph of Arimathea's imprisonment at the hands of the Jewish priesthood, following his collection of the Holy Blood using the cup of the Last Supper, and his subsequent release by Titus (his father Vespasian in the story), was known to the monks of Lindisfarne. Unfortunately, however, there are certain flaws in this theory, since the account found in the Grail romances concerning Joseph's imprisonment after the Crucifixion is loosely based on existing apocryphal texts such as the fifth-century *Evangelium Nicodemi* ('The Gospel of Nicodemus'). Also known as the *Acta Pilati* ('Acts of Pilate'), this work was said to have been translated from Hebrew to Latin by Nicodemus, a Pharisee and important Jew who, according to the Gospel of John, came to Jesus at night in order to learn how he might be born anew.[175]

The *Evangelium Nicodemi* first became widely known in Britain during the eighth century and was still in circulation across Europe when the first Grail romances were written in the last quarter of the twelfth century. It speaks of Joseph's imprisonment on the day of the Crucifixion, but says he was released at midnight on the Sabbath when Jesus entered his cell and transported him instantaneously to his home town of Arimathea in order to demonstrate the power of the Resurrection to the Jewish priesthood. There is no mention of him remaining in prison for 42 years, as is the case in the Grail romances. Moreover, the *Evangelium Nicodemi* never alludes to any vessel associated with the Last Supper and given into the possession of Joseph of Arimathea, or of his subsequent collection of the Holy Blood at the time of the Crucifixion. In fact, not only was the Grail of the romances apparently unknown before Chrétien de Troyes' *Perceval*, but there are no specific traditions prior to this time connecting Joseph of Arimathea with blood-relics. Indeed, other than a couple of examples of Romanesque art from churches in France which are *assumed* to show Joseph of Arimathea in the course of collecting the Holy Blood at the Crucifixion, nothing exists to link him with this tradition until the end of the twelfth century. Despite this, there *is* a tradition concerning the collecting of the Holy Blood before this time, but it involves *not* Joseph but his companion Nicodemus. For instance, Jacobus de Voragine, Archbishop of Genoa, who compiled the *Golden Legend* (c. 1267), records in another work entitled *Chronicon Januense*, written post-1277, that '. . . in certain books of the English (Anglorum) is found the statement that when Nicodemus took down Christ's body from the cross, he also collected the sacred gore which was still moist, and which had been ignominiously spilled about, in a certain vessel of emerald (*vase emeraldino*).'[176] Even though de Voragine *might* have been influenced by the existence of Genoa's *Sacro Catino* in his reference to the vessel being fashioned from emerald, his words imply that there existed a strong tradition that Nicodemus, and not Joseph of Arimathea, was keeper of the Holy Blood.

FÉCAMP'S STORY

Take, for example, the two blood-relics kept at Fécamp Abbey in Normandy, which are said to have been collected by Nicodemus. They are referred to in a treatise dedicated to the third abbot of Fécamp, who died in 1107,[177] and so they were unquestionably there before the end of the previous century. According to Jessie Weston in her important book *The Quest of the Holy Grail*, published in 1913, a minstrel fraternity was founded by the first abbot of Fécamp in 1031 with the express purpose of spreading the reputation of the abbey, indicating that the story of its blood-relics was certainly popular by this time and was thus most probably based on an even earlier tradition.

The story starts with the preparation and burial of Jesus's body by Joseph and Nicodemus, derived from the account in John's Gospel. However, instead of Joseph taking the lead in what happened next, it is Nicodemus who, noticing the dried blood around the wounds on the hands and feet of the Saviour, scrapes some away with a knife and conceals it inside a leather glove.[178] On his deathbed, Nicodemus entrusts the relic to his nephew Isaac, who afterwards comes under threat from the Jewish authorities. Having learned in a dream that Palestine is about to be invaded by Roman legions, he decides to seal the blood-relic in two lead receptacles, which are inserted into a fig tree growing close to the shore. The holes in which they have been placed close up to conceal the relics, and eventually a high tide uproots the tree and washes it out to sea. The tree travels miraculously across the water until it comes eventually to the coast of pagan Gaul, i.e. France, where its precious contents are found and removed. Even though the blood-relics at Fécamp were perhaps present by the end of the tenth century, they were subsequently hidden within a pillar attached to the high altar and not 'found' again until 1171, the knife used by Nicodemus to collect the Holy Blood being discovered at the same time. Thereafter, Fécamp became northwest France's most important place of pilgrimage, bringing it incredible wealth and making it one of the most influential religious houses in Western Europe.

MORE BLOOD-RELICS

In addition to the story behind the blood-relics of Fécamp in France, Nicodemus is connected with the legend surrounding a holy relic known as the *Volto Sancto*, or Holy Face, of Lucca.[179] This asserts that after the Crucifixion Nicodemus was persecuted by the Jews, who whipped him and turned him out of his house. He was then taken into the home of Gamaliel, a rabbi and teacher of St Paul, where he spent his time whittling the likeness of Christ's image. Yet unable to finish it, he fell asleep discouraged and weary, at which an angel appeared and completed the carving overnight.[180] It is said that on his deathbed the sculpture – which in its present form looks like a regular crucifix – was bequeathed to a 'loyal' follower named Issachar, who has to be one and the same as Isaac, Nicodemus's nephew, in the Fécamp story. Thereafter the relic was venerated secretly for many generations until the iconoclastic period of the Byzantine Empire, when sacred idols risked destruction. It was then that a devoted Christian named Selenco, who was at that time the guardian of the Holy Face, is said to have sold it to an Italian bishop named Gualfredo or Walfried, who had been told in a vision to go to a hospice at Ramleh in Palestine and there seek that which God wished to command into his care. Afterwards, it was taken to the port of Joppa (the ancient name for Jaffa), where it was carefully placed on an unmanned vessel that miraculously carried it to the mouth of the River Magra, near Luni in Italy, which it reached on Good Friday in 742. Two phials of Holy Blood are said to have been found in the neck of the image, presumably collected by Nicodemus at the time of the Crucifixion. One was given to the town of Luni, while the other blood-relic, along with the Holy Face itself, was given to the neighbouring town of Lucca, where both remain to this day. Although there is no written evidence that the *Volto Sancto* reached Italy as early as 742, it was certainly there by 1100, for it is recorded that the English king William Rufus would swear oaths in its name.

In biblical tradition, Nicodemus appears only in John's Gospel, where he is described as 'a man of the Pharisees' and as 'a ruler of the Jews', titles which are never quite explained.[181] Other than the references to him coming by night to learn the teachings of Jesus and to understand how a person might be born anew, the only other mention of him before the Crucifixion is when he addresses the dreaded Sanhedrin, the council of priests and elders under the control of the High Priest Caiaphas. In the knowledge that they are plotting to condemn Jesus, he asks: 'Doth our law judge a man, except it first hear from himself and knew what he doeth?' to which they answer: 'Art thou also of Galilee? Search, and see that out of Galilee ariseth no prophet.'[182] In all four Gospels it is Joseph alone who goes to see the Roman governor Pontius Pilate in order to secure the body of Jesus. Yet in John's Gospel Nicodemus helps Joseph remove the body from the Cross and prepare it for burial in the sepulchre. It tells us also that Nicodemus provides one hundred pounds in weight of mixed myrrh and aloes, which are placed in the linen bound around the body.[183]

Nicodemus's omission from the three Synoptic Gospels is suspicious, and might indicate that his name was deliberately expunged at a very early date for reasons that might never become clear (either that, or his name was an interpolation into the Gospel of John, a much less likely possibility). Since he cautiously defends Jesus before the Sanhedrin, and later takes part in the preparation and burial of his body, Nicodemus was obviously a significant player, and one who somehow became associated with the collection of the Holy Blood in precedence over Joseph of Arimathea.[184] It is not known how old the stories connecting Nicodemus with the blood-relics of Jesus really are, since it has been impossible to determine the true age of the legends surrounding the Holy Face of Lucca and the knife and blood-relics of Fécamp. Moreover, it has also proved difficult to trace the origins behind the legend concerning the collection of Jesus's Holy Blood, a tradition so intimately connected with the concept of the Holy Grail. However, a brief excursion to look at the development of the Crucifixion scene in Christian art does throw some light on the evolution of this tradition.

HOLY BLOOD IN CHRISTIAN ART

It is clear that when the first Grail romances were being composed at the end of the twelfth century, Joseph of Arimathea had become the favoured receiver of the Holy Blood. Whether connected or not, ivory carvings of the Crucifixion fashioned in Germany earlier that same century have a chalice at the base of the Cross where, usually, a skull is shown. It is specifically positioned in order to receive the blood of Jesus, which will ooze down from the wounds in his chest and feet. That the chalice shown in the ivory carvings is there to collect the Holy Blood is confirmed by other contemporary, or slightly earlier, illustrations of the Crucifixion from Bavaria which show the Roman soldier Longinus piercing Jesus's side and the flowing blood being caught in a chalice held by an unidentified male individual at the base of the Cross.[185]

A Crucifixion scene from an illuminated manuscript dated to c. 980 known as Egbert's Psalter shows an even more compelling scenario at the foot of the Cross (see Plate 12). Blood flows as a stream from the wound in Jesus's right breast into a chalice held by a small red-robed male figure wearing a crown. More blood flows from the wounds in Jesus's feet down towards the skull of

Adam, the first man, who was said to have been buried on Calvary Mount, hence its alternative name of Golgotha, 'the place of the skull'. To the left of the cross are three women, one of whom, Mary Magdalene, is reaching out towards the blood stream as if trying to control its flow. On the right-hand side are three figures: Longinus with his spear, a youthful John the Evangelist and an elderly bearded individual, partially obscured, identified as Joseph of Arimathea.[186] Thus by process of elimination, the small figure collecting the Holy Blood must be Nicodemus, the crown signifying that he is 'a ruler of the Jews'. Confirming Nicodemus's role in the collection of the Holy Blood are medieval legends that speak of him using the cup of the Last Supper for this purpose.[187] Curiously, Egbert's Psalter was presented to Egbert of Trier (c. 950–93) by two artist monks of the famous monastery of Reichenau, located on an island in Lake Constance, Italy, which gained its own famous blood-relic in 925,[188] perhaps the reason why the collection of the Holy Blood is emphasised in this illustration.

Going back still further, a Crucifixion scene from the so-called Stuttgart Psalter, thought to have been painted in northern France c. 820/30 (see Plate 16),[189] shows Jesus on the Cross with a chalice floating in midair before him. It stands between a lion and a unicorn that rear up towards him in an aggressive manner thought to symbolise Jewish hostility. However, the fact that the unicorn's horn virtually pierces Jesus's left breast seems to link it with the wound itself. To the right of Jesus stand Longinus and his accomplice Stephaton (mentioned only in medieval legend), yet infinitely more interesting are the two male figures beneath the Cross who carry what appears to be a large blanket. One of them holds a knife in his right hand, making it clear that he is Nicodemus (it was he who used one to collect the dried blood), identifying his accomplice as Joseph of Arimathea, the blanket being the linen shroud in which they intend to wrap Jesus's body. The importance of this picture is that it demonstrates how, as early as the first half of the ninth century, Nicodemus was seen as the guardian of the Holy Blood. Joseph's involvement in the whole affair came much later, and was probably inspired by a certain amount of chalice symbolism that had loosely become associated with his role in the burial of Jesus.

The Holy Sepulchre in which Jesus had been interred was believed to have been owned by Joseph, and since the chalice was occasionally used as a metaphor for the place of Christ's burial, this vessel became linked with Joseph of Arimathea prior to the writing of the first Grail romances.[190] However, the chalice-sepulchre symbolism bore no direct relationship to the tradition concerning the collection of the Holy Blood. Despite this fact, Joseph's connection with the chalice blended well with the story of the Wandering Jew to elevate him into the disciple of Christ who crossed continents in order to spread the word of God, taking with him the secrets of the Grail, seen as the cup of the Last Supper.

At the end of the day, the mere existence of these Crucifixion scenes showing Jesus's blood being collected in a cup ably demonstrates that the concept of the

Holy Grail was not invented by the first writers of the Grail romances; it existed hundreds of years beforehand. The only thing which changed in the twelfth century was that the cup or receptacle used to collect the Holy Blood became known as a *graal*, from the *langue d'Oc* word *grasal*, *grazal*, *grezal*, *gresal*, etc., meaning a pot in which to put liquid.

REVEALING THE FRANKS CASKET

I felt it unlikely that the little man holding the cup on the Franks Casket panel showing the sack of Jerusalem was Joseph of Arimathea. I thus examined more closely the central figure seated above him holding his own cup. Everything about him – his look, the fact that he is seated in such a grand chair and is the focus of the scene – suggested that he was in fact Jesus. To the left of him are two male figures facing each other, one of whom (on the left) appears to be tugging at, or pulling, the long hair of the other. Certainly, this was my initial impression, but the awkwardness of the puller's hand seemed to imply another possible solution. It looked to me as if this figure was using a curved knife or sword to sever the other man's ear. Even though the image was more abstract than realistic, the idea would not leave me, until I realised what it might represent.

The Gospels relate how when Judas betrayed Jesus with a kiss in the Garden of Gethsemane – located outside the city of Jerusalem, over by the Mount of Olives – the disciple Peter drew a sword and cut off the ear of Malchus, a servant of the high priest Caiaphas, who had accompanied the Temple guards intent on seizing Jesus. Seeing what had happened, Jesus picked up the severed ear and healed Malchus of his wound. If this really is what the panel on the Franks Casket shows, then it could mean that the two figures to the right of Jesus represent Judas approaching Jesus in the company of one of the Temple guards. Yet if this was so, why is the 'Jesus' character on the Franks Casket

Fig. 3. Scene from the Franks Casket. What is the identity of the seated figure, and what is the cup that he holds? What are the two men doing to his left?

bearing a cup and why is there another smaller figure at his feet holding either the same or a similar cup?

Turning to the relevant passages in the Bible, I was disappointed to find that two out of four of the Gospels (Luke and John[191]) assert that Peter removed Malchus's *right* ear, whereas it is the *left* 'ear' that is being severed in the scene depicted on the Franks Casket. The other two Gospels (Matthew and Mark[192]) mention only that the servant's ear was severed, without any reference to which one. I was ready to dismiss the whole exercise as a waste of time when, on examining various examples of Jesus's betrayal by Judas in Christian art, I found that Peter is occasionally shown removing Malchus's *left* ear, instead of his right one. This has been done to keep the perspective of the picture, with Peter severing Malchus's ear to the left of Jesus as Judas and the Temple guard approach from the right.

I felt that I was back in business, and could now take the matter further. Below and to the left of the scene showing what I believed were events that occurred in the Garden of Gethsemane is the word *dom*, 'Doom', or 'Judgment'. Because the principal theme of the panel is the destruction of the Temple of Jerusalem, it most probably refers to the belief current among Christians from around AD 150 onwards that this catastrophic event in the history of the Jewish race was divine retribution, or *judgment*, for the manner in which they had treated Jesus and denied the Resurrection. Such hateful views were derived from prophetic statements made in the Gospels that allude to the fulfilment of ancient scriptures. For instance, in the Gospel of Mark, before Jesus is apprehended in the Garden of Gethsemane, he addresses his would-be captors in the following manner: 'Are ye come out, as against a robber, with swords and staves to seize me? I was daily with you in the temple teaching, and ye took me not: but *this is done* that the scriptures might be fulfilled [original emphasis].'[193] Then, of course, there was Jesus's assertion that the Temple would be destroyed in three days, i.e. at the time of the Crucifixion, following the incident known as the 'Cleansing of the Temple', where he and his disciples entered its sacred precincts and overturned the stalls belonging to the money-changers. In the minds of those who compiled the Gospels, the scriptures prophesied that following the appearance of the Messiah the Temple would be torn down and its corrupt Sanhedrin priesthood replaced by a new order, and for the followers of Jesus that day had arrived.

Such ideas were fuelled in the early centuries of the Christian era by pseudo-gospels such as the *Evangelium Nicodemi*, which told how Jesus was condemned by the Jewish priesthood. Similar to the Gospels, it spoke of how, when Jesus expired on the Cross, the sky darkened and the veil of the Temple was rent asunder, omens of what was to come.[194] Anti-Semitic sentiments of this sort filtered through to Anglo-Saxon Britain and might well have been responsible for the single word 'judgment' on the Franks Casket. If so, then it provides a perfect platform to present the scene of Jesus's betrayal into the hands of the Jews who 'brought against him one false accusation after another'.[195] This established, I returned to the central issue of the scene in question – the seated 'Jesus' bearing the cup. Exactly what was this cup, and who was the smaller figure beneath him who also bore a cup? Turning to the Gospel of John, the answer seemed to be provided immediately after Peter severs Malchus's ear, for it records: 'Jesus therefore said unto Peter, "Put up the sword into the sheath: the cup which the Father hath given me, shall I not drink it?" '[196]

AGONY IN THE GARDEN

The use of the cup as a metaphor here is pre-empted not only by the events of the Last Supper, which had occurred just hours beforehand, but also by those in the Garden of Gethsemane when Jesus calls upon Peter, James and John in order that they might watch over him for an hour or so.[197] Once in his company, the disciples are unable to keep awake, causing Jesus to move away slightly and, according to Mark's Gospel, cry out: 'Abba, Father, all things are possible unto thee; remove this cup from me: howbeit not what I will, but what thou wilt.'[198] The other Synoptic Gospels go further by stating that thereafter an angel appeared to Jesus, giving him inner strength to face his agony, after which sweat from Jesus's head fell as drops of blood on to the ground.[199] It is an incident used by Bible scholars to demonstrate the authenticity of the Gospel account, since 'sweating blood' is a rare medical disorder known as hematidrosis, occasionally achieved by someone who, like Jesus when in the garden, is under extreme mental strain. More significant, however, is the nature of this event, known as Christ's 'agony in the garden', with the vessel being referred to as the 'Bitter Cup'. It is usually taken to signify the martyrdom or sacrifice that Jesus knows he must make through crucifixion in order to bring salvation to the world. The 'agony in the garden' scene shows that it is something he only reluctantly accepts, knowing that there is no other way, and that he must now die a horrible death. It is a popular theme of depiction in Christian art, whereby Christ is seen on his hands and knees praying as either an angel or the hand of God materialises before him holding a chalice, symbolising the Bitter Cup. Other variations show the chalice appearing to Christ in a blinding light, exactly as the Holy Grail was said to manifest to King Arthur and the Knights of the Round Table in the medieval romances.

Yet what is quite clear is that the Bitter Cup makes its first appearance on the occasion that James and John, or Salome on their behalf, ask Jesus whether they might sit in glory either side of him, to which the Lord says that this is not for him to decide. However, before they may enter the kingdom of heaven he asks them if they are able to drink from the cup that he drinks from and take the baptism that he has taken. In reply, they say they *will* drink of the same cup and take baptism, not realising that this decision will not only mean them partaking in the goodness of the cup, but also that they, too, will now face almost certain death through martyrdom. In other words, this response from Jesus takes the form of a prophecy, foretelling both his own Crucifixion and the death of James and John.

As is recorded, James, the son of Zebedee, styled 'the Great', was eventually put to death by the Jews at the order of Herod Agrippa in AD 42. Yet John, although twice subjected to martyrdom, first when he was plunged in a cauldron of boiling oil and later when he was forced to drink from the Poison Chalice, survived on both occasions and lived to a ripe old age, at least according to apocryphal tradition. Certainly, this was one of the reasons why the Poison Chalice, being associated with the Bitter Cup, became an emblem of John the Evangelist, since it signified his conquest of martyrdom. Moreover, the cup came to symbolise not just the martyrdom of Jesus, or James and John, but every Christian saint or martyr who received baptism, drank from the communion cup, and then gave their life in the name of Christianity. This is why the Whore of Babylon in John's book of Revelation holds the cup containing the blood of the saints and martyrs – it is the same cup, now full of the blood of all those who have sacrificed their lives in the name of God, including Jesus himself.

When Jesus announced that the wine in the cup of the Last Supper signified his blood, he was implying that through his upcoming martyrdom on the Cross everybody who would afterwards partake of its contents would be able to enter, or at least experience, the kingdom of heaven. This view must be seen from the perspective of the earliest Christians, who lived at the same time that the Synoptic Gospels were being compiled by the evangelists. Despite the hostile world in which these people must have lived, they would desperately have wanted to convey a message designed to encourage further Jews or Gentiles to dedicate their lives to the faith of Christ.

Bible scholars accept that the Last Supper was not a normal Jewish Passover feast, even though it is referred to as such in the Gospel of Luke,[200] for it took place one day too early and featured the communal use of bread and wine. Despite its uniqueness, this style of communion meal was adopted by the earliest Christians, probably in mimicry of the gospel account of the Last Supper, although now with its own unique elements. For instance, it would occur during the so-called Paschal vigil kept on the night before Easter Sunday, the day of the Resurrection,[201] which would include baptismal initiations followed by a specific *perikope*, or 'section', read out from Mark's Gospel, the only time in the year that this would happen.[202]

THE SECRET GOSPEL

Integrally connected to this nocturnal rite of great mystery is the Secret Gospel of Mark, known to exist only from a single reference in a letter, written c. 200, from Clement of Alexandria (d. 213) to one 'Theodore', of whom nothing more is recorded. A copy of it was discovered in 1958 in the library of the monastery of Mar Saba in the Judean desert by noted Bible scholar Morton Smith. His linguistic analysis of the letter, and the fragments of the Lost Gospel it contains, led him to conclude that it predates the formulation of the canonical, i.e. regular, Gospel of Mark, and existed certainly before AD 90.[203] Smith speculated that it had been written by Mark when in Rome with Peter. Then, sometime around AD 60–3, it was taken by Mark back to Alexandria, where he had already established a religious community of his own. Copies of the Secret Gospel eventually came into the possession of Clement and his followers, although the letter makes it clear that one copy at least had fallen into the hands of a Gnostic teacher from Alexandria named Carpocrates, who flourished c. 125–60. His followers, the Carpocratians, now used it in a blasphemous manner to express their founder's own licentious form of the Christian faith – at least, this is how Clement saw it. More importantly, the passages cited from the Secret Gospel, which include an account of how Lazarus was raised from the dead and subsequently underwent a nocturnal baptism in the company of Jesus, fell within the *perikope* from Mark's Gospel read out during the night-long Paschal vigil, something which continued to take place in Clement's day. In other words, this sequence of quotations originally contained passages that were either deliberately left out of Mark's Gospel, or were expunged before AD 90 because of their controversial nature.

The significance of this extraordinary knowledge is that the above-mentioned *perikope*, identified as Mark 10:13–45, includes the story of James and John asking whether they might sit in glory with the Lord, and Jesus responding by asking them whether they are able to drink from the same cup as him and undergo the same baptism.[204] This implies that the cup-and-baptism story concerning James and John was aimed directly at those candidates for baptismal initiation at the Paschal vigil, who would afterwards drink from the communion cup for the first time. Thus acceptance of the Bitter Cup was a double-edged sword. On the one hand receiving baptism and drinking from the communion cup would bring the initiate within sight of the Light of God and the kingdom of heaven, yet on the other its acceptance might well condemn them to a long and painful death as a martyr, like James, or indeed Jesus. Such a profound concept would not have been lost, keeping alive the sheer potency of the cup or chalice as a primary symbol of Christian martyrdom across the centuries.

Through the heterodox, i.e. unorthodox, Johannine communities of Palestine and Asia Minor, a knowledge of the communion meal of the Paschal vigil, and the significance of the Bitter Cup, would seem to have been carried into medieval times by Christian sects such as the Manichaeans, Luciferans, Bogomils, etc. This enabled it to manifest finally as the communal meals of the Cathars, during which *perfectae* would administer *consolamentum* for those candidates ready for reception into the religion. This then was the origin of the *Secret Last Supper* alluded to in the title of the heretical work of this name used by the Cathars. Remember, this features a discourse between Satan and John the Evangelist, the Beloved Disciple and first priest of Christ, whose memory was finally usurped by that of Joseph of Arimathea. Thus the 'secrets' of the Grail expressed in the special 'service' held around a table, mimicking that of the Last Supper, are probably an echo across the centuries of the nocturnal communion meal of the Paschal vigil, while the poignant symbolism of the Bitter Cup would seem to have become the role model for the medieval concept of the Holy Grail.

For me, the scene on the Franks Casket panel depicting the destruction of the Temple shows Jesus holding the Bitter Cup, which is being offered to, or taken away from him by, the smaller cup-bearing figure beneath his chair. He can be seen either as a Christian accepting the communion cup following his baptismal initiation, or as Jesus's priestly successor, who the Gospel of John implies was not Peter, the founder of the Roman Church, but the Beloved Disciple, John himself. If this assessment of the panel is correct, then it really does show the oldest-known representation of the drinking vessel that became known as the Holy Grail. I equally respected Yuri's own view that this same figure on the Franks Casket was Joseph of Arimathea holding the cup of the Last Supper, even though it was something we passionately debated that New Year's Eve around a large table in the Indian restaurant, where Sue and I enjoyed our meals in the company of several close friends. Furthermore, we knew also that the following morning, before travelling back to Essex, we intended to find out what we could about the Templar Stephen de Staplebridge, the alleged one-time keeper of the Head of God.

11. THE APOSTATE

When on earth my name was Stephen de Staplebridge, and I declare, God save, that this is my story.[205] A nobleman by birth, and of the knightly class, I was received into the virtuous Order of the Poor Fellow-Soldiers of Christ and Temple of Solomon on the Feast of the Assumption of the Blessed Virgin Mary in the year of Our Lord, 1295. It took place at the preceptory of Keele in the shire of Stafford, and was presided over by my lord Guy de Forester, the Master of the Temple in England. Present also on this occasion were chaplains John de Reives and Henry de Daumari, and Brother Hugh, the macebearer. I accepted my duties to God, in his mercy, and a short while later, in the year 1297, I was received into the second order, the *Templi Secretum*, although this time the rites were conducted behind closed doors so that the profane might not know their sacred nature. It took place at Lydele, and the receptor this time was none other than the new Master of the Temple, Brian de Jay, a man of forthright spirit. Thereafter I was able to travel with better freedom to pursue the path which God had set forth for me. For ten years all went well, until in October 1307 the King of France, Philip the Fair, with the aid of His Holiness Pope Clement V, declared that our Holy Order was guilty of committing many heinous crimes against the Lord Jesus Christ, and other evil mischiefs which cannot be spoken.

I was able to elude capture by taking flight from Lydele, hiding my face beneath a cloak and cowl, and joining with other fugitives. I was hunted down by the bailiffs of Our Lord the King. During this time, my brethren's duties were manifold, and ever did we think that one day the *Magister Templi*, Jacques de Molay, and our fallen brothers in France, would be absolved of the evil crimes levelled against them, and that our full dignity would be restored.

It was in the year 1311, close to the time of midsummer, that whilst attending to business at New Sarum, in the shire of Wiltshire, I was arrested by the officers of Our Lord the King and taken in chains to Newgate Prison in London, where I was given up to the Chief Inquisitors. None of them had any sympathy for the plight of the Holy Order, for they wished only to extract false testimony from myself and those of my brothers in custody at this time. I was brought for questioning before Their Graces the Bishops of London and Chichester, and then dragged to Saint Paul's Church where I was again accused of great blasphemies and made to confess my sins. Under pressure of torture, and worse still a painful death, I told them a little of my reception into the two orders, and then begged for mercy. I was absolved by His Grace, the Bishop of Chichester, and released from interrogation.

For too long I was kept in gaol, as my brethren tore at their chains and went mad by the day, and then without warning, in the year 1313, I was sent to do penance at the priory of Our Lady at Merton in the shire of Surrey, which is a holy house of the Order of the Blessed Saint Augustine. To keep me, they were awarded four pence daily, and for a while I accepted the duties given to me and attended their services as a poor canon of Christ. Yet the priory was more thrifty than many I have known, and His Grace the Prior and his canons suffered badly from this poorness. I could not endure their virtuous lifestyle, and longed to live in all honour and dedication among my brethren, whose wills had not gone astray. This was even when in the year 1312 the Council of Vienne, headed by His Holiness Pope Clement V, and other men of the Holy Church, dissolved our Order because of the false testimonies offered by those enemies whose mischiefs were enough to see it trodden into the dirt. It was with these thoughts that I took leave of the priory and reverted to being a fugitive once more. In faith, I survived, moving by night and resting by day, in the knowledge that my fellow brethren still convened in secret to exact the duties of Our Lord God and the Blessed Saints, and to make plans for a new order to continue the ideals of old.

After a while, time enough for me to complete what I was meant to do for my brethren, I journeyed once more to New Sarum and was apprehended by the town's bailiffs. They took me in chains back to Newgate where I was hauled before no less than fifteen bishops who insisted that I should reveal more of the *Templi Secretum*, but I said nothing, and was allowed to return to gaol, there to rot with the filth of the streets.

Then, in the year 1319, the Prior of Christchurch in Dorset, whose canons like those at Merton Priory followed the rules of the Blessed Saint Augustine, was instructed by His Grace the Bishop of Winchester to receive me into its house. Yet since I was an apostate, he was told that I should not be allowed to advance beyond the first tonsure, for fear that I would seek my freedom, or else beguile the minds of the canons with false ideas. Here, as a simple novice, I remained until my life became lost in the mists of time, and no more was known of me until I was awoken from my slumber in the year of Our Lord 2001 by those who now search for the relics of our Order.

STEPHEN DE STAPLEBRIDGE

This true and factual account of the life of Stephen de Staplebridge (or Stapelbrigge, Stapelbrugge or Stapelburgh) was provided by Ken Tullett, the archivist at Christchurch Priory (all except the ending, that is). His own introduction to this Templar knight came following the chance discovery of a Purbeck coffin lid in the church of St Michael's Loft, built in the fifteenth century over the site of the priory's Lady Chapel. On the slab's flat surface is a cross pattée (the so-called Maltese cross) enclosed in a circle attached to a long shaft, besides which is a crudely carved sword. He brought it to the attention of Professor Kemp at the University of Reading, who felt that it dated to around the middle of the fourteenth century, prompting Ken Tullett and his colleague, the late Ray Lax, to conclude that it might have marked the grave of a Knight Templar. Yet the Order, of course, had been suppressed some forty years beforehand, which would mean either that the artefact dated from earlier or that somehow the Templar symbolism had been allowed to be carved into the lid. Then, on examining the priory's records, the two men found reference to Stephen de Staplebridge and wondered whether it might have belonged to him. The incredible amount of information they have unearthed on this rebel Templar, and the family that shares his surname, must be commended, and I was most gratified to receive a copy of their research notes.

I was given Ken Tullett's name by Geoff Wilson, the owner of the Manor House at Templecombe in Somerset, when we visited him on New Year's Day 2002. This followed a trip out to Stalbridge, just over the border in Dorset, which produced nothing whatsoever on Stephen de Staplebridge. Additionally, a brief meditation using the Templar panel as a focus inside Templecombe's church of St Mary also produced very little, despite the accompaniment of a Welsh harp played by Yuri Leitch. This lack of new information had been quite a surprise, especially as the New Year is often a microcosm of that which will occur over the coming twelve months. Despite this, when Yuri and our friend Paul Weston had departed back to Glastonbury, Richard, his partner Pandora, Sue and I went on to see Geoff Wilson, who cordially invited us into his medieval manor, which incorporates the surviving fragments of the Templar preceptory's main gatehouse, through which the old Bristol road would once have passed. Geoff pointed out the old spiral staircase that had led to the upper floor of the building – steps which must have been climbed by a great many Knights Templar before the suppression of the Order in England in 1308.

Geoff Wilson did not have a lot on Stephen de Staplebridge. Indeed, he only really became aware of his existence after being contacted by Ken Tullett, who asked very similar questions to those I had put to him. For example, if this knight had come from nearby Stalbridge, the medieval Staplebridge, was he inducted into the Order at Templecombe? The answer proved to be no, for the preceptory was almost certainly an 'initial training establishment' for those young men destined for the Crusades in the Holy Land. In other words, it was more Colchester barracks than the Royal Military College, Sandhurst. As far as Ken Tullet has ascertained, it did not receive those of a knightly class, which Stephen de Staplebridge would certainly seem to have been. For instance, he is described in David Wilkins' *Concilia Magnae Britanniae et Hiberniae*, a four-volume work, published in 1737 and containing a comprehensive account of the trials of the Knights Templar (it was this book that the spirit of Crowley had told us to read if we wanted to learn more about Stephen de Staplebridge), as *milicie*, i.e. a knight. It says also that he gave his testimony in French ('in lingua Gallica'), which meant that he saw himself as a nobleman. Therefore, even though he might have been familiar with the preceptory at Templecombe, he was received into the Order at the preceptory of Keele in Staffordshire.

A connection with Staffordshire I found particularly interesting, as I had previously come across a series of stone coffin lids which belonged to Knights Templar from Keele. They are to be seen up against the outside wall of the church of St Lawrence at Biddulph, a town north of Stoke-on-Trent. These grave slabs were probably transferred here from nearby Hulton Abbey, which, being a Cistercian house, had ties with the knights at Keele. Just like the coffin lid discovered in the church of St Michael's Loft at Christchurch, each one bears a cross pattée at the end of a long shaft, alongside which are carved weapons representing those which were buried with the knight, usually his sword or axe. Yet, strangely, I was in two minds whether the coffin lid found at Christchurch Priory did actually mark the grave of Stephen de Staplebridge. Firstly, Ken Tullett uncovered no firm evidence that he died and was buried in Chris-tchurch Priory and, secondly, I doubted very much whether the prior would have buried a former Knight Templar with full military honours, complete with his sword. Much more likely is that, as a canon, he would have been given a more simple grave slab bearing not a cross pattée and sword, but a plain cross. Yet on the other hand, if he had remained a Templar through until the end, and was a nobleman, then he might well have persuaded the prior that if he lived like a Templar then he should die and be buried like one too.

THE CONFESSIONS

What Geoff Wilson *was* able to show us were certain references in books concerning Stephen de Staplebridge's confessions at his initial trial. As a 'fugitive Templar', he was arrested in June 1311 by the king's officers at New Sarum (modern Salisbury), in the county of Wiltshire and, in the presence of the Bishops of London and Chichester on 23 June, made what are described as 'the first confessions comparable to those [of his brethren] in France'.[206] He admitted that there were two admissions into the Order, the first of which was 'licit and good' and the other 'against the faith'.[207] He said that he had been received by both methods, in the first instance 'in an honest manner' and on the second in the manner described. This had taken place at Lydele, thought to be the preceptory of Lydley in Shropshire (on the site of which was built Penkridge Hall, near Leebotwood). The receptor on this occasion was Brian de Jay, Master of the Temple in England 1296–8 (and Master in Scotland 1286–92), something which instantly marks de Staplebridge out as important, since it cannot have been often that such a high-ranking Templar would preside over an investiture of this type, even though de Jay did in fact come from Shropshire. Curiously, Brian de Jay was later to support the cause of Edward I, King of England, against the Scots, leading to him breaking with Templar rule and becoming the model for the evil Templar, Sir Brian de Bois Guilbert, in Sir Walter Scott's novel *Ivanhoe*.[208] De Jay was killed eventually in 1298 bearing arms against Scotland at the Battle of Falkirk, supposedly at the hands of William Wallace himself.

According to Stephen de Staplebridge's own account of his reception into the second order, a cross was brought in and then, in the presence of two brothers with drawn swords, Brian de Jay informed him: 'It is necessary for you to deny that Jesus Christ is God and man, and to deny Mary, his mother, and to spit on this cross.'[209] Allegedly, he had told his confessors that he was 'frightened' when forced to do this, but went ahead anyway, making the requisite denials, although he claimed that it was 'by the mouth, and not in the heart', and that he spat not on the Cross but on the hand next to it.[210] Apparently, the reception, which he said was quite usual in the Order, had occurred at dawn. In addition to this, Stephen de Staplebridge spoke of how members of the Order were told not to believe in the sacrament, how the *Magister Templi*, Master of the Temple, was able to give absolution of sins, and that homosexuality was allowed (this being one of the charges levelled against the Knights Templar by Pope Clement V in 1307). Additionally, de Staplebridge is on record as saying that he was aware that a fellow knight, Walter Bachelor, about whom various Templars had been questioned, died 'in prison through torture'.[211]

TEMPLI SECRETUM

Lastly, Stephen de Staplebridge stated that 'the Order's errors had originated in the diocese of Agen' in Aquitaine,[212] where a major Templar *commanderie* was located, with the implication that the fault lay with one Roncelin de Fos, Master of Provence, who was Master of the Temple in England 1252–6, and again Master of Provence 1260–78. De Fos is a very important player with respect to understanding the inner order of the Templars, for just as de Staplebridge asserted, there is a strong belief among aficionados of the Templar mysteries that it was he who instituted the *Templi Secretum*, 'secret temple', which included denying that Jesus was God and spitting and trampling on the Cross. Roncelin de Fos was born at Fos-sur-Mer, a small port not far from Marseilles in Provence. His entire family were already involved in the Knights Templar, and held deep memories of the massacre of the Cathars, particularly the thousands who were slain alongside Catholics at Béziers on 22 July 1209, the feast-day of Mary Magdalene, whom the Cathars revered as the spiritual bride of Jesus Christ (see Chapter 18). Roncelin de Fos excelled himself from an early age, and soon became a vassal for the King of Aragon, under whose control were the Templars of Roussillon and Aragon, with their preceptory at Le Bézu, founded in the mid-thirteenth century so near to Rennes-le-Château.

Most significant of all was that the name of Roncelin de Fos is found on a strange Templar document alleged to have been discovered in 1794 in the Corsino Library of the Vatican Archives by Friedrich Münther, Bishop of Copenhagen, and/or in a Masonic library in Hamburg, Germany. Known variously as the 'Statutes of Roncelin', 'The Secret Rule' and 'The Book of the Baptism of Fire', it sets out the Secret Statutes of the Knights Templar.[213] It bears at its base the name Robert de Samfort, Procurator of the Templar Order in England in 1240, although Roncelin de Fos is said to have had a hand in its composition. Despite the fact that its authenticity is dismissed out of hand by modern Templar historians, it is worth investigation as the document contains some very important statements pertinent to our quest for the Holy Grail and the Head of God. For instance, a candidate's reception into the *Templi Secretum*, which would involve a receptor and three brothers as witnesses, included both a ritual and a *consolamentum*. This was the Cathar name for their variation of the nocturnal communion meal practised by the early Christians – the very rite which inspired the concept of the Bitter Cup and thus the true origin of the Holy Grail. Indeed, the Secret Statutes actually refer to the fact that 'Albigensis', i.e. Cathars, as well as members of other heretical and very Gnostic sects, are to be allowed admittance into the *Templi Secretum*.

Jesus is referred to in the ritual and *consolamentum* described in the Secret Statutes simply as 'Mary's son called Jesus', while, again as with the Cathar reception, verses of John's Gospel are read out during the oration. The so-called 'Third Prayer' is called 'The Baphomet' and opens with a reading from the first verses of the Koran, after which the receptor adds: 'One master, one faith, one baptism, one God father of all and who in invocation of God's name shall be saved.' After this he raises the neophyte and anoints his eyelids with consecrated oil, with the words: 'I want to anoint you, friend of God, with the oil of Grace, so you may see the light of your fire baptism for so it shines for thee and for all of us on our path of truth and eternal life.'

At this point, an 'image of Baphomet', almost certainly a head reliquary, is 'retired from its shrine' as the receptor says: 'The people that walked through darkness have seen a great light and it has shone for all those sitting in the trees of the dead. There are three that pay homage to God and the world and [these] three *are Saint John* [my emphasis, although who the *three* Johns are is not explained].' Thereafter, all brothers shout out 'Yah Allah', which means 'Splendour of God', at which they kiss the image and touch it with their belts (the waist cord of their robe). Once the ritual is over, the consoled, or chosen one, is then led to the library archives where he learns about 'the Divine Science, of God, young Jesus, the true Baphomet, the new Babylon, of [the] nature of things, of eternal life, as well as: the Secret Science of the Great Philosophy: Abrax and the talismans. These things must be rigorously hidden to the ecclesiastics admitted in the Order.'

Here then was the origin behind Richard's reference to a Templar-inspired 'baptism of fire', which Bartzabel and then Crowley had instructed him to take before the Baphomet statue in Hastings Caves. In the Cathar *consolamentum* the candidate receives the Holy Spirit in a manner likened to how the disciples received the divine fire at Pentecost, seen by some Christians as the fulfilment of the Baptist's prophecy that the one who would come after him, i.e. Jesus, would baptise not with water but with the Holy Spirit and fire.[214] This, then, is why the reception into the *Templi Secretum* was known as the Baptism of Fire, since it borrowed directly from the Cathars' own *consolamentum*. This realisation does not authenticate the document, but it certainly shows that whoever composed it had a profound understanding of Cathar religious practices. More significantly, it is known that even before the fall of the last Cathar stronghold of Montségur in 1244, various noblemen from families with known Cathar affiliations joined the ranks of the Templars of Roussillon-Aragon, whose administrative centre was at Mas Déu.[215] Did they bring with them knowledge not only of the *consolamentum* but also of other unorthodox religious practices, including a greater understanding of the true origins of the Holy Grail? With

Roncelin de Fos's own associations with the Aragonese king, might he have constructed the rituals for a knight's reception into the Order's inner chapter based on the new-found Cathar influence among the Templars of Roussillon-Aragon?

That Stephen de Staplebridge had undergone a ritual and *consolamentum* similar to that described in the Secret Statutes is most certain, especially as he cited Roncelin de Fos as being responsible for leading the Order astray. Exactly why he should have admitted this is difficult to determine, although he seems certainly to have been privy to the organisation and infrastructure of the *Templi Secretum*. Whatever the reason, the likelihood is that his second reception involved him kissing 'the image of Baphomet', very probably a head reliquary, and perhaps even the one Richard saw in his dream being used in a bizarre ritual at Garway in Herefordshire. Here in 1294, Jacques de Molay, the Master of the Temple and former Grand Preceptor in England, had received John de Stoke into the *Templi Secretum*, confirming the place's significance to the Order's inner chapter. In his vision of the ritual that had apparently taken place here, Richard saw seven knights lying in a star pattern in the presence of not only de Staplebridge and the head reliquary, but also a scantily clad woman holding a cup, who probably represented the Gnostic concept of Sophia, female 'wisdom'.

A link here between the Templars and Gnosticism seems certain, for the reference in the Secret Statutes to 'Abrax' alludes to a demiurge called Abraxas. He was venerated principally by the followers of Basilides, an Alexandrian Gnostic, who flourished c. 120–40. Abraxas took the form of a composite deity with the head of a rooster, the body of a man – his legs replaced by two snakes – and with a shield symbolising the sun in one hand and a flail in the other. In another form, he bore the head of a lion, very plausibly the origin behind the myth that the Templars venerated a demon in the form of a cat. Abraxas was seen as controller of time through the movement of the sun, a supposition confirmed by the fact that the numerical value of his name is said to add up to 365, the number of days in a solar year, and the amount of aeons, or ages, over which he rules. In addition to appearing in the Secret Statutes, Abraxas, or Abrasax as he was also known, features as the image on a counter seal of Templar origin, confirming the influence that Gnosticism held within the Order. To the right of his engraved image are the seven stars, representing the seven planets and the seven spheres of existence, while inside a border are the words *Templi Secretum*, confirming the seal's use as a sign of the Order's inner chapter.

In addition to the Templars' interest in Abraxas, a Gnostic demiurge, Professor Hugh Schonfield has determined that by using something called the Akbash Cipher, a complex code developed originally by the Essenes (a religious sect that thrived in Palestine around the time of Christ), the word Baphomet transforms into 'Sophia'.[216] This is unlikely to be coincidence, and probably reflects some kind of dual polarity between the two forms, male and female, exactly like Baphomet and Babalon in the occult doctrine practised by the

Crowley-influenced organisation known as the OTO. It has to be remembered that they inherited ideas and practices from pre-existing Templar groups that claimed descent from the original Knights Templar.

Then we come to some very strange graffiti, of probable Gnostic-Templar origin, to be seen in the church of St Michael at Garway. Above the opening of the piscina, which is shaped like the head and torso of a person, are various interconnected images. Directly above the 'head', positioned like a crown, is a triangle with hatching, very possibly a representation of the Great Pyramid (witnessed by Crusaders while out in the Holy Land), over which is an equal-armed cross inside a circle – the two being linked together by a square box. This sits within a pair of 'wings', which are either just that, wings, like those which flank the sun-disc in Ancient Egyptian art, or they denote the cross section of a bowl, plausibly signifying the cup of the Eucharist. Each side of the 'head' are other carved forms – to its left is a fish, a Christian sign denoting Christ, and to the right is a snake, the Gnostic symbol of knowledge and wisdom very much associated with Sophia. Whatever the true symbolism of these graffiti, their nature suggests that those who carved them were familiar with the Gnostic Christian mysteries.

Finding links between the Knights Templar and the unorthodox Christian beliefs of the medieval Gnostics is nothing new. The nineteenth-century Austrian Orientalist Baron Joseph von Hammer-Pürgstall was the first to suggest that Baphomet, as the *bapho metis*, or 'baptiser of wisdom', derived from Gnostic sources and that he was worshipped as an androgynous figure depicted on certain thirteenth-century stone caskets. Moreover, the Gnostic–Templar relationship was greatly expanded in a book entitled *La Doctrine Secrète des Templiers* ('The Secret Doctrine of the Templars') by French scholar Jules Loiseleur, published in 1873. He proposed a direct descent from the Manichaeans through the Luciferans, Bogomils and Cathars to the Knights Templar, and wrote that the *consolamentum* of the Cathars heavily influenced certain Templar rituals.[217] More controversially, Loiseleur proposed that the Templars' denial of Jesus's divinity and their spitting and trampling on the Cross derived from the Cathar belief that Jesus had been the lover, companion and bridegroom of Mary Magdalene, which proved that he was flesh and blood, the son of Mary, and not God incarnate (see Chapter 18).[218]

THE MIND OF STEPHEN DE STAPLEBRIDGE

Returning to Stephen de Staplebridge, I discovered that before the end of his first trial the Templar knight did something very curious indeed:

> And then bending with knees to the ground, with eyes uplifted and hands clasped together, with tears, sighs and laments, he devotedly asked for the mercy and grace of the Holy Church; and that there should be enjoined on him a salutary penance for what he had done, saying that he did not care about the death of the body, nor about other torments, but only for the safety of the soul.[219]

Initially, this might sound like the words and actions of a man full of remorse for the ills that he has done, but something does not add up. Firstly, we know that many such confessions were extracted under torture, or with the threat of painful death by torture (as was the case with his fellow brother Walter Bachelor) and, secondly, this is a man who, after being given the chance to do penance at the Augustinian priory of Merton in Surrey, quickly goes absent without leave. He was then caught again at New Sarum (what importance did this place hold for him?), and dispatched eventually to the Augustinian priory of Christchurch. Yet due to his blatant troublesome nature, the prior there was told not to advance him beyond the first level, or tonsure, most probably because the clergy feared that he would incite unrest among the canons. In my opinion there seemed every reason to suspect that Stephen de Staplebridge's actions in front of the Bishops of London and Chichester imply a ruse so that he might forgo torture and possible death and, instead, be given a 'soft sentence' which he knew would allow him to escape when the opportunity arose.

Another historical source spoke of Stephen de Staplebridge as one of the two Templars listed in connection with the preceptory at Lydley in Shropshire, when in 1308 the Order's confiscated estates there were valued at £44. The preceptory's warden, Henry de Halton, gave himself up, but as Evelyn Lord in *The Knights Templar in Britain* admits, 'Stephen de Stapelburgh' escaped, 'threw off his robe and fled to Salisbury where he was eventually arrested'.[220] More significantly, Lord refers to him as 'the apostate', the rebel, a fitting epithet for a knight who defied his would-be captors for so long. He was indeed an apostate, and one who quite obviously did not let his belief in the rule of the Templars die when the Order was officially dissolved.

THE GREAT SOCIETY

Since the Templars in England had nearly three months grace between the arrest and imprisonment of their French brethren and the issuing of the warrant for their own arrest, many of them simply vanished before the king's bailiffs had a chance to raid their preceptories. Often the Templar properties in England were found to be deserted or manned by just one or two caretaker knights, the rest having already gone underground (any treasures or gold having also mysteriously disappeared in the process). It is known that the rebels shaved off their traditional long beards, threw away their white surcoats and took on new identities and professions in order to evade arrest. They probably utilised a series of safe houses, or 'lodges' (maybe a barn, croft or gamekeeper's hut), in order to go about their business unhindered by the authorities. Moreover, there is some suggestion that, as John J. Robinson in his remarkable book *Born in Blood: The Lost Secrets of Freemasonry* argues, these fugitives formed themselves into secret enclaves, or 'lodges' (after the places where they could meet in safety), under the control of a much more widespread mutual aid and protection society, whereby its members recognised each other using covert charges, handshakes, signs and catechisms. Known as the 'Great Society' – a term which first appears following the Peasant's Revolt of England in 1381 to denote those who ignited and controlled the country-wide insurrection against the existing feudal system – this shadowy organisation remained underground for four centuries and resurfaced into the public eye as the Ancient Order of Free and Accepted Masons, or Freemasonry, in London during the first quarter of the eighteenth century.[221]

In order to back up his groundbreaking theories, Robinson provided stunning evidence that Freemasons did not originate among medieval stone-building guilds, a view popularly believed by researchers and writers of Masonic history, as well as by Freemasons themselves. Much of the Masonic symbolism connected with the tools and paraphernalia associated with Craft Masonry, he argues, derive either from its roots in medieval Templarism, or from a more acceptable 'history' of Speculative Masonry created in the seventeenth century to hide its true origins.

One prominent symbol used by Freemasons in Masonic lodges (in addition to that of the chequerboard mosaic pavement, the compass and the square) is the circle, divided into four parts. This is composed of the circle itself, a point at its centre, and two parallel lines – one on each side of the circle. In Masonic lore the circle is taken to symbolise the boundless universe, while the centre point is the individual Mason and the parallel lines the 'staffs of St John the Baptist and St John the Evangelist'.[222] Robinson argues that the first usage of this device derives from his proposed medieval mutual-protection society for fugitive Templars, whose members would draw the circle in four parts in the earth at their makeshift lodges, something that recalls the rotundas which emulate the Church of the Holy Sepulchre in Jerusalem, which was behind the design of many Templar round churches.[223] If this is so, then it is yet further evidence for the devotion among the Templars to the two Johns – John the Baptist and John the Evangelist.

Somehow, I envisaged Stephen de Staplebridge belonging to just such a band of outcasts, clearing up unfinished business on behalf of his beloved Order. Yet even if this were so, was he responsible for the disposal of certain Templar relics such as the Head of God? Did Stephen de Staplebridge's knowledge of Roncelin de Fos, with his connections to Provence and the King of Aragon, begin to make sense of why this head reliquary might have made its way to the French Languedoc following the fall of the English Templars? Only time would tell whether or not it had left the country through the actions of Stephen de Staplebridge and his fellow apostates, but for the moment I was beginning to better understand why the rebellious life of this Templar knight was being revealed to us, and felt sure that we had not heard the last of him yet.

12. THE CROWN OF MITHRAS

I slept, and before me was a celebration. Hundreds, no, thousands of people were taking part in a colloquial festival. There were crowds, all laughing, joking and invoking some kind of ancient power. They stood on the slopes of a green hill, together as one, doing something bizarre, something absurd. A human head was being rolled down a slope, like a ball of cheese, and everyone was cheering its tumbling movement. I wanted to turn away, but could not. It was being shown to me for a reason. They all whooped with joy, bringing a climax to the day's activities, which took place on 5 May, a date linked to this bizarre fixture.

The bloodied cranium, complete with skin and hair, rolled over and over until it reached a stone gateway at the base of the slope and passed through it before coming to a halt. Back on the grassy slope, elders of the community emerged from the crowd to make themselves known. Everyone parted to allow these seven raggedy individuals, both male and female, to link hands in the middle of a large clearing. At that moment, two large dogs barked out from beneath the feet of the spectators and entered the ring of men and women, where they began fighting ferociously – one biting the other on the nose, causing blood to fall on the earth. The rustic guardians screamed and screamed, raising the power to a point of utter ecstasy. Flashes of the head continued to fill my dream, still rolling over and over, like a video clip being replayed again and again. I was at the place of the head; yes, where we would find the great oak at the centre of it all. Then, all of a sudden, I saw Richard saying to me, 'I told you we had to go to Head-culm.' It was a name that kept going around my brain, and would not leave it . . .

Thursday, 10 January 2002. I woke up from an amazing dream. It was four o'clock in the morning, and my mind was buzzing with the imagery I had just witnessed. Head-culm – it was a place-name, the centre of the great circle we had envisaged overlaying part of southeast England. Somehow, what I had just viewed was a clue to its discovery. Forced to get out of bed, leaving Sue peacefully asleep, I scribbled down what I could remember of the details before pulling out my copy of *The Concise Oxford Dictionary of English Place-names*, by Eilart Ekwall, looking for somewhere called 'Head-culm', or even 'Headcombe'. If where I saw was in Kent, or Sussex, then it would make sense. I picked through the pages until I found those entries starting with the letter H. There was no 'Head-culm', or 'Headcombe', but there was a 'Headcorn',[224] and it was in Kent!

My heart raced, and felt like it had skipped a beat. Yes, this was what I had dreamed about – the head rolling over and over again. It must have been

Headcorn. Reaching for my copy of Arthur Mee's *The King's England: Kent* – one volume in a brilliant series on the topography of England produced during the 1930s, and never bettered – I excitedly looked up 'Headcorn', and read the entry. There was mention in the first paragraph of 'a living giant at which it is said that Queen Elizabeth wondered',[225] and so I read on with bated breath, and found this:

> . . . what most travellers will love best in Headcorn is one of the greatest natural monuments for a thousand miles around. It is a mighty oak, a giant of the centuries, whose roots are said to reach for 60 feet [18 metres], and whose trunk is certainly 42 feet [12 metres] round. They will tell you in Headcorn that it is the oldest survivor of the original forest of the Weald, and that one of its branches centuries ago reached to a window of the prison above the church porch, so that a prisoner was able to set himself free with the aid of it.[226]

What an incredible discovery. Yet the strange thing is that the great oak at Headcorn is not mentioned at all in the book's index, and so when I had looked at it earlier for possible candidates for Richard's gnarled old oak tree, only two places had entries under 'Trees', and neither of them were for Headcorn. Satisfied by what I had found, I went back to bed, and slept unhindered this time.

THE CIRCLE DRAWN . . .

After a few hours' more sleep, I got up and found very quickly my scrawled notes from the previous night. Following breakfast, I took a cursory look at a large-scale map and tried to see whether Headcorn – a medieval market town south-southeast of Maidstone – might be close to the centre of our proposed circle of sites. On paper it actually looked good – it was 17 kilometres (10 miles) due south of Stockbury, right in the direction that Richard felt the centre point would be found (although further away than I had anticipated). Excited now, I reached for a compass and used Headcorn to form a huge circle with Hastings at the limit of its circumference.

Not only did the resulting circle, 68.5 kilometres [43 miles] across, make some kind of wild sense, but as the pencil completed its task I saw that it went exactly through Saltwood Castle in Hythe, which Crowley had specifically told us would be found at its east-southeastern extremity – exactly where it is. In addition to this, it sliced through Canterbury, the location of Richard's dream about being crowned King Mithras in the cathedral crypt, where he also encountered Babalon. In fact, looking more closely, I found that the line did not just go through Canterbury, it passed through the cathedral itself!

But there was another surprise in store. At the circle's northwestern extreme, near the town of Sevenoaks, something else of possible significance became apparent. Falling just a kilometre or so beyond its perimeter was Ide Hill, the so-called 'dome of Kent', due to its famous tree-lined summit, where back in

1989 Helen Laurens had unearthed, among other things, the silver-plated chalice with an inscribed serpent line rising out of the bowl – the same artefact that Richard had dreamed about in connection with our search for the Grail cup.

There was, however, some disappointment, for when I came to divide the circle into seven parts, using Hastings as the starting point, I found that neither Hythe nor Canterbury fell anywhere near the correctly orientated angles of the internal heptagon. Only Ide Hill conformed to the star's rigid geometry, falling just beyond the tip of its northwestern point, a realisation which could not be ignored. Had I really found Crowley's so-called Star of Babalon, a landscape design of gigantic proportions, or was I wrong? The significance of the tree argued against a mistake, but still I required some confirmation. And what was I to say to Richard? This was so important that, for the moment at least, it was best to say nothing, other than to announce that I had experienced a strange dream which had directed me to a great oak that I felt might mark the centre of the great circle. In this way there was a good chance that he would independently either confirm the significance of Headcorn, or determine the true location of the centre point, without being influenced by my own opinions on the subject.

KING JOHN'S OAK

What I needed was to find a local historian in Headcorn who could tell me a bit more about the place, and, of course, the tree. I managed to track down a very helpful man named Leslie Daniels, who lived in the town. He confirmed that the tree stood on the edge of the churchyard, as Richard had predicted, while the old pictures showed that its trunk was split down the middle, making it possible to enter inside its hollow interior. More important, it was known as King John's Oak (also the Headcorn Oak or River Oak, due to its position near water), and was connected with a very interesting local legend. King John, who ruled England between 1199 and 1216, is said to have sat beneath its branches and watched bull-baiting. This seemed a strange sport for the townspeople of Headcorn to have become involved in, making me question whether or not there was any record of them actually conducting such barbaric practices in years gone by. The answer from Leslie Daniels was no, so I wondered whether the whole thing might not be symbolic of something else, like the head-rolling ceremony of my dream which, I presumed, was simply a mental vehicle to convey to me the importance of the word 'head'.

King John's connection to Headcorn's bull-baiting legend might well be linked with an important event in English history. Tradition insists that the king stayed locally on the occasion that he surrendered his crown to Rome, after his kingdom was placed under an Interdict (the debarring of all ecclesiastical functions and activities), while he himself was excommunicated by the Pope. According to one contemporary account of the meeting, it took place 'in the house of the Templars near Dover',[227] a reference either to the Order's preceptory at Temple Ewell,[228] situated outside the seaport of Dover, or another

Fig. 4. Aleister Crowley's Star of Babalon overlaid on a drawing of Headcorn's King John's Oak. Did he leave a chalice, representing the 'Cup of Babalon', within its hollow interior?

Templar house on Dover's Western Heights. Two Templars, one probably John's close adviser and confidant Aymer de Saint Maur, Master of the Temple in England,[229] acted as mediators between the king and the papal legate, apparently moving between rooms in order to consult each party, who refused to sit at the same table. During this act of submission, which occurred on 15 May 1213, the crown of England and Ireland was handed to the Pope, after which the king received it back, although now only as a vassal of Rome. King John recognised the Pope as his overlord and received absolution, for which service he paid nine gold marks, borrowed, it is said, from the Templars![230]

That King John might have stayed in the vicinity of Headcorn prior to relinquishing his crown associated the whole bull-baiting episode with the concept of kingship, almost as if he needed to gain divine acceptance of his intended actions by visiting the ancient oak. Then I came across a fact that made me think more closely about Headcorn's bull-baiting episode and its links with kingship. In the cult of the Persian god Mithras, which spread across the Roman Empire and reached Britain around the same time as Christianity, the central focus was the god's combat and ritual killing of the bull. Moreover, the practice of bull-baiting was once conducted in the name of Mithras.[231] A bull was let loose and bulldogs, or pit bulls, would be allowed to pursue, torment and tear apart the animal, imagery integral to reliefs in Mithraism known as the *tauroctony*, which show Mithras slaying the bull as his dog rips at the bovine's flesh. It is symbolism based wholly on the celestial heavens, and Mithras's associations with the constellation of Taurus, which marks the dawn of the age of Mithras in astrological terms.[232] Mithras's crown of seven rays was, of course, the sun-disc given to his companion Helios or Sol Invictus, who was really an aspect of himself in his role as the sun-god. Similar to Abraxas in Gnostic tradition, Mithras/Sol Invictus controlled time through the annual movement of the stars across the line of the sun's ecliptic, the reason why he is usually shown with the signs of the zodiac around him. Also like Abraxas, the numerological value of the name Mithras (Mithra) adds up to 365, the number of days in a solar year. Did any of this suggest that King John had taken over the role of Mithras in the bull-baiting legend, which probably existed in some form before his association with Headcorn?

TAURUS THE BULL IN HEAVEN

In my dream I knew the head-rolling ceremony had occurred on 5 May, possibly as part of a yearly celebration. Turning to astrology I noted that this date fell when the sun is in the constellation of Taurus, which falls each year between 21 April and 21 May. A little bit of checking also revealed that Headcorn's annual festival was on May-Day Bank Holiday Monday, meaning it would take place on Monday, 6 May that year. Was it on Sunday, 5 May, or at least around this time, that we were meant to find the Grail cup which Richard now felt might be hidden in the vicinity of the great oak at the centre of the great circle of sites?

It was then that I found out something of immense frustration and sadness. Leslie Daniels informed me that King John's Oak was razed to the ground under somewhat mysterious circumstances on the night of 25 April 1989. Everything had been quiet when a local man out walking his dog passed the tree around eleven o'clock that evening. Yet according to local reports, sometime around midnight two men on motorbikes turned up and set fire to its hollow interior.

Fig. 5. King John's Oak, Headcorn, from the Headcorn Parish magazine, 1887.

By the time that anyone got there, the tree was a blazing wreck, and all that remained was a crater of charred wood filled with burned debris, and a small halfpipe-like section of the trunk. There seemed to have been no obvious motive for this wanton destruction, and the whole thing was put down to an act of mindless vandalism. Curiously, just two days later, on 27 April 1989, the silver-plated chalice was unearthed at Ide Hill, begging the question of why Richard should have dreamed about the retrieval of this artefact, whatever its symbolism. Not wishing to stretch the coincidences too far, I noted that these two dates – 25 April and 27 April – also fell within the astrological month of Taurus. What is more, even despite the calendar changes in England and its colonies in 1751, King John's surrender of his crown to Rome on 15 May 1213 occurred either during, or on the cusp of, this same astrological month, meaning that he visited Headcorn when the sun was in the sign of Taurus.

Taurus, the bull in heaven so much associated with the cult of Mithras, is ruled by the planet Venus, which, in its personification as the goddess of sex and love of the same name, is recognised to be the root behind the Whore of Babylon of St John's book of Revelation, as well as Crowley's inspiration for Babalon, the divine being, or Scarlet Woman, whom he saw as incarnated through his succession of mistresses. Were these eclectic clues pointing towards some importance between the landscape geometry discovered on the Kentish and Sussex landscape and the Roman cult of Mithras? As I knew, the religion's outer order had seven degrees of initiation, perhaps signifying the seven-pointed Star of Babalon (seven and the seven-pointed star were also sacred to Near Eastern goddesses of sex and love, such as Venus, Ishtar and *al-uzza*, the last of whom thrived in the pre-Islamic Arab world).

Somewhat bizarrely, I was to discover that just 3 kilometres (2 miles) northwest of Headcorn, close to the small hamlet of Hawkenbury, is a place called Babylon Farm, situated in Babylon Lane. At first this did not seem too important. However, when I investigated this place-name I found that there are only a handful of locations in Britain called Babylon, making its presence at the centre of Crowley's proposed Star of Babalon somewhat eye-opening if nothing else.

Just three days after the dream that revealed the importance of Headcorn, Sue and I travelled to Kent to visit the town's medieval church of St Peter and St Paul. Although King John's Oak is now no more than an overgrown crater of burned wood, a cutting was taken in the 1940s from which has grown a new tree that today thrives in the churchyard. Underneath it, Sue and I visualised Richard picking up new information on Headcorn in the hope that he would independently confirm what we had found out already. The result of this exercise was quite extraordinary. Exactly 24 hours *before* our visit, which he was unaware of, Richard had again glimpsed the old gnarled oak in vision, the first time he had done so for some while. As before, he saw it standing at the edge of the churchyard, close to the church's south porch, which was correct. On each side of the tree he could see iron railings, and close to its base were

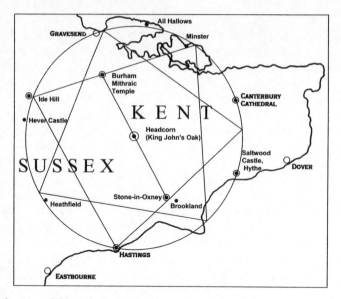

Fig. 6. The seven-fold circle known as the 'Star of Babalon' overlaid on the landscape of Kent and Sussex. Key and secondary sites are marked, as are the Mithraic sites of Burham and Stone-in-Oxney, aligned on and equidistant from the centre point at Headcorn.

a few gravestones, which was also the case, even though the railings have now all but rusted away. More significantly, and the point which finally convinced me that we had found the right place, was his statement that he could see an upright pole within the tree's hollow trunk. There had indeed been a wooden pole at its centre which helped support the ageing giant's enormous trunk, and although it burned down in the fire, its stump was still visible in the centre of the burned-out crater. The only factor that he had still not picked up on about the tree was how it had been destroyed by fire some years beforehand; presumably, that would come later.

THE PLACE-NAME GAME

I examined next the etymology of Headcorn's place-name. *The Concise Oxford Dictionary of English Place-names* cites the oldest forms of the name as *Hedekaruna* (c. 1100), *Headcrone* (1226) and *Hedecrune* (1240).[233] He suggests the second element derives from the Old English *hruna*, meaning 'a fallen tree' or 'fallen trees', with the first element stemming from the personal name 'Huda'.[234] However, Leslie Daniels sent me photocopies of a book on Kent place-names by J.K. Wallenberg, written in 1934, which throws better light on the subject. According to him, the Middle English *crune*, or *corune*, as well as variations of the name in other European languages, means 'crown', implying 'something having the circular form of a crown' or 'the rounded summit of an elevation'.[235] Yet since Headcorn's topography is relatively flat, Wallenberg speculated that the use of the name could be similar to the Old English *hring*, 'ring, circle', or *hwēol* 'wheel, circle'.[236] The fact that I had just used Headcorn to draw a great circle or ring 68.5 kilometres [43 miles] across, made this interpretation that much more appealing.

Looking at the first element of the Headcorn place-name, Wallenberg concluded that it perhaps derived from the Old English *heafod*, 'head', and so proposed a full translation as 'the chief crown-formed topographical object',[237] even though he was still at a loss to understand how it might relate to the local landscape. He did, however, point out that a kilometre or so northwest of the town was a hill with a rounded elongated appearance which might be important, near to which is Babylon Farm!

What clinched the 'chief-crown' or 'head-crown' derivation of the Headcorn place-name is a corrupted form from the fourteenth century preserved in the name Pinkhorn Farm, again located near Babylon Farm. Even earlier, it had been Pendcrune and Pencrone, among other variations.[238] Whereas Wallenberg had suggested that the first element might stem from the Old English *gepyndan*, 'to shut up', or *pynding*, 'dam' (or, indeed, *penn*, 'enclosure'), I felt it was more likely to have come from the British *pen*, 'chief', 'head', 'top', 'summit', 'end', which Ekwall saw in the place-name Penge, found in the neighbouring county of Surrey.[239]

Should the place-name interpretation of Headcorn offered by Wallenberg, i.e. the 'chief' or 'head-crown', not derive from a local hill, which is possible (especially when I thought about my dream), then it had to have some other value. Either it related to a now-lost prehistoric site of circular significance, or Headcorn really was seen as the 'crown' of a whole series of outlying places linked to it like the spokes of a wheel. Local history records that several ancient drovers' paths once converged on Headcorn from all over the great forest that covered the Weald of Kent. So if King John's Oak did exist at this time, and certainly it is thought to have been at least 1,000 years old when it was destroyed, the chances are that it would have been the focus of the local community, maybe why it was linked with bulls and kingship rites that reflect elements of a far older cult of the Roman god Mithras. This makes better sense in the knowledge that the whole idea of a reign, or rule, of a king derives from the same word-root as 'ruler', a measuring instrument, while thrones (originally standing stones, stone armchairs or ancient trees, like the Yggdrasil of Norse mythology) were often sited at the geographical or political centres of kingdoms.

My mind kept returning to Richard's dream in which he was offered the Crown of Mithras by Aleister Crowley in the crypt beneath Canterbury Cathedral. Since it occurred the night prior to our trip to Stockbury, where we first searched for the centre of the great circle, then perhaps it was yet another clue to Headcorn, which was to be seen as the 'chief' or 'head-crown' of seven rays, the Crown of Mithras, the Crown of the Heavens and, very much, the Crown of the Land. Yet all of this I would withhold from Richard, certainly until we had a chance to conduct a psychic session on the matter to see what he might come up with himself. Beyond this was the deeper question of whether or not the Grail cup would be found somewhere in the vicinity of the site of King John's Oak. Richard had suggested that it *might* be found here, but what of the reality of this statement? Now that we had presumably found the right location, what then were we to do next? Were we to use a spade to start exploring the soil around the remains of the old trunk, or was there another solution altogether? Hopefully, all would be revealed when next the three of us got together to try and find some answers.

Thursday, 17 January. With a certain sense of expectancy, we began the psychic session at our home in Leigh-on-Sea in the usual fashion, and waited eagerly to see what Richard might experience on this night. Even before it had begun, with his eyes still wide open, he saw the spirit of Aleister Crowley enter the room and move across to where Sue sat on a sofa. Without any introduction, he knelt down and kissed her, and then just reverently remained in this position for some while, his head bowed. Richard said that he was ignoring us, and saying only: 'Prepare ye for the way of blood. For this is the rite of our Lady Babalon.'

There was something we needed to do, Richard said, before explaining that Crowley was now joking about 'the name of the place', referring to the location of the old oak. Seated in an easy chair in the candle-lit room, he could see the tree again, this time shrouded in greyness and battered by constant wind squalls. Crowley, still kneeling before Sue, spoke of it being somewhere with a name comprising 'head' and 'corn', with corn being 'the most ancient symbol of fertility. What better place to put the cup of my lady.'

So, finally the name 'Headcorn' had come up independently via Richard's own psychic talents. Yet still Sue and I refrained from confirming whether his words were correct or not.

'He put it here not long before his death,' Richard offered next. 'He says, "I visited it in 1946." And now I see Crowley moving the cup there. I see it as silver, but that could just be symbolic, I don't know. The tree was different then. He's putting it into, like, a hollow in a large branch, but whether it's still there . . .'

Where exactly was the cup now?

'All I can see is Crowley standing by the tree, and it's just in front of the . . .' There was a moment's pause. Then Richard shook his head, and said, 'Can't be, someone would have taken it. It's almost in front of the pole . . . in the tree.'

Was it buried?

'No, not buried,' he replied.

Was it still retrievable?

Crowley answered this one directly using Richard's vocal chords: 'If you come when I tell you, then you shall have it.'

This was promising at least.

'He's saying something else,' Richard continued. 'I'm only going to say what he says. Don't take this as disrespectful: "Just as the unicorn will only come to the virgin – the cup may only be retrieved by the harlot of my whoredom." He's very concerned over who comes to retrieve it.'

So, he was talking about Sue, then . . .

'She embodies my Lady Babalon,' Crowley confirmed.

OK. I would listen on. But when and how, Mr Crowley? When and how?

'She will retrieve it with her own hands,' he said next.

How?

'She will reach beyond the void.'

Could he direct her to the exact spot?

'You will come . . .'

When?

Richard answered: 'He's not telling me. I'm getting a feeling, "Beltane", but he's not telling me.'

Beltane is the old Celtic name for the annual celebrations that took place in Britain on the May cross-quarter day, the half-way point between the spring equinox and the summer solstice, 5 May by the current calendar (although fixed today as 1 May, May Day). It fell during the astrological month of Taurus and made sense of my dream, which had highlighted the date 5 May. It was around this time that we should make our attempt to achieve the cup, I was certain of that now. Yet what about the tree?

Ask Crowley to show you the tree.

'Very windy,' was all he could get out.

Tell him what has happened.

'It is wizened and old.'

Somehow, Richard was not picking up on the tree's current condition. Again, I asked him what had happened here.

'Fear not, you may have it,' Crowley responded next.

He was back on the subject of the cup.

'Look to the centre of the star,' he now said.

We were doing that already.

Richard broke off his concentration and took a break, bringing an end to the evening's session. So I was right about Headcorn. Not only had my own psychic ability been vindicated, but it was important to remember that Richard had first glimpsed King John's Oak even before I had wrongly assumed Stockbury to be the centre of the Star of Babalon in December. Only now did we reveal to Richard that the great oak he had seen was indeed located at Headcorn, and that this is where Sue and I had been the previous weekend. Moreover, I told him that the tree was destroyed back in April 1989, something which actually quite annoyed him, for the Crowley in contact with us was clearly unaware of this fact. Indeed, from Richard's vivid description of the tree, I calculated that he was viewing the churchyard from a southerly perspective as it might have appeared sometime around the 1940s or 1950s. For me at least, it was a beautiful example of how the psychic mind is sometimes unable to update place memories, even after a traumatic event has occurred at the site in question.

We had now been presented with the possibility that some representation of a Grail cup was placed in the hollow of King John's Oak, Headcorn, by Crowley, just one year before his death in 1947. It made little sense of anything other than the period in which Richard had seen the tree, especially as Crowley rarely travelled from his lodgings in Hastings, where he resided for the last two years of his life, and no such trip is recorded. Yet it is *possible*, however unlikely, that someone had driven him to Headcorn, or placed the cup there on his behalf, raising the question of how he might have come to learn of Headcorn's magical significance in the first place. Clearly, Aleister Crowley would have been amused by the Babylon place-name, recalling his own Lady Babalon, but surely this can have meant little more to him than a nod from the cosmic joker to confirm that he was at the correct place. For the time being, all we could do was abide by the psychic information and focus our attentions on culminating our quest to find the Grail cup on or around Sunday, 5 May, the eve of Headcorn's own annual celebrations.

13. THE CUP OF JANUS

Whether or not I was awake or asleep, I recall seeing the darkened interior of a cold, empty church lit by torches that revealed four knights in medieval-style dress, kneeling one each side of a box-shaped stone altar. They were placing a thick gooey substance on charcoal embers that burned inside the stone's curved surface. From this fusion came a strong acrid smoke that rose upwards to create a dense fog, filling the church. The knights inhaled it in order to induce visions, making me think that it was a powerful narcotic of some kind. So strong was it, that I could almost taste it.

From beyond the fog emerged an apparition, at least I felt it was an apparition – an Eastern-looking man, a mystic to be sure, old, strong, dignified and with a white beard. He stood there dressed in a crimson robe and matching silk turban, looking like some fairy-tale wizard. Did he originate from Persia, or somewhere like that, where the cult of Mithras had its beginnings? Was he attempting to convey knowledge to them of his ways, his essence, and his teachings? No answers came as the scene faded away, and I fell into a deep slumber.

Tuesday, 29 January. I woke up very suddenly, my thoughts struggling to hold on to the full contents of the inspiring, though somewhat disjointed, dream. The church, I seemed to know, even though I had never been there, was the imposing medieval edifice that dominates Stone-in-Oxney on Kent's Isle of Oxney, separated from the nearby Romney Marsh by the River Rother. Here is to be found an unusual stone altar, thought to come from a long-lost Roman temple of Mithras, this much I knew. Rectangular in appearance, it is 60 centimetres (24 inches) long by 55 centimetres (22 inches) wide, and 102 centimetres (40 inches) high, and has a concave basin-like surface that I later found shows signs of burning. Until 1753 it was kept inside the church, but in this year a local vicar had it 'restored' and positioned next to the vicarage, where it was used as a mounting-block for horses. Then in 1926, when its true archaeological value was realised, the stone was carried back inside the church, where it has since remained beneath the bell-tower.[240]

Each side of the stone altar bears the carved relief of a bull, the most likely reason why it has been associated with the god Mithras. That the place-name Stone-in-Oxney probably means something like 'stone in the place where oxen were kept' only deepens the mystery, especially as a large metal ring, once used to tether an animal, perhaps a bull or horse, is attached to one side. Clearly, altars come from temples, and so it has been suggested either that a temple of Mithras once stood on the site of the present church, or that one existed nearby.

If the dream vision was more than simply imagination, which I had to assume, then who were the four knights who had gone to Stone-in-Oxney to induce visions in order to conjure the Eastern mystic into visible appearance? I had the distinct feeling that this character lived in Persia, and that the knights were, like us, on some kind of Grail quest, which they saw as seven-fold in nature. For them, it was like seven degrees of initiation, a road I felt we too would have to go down at some stage. However, for the moment the greater puzzle was why it should have been important for me to see these knights invoking an Eastern mystic at a Roman altar connected with the god Mithras. It was a problem partially solved by another vivid dream experienced a short while later.[241]

I found myself before a conical mound in five stages, like some huge wedding cake crafted out of earth, with each step representing a different state of being, or level of consciousness. The first four tiers corresponded to the four elements – earth, air, fire and water – while the top tier signified the amalgam of all four, the ultimate force, the Fifth Element, Ether, or Quintessence. More than this, I knew somehow that this tiered mound expressed five sacred principles of Sufism, the inner teachings of Islam, a subject I was unfamiliar with. It was wisdom derived from Persia, embracing ideas inherited from the cult of Mithras. Furthermore, through their links with the Knights Templar at the time of the Crusades in the Holy Land, or indeed the Moorish occupation of Spain, Sufi philosophy entered medieval Europe. From this fusion of mystical ideas came a new-found awareness of the five-fold principles of spirituality, represented by the five-pointed star, the pentagram, which became not only the heraldic device of Gawain, one of the achievers of the Grail in the romances, but also a primary symbol in Freemasonry and Western occultism.

The next day I read, for the first time, the only book I possessed on Sufism – Sufism: Its Saints and Shrines by John A. Subhan, published in 1970. It introduces the whole concept of the Sufi, who embraces a form of religious mysticism expressed not through outward performance, but via the activities of the inner self. The foundation of Sufism, which is made up of a whole series of sects across the Islamic world, is credited to the prophet Mohammad (570–632), even though there is no real evidence of its existence until some 200 years after his death.[242] Yet there can be no doubt that Sufism was inspired by pre-existing religious ideals derived from Mithraism, Gnosticism, classical Neo-Platoism, Persian, Indian and Buddhist thought, Graeco-Egyptian alchemy and even orthodox Christian and Egyptian Coptic beliefs. All of these played some role in its evolving system of contemplative mysticism. However, despite the constant spread of Sufism throughout the Islamic world, it was not recognised by orthodox Islam until the end of the eleventh century.[243]

One form of Sufi philosophy based on principles borrowed from Gnostic and Johannine principles is Nūru'l-Muhammadiyya, the 'Light of Mohammad'. Like John's Gospel, it expounds the concept of the Light of God, and compares the Logos, the 'word' of God, with Mohammad, whom it sees as behind the creation of all things. It is a teaching that places into the mouth of Mohammad sayings such as: 'The first thing which God created was the Light of the Prophet' and 'I am the Light of God and all things are from my light.'[244]

In order to access that part of him or her which is divine, i.e. the spirit, the Sufi mystic utilises five concentration points, or *latīfa*, which, although existing in *'Alam-e-khalq* (the World of Creation), i.e. the Microcosm or material world, are reflected in *'Alam-i-Amr* (the World of Command), the Macrocosm or immaterial world. Viewed as 'the organs of spiritual communication with God', in ascending order of importance they are given as: *Qalb*, 'heart' or 'mind', associated with the 'Throne of God' (colour yellow, location left side of body), *Rūh*, 'spirit' (red, right-side of body), *Sirr*, 'the secret' or 'consciousness' (white, solar plexus), *Khafi*, 'the hidden' or 'mysterious' (black, forehead), and *Akhfa*, 'the deeply hidden' (green, centre of chest).[245] The lower four correspond to the four elements of western tradition, while the fifth *latīfa*, *Akhfa*, relates to the innermost consciousness of the individual, the Ultimate Unseen, *Ghayb-ul-Ghaib*. Moreover, each *latīfa* comes under the control of a different prophet: *Qalb* is said to be beneath 'the foot of Adam', *Rūh*, *Sirr* and *Khafi* are under the feet of Abraham, Moses and Jesus respectively, leaving *Akhfa*, the highest communication point. This comes under the dominion of Mohammad, who enables the spirit of the mystic to perceive the closeness of God's presence.[246]

It is the will of every Sufi to awaken the five *latīfa* (pl. *latā'if*) in turn (starting with yellow and ascending in order through to the green ray of *Akhfa*) so that they might become closer to remembering the ways of God, through which they will receive *Tajallī*, Divine Illumination. This is achieved through the process of *dhikr*, or 'remembrance', i.e. active contemplation using strict meditational practices. As each new *latīfa* is attained, the Sufi becomes at one with the prophet in question and moves ever nearer to the Light of God.[247]

THE SEARCH FOR JAM'S CUP

The most significant aspect of the Sufi concept of the *latā'if* is that the perceived spiritual journey to regain the divine knowledge, lost originally by Adam at the time of the Fall of Man, is symbolised by the search for a sacred vessel called Jam's Cup.[248] Jam is Jamshid, the most ancient of the Persian *shahinshah*, the legendary 'King of Kings', who owned a precious wine-cup (*Jām-i-Jam*), often compared with the western concept of the Holy Grail. Persian and Urdu literature assert that it bore on its surface seven lines or rings, known as *khatt-i jam*, representing the seven spheres of existence.[249] When full, the king could gaze upon the still surface of the wine and see mirrored within it the whole world, and all events past and future.[250] Once emptied down to the dregs, the magic reflecting surface vanished, and the vision could no longer be seen. The journey to find Jam's cup is generally unachievable, yet because in man's heart there remain traces of the 'effulgence of divine knowledge' (i.e. the spirit, or divine spark), he will come to comprehend the Lord Most High.

This, then, is the true path of the Sufi mystic. The parallels with our own search to find, or at least understand, the Grail cup were striking, especially in the knowledge that *Akhfa*, the highest *latīfa*, corresponds to the colour green, which in occult philosophy is associated with the planetary influence of Venus, which rules the astrological influence of Taurus. Somehow this Sufi wisdom could, I felt strongly, be used to access the inner workings of the great circle of sites before we visited Headcorn on Sunday, 5 May, most probably through some form of creative visualisation utilising the *latā'if* colour sequence from yellow (*Qalb*) through to green (*Akhfa*).

What then was the link between Sufi wisdom concerning the *latā'if* and the cult of Mithras? Even though this pagan religion is generally thought to have only seven degrees of initiation, each one under the control of an immortal spirit, I discovered that there were in fact another five degrees practised by its initiates, making twelve in all. The highest of these, the twelfth degree, was known as 'King of Kings', because it could only be attained by the *shahinshah* himself.[251] The first such legendary ruler was Jamshid, owner of the famous wine-cup, a vessel very much associated with the concept of kingship.

It is worth recalling that the model for all modern crowns is the so-called royal *farr*, symbol of the *shahinshah*'s divine countenance. In Persian myth it is portrayed as a semi-intelligent embodiment of divine power preserved within a ring of light the size of a crown, and passed on from one king to the next.[252] Eventually, it came to signify the golden sun-disc, usually shown with either seven or twelve rays, which over the millennia solidified into the golden circlet, or crown, traditionally worn by kings. The act of transferring the divine countenance, or crown, from one king to another, became known as the 'coronation', from the Latin root *corona*, meaning 'crown'. That Headcorn's place-name was originally *Hedekaruna*, which probably translates as the 'chief' or 'head-crown', seemed strangely relevant, especially when all of these musings were taken into consideration. Was it an ancient place of kingship, where kings were crowned? Was this concept embodied in the legend of King John watching bull-baiting beneath Headcorn's great oak prior to submitting the crown of England and Ireland to the Pope's prelate on 15 May 1213? More pressingly, did this concept of the divine king relate specifically to the concept of the Holy Grail, which contained the blood of the ultimate Christian king, Jesus himself?

Monday, 1 April. Having not spoken to Richard for some while (I had been extremely busy completing a book about the Egyptian pharaoh Tutan-khamun,[253] which meant no real communication with the outside world for weeks on end), I finally got a chance to bring him up to date on some of the more recent developments in our quest. He had not picked up anything of note himself, but listened keenly on the other end of the line.

I informed him about the Mithraic altar at Stone-in-Oxney and the ritual apparently conducted there by four knights. This seemed to trigger something in Richard's imagination. 'As you're speaking now, I can see a church, which seems shrouded in mist,' he began. 'To get to it, you've got to cross a very boggy landscape, which seems to be sparsely inhabited. There's something important about this church – Mithraic connections, I feel. It's near this Mithraic altar, which I have been to, once, in fact on the same day that I was taken to see Hastings Caves a few years back. Yet I don't know this church at all.'

'Go on,' I urged.

'I can see carved panels, linked in some way with agriculture and the zodiac.' He fell silent for a moment. 'I can also see Janus, connected with the cup. I see him with it in his hand.'

Janus was, of course, the twin-faced god of Roman mythology, god of all beginnings, guardian of doors and gates, who sees everything past and future. I was not, however, aware of him being associated with a cup, or with Mithras.

'The people locally hold some kind of pseudo-Mithraic knowledge preserved in folk beliefs and customs, reflected in these panels, which I think are on *a font*,' he announced. 'There's also a strange-looking pagoda next to the church.'

A pagoda? What did he mean?

'Some sort of separate tower, I think.' There was further silence, before, 'St Augustine. The church, it's dedicated to St Augustine. Don't know how I know that, but it just is.'

It could easily be checked out.

'I see Janus holding the cup again. I think it's on one of these panels, and Crowley. He's in my mind now, saying, "Remember the figure by the fire." It's another panel, which shows a weird-looking alchemist at a forge.'

Anything else?

'I also see some Mithraic figure slaying a bull,' Richard continued. 'It's yet another panel on this font, which, as I said, is linked in some way to the signs of the zodiac.'

Any more? This was getting interesting.

'Some sort of connection between Mithras and Janus, something to do with primordial chaos, and accessing cycles of time.'

Where was this church? Did he have any idea?

'No, but I feel there's a church ruin nearby. There could be more Mithraic connections here.'

BROOKLAND'S GREAT TREASURE

With Richard still on the telephone, I tried to identify the church in question. After flicking backwards and forwards through *The King's England: Kent*, I realised that he was talking about Brookland church, located on Romney Marsh, just 5 kilometres (3 miles) away from Stone-in-Oxney. In the churchyard, it said, is a 500-year-old, eight-sided, detached timber belfry, like a pagoda, 'where the monks used to go to pray',[254] which had to be what Richard was seeing. He was also right to predict that the church is dedicated to St Augustine, and that it possesses a font of extraordinary significance. Made of lead – one of only thirty-eight in England – its circular bowl displays a unique series of panels, forty in all in two tiers of arches. One tier shows the twelve signs of the zodiac, almost repeated twice, while beneath them are scenes depicting the twelve labours, or seasonal activities, associated with the corresponding month of the year.

According to Arthur Mee, the panels on the Brookland font included 'a man with a Saxon horn, a rustic pruning a tree, a ploughman at his work. A rider with a hawk on his wrist, twins with quaint hats, a swineherd knocking down acorns for a pig' and, more significantly, 'a butcher killing an ox',[255] this last one being the Mithras-inspired imagery suggested by Richard. An accompanying illustration displayed more of the panels, and next to the 'butcher killing an ox' was one representing January, which shows Janus seated at a table (see Plate 23). In his right hand is a sceptre – denoting control over the cosmic axis – while in his left hand is a *cup*. The panel on his right shows a cowled smith at his forge, clearly the 'weird alchemist', or 'figure by the fire' referred to by the voice of Aleister Crowley. There seemed little question that the sheer existence of this font was of paramount importance to our quest for the Holy Grail. Yet to find that it was so close to Stone-in-Oxney, where the Mithraic altar was located, had to mean something to us.

'This Janus figure,' Richard began again, 'he's important somehow – something to do with us finding the cup. I can see this ruin again. I think it's the Chapel of Abominations.'

THE CHAPEL OF ABOMINATIONS

The Chapel of Abominations was a partly ruined chapel in a wood somewhere in southeast England that we had been hoping to find ever since it had first cropped up during a psychic session at Leigh-on-Sea back in December.[256] When first observed, Richard described seeing a group of Templar-inspired occultists in black cowls conducting some kind of ritual in a clearing within sight of the structure. In front of them was a young, attractive woman lying naked on her back, her arms and legs outstretched to form a star pattern. On her bare navel was a silver chalice, which they were using in order to link in minds with the actual Holy Grail, Crowley's Cup of Babalon.

The date, Richard felt, was 1952, and the individuals, he seemed to think, might have been connected with the *Ordo Templi Orientis*, the OTO. Back in 1912, the then head of the Order, Theodore Reuss, had given Crowley a charter to establish a British branch, which he acted as head of until his death in 1947. Afterwards, the Order's Grand Treasurer General, Karl Germer, gave a young man named Kenneth Grant, who had been Crowley's secretary for a while in Hastings, a charter to operate the OTO's first three degrees in Britain. However, for reasons that have remained a matter of dispute to this day, Germer expelled Grant in 1955, prompting him to assume overall control of the Order. It henceforth became known as the Typhonian OTO, after Typhon, the Greek name for the Egyptian god Set, venerated extensively in ancient Egypt c. 1800–1575 BC. For Grant, this 'Typhonian' age was the last time in Egyptian history that the 'stellar wisdom' was openly recognised and understood, before it was forced underground, and since that time has been known only to certain magico-religious groups, cultures or religions existing in isolation across the world.

Between 1955 and 1962, and plausibly even before this time, Grant operated the so-called Nu-Isis lodge as the inner cell of the Typhonian OTO. It was established in order to open inner gateways to wider and deeper vistas of consciousness, and to align the stellar wisdom of ancient Egypt and before with the current of Thelema, the name Crowley gave to his own magical system of communication with non-human intelligences. The members of the Nu-Isis lodge embarked on a series of important workings, both indoors and outdoors, using the mediumship of different psychic conduits, including Grant's own wife, the artist Steffi Grant; indeed, much of what they did during this period parallels very well modern-day psychic questing activities, something he alludes to in his most recent non-fiction work.[257] Grant's first book, *The Magical Revival*, published in 1972,[258] led to a genuine renewal of interest not just in the 'magick' of Aleister Crowley, but also the OTO, which today operates in two forms – Grant's Typhonian OTO and the American-based Caliphate OTO, which derives from those supporters who remained loyal to Germer.

Although the individuals who had seemingly visited the ruined chapel in 1952 had not found what they were looking for, we now had a chance to succeed where they had failed, and find the true Grail. Incidentally, the OTO's 'lamen', or chief emblem, is composed of an almond-shaped oval, inside which is the eye in the triangle from which emerge rays of light. Beneath it is a dove, symbol of the Holy Spirit, descending into the Gnostic Grail from which emerges a blazing rose bearing the cross pattée of the Knights Templar.

During the psychic session in which we had first been introduced to the existence of the ruined chapel, Richard said the scene showing the robed figures and the woman spread-eagled on the ground had suddenly changed to that of him and I standing back-to-back by the ruins, our heads together, like the Roman god Janus. Sue had replaced the young woman, and on her stomach was also a chalice or cup, from which radiated rings of emerald-green energy that pulsed out into the surrounding countryside. The coming together of all these different elements at the chapel, which seemed important in its own right, perhaps even with connections to the Knights Templar, would psychically propel us forward into France, where we would take up the quest for the Head of God. The sheer fact that the vision of the ruined chapel had shown us doing the ritual with the Grail cup in our possession implied that we *would* find it, otherwise the whole scene made no sense whatsoever.

Crowley's voice had referred to the ruins, already reclaimed by nature, as the 'Chapel of Abominations', a term which appears in a short prose piece written by him entitled *Liber CLVI* (156 in Roman numerals), also known as *Liber Cheth vel Vallum Abiegni*, with 156 being the numerological value of the name 'Babalon'. It was the work we had been told by him to read back in November, yet, due to a certain amount of confusion on our part, had failed to do so. With the somewhat revealing subtitle of 'The Ritual of the Holy Graal', it starts as an address to Babalon, before she then answers in her own words. The text alludes to 'the secret of the Holy Graal, that is the sacred vessel of our Lady the Scarlet Woman, Babalon', before describing a symbolic ritual in which a devotee's blood is offered to her in a 'golden cup', in order 'that thou attain to the Sacrament of the Graal in the Chapel of Abominations'.[259]

The 'Chapel of Abominations' is mentioned also in *Moonchild*, Crowley's classic work of fiction published in 1929. Here it is the place where the character Lisa la Giuffria is initiated into a magical order following a lengthy vigil.[260] However, in this instance it is described simply as a bell-shaped cave, cut out of the living rock with a bare altar and a magic circle inscribed on the floor,[261] indicating that Crowley did not have in mind a genuine ruined chapel when he first conceived of such a place.

That Richard and I would have to stand back-to-back, heads together, during the intended rite of passage at the ruined chapel had initially seemed strange. However, the entrance of the Roman god Janus into this complex saga, via the lead font at Brookland church, now made better sense of this information. We derive the name January from Janus because his two faces, both generally male and bearded (although occasionally with one female), respectively look backwards to the year that's been and forward to the year that is to come. Thus he becomes the seer, the knower of all things, past and future, whose moment is the transmission point between one cycle and the next, which in ancient times was the five-day period between each year of 360 days, the origin behind the saying 'a year and a day'. Indeed, I discovered that in some legends Janus held the number 300 in one hand and the number 65 in the palm of the other, providing the number of days in a solar year, making him a *kosmokrator*, a keeper or controller of cosmic time, like the Persian god Mithras and the Gnostic demiurges Ialdobaoth and Abraxas. In many ways, the god's double-headed attributes corresponded with his Christian counterparts, John the Baptist and John the Apostle, who look, respectively, towards the longest and shortest days of the year.

Richard and I were to mimic Janus in the presence of the Grail cup at the so-called Chapel of Abominations, providing us with a nexus point in time whereby we could leave behind that which we had already achieved and project ourselves forward to where we needed to be in the future. At the same moment, Sue, acting as an embodiment of Venus or Babalon, would use both the cup and her personal energies to create the necessary power to allow our collective minds to lock into the site's own energy matrix to make this happen. As mad

Fig. 7. Janus, the Roman god of all beginnings, with one face bearded, the other beardless. In Freemasonry they became the faces of the two Johns – John the Baptist and John the Evangelist.

as it seemed, similar bizarre acts had worked in the past, and so we no longer doubted psychic instructions of this type or nature. All we needed to do was just go with the flow and see where it led us. However, before journeying to the Chapel of Abominations, we had first to find not just the ruin itself, but, more essentially the Grail cup, which we sincerely hoped would be retrieved from the vicinity of the old tree at Headcorn; only time would now tell whether this was correct or not.

14. PUZZLES IN STONE

Sunday, 28 April. Beyond the gatehouse marking the entrance to Shugborough Hall Country Park, the car cruised slowly along the Tarmac road, past an assortment of obelisks, follies and temples. We came eventually to the great mansion reconstructed in the mid-eighteenth century by Thomas Anson, the MP for Lichfield, with the help and aid of his younger brother George, Admiral Lord Anson. Hopefully, we would at last find out why, during a meditation in December, Richard had found himself thrust away from seeking the mighty oak at the centre of the great circle of sites in southeast England to look instead at a curious carved cat atop a stone urn, located somewhere in the grounds of Shugborough. Beneath it on a pedestal was, apparently, a coat of arms, or an inscription, or something, which he felt would be a key to understanding not just our quest to find the Grail, but also the Templar relic known as the Head of God.

Sue and I had come here with our friends from Stafford, the fantasy writer Storm Constantine and her husband Jim Hibbert. Richard was unable to join us due to prior commitments at home, but I had agreed to ring him if anything was found. As the rain began to beat down incessantly, and the others sought cover, I continued to study the carved reliefs on a whole range of stone urns showing classical scenes. I saw goats, satyrs and, just occasionally, the great god Pan, but never cats. After sheltering for a while in a small temple, the search continued and all at once our party came across the famous Shepherd's Monument. What is more, standing alone on an island between a river divided into two channels, one natural and the other dating only to the eighteenth century, was a bulbous urn on which I could just make out a curled-up domestic cat, frozen in stone.

'That's the Cat Monument I told you about, Andy – the one I did the story on,' Storm announced, before looking a little confused. 'But I don't remember the cat being on top of an urn.'

As we reached the Shepherd's Monument, which I noticed faced out towards the Cat Monument, I asked her briefly to recall the story she had written.

'It was years ago, really,' she mused, pausing on the edge of the bank. 'I would come over here a lot, and was always drawn to the monument, as I love cats. The story is about a young woman who becomes transfixed by the whole thing and starts to take on attributes of the person who built it.'[262]

I looked up at the Shepherd's Monument with its slightly more cramped version of Nicholas Poussin's painting *Les Bergers d'Arcadie* ('The Shepherds of Arcadia'), here transposed mirror fashion. On the tomb, or sarcophagus, being examined by the shepherds and shepherdess of the picture, was the legend *ET IN ARCADIA EGO*, while carved in stone beneath the relief were the ever-mysterious sequence of letters:

O U O S V A V V
D.   M.

The whole structure looked impressive, and I hardly felt, as Richard had suggested, that it was a 'red herring', here simply to throw writers and researchers of the Rennes-le-Château mystery off the true scent. Since its representation of Poussin's painting faced out towards the Cat Monument, which would have been seen more clearly before trees grew up, blocking its view, I suspected that the two monuments bore some kind of inter-relationship which might only be understood if they were studied together, and not individually.

But how were we to reach the Cat Monument and examine it closely? Storm said she knew – it was via an oriental footbridge next to the Chinese House, located nearby. Yet finding it chained off from the public, I waited for a clear moment before swiftly navigating the obstacle and stepping on to the bridge that spanned the extension of the River Sow, created in Thomas Anson's day.

GRIFFIN-GUARDED VASE

Marching across to our goal, I came to a halt, camera in hand. Everything I saw that afternoon had to be captured on film, just in case I missed something with the naked eye. The cat lounging on top of the stone urn is of normal size and proportions, and seems to be looking out across the water towards the Shepherd's Monument, convincing me even more of a relationship between the two structures. I was later to read that the cat is thought to commemorate either a pet that accompanied Admiral Lord Anson on his circumnavigation of the globe between 1740–4, or a Persian called Kouli-Khun belonging to Thomas Anson, this last idea being the preferred choice of Shugborough's guidebook writer.[263] Yet this explanation is unlikely, says Storm, for as a cat lover herself she is convinced that the carving does not show a Persian. Whatever the answer, the fact that no one seems to know exactly what the cat represents leaves it open to the possibility that, as Richard had proposed, it recalls the demon in the form of a cat supposedly worshipped during secret ceremonies by the Knights Templar, a better explanation by far!

Underneath the urn is a pyramid-shaped stone plinth with concave sides. Emerging from the corners are the heads of four goats with curled horns, each one supporting looped stone garlands that hang loosely across its four sides. The official explanation for the presence of the goats' heads is that they represent a Corsican flock kept in the gardens by Thomas Anson, and, certainly, this breed of goat definitely has curled horns. However, to consider that these carvings might in fact signify the designer's belief in the continuing influence in our lives of Pan, whose semi-mythical realm of Arcadia features in the legend carved on the tomb in Poussin's painting, was also quite possible. This theory became infinitely more plausible when I discovered that the monument's designer was none other than architect, astronomer, mathematician, Druid and apparent Philadelphian Thomas Wright of Durham.

According to the guidebook, he built it in 1749, around the same time as the Shepherd's Monument, erected c. 1750–5, and the pagan altar to Mithras at Wrest Park in Silsoe, Bedfordshire.

Beneath the pedestal supporting the urn is a rectangular stone plinth, on the front of which, facing the Shepherd's Monument, is a stone tablet showing in raised relief two griffins rampant that flank a rococo-style vase. Since the structure bears no other inscription or 'coat of arms' as Richard had hoped, then this tablet was obviously what we had come to see, although I struggled to see why. In classical mythology griffins were composite creatures with the head and body of a lion and the claws and wings of an eagle; they were also said to guard buried treasure. Yet the significance of the vase was a little more difficult to determine, for the moment at least.

Having finished taking pictures, and allowing the others time to inspect the monument, we exited the island and headed back to the Shepherd's Monument for a breather. What exactly was the key to unravelling this strange puzzle? All I knew was that Poussin's *Les Bergers d'Arcadie* appears to show real topographical features in the landscape around Rennes-le-Château, more specifically three sites – the peak of Pech Cardou, the ruins of a castle tower on a promontory called Blanchefort and, on the extreme right, the hill of Rennes-le-Château. All this might be so, but here at Shugborough the painting is transposed, mirror fashion. Why was this done? No one has ever really addressed this enigma, and yet it had to be a key to understanding the role of both monuments.

There was only one way to learn more, and so I rang Richard to see what he might have to say about the day's discoveries.

'As you say this,' he started, intrigued by the whole thing, 'I feel there's some kind of alignment from the Shepherd's Monument to the Cat Monument. Some clue that we need to know about.'

And then it struck me like a flash of inspiration. If you were to stand *behind* the Shepherd's Monument, and made it semi-transparent, then you would see its representation of Poussin's *Les Bergers d'Arcadie* the *right way round*. Moreover, beyond the structure, directly in line with the eye, would be the Cat Monument, making it appear as if this, too, was framed within the picture. Aligning the two monuments, I quickly realised something else. The Cat Monument was not exactly dead centre if viewed from behind the Shepherd's Monument – it was slightly to the right of centre. This implied that it aligned closely to the position of Rennes-le-Château as viewed from the painting's perspective of Poussin's Tomb, which was located until 1988 just beyond the road between the town of Arques and the village of Serres, at a site known as Les Pontils. Thus the symbolism on the monument, presumably the griffins flanking the vase, seemed somehow indicative of the treasure of Rennes-le-Château. This alone was a remarkable realisation, and I wondered why no writer or researcher had ever considered that the Cat Monument might be important in some way. Yet what Richard had said was probably right – they had only ever concentrated on the Shepherd's Monument, and in doing so had failed to see what was burning into their backs.

I was sufficiently taken by the blatant perspective of the two monuments at Shugborough for the matter to play on my mind beyond the trip to Staffordshire. The whole thing bugged me, and would not leave my thoughts. Did the presence of the vase on the tablet indicate that the Grail was now to be found somewhere around Rennes-le-Château, or did it signify that there was another treasure there – the imagery simply revealing that it was guarded by two griffins, symbolic perhaps of architectural clues found in buildings scattered about the area? Five statues of saints erected in the church at Rennes-le-Château by Berenger Saunière during his restoration of the building are thought by some to be positioned in such a way that the first letter of each of their names spells out the word 'graal', French for Grail. Did he possess some knowledge of the holy vessel's whereabouts locally, or was this clue more subtle than that?

Perhaps the real Grail was in France, and the vase seen on the tablet was the one that we were meant to find, meaning that we could now move on to search for the Head of God, the supposed idol of the Templars. No, this did not make sense, as we had a date with Crowley at Headcorn in a week's time, and there was every chance that we might pick up the cup then.

Fig. 8. The imaginary view from behind Shugborough's Shepherd's Monument across towards the Cat Monument, both designed by astronomer, architect and mathematician Thomas Wright (1711–86). Does the alignment indicate the importance of Rennes-le-Château?

THE RED SERPENT

Then came a major breakthrough. I was reading *The Templar Revelation* by Lynn Picknett and Clive Prince, two writers very well known to me. Immersed in its strongly argued theories concerning the true identity of Christ, I turned to a chapter concerning the mysteries of Rennes-le-Château. It spoke of a very brief but highly strange tract entitled *Le Serpent Rouge* ('The Red Serpent'), which some people feel is a key to revealing its innermost secrets. Divided into thirteen sections, representing each of the twelve signs of the zodiac with the addition of a thirteenth sign, Ophiuchus, the serpent, it was the entry for Leo that drew my attention. Something in its words struck me like an arrow piercing my soul as the image of the twin griffins supporting the vase flashed before me once more:

> I am aware of the scent of the perfume which impregnates the sepulchre of the one I must release. Long ago her name was ISIS, Queen of the benevolent springs, COME TO ME ALL YOU WHO LABOUR AND ARE HEAVY LADEN AND I WILL GIVE YOU REST. Others knew her as MAGDALENE with the celebrated vase full of healing balm. The initiated know her to be NOTRE DAME DES CROSS.[264]

Although there is ample evidence that this document, deposited under mysterious circumstances in the Bibliothèque Nationale, Paris, in 1967, is just some kind of prank to keep alive the mystery of Rennes-le-Château, I was not concerned with its authenticity. It was the reference to the 'vase full of healing balm' that compelled me, for it was very obviously the vessel from which Mary Magdalene poured the expensive ointment used to anoint the head and/or feet of Jesus just days before the Crucifixion. Did the vase carved in high relief on the Cat Monument signify this same holy vessel, and was it in any way representative of the Grail cup that we sought? It made sense of what was known about Rennes-le-Château and its mystery, for the church there is dedicated to Mary Magdalene, and if you were to be there at dawn on 22 July, her feast day, the sun would be seen to rise directly over the ruins of Blanchefort. If this sighting line is extended beyond Blanchefort it reaches the church of St Anne at Arques – once dedicated to John the Baptist and said to contain a relic of the saint in the form of a finger bone[265] – before crossing the threshold into the town's cemetery.[266]

POUSSIN'S TOMB

This simple alignment virtually follows the sighting line in the opposite direction, from Poussin's Tomb to Rennes-le-Château, making sense of how, through a pairing with the Shepherd's Monument, the Cat Monument signifies both Rennes-le-Château and the Magdalene. It made sense too why griffins flanked the vase, for, traditionally, the treasure they guard is not any old treasure, but *gold*. John Milton, the famous English poet and visionary of the seventeenth century, muses on the griffin and its role in Book II of his monumental work *Paradise Lost*:

As when a gryphon through the wilderness,
With winged course, o'er hill and moory dale,
Pursues the Arimaspian, who by stealth
Had from his wakeful custody purloined
The guarded gold.[267]

The 'gold' which the Griffin guards is in fact the wealth of the sun at dawn, the gold in the east, and what better metaphor could there be for a revelation illuminated by the first rays of the sun, a knowledge shared only by a select few who understand the true potential of the magical landscape around Rennes-le-Château. It felt fitting that at the end of the sunrise alignment was the church of Arques, once dedicated to John the Baptist, whom the Gnostics equated with the sun-god Helios. Beyond all this was the compelling fact that in classical mythology a griffin's talon was so large that it could be fashioned into a drinking cup. In doing so, it became a magical vessel able to detect poison in any liquid poured into it, recalling the Poison Chalice of John the Evangelist, whose symbol as one of the four evangelists was the eagle, one half of the mighty griffin.

In addition to all this, the place-name Arques was phonetically similar to the Latin *arca*, meaning a 'box' (and also a 'secret'), and the only additional feature in the variation of Poussin's *Les Bergers d'Arcadie* found on the Shepherd's Monument is a box, or casket. It rests on the tomb once thought to have existed at Les Pontils, the site of the more famous Poussin's Tomb, or Tomb of *Arques*, constructed as late as 1903.[268] Lastly, and this is the freakiest fact of all, when Poussin's Tomb was opened at one point to remove the bodies of two women, the mother and grandmother of one Louis Lawrence, who died in 1954, it was found to contain the mummified remains of two cats.[269] How they came to be interred, nobody could say.

Now it might seem difficult to understand where exactly the Anson family and their architect friend Thomas Wright fit into a modern-day French mystery which only began in the late nineteenth century when a simple curé of Rennes-le-Château apparently chanced upon something of immense value connected with his church. However, it is a fact that knowledge of a great treasure existing somewhere in the Aude valley, which Rennes-le-Château overlooks, goes back many centuries, and there is every reason to believe that it was known about when Poussin painted his famous painting in 1640. By virtue of the apparent topographical features in this picture, along with the legend on the tomb it shows, this area had come to be associated with Arcadia, the mythical realm of Pan – a paradise on earth where a golden treasure of immense monetary and/or spiritual value awaited discovery. Although oversimplifying the facts here, it is quite likely that this mystery inspired freethinkers of the eighteenth century, people like the Ansons and Thomas Wright, who alluded to what they knew in stone puzzles. Yet none of this would have been known to Berenger Saunière when in 1885 he became parish priest of the church of St Magdalene at Rennes-le-Château and unexpectedly stumbled upon the key to a mystery which was already hundreds, if not thousands, of years old. Whether it had anything to do with why statues of the saints in his church were positioned in such a manner that their names spell out the word 'graal' is still unclear, but it is a clue to the secret nevertheless!

We had obviously been drawn to Shugborough for a specific reason, and that appeared to be connected with Mary Magdalene, a name linked both with Rennes-le-Château and southern France in general. What were the Cat Monument, the Shepherd's Monument and Saunière's saintly message really trying to show us? Was it that the Holy Grail was connected in some way with the Magdalene, who in Gnostic/Manichaean tradition was considered the shepherdess who brought back to the fold the lost eleven disciples following the Resurrection?[270] All I knew was that in a few days' time we would depart for Headcorn in search of the Grail, and that in the meantime I should explore more fully the mysteries of the Magdalene in order that we might better progress on to the next stage of our ever-unfolding psychic quest.

15. THE MAGDALENE

Mary Magdalene is arguably one of the most enigmatic and misunderstood figures in the whole of the New Testament. She features very little in the Gospels, and yet to Christians worldwide Mary has become the ultimate symbol of the reformed sinner and penitent saint, through some misrepresentation of her life as a lady of the night, redeemed of her sins by Jesus himself. Yet it was only after the chance discovery in 1945 of a whole corpus of Gnostic literature in Egypt that the world came to learn of her true place in the Early Church, her existence having been virtually annihilated by orthodox Christianity.

It is a story that slowly unfolds to become the next stage in the discovery of the Grail, but to understand her place in this saga I would have to start with the Gospels to see how they portrayed the woman whom British Magdalene writer and champion Lynn Picknett sees as the most important woman in history.[271]

The Magdalene (from the Hebrew *magdal*, 'tower') makes her first appearance in Luke's Gospel, where she is mentioned as one of the women that Jesus 'healed of evil spirits and infirmities', who ministered to their master and his disciples 'of their substance'.[272] Nothing is told of her past or her character; she is simply cited as someone 'from whom seven devils had gone out',[273] and as a follower of the Lord. She does not reappear until the Passion, when Mary is said to have watched her Saviour suffer on the Cross. She then returns to play a prominent role in the finding of the Empty Tomb and goes on to become the first witness to the resurrected Jesus.

In her absence we hear of another Mary who the Roman Church accepts is the same person as Mary Magdalene, and this is Mary of Bethany, the sister of Martha and Lazarus. They are a family who lived in Bethany, a village 'high unto Jerusalem, about fifteen furlongs [3 kilometres] off.'[274] Apparently, Jesus would go there often on his travels, and in Luke's Gospel we read that after the Ascension he led the disciples and those that were with them out to Bethany where he thereafter ascended to heaven.[275] The house belonged to Martha, the elder of the two sisters, although it is Mary who was said to have 'sat at the Lord's feet, and heard his word',[276] meaning that she followed his teachings. That Mary devoted her life to Jesus, instead of helping her sister prepare the meals when he came to stay, grieved Martha enough for her to bring the matter to his attention. He simply told her not to be troubled by this as Mary had chosen 'the good part, which shall not be taken away from her'.[277]

This is Mary of Bethany's introduction to the Gospels. Yet much later on in Jesus's ministry she is responsible for what might be taken as one of the most profound events in his life.

THE ANOINTING OF JESUS

This event happened when Jesus and his disciples were in Bethany, and because the story alters from gospel to gospel they are treated individually.

Matthew tells us that two days before the Passover, that is the day before Jesus's triumphant entry into Jerusalem on the back of an ass, to be followed later that week by the Last Supper and his betrayal at Gethsemane, Jesus and the disciples went to the house of 'Simon the Leper', a man of whom nothing is known but his name.[278] As they enjoyed 'meat', a woman having an 'alabaster cruse' – the English translation of the original Greek word *alabastron,* meaning an unguent jar or vase – containing 'exceeding precious ointment' came up to Jesus and poured its contents over his head.[279] It was an action that the disciples had obviously not been expecting as they bemoaned it as a complete waste of good ointment, which could otherwise have been sold and the money given to the poor. In response, Jesus said that there would always be poor, but he would not always be around.[280] He also suggested they leave the woman alone: 'For in that she poured this ointment upon my body, she did it to prepare me for burial. Verily I say unto you, Wheresoever this gospel shall be preached in the whole world, that also which this woman hath done shall be spoken of for a memorial to her.'[281]

In Mark's Gospel the anointing also occurs in the house of Simon the Leper two days before the Passover, but this time the reader is informed that the expensive ointment poured from the 'alabaster cruse' is, in fact, spikenard (Hebrew *nerd*).[282] This is a very costly essence extracted from the root of an Indian plant of the family of *Valerianæ,* which grows exclusively in the Himalayas. Since a prized ointment would have fetched a high price at market, it is unlikely to have been the sort of thing somebody might have thrown around without good reason. Once again, the unnamed woman pours the precious ointment over Jesus's head, and the disciples complain, saying that it could have been sold for 300 denarii.[283] As before, he rebukes them, saying that the poor will always be poor and he will not always be around, and that she has 'anointed my body aforehand for the burying'.[284] This is stronger language than Matthew, suggesting that what she did was no spontaneous act of devotion.

Moving on to Luke's Gospel, what is quite obviously the same incident has altered considerably. No date is given, and this time the anointing occurs in the house of a Pharisee, one of the three main Jewish sects in Palestine (the others being the Sadducees and the Essenes). It is carried out by 'a woman which was in the city, a sinner',[285] who, because she remains unnamed, has become known as Luke's Sinner. With her 'alabaster cruse of ointment'[286] she stands behind Jesus weeping, and then begins to wet his feet with her tears. She then wipes them with her hair before anointing each one.[287] The Pharisee, now named as Simon, and thus almost certainly the same as Simon the Leper, tells Jesus that if he was a prophet then he would know that this woman was 'a sinner'.[288] What type of 'sinner' is not stated, although it is generally taken that she was a harlot from the city, for ladies of the night wore their hair down, while decent women covered their heads, and the sinner's act of drying his feet with her hair seems to emphasise this role.

Jesus rebukes Simon, saying: 'Seest thou this woman? I entered into thine house, thou gavest me no water for my feet: but she hath wetted my feet with her tears, and wiped them with her hair. Thou gavest me no kiss; but she, since the time I came in, hath not ceased to kiss my feet. My head with oil thou didst not anoint: but she hath anointed my feet with ointment.'[289] As a sinner, he then absolves her, which at 'meat' causes murmurs among the disciples, who ask how it is that Jesus can forgive such sin.[290]

Turning to John's Gospel, which has a different root of construction to the three Synoptic Gospels, we learn that the anointing took place at Bethany six days before the Passover,[291] instead of the two days cited in Matthew and Mark. What is more, it occurs not in the house of Simon the Leper, or Simon the Pharisee, but in the home of Martha, as she prepares supper for Jesus and his disciples.[292] This time the anointer is named as 'Mary', presumably Martha's sister, and she is said to have taken 'a pound of ointment of spikenard, very precious, and anointed the feet of Jesus, and wiped his feet with her hair: and the house was filled with the odour of the ointment'.[293] Thus, John's Gospel complies very well with the account given in Luke, even though Luke's Sinner is not named and the incident appears to take place elsewhere in Bethany. After the anointing of Jesus, Judas Iscariot, who would later betray his master, is named as the disciple who takes offence at what she has done, pointing out that the ointment would have fetched 300 denarii,[294] which could have been given to the poor. Yet, as in Matthew and Mark, Jesus responds: 'Suffer her to keep it against the day of my burying.'[295]

Bible scholars and churchmen are very mixed about what exactly this powerful episode in the Gospels actually represents, or who exactly the woman with the alabaster jar might have been. Even though she is identified clearly as 'Mary' in John's Gospel, the fact that she becomes an anonymous sinner in Luke's Gospel, and goes unnamed in Matthew and Mark, has led them to assume that two, or possibly three separate incidents are referred to, each one involving a different woman. However, in the knowledge that Mark, the oldest of the Gospels, was not written in its present form until around AD 70, and John's Gospel was not put together until the final years of the century, there is every reason for a confusion of facts relating to what seems obviously one single event. It occurred in a Bethany house just prior to Jesus's Passion, and was unquestionably an act of anointing conducted by Mary, a woman who was not just a follower of Jesus but also a confidante with whom he shared the gravity of his imminent fate.

Exactly what Mary was trying to achieve when she anointed Jesus takes us away from orthodox Jewish practices during this age. There is some suggestion that the act mimicked the ancient Israelite tradition of anointing kingly candidates in order to make them inviolate to danger, and to give them a special relationship with God. In this ceremony, which took place in the Temple of Jerusalem, the divine spirit would enter the new king enabling him to become the 'Anointed of Yahweh'.[296] If this was so, then it would mean that Mary saw Jesus not only as a King of the Jews – the title daubed on the plaque nailed to the Cross, following Pilate's question to Jesus asking whether he is indeed 'King of the Jews'[297] – but also as *Christos*, the 'anointed', prophesied as coming in the scriptures. This was the Greek form of the Hebrew word rendered 'Messiah'. Of course, to St Paul's Gentile Church, and all Christians today, he was and still is Jesus, 'the Christ', the Anointed One. This would fit in well with the idea that Jesus was trying deliberately to fulfil ancient prophecies concerning the coming Messiah found in the books of Isaiah,[298] Daniel[299] and Zechariah,[300] to name but three.

That Mary was chosen, or indeed took it upon herself, to carry out such a divine mission makes her a very important person indeed, for in Near Eastern pagan religions, which flourished at the time of Jesus and undoubtedly influenced Jewish religious customs and practices, the anointing of a sacred king was performed by a chosen priestess. She was seen as the personification of a love goddess, such as Venus, Astarte or Anath, and the act would be followed by some form of 'sacred marriage' to the king as the incarnate god, with her acting as his spiritual bride. That Mary would appear to have been anointing Jesus for burial, in line with the Jewish custom of anointing a deceased partner before burial, tends to bear out a comparison with pagan religions since the priestess, as the divine widow, would lament and mourn the symbolic death of the god-king before he was reborn anew the following spring.

From a Jewish point of view, the role of the Israelite king, as the Anointed of Yahweh, is no better expressed than in the Canticles of Canticles, or 'Song of Songs', traditionally credited to King Solomon and included in the Old Testament. They set forth the mutual love between a king as the bridegroom and his bride, the Shulamite Woman, something understood by Christians as an example of the relationship between Christ and the Church. The Canticles come together to form a very beautiful, and highly sensuous, work, and at one point the fact that the bride's spikenard sends forth its fragrance across the table to the king is deliberately described.[301] That spikenard was used also in Jesus's anointing ceremony cannot be coincidence, emphasising that Mary's actions are *meant* to be seen as fulfilling some kind of scriptural prophecy in which Jesus is recognised as embodying the Christ, the Anointed. During the twelfth century, the great religious figure Bernard of Clairvaux wrote a treatise on the Canticles and compared the bride with Mary of Bethany. Bernard was a leading light in the establishment of the Knights Templar, writing their Rules and supporting their cause before the Pope in Rome. He also showed a keen interest in the cult of Mary Magdalene, which in his native France was reaching epidemic proportions in his day.

MARY MAGDALENE

Martha and Mary of Bethany feature also in the story of the raising of their brother Lazarus from the dead, which, although only found in John's Gospel, was also present (as we have seen) in the Secret Gospel of Mark as cited in the letter from Clement of Alexandria to a man named Theodore discovered by Morton Smith in 1958.[302] That Jesus's greatest miracle was not included in the standard version of Mark's Gospel, or indeed any of the Synoptic Gospels, says something about the nature of that incident. Either it took the form of some kind of symbolic death and rebirth that Lazarus underwent with Gnostic overtones, or there were good reasons to avoid mentioning the Bethany family wherever possible. Certainly, the fact that Mary is not named as the woman who anointed Jesus in any of the Synoptic Gospels is very telling indeed, and has led to the confusion surrounding her involvement in this hugely symbolic act.

That Mary of Bethany 'sat at the Lord's feet, and heard his word',[303] and, as Luke's Sinner, did not stop kissing Jesus's feet, establishes her character as a woman devoted to her master. Her overwhelming acts of affection will become important, but the moment after anointing Jesus, Mary of Bethany disappears entirely from the Gospels. She is replaced just a few days later – maybe just 48 hours later if we accept Matthew and Mark – by a woman who seems to absorb her role completely, and that is Mary Magdalene. Matthew tells us that as Jesus suffered on the Cross 'many women' watched from afar.[304] They are the same women that had followed him from Galilee, ministering to him, and are named as 'Mary Magdalene, and Mary the mother of James and Joses [a.k.a. Jose – see below] and the mother of the sons of Zebedee', i.e. Salome.[305] The same list is given in Mark,[306] nothing is said in Luke, while in John the women who watch – not from 'afar' this time, but remaining 'by the cross' – are given as 'his mother [i.e. Jesus's mother, Mary], his mother's sister, Mary the wife of Clopas, and Mary Magdalene'.[307]

After Joseph of Arimathea removes Jesus's body from the cross, the so-called Deposition, he prepares it for burial in a rock-hewn sepulchre. John tells us that Nicodemus, who had helped him in this task, came by night bringing 'a mixture of myrrh and aloes, about a hundred pound weight'.[308] These spices would have been placed inside the linen used to wrap the body for burial, after which the tomb would have been sealed by a large stone slab, rolled into place across the entrance doorway.

In Matthew, after Joseph of Arimathea had departed from the sepulchre, Mary Magdalene is said to have stayed there with 'the other Mary, sitting over against the sepulchre'.[309] Mark says that it was 'Mary the mother of Jose' who was with the Magdalene who 'beheld where he was laid'.[310] Luke, on the other hand, tells only that 'the women, which had come with him out of Galilee, followed after, and beheld the tomb, and how his body was laid'.[311] Yet he adds that 'they returned, and prepared spices and ointments. And on the Sabbath [i.e. the next day, Saturday] they rested according to the commandment.'[312] All this clearly reminds us of how the anointing of Jesus by Mary of Bethany pre-empted the Magdalene's role of preparing the body for burial with 'spices and ointments'.

The Gospels then move forward to the night of the Sabbath, and speak of how as dawn breaks Mary Magdalene, either on her own or in the company of one or more Mary, returns to the tomb and finds it empty. Generally, an angel who is present, and has rolled away the stone, tells her, or the group of women, to go to the disciples and inform them what has happened, but, of course, when she/they do so, there is complete disbelief.[313] In Matthew, after the women depart from the tomb they encounter Jesus, whom they hold by the feet (recalling Mary of Bethany's own acts of affection), and worship.[314] In Mark, 'Mary Magdalene, and Mary the mother of James, and Salome' come to the tomb bringing 'spices, that they might come and anoint him',[315] as they do also in Luke.[316] Afterwards, Mark says that Jesus appeared to Mary Magdalene alone.[317] In Luke, the women return to the tomb bringing with them the disciples and Jesus is there. He speaks to them and those that are with them, and afterwards he leads the party out to Bethany, where he blesses his disciples before ascending to heaven.[318] The implication of this story is that the Ascension took place at Bethany, where Jesus had earlier been anointed by Mary.

Finally, there is John's account of the events. He says that on the first day after the Sabbath Mary Magdalene went alone to the tomb when it was still dark, and saw that the stone had been removed from the entrance.[319] Without further thought, she ran to find the disciples and came across Simon Peter, i.e. Peter, and 'the other disciple, whom Jesus loved', presumably John, and told them what had happened.[320] Peter and John then ran to the tomb, John reaching it first. Yet he did not go inside, and instead waited for Peter to confirm the tomb was empty before entering himself.[321] John then records that they did not know what had happened, since they were unaware of the scriptures that prophesied that the Messiah would live again.[322]

Even after the two disciples depart from the tomb, Mary, who has rejoined them, remains behind weeping, and then sees 'two angels in white' where the body had lain.[323] They ask her why she is weeping, and in response she tells them that it is because they have taken away the Lord, to where she does not know.[324] Mary then turns around and sees Jesus standing there, but does not recognise him. He asks her why she weeps, and whom she seeks, but somehow she manages to mistake him for the gardener.[325] Yet then he addresses her by name and she replies 'Rabboni', i.e. rabbi, which becomes her moment of recognition.[326] But as she moves to embrace him, he says to her, 'Touch me not, for I am not yet ascended unto the Father.' Instead, he asks her to go to his brethren and tell them what he has told her, and what she has seen, which she does.[327]

APOSTLE TO THE APOSTLES

This ends the entries in the Gospels for the woman known as Mary Magdalene. She appears nowhere else afterwards – not in Acts, nor in any of the letters written by the apostles; it is as if she vanishes completely. Yet in the few brief passages in which she does feature in the Christian testament, it is clear that the Magdalene took over the role begun by Mary of Bethany. She brings spices and ointments to the tomb, and is also the leader of Jesus's women followers who arrive at the tomb and find it empty. In John, the only Gospel likely to have been written by an eyewitness to the events surrounding the Crucifixion, it is the Magdalene alone who encounters Jesus, and then announces the fact that he has arisen to the disciples, making her the first messenger, or 'apostle', to convey the good news, or 'gospel', of the Resurrection. To the martyr, presbyter and antipope Hippolytus (d. 236), the first writer ever to link the Canticles with Mary Magdalene,[328] she became *apostola apostolorum*, the 'apostle to the apostles',[329] an epithet that establishes her as one of the most important women in the foundation of the Christian Church.

If the Magdalene can be identified with Mary of Bethany – which she was as early as the second century[330] – then her role as the anointer of Christ makes her the bride to the bridegroom of the Canticles, and in pagan terms the priestess to the king, the goddess to the god. She should have set the pace for the significant role of women disciples in the Church, and in Paul's Gentile Church there *were* originally women who became leaders of communities, missionaries, deacons, prophetesses and teachers, all of whom he saw as fellow workers, without any kind of sexual prejudice.[331] Yet very gradually, due to a denigration of women's rights by the Roman Church (see below), they would never again achieve full equality. Today, despite the emergence of equality for men and women alike, women priests are still banned by the Catholic Church, and just about tolerated by most of the Anglican Church.

THE GNOSTIC MARY

Even though Mary Magdalene disappears from the New Testament after the Ascension, today it is clear that she *did* play a major role in the development of the Early Church. This we know because of a chance discovery in December 1945 at a place called Nag Hammadi in Upper Egypt of an earthenware jar, which had remained *in situ* for some 1,600 years. Inside it were various ancient papyrus codices written in the Egyptian Coptic language, and these were found to contain over fifty distinct works of Gnostic origin, most of them completely unknown to the modern world.[332] Some feature the Magdalene before the Ascension, including her special relationship with Jesus, while others speak of her role after this time, particularly her visionary capabilities, her leadership of the remaining eleven disciples and the incredible enmity that clearly existed between her and St Peter. Moreover, the simple fact that Mary of Bethany does *not* appear in the Gnostic gospels, even though her sister Martha *does,* is surely evidence in favour of this Mary being identified with Mary Magdalene.

The Nag Hammadi Library, as it has become known, seems to make better sense of the Magdalene's relationship with Jesus. For instance, in the Gospel of Philip, an early Gnostic Christian work which has proved of immense embarrassment to the institutional Church, we read that there were 'three who always walked with the Lord: Mary his mother and her sister and Magdalene, the one who was called his companion. His sister [sic] and his mother and his companion were each a Mary.'[333] The original Greek form of the word translated by scholars as 'companion' is *koinonos*, which actually implies much more than simply one who keeps company with another, for it *can* refer to a consort or, more accurately, a sexual partner.[334] If this was so, then being on such intimate terms with Jesus – whether on a physical level, or a spiritual level, or both – would explain why she prepared the spices and ointment for his body before burial. Yet it is what the Gospel of Philip goes on to say that most bears out the fact that Mary was his lover, for we read: 'And the companion of the [Christ was] Mary Magdalene. [He loved] her more than [all] the disciples [and used to] kiss her [often] on her [lips??].'[335] Since it does not say anything similar about any other person in Jesus's retinue, it becomes blatantly obvious that Jesus and she were very close indeed – the reason why it was her alone who came to learn of his impending fate, and why she was the one who anointed him.

PETER'S ENMITY

Moving on to the Gospel of Mary – written in the late first century or early second century,[336] and named after the Magdalene – we find her in charge of the apostles, who are downhearted that their master has departed from them. Mary gets up and rouses their spirits, prompting Peter to ask, 'Sister, we know that the Saviour loved you more than the rest of women. Tell us the words of the Saviour which you remember – which you know [but] we do not, nor have we heard them.'[337] She then begins to talk about a vision of Jesus that she has received, and the details of that dialogue, prompting Andrew, Peter's brother, to dispute the fact that this is what their master had said, since her ideas seem strange. Peter agrees, saying, 'Did he really speak with a woman without our knowledge [and] not openly? Are we to turn about and all listen to her? Did he prefer her to us?' In response, Mary weeps, saying: 'Do you think that I thought this up myself in my heart, or that I am lying about the Saviour?'[338] Levi consoles her, pointing out that Peter has always been hot-tempered, and then confronts him with the words: 'Now I see you contending against the woman like the adversaries. But if the Saviour made her worthy, who are you indeed to reject her? Surely the Saviour knows her very well. That is why he loved her more than us.'[339]

In the Gospel of Mary – which was in circulation before the discovery of the Nag Hammadi Library – the Magdalene was able to receive visions, allowing her direct dialogue with the ascended Christ, something which the male disciples just could not accept, especially as she was a woman. What is more, they knew full well that Mary had some kind of special relationship with their master, which the male disciples found difficult to handle. Moreover, she had taken on the role as the group's spiritual leader, which was perceived as a direct threat to Peter's own assumed authority over the apostles.

This enmity against Mary is something which appears to have been brooding for some while, for even before the Crucifixion the Gospel of Thomas, also known about before the Nag Hammadi discovery, tells us that at one point Peter exclaims: 'Let Mary leave us, for women are not worthy of life.'[340] In answer to this, Jesus had apparently said, 'I myself shall lead her in order to make her male, so that she too may become a living spirit resembling you males. For every woman who will make herself male will enter the kingdom of heaven.'[341] This peculiar concept of a woman becoming male in order to enter the kingdom of heaven stems from the Gnostic belief that the spirit, the divine spark trapped inside a person's soul, was originally male, even if the outer shell is now female. However, this was certainly not a view adopted by all Gnostic sects, many of which saw men and women as equals, and placed women in roles such as deacons and even priests.

'I AM FEARING PETROS'

In another Gnostic text known as the Dialogue of the Saviour, Jesus provides secret teachings to Judas, Matthew and Mary Magdalene,[342] who listened and 'understood completely'.[343] This theme of total understanding is found also in the Pistis Sophia ('faith-wisdom'), a work of late third-century composition. Here the ascended Christ appears before his disciples in a brilliant light and tells his closest followers how he has rescued Sophia, female wisdom, his spiritual bride or partner, from her exile in the twilight zone between the Pleroma (the heavens), and the Cosmos, and in so doing has restored her to the Fullness. Elsewhere, Mary is herself seen as the 'Spirit of Wisdom', the personification of Sophia, making it more clear why, on a spiritual level at least, she was viewed as Jesus's bride, consort or partner.[344]

In the Pistis Sophia, Jesus next asks his pupils to provide questions for him, to which he gives a lengthy reply by way of a dialogue. It is the Magdalene who asks 39 out of 46 questions, hence the alternative name for this text, which is 'Interrogations of Mary'.[345] Jesus commends Mary over and over as 'happy beyond every woman',[346] but then Peter rises and boldly tells Jesus, 'My Lord, we are not able to bear with this woman, saying instead of us; and she let not any of us speak, but she is speaking many times.'[347] Mary later admits to Jesus that 'I am fearing Petros [i.e. Peter], because he is wont to threaten me, and he hateth our sex.'[348]

Clearly, there was no love lost between Mary and Peter, who each vied for Jesus's undivided loyalty during his life, and continued the rivalry after the Ascension. Even though this might explain why so little is told about her in the Gospels, the role she played in the anointing of Jesus, the Deposition, the finding of the Empty Tomb and her encounter with the resurrected Jesus was too important, too well established, to be ignored. The enmity towards her also begins to answer the question of why key stories relating to the Bethany family, such as the raising of Mary's brother Lazarus, Jesus's greatest miracle, were removed from the Gospel of Mark. If the Magdalene really was as important as the Gnostic gospels imply, then what else has been whitewashed about the role she played in the foundation of the Christian Church? In my temporary excursion from questing activities in advance of our trip to Headcorn, I had now to explore the more or less androgynous relationship that seemed to exist between Mary Magdalene and John the Evangelist, which becomes the key to unravelling the real origins of the Holy Grail.

16. THE BELOVED DISCIPLE

In the *Philosophumena*, a work written by Hippolytus about AD 220 condemning the Gnostic heresies, it records that the sect called the Naasenes, who took their name from the Hebrew for 'serpent', claimed that their secret teachings were given by Jesus to James the Less, 'the brother of the Lord', who passed them on to his successor Mariamne.[349] There is a strong case for suggesting that this Mariamne, a corruption of Miriam, the Hebrew form of Mary, is none other than Mary Magdalene. If this was so, then she must have been a leader of the first Christians, which supports what the Gnostic gospels have to say about her. Indeed, in the Pistis Sophia, Jesus says at one point: 'Mary Magdalene and John the virgin will surpass all my disciples and all men who shall receive mysteries in the Ineffable, they will be on my right hand and on my left, and I am they and they are I.'[350] Since this statement was written perhaps 150 years after their age, it must be assumed that the Gnostic writer of the Pistis Sophia obviously believed this to have been the case. To him or her Mary and John shared a dual role which was at one even with Christ himself, for as he says: 'I am they and they are I'. John's epithet of 'the virgin' was applied to him from a very early date, and stems from his own alleged relationship with the Magdalene, which will now steer us not only back towards the Grail mystery, but also towards its final secrets.

Early Christian legends not only link Mary and John together as companions, but also assert that they were married at the wedding of Cana, where, according to John's Gospel, Jesus turned water into wine. The story goes that on meeting John, Jesus asked him to give up his marriage and become his disciple, leaving Mary to sink into a world of whoredom – the reason why she turned to him for absolution of her sins and was purged of 'seven devils'.[351] Clearly, this was not how Jesus first came into contact with John, for we know that, as the Beloved Disciple, he and Andrew were followers of John the Baptist who swapped allegiance after Jesus was baptised by him. However, the story that John the Evangelist was the bridegroom at the wedding of Cana goes back at least to the sixth century, since it is quoted by St Augustine, even though he fails to give the name of the bride.[352] The story developed more fully in the centuries that followed. Yet how it originated, scholars have no idea, although it does serve to highlight the unshakeable link between these two characters, so important to the life of Jesus.

In the late sixth century, Gregory of Tours (544–95), a historian of the Franks, was to speak of Mary Magdalene ending her days at Ephesus in Asia Minor, where John is thought to have become its first bishop. Her flight to Ephesus is confirmed by Modestus (d. 634), patriarch of Jerusalem, who tells us:

. . . after the death of Our Lord, the mother of God and Mary Magdalen joined John, the well-beloved disciple, at Ephesus. It is there that the myrrhophore ['myrrh-bearer'] ended her apostolic career through her martyrdom, not wishing to the very end to be separated from John the apostle and the Virgin.[353]

So after spending her final years in the company of John and, seemingly, Mary the mother of Jesus, the Magdalene was martyred and, according to tradition, was laid to rest in an elevated sepulchre on Mount Celion, near the entrance to the Cave of the Seven Sleepers.[354] They were seven young Christian men who went to sleep in a cave during the persecutions of Decius, Emperor of Rome (c. 249–51), and woke up, Rip van Winkle-style, nearly 200 years later during the reign of the Christian Emperor Theodosius II (d. 450). Her tomb at Ephesus was venerated as early as the sixth century, and it is from here that the first evidence of her cult begins to emerge. There exist numerous accounts of prominent figures of the day visiting her tomb, yet by the twelfth century it was said to be empty. Probably, this had something to do with the fact that her remains had apparently been translated (i.e. ceremoniously moved) to Constantinople in 886 under the authority of Emperor Leo VI (886–912), the Philosopher. They were placed alongside those of her 'brother' Lazarus, who is also said to have journeyed to Ephesus, where he became its bishop for forty years.[355] A similar claim was made for John the Evangelist, and, indeed, some scholars have theorised that Lazarus – named as 'the youth whom Jesus loved' in the fragment from the Secret Gospel of Mark where he is raised from the dead – was the true Beloved Disciple.[356]

Despite the supposed translation of the Magdalene's remains to Constantinople, the church of S. Giovanni Laterano (St John Lateran) in Rome, built on the spot where John the Evangelist is supposed to have defied death after being immersed in a cauldron of boiling oil, set up an altar to the Magdalene and claimed to possess her headless remains. Other claimants regarding the possession of her head, and even her entire body, stem almost exclusively from churches in southern France, where medieval legends arose to suggest that it was there that the Magdalene ended her days (see Chapter 18).

THE FOURTH GOSPEL

As I examined the connections between Mary and John's legendary lives, some kind of inter-relationship began to emerge, highlighted by recent attempts to champion Mary Magdalene not only as the true Beloved Disciple, but also as the author of the Fourth Gospel, credited normally to John the Evangelist. These ideas, proposed in 1998 by Catholic scripture scholar Ramon K. Jusino,[357] derive from the plausible premise that Mary, and not Peter, emerged as the outright leader of the Early Church. He believes that she went on to compose the original stage of what became the Fourth Gospel sometime between the mid-50s and late 80s, alluding to herself merely as the disciple and apostle whom Jesus loved. This, of course, is exactly the same way that the Magdalene is described in some of the Gnostic gospels, as we have seen. For instance, in the Gospel of Philip we read that Jesus '[loved] her more than [all] the disciples', while in the Gospel of Mary it says: 'Surely the Saviour knows her very well. That is why he loved her more than us.'

The Fourth Gospel bears distinct Gnostic leanings, the reason why Jusino suggests that it was readily adopted by the emerging Johannine community of Ephesus, whom he sees as followers of an individual named John the Presbyter, a separate person to the disciple John, the son of Zebedee. They were motivated by a more dualistic and wisdom-orientated Christianity, inspired by the concept of direct communication with God, something which would later re-emerge both in Cathar tradition and within the Grail romances. However, a schism then occurred among the Johannine community, whereby one branch veered more heavily towards outright Gnosticism, while the other faction amalgamated and merged with the Church of Rome. Yet these institutional Christians had no place for women playing active roles in the Church, thus the only way that the Fourth Gospel could be accepted by them was for a redactor to change the Beloved Disciple, i.e. Mary Magdalene, *into a man*. Yet since the Magdalene played a key role in events already popularised in the earliest forms of the Synoptic Gospels, such as the witnessing of Christ's suffering, the finding of the Empty Tomb and as first witness to the resurrected Christ, the redactor awkwardly rewrote her back into John's Gospel as someone quite apart from the all-male Beloved Disciple. However, in so doing they created textual flaws that are apparent to any scripture scholar. On the other hand, the section of the Johannine community that retained its connection with Gnosticism and the Magdalene continued to see her as Jesus's bride or partner, whom he loved more than any other disciple. With the spread of Gnosticism throughout Asia Minor and the Near East in the second and third centuries, the Magdalene retained her prominence in their gospels, the reason why she is named as such in the fourth-century Nag Hammadi Library.

Jusino's theories are derived from internal evidence in the Fourth Gospel, and also from references to the Magdalene in the Gnostic gospels. Despite their utter persuasiveness, his conclusions fail to explain certain fundamental issues concerning the Fourth Gospel. For example, if the Beloved Disciple is not John, the son of Zebedee, then why does this disciple, so prominent in the three Synoptic Gospels, not feature anywhere in the Fourth Gospel? Moreover, if Mary Magdalene was the Beloved Disciple, then what was she doing fishing in a boat with male disciples on the occasion that he/she noticed the resurrected Christ on the shoreline, and says to Peter, 'It is the Lord'?[358] Surely, it makes more sense for this person to have been John, the son of Zebedee, who – along with James, Peter and Andrew – was a fisherman.

That John, as the author of the Fourth Gospel, referred to himself simply as the 'the disciple whom Jesus loved' should not be seen as peculiar. His contemporary, St Paul, does exactly the same thing in his Second Epistle to the Corinthians. He describes the visions and revelations granted to him by God, but speaks in the third person: 'I know a man in Christ . . . such a one caught up even to the third heaven . . . And I know such a man . . . he was caught up into Paradise . . . On behalf of such a one will I glory: but on mine own behalf

I will not glory.'[359] In addition to this, there is ample evidence from the early Church Fathers that John wrote his own Gospel.[360]

LEONARDO'S LADY M

Although at the present time I am unable to accept that Mary Magdalene was the Beloved Disciple, who thus wrote the Fourth Gospel, such inspired ideas were themselves highly significant, for the dual worlds of Mary and John seem inextricably linked, almost as if they grew to become two sides of the same coin. It was a matter picked up on by my colleagues Lynn Picknett and Clive Prince in their monumental book *The Templar Revelation*, first published in 1997. They discuss the fact that Leonardo da Vinci's famous fresco of the Last Supper in the refectory of the convent of Santa Maria delle Grazie in Milan (1495–99), contains a whole series of peculiar irregularities that do not derive from gospel accounts of the event.[361] Among them is the manner in which John the Evangelist is portrayed sitting at Jesus's right-hand side. Instead of leaning into his Master's bosom as is emphasised by his role as the Beloved Disciple of John's Gospel, he leans exaggeratedly away from him, straining his ear to hear Peter ask who it is that will betray their master. Oddly, Peter's right hand, which gestures towards Jesus, palm upright, is aptly positioned to seem as if he is making a cutting stroke across the throat of the Beloved Disciple, a reference perhaps to the beheading of John the Baptist, who was his master before becoming a follower of Jesus. More peculiarly, John is depicted quite clearly *as a woman*.[362]

I knew that it was standard practice for artists to depict the apostle John as an effeminate young man, since it contrasted well with his older form as the evangelist holding the Gospel attributed to him. However, there seems little question that Leonardo da Vinci (1452–1519) was, in this instance, portraying John as a female with a pretty face, petite breasts, delicate hands and gold necklace around her neck. Why? One clue is in the shape made by the position of Jesus and John together, which makes 'a giant, spread-eagled "M", almost as if they were literally joined at the hip but had suffered a falling out', as Picknett and Prince aptly put it.[363]

The two authors go on to identify this 'Lady M' as Mary Magdalene, who they feel in Leonardo's painting replaces John as the Beloved Disciple at the table of the Last Supper.[364] Such a revelation begs the question of why such a famous artist would have wanted to put his neck on the line and swerve away from conventional Christian iconography so much that he risked being accused of blasphemy. Did he know something about the Fourth Gospel's Beloved Disciple that went against orthodox tradition? Remember, if Jusino is correct and the Beloved Disciple *is* Mary Magdalene, then it is *her* sitting at the right-hand of Jesus, and *not* John. The authors of *The Templar Revelation* propose that Leonardo was exposed to an underground stream of knowledge, which came via the Templars and Cathars from early Christian Gnostic sects, and stemmed originally from those followers of John the Baptist who joined Jesus's entourage, i.e. Andrew and the Beloved Disciple. The existence of an underground strain of knowledge passing through time from person to person makes sense, especially in the knowledge that the Freemasons and the Templar revivalists of the eighteenth and nineteenth centuries both saw John the Evangelist as their legendary founder. What is more, Leonardo da Vinci was obsessed by the concept of the androgyne, and often painted them into his pictures – the *Mona Lisa* being the most obvious example.[365]

Did the life of the Magdalene become so confused with that of John that the two occasionally merged into one androgynous figure? Is this what Leonardo da Vinci was attempting to convey by painting John as Lady M? The words spoken by Jesus to Peter in respect to Mary Magdalene as given in the Gospel of Thomas now become more relevant, and should be read very carefully indeed: 'I myself shall lead her in order to make her male, so that she too may become a living spirit resembling you males. For every woman who will make herself male will enter the kingdom of heaven.'

The idea of the androgyne was something of immense importance to the earliest Gnostic Christians, who practised initiatory baptisms, carried out naked, whereby both men and women achieved a kind of reunification with God by becoming like Adam, the first man, before a rib was taken from him to create Eve, the first woman.[366] In other words, the initiate would have to become bisexual, in a spiritual sense at least, since it was believed that the 'image' of God, and thus the soul itself, was bisexual (and only took on gender at birth).[367] This transformation was reflected by the asexual clothing, appearance and lifestyle the initiates would thereafter adopt for the rest of their lives. Such individuals were known in Greek as *monachus* (*monachoi* in plural), quite clearly the root of the word 'monk', used to describe a Christian ascetic. Yet for the Gnostic *monachoi*, they were now eligible for a more secret initiation in a place known as the Bridal Chamber, where both males and females became 'one', even if they were not afterwards treated as equals. Indeed, if the female was to become a 'living' spirit, then she had to adopt a male personality, thus helping to explain the strange statement in the Gospel of Thomas.

Exactly what took place during the 'Mystery of the Bridal Chamber' remains obscure, with orthodox Christians assuming, rightly or wrongly, that it involved sexual practices.[368] Certainly, it is known from certain Nag Hammadi texts that it involved 'becoming one' with the Bridegroom, establishing the 'germ of light in the bridal chamber', and 'receiving grace and the Spirit'.[369] For the sect of Gnostics known as the Valentinians it was a kind of 'sacred marriage',[370] *Hieros Gamos* like that practised by the god-king and his chosen priestess, not just in the pagan religions of the Near East, but also by the very earliest peoples of ancient Mesopotamia (modern-day Iraq), such as the Sumerians and Baby-lonians.[371] What is more interesting, however, is that the 'Mystery of the Bridal Chamber' was compared with the union of the Saviour, i.e. the ascended Christ, 'with the previously barren Sophia – also represented by the peculiar legends of Christ's association with Mary Magdalene'.[372] Although John the Evangelist is not associated with this tradition in any existing Gnostic documents, the fact that he was seen to have been the bridegroom of Mary Magdalene certainly suggests that in the minds of some early Christian sects the couple might well have become 'one' to form the perfect androgyne, compared with the bisexual Adam before the creation of Eve, in order to join in perfect union with Christ. Did such ideas live on within the underground stream and, along with the androgyne nature of Baphomet, go on to inspire the androgynous art of Renaissance painters such as Leonardo da Vinci?

MARY'S GRAIL

Acknowledging that he would one day drink from the same cup as Jesus, i.e. face martyrdom because of his faith, along with his perceived role as priest at the Last Supper, led John the Evangelist to become the first Grail-bearer. It is this same cup, with its emerging serpent, a symbol of Sophia, the 'spirit of wisdom' embodied by the Magdalene, that becomes his emblem as the Beloved Disciple. So if he is temporarily exchanged with the other half of his persona, Picknett and Prince's 'Lady M', identified as Mary Magdalene, does this enhance our knowledge of his cup symbolism? Indeed it does, for the Magdalene's own symbol is the *alabastron*, the unguent jar or vase that contained the spikenard used to anoint Jesus. In Christian art, the Magdalene is invariably shown with this vessel either held in one hand or placed at her feet. Moreover, from medieval times onwards her vase is occasionally upgraded to a chalice, or 'ciborium',[373] into which descends a dove, symbol of the Holy Spirit. This same bird signified divine love in Jewish mysticism, and was not only a symbol of the Shulamite Woman in Solomon's Song of Songs but also a totemic device of Near Eastern pagan goddesses of sex and love – their attributes being absorbed into the cult of the Magdalene; the dove even becoming Mary's personal emblem via this route.[374] In addition to this, some of these love goddesses were shown bearing a cup, filled with the waters of life, representing their association with the fecundity of the land. Sacred springs and pools were also associated with this aspect of their devotion. So was there some connection between the Magdalene's *alabastron* and the origins of the Holy Grail, identified in the medieval romances primarily as a receptacle of the Holy Blood?

The answer is a very definitive yes. In a second-century work of Gnostic origin entitled the First Gospel of the Infancy of Jesus Christ it records that after Jesus was circumcised in a cave (usually on the eighth day), a 'Hebrew woman' took the bloodied foreskin ('others say she took the navel-string') and preserved it in 'an alabaster box of old oil of spikenard'. Her son was a druggist, and he was told that under no circumstances was the box to be sold, even though he would be offered 300 denarii for it. Many years later, the vessel was procured by 'Mary the sinner' and used by her to anoint Jesus on the head and feet, after which she wiped the ointment away with her hair.[375]

Another Magdalene-linked blood-relic is a phial of unknown origin, housed until the eighteenth century in the sixteenth-century Tommaso Lombardo tabernacle, found in the sacristy of the church of the Friari in Venice. It supposedly contained drops of Jesus's Holy Blood mixed with the spikenard unguent used by the Magdalene to anoint Christ.[376] This item, donated to the church in 1479, was removed from a church in Constantinople when the city was sacked by the Crusaders in 1204, although what its provenance might have been, and what became of it, is unclear.[377]

THE HOUSE OF SIMON THE LEPER

Then we come to the connections between the anointing of Jesus and the events surrounding the Last Supper. Matthew and Mark both state that the former took place two days before the Passover at the house of Simon the Leper at Bethany, while Luke says it occurred at the home of Simon the Pharisee. In John it was held at the house of Martha, Mary and Lazarus in the same village. Knowing therefore that the *alabastron* seems to have been a blood-relic receptacle even before the anointing, I found it curious that medieval legends, and in particular Robert de Boron's *Joseph d'Arimathie*, insist that the Last Supper occurred in the house of Simon the Leper.[378] Moreover, afterwards when Jesus was arrested, de Boron says that upon Jesus's seizure by the Jewish authorities a Jew went to Simon's house and found the vessel used at the supper. He took it to the Roman governor Pontius Pilate, who on the occasion that Joseph of Arimathea pleaded for the body of the Saviour, gave the cup to him, knowing that he loved this prophet very much.[379] One medieval legend has it that Joseph of Arimathea took the vessel himself from the house of Simon the Leper,[380] while Jacobus de Voragine tells us in his *Chronicon Januense*, c. 1277, that a 'certain vessel of emerald (*vase emeraldino*)' used at the Last Supper was taken by Nicodemus to collect 'the sacred gore which was still moist, and which had been ignominiously spilled about'.[381] These stories link the house in which Mary of Bethany anointed Jesus with the location of the Last Supper, and imply that there is some overlap between the unguent jar of the Magdalene and the cup (or *catinus*, i.e. meat dish) of the Last Supper – both of which came to be regarded as receptacles of the Holy Blood.

CATCHING THE BLOOD

In this context, there exist several medieval depictions of Mary catching the Holy Blood in a cup-like vessel,[382] others that show her catching the blood that flows from the feet of Jesus using her hands (see Plate 21),[383] and still more where she is using her long hair to wipe the blood from his feet.[384] The Magdalene's place at Jesus's bloodied feet recalls the carved reliefs of the Crucifixion from Germany, dating from the eleventh and twelfth centuries, which show a chalice at the base of the Cross. It is quite clear that although Crucifixion scenes showing Joseph of Arimathea collecting the Holy Blood spread across Europe only after the appearance of the first Grail romances, separate traditions saw both Nicodemus and the Magdalene taking on the same role. One medieval legend even has Christ appearing to her after the Crucifixion and giving her, and not Joseph of Arimathea, the Grail,[385] while an alabaster flask of Holy Blood in the church of St Maximin in Provence, which liquefied every Good Friday, was said to have been collected at the time of the Crucifixion by Mary Magdalene.[386] More importantly, accounts of her part in

Plate 1 *(right)* Aleister Crowley (1875–1947) in Arab-style dress. Why did this long-dead occultist become the unlikely spirit guide in a quest to find the Holy Grail?

Plate 2 *(below)* The horned statue in St Clement's Caves, Hastings. Does it represent Baphomet, idol of the Knights Templar? Why did the Grail quest have to begin here?

Plate 3 *(above)* Nineteenth-century conception of a Knights Templar rite practised by French Freemasons, with Baphomet carried in procession.

Plate 4 *(left)* The Holy Grail manifesting to King Arthur and the Knights of the Round Table, from a fourteenth-century French manuscript. Could the true Grail really be found?

Plate 5 *(left)* John the Baptist beheaded at the hands of Herod, from a stained glass window in St John's church, Glastonbury. Was his head venerated by the Templars, who saw him as their patron?

Plate 6 *(below)* Medieval panel found at Templecombe in Somerset. Does this mesmerising face executed by the Knights Templar show Jesus Christ or John the Baptist?

Plate 7 *(above)* Nicolas Poussin's *Les Bergers d'Arcadie*, painted c. 1640. Does it really show the landscape around Rennes-le-Château in southern France?

Plate 8 *(right)* Joseph of Arimathea holding two cruets containing the blood and sweat of Christ, from a fifteenth-century stained glass window at Langport, Somerset. How did this lesser-known follower of Jesus become the bearer of the Grail in medieval tradition?

Plate 9 *(left)* Chevalier Andrew Ramsay (1686-1743), a Scottish born philosopher and quietist, who introduced Templar degrees known as Ramsay's Rite to French Freemasonry.

Plate 10 & 11 *(above)* The Franks Casket, c. AD 700–750, and, inset, the panel showing the destruction of the Jerusalem Temple. Does it show the oldest known representation of the true Grail?

Plate 12 *(left)* Illustration from the Egbert's Psalter, c. AD 980, showing the Crucifixion. Why is Mary Magdalene gesturing towards the flow of the Holy Blood, and who is the crowned figure collecting it in a Grail cup?

Plate 13 The Bitter Cup appears to Jesus as he suffers the Agony in the Garden at Gethsemane before the Crucifixion, from a stained glass window at Beauchamp Roding in Essex. Is the significance of this communion cup the true origin of the Grail legend?

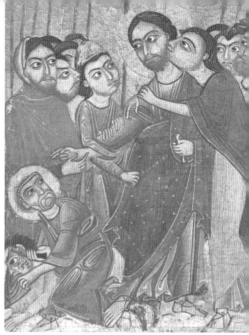

Plate 14 The Betrayal of Jesus from the School of Pisa, second half of the twelfth century. That Malchus's left ear is being severed by St Peter instead of his right ear – as stated in the Gospels of Luke and John – bears out the significance of the Franks Casket scene showing the destruction of the Temple.

Plate 15 Counter seal of the *Templi Secretum*, the Templar's inner order, showing the Gnostic god or demiurge Abraxas beneath seven stars signifying the seven heavens. Did the Order protect the holy relic known as the Head of God?

Plate 16 Illustration from the Stuttgart Psalter, c. AD 850, showing the Crucifixion scene with the Grail cup suspended in mid air. Who are the two small figures, one seen holding a knife, carrying a blanket between them?

Plate 17 (*above*) Strange carvings around the torso-shaped piscina in the Knights Templar' church at Garway, Herefordshire. Are they Gnostic in origin? What do they mean?

Plates 18, 19 & 20 The Shepherds Monument at Shugborough Park in Staffordshire (*above*), showing Poussin's *Les Bergers d'Arcadie* transposed, mirror-fashion. Does it divert attention away from the nearby Cat Monument (*left*), with its unique stone plaque showing the griffon-flanked vase (*below*)?

+ Sča(h)aria Oʒagralerii aporiæ apoliola +

Plate 21 (*left*) Were the Gnostics correct in naming the Magdalene, seen here (standing) in her guise as Apostle to the Apostles, as Jesus's true successor?

Plate 22 (*below*) Section of Leonardo da Vinci's *The Last Supper*, showing the Beloved Disciple on his right-hand side. Is this figure John-the-Evangelist, Mary Magdalene or both of them combined?

Plate 23 (*left*) Two-faced Janus, Roman god of all beginnings, representing the influence of January, as seen on the lead font at Brookland, Kent. What part does he play in the quest for the Grail?

Plate 24 (*below*) What symbolism is concealed in this image of the Holy Family by Albrecht Dürer, dating from c. 1512. Behind them is John the Evangelist, with his arm around Mary Magdalene, and a hook-nosed old man, identified by Dürer as Nicodemus.

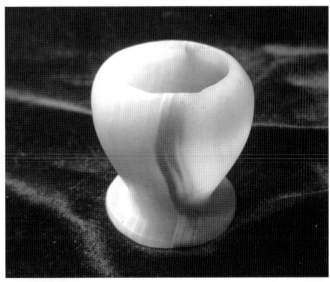

Plate 25 (*left*) How did this stained glass window showing John the Evangelist holding the Gnostic Grail in Hodnet church, Shropshire, become important to the Grail quest?

Plate 26 (*below*) The Marian Chalice. Is this the Magdalene's alabastron, as well as the most authentic Grail in existence today?

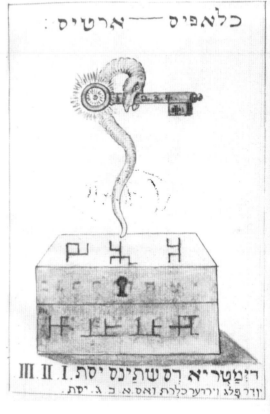

Plate 27 (*above*) Graham Phillips examines the broken eagle statue inside the caves at Hawkstone Park, Shropshire, behind which a small cup, thought to be the Marian Chalice, was found during restoration work in 1917.

Plate 28 (*right*) Illustration from the manuscript *Aleph*, dated 1802 and written by Archarion, a German Rosicrucian. Does the serpent holding the key help reveal how to unlock the secrets of the Grail?

Plate 29 (*above*) Sue Collins and Richard Ward stand next to St Frideswide's shrine in Christchurch Cathedral, Oxford, on Saturday 19 October 2002, shortly before the discovery of the key at Binsey.

Plate 30 (*right*) St Frideswide, from a medieval stained glass window in Christchurch Cathedral, Oxford. Does this Saxon saint guard Binsey's holy well?

Plate 31 (*above*) Antique key with magical sigils unearthed close to St Margaret's Well.

Plate 32 (*right*) Heraldic shield showing three crowned female heads above an ox crossing a ford, as found on the pulpit in Binsey's church. Do these heads affirm a link between St Helen, the Three Crowns and St Margaret's Well?

this powerful act predate those of Joseph of Arimathea by at least two centuries. As previously noted, an illuminated scene of the Crucifixion preserved in Egbert's Psalter, dated to c. 980, shows Longinus piercing Jesus's side and blood flowing down into a cup held by a small crowned figure identified as Nicodemus. On the left-hand side stands the Magdalene, who reaches out and virtually touches the stream of blood as if honouring, or even controlling, its descent. It is difficult not to conclude from this painting that Mary is the one ensuring that the Holy Blood is being caught in a vessel by Nicodemus, who seems subservient to her.

Thus through the shedding of Jesus's blood and its collection, if not by herself then by Nicodemus, Mary appears to be fulfilling Christ's simile of the Bitter Cup, the ultimate symbol of his agony and martyrdom, which also features as the communion cup of the Last Supper and the Paschal vigil. The vessel containing Christ's blood encapsulates this extraordinary power, which although originally symbolic in nature was quickly replaced in the early Christian era by real containers of supposed blood-relics that were seen to embody this same divine potency. Remember, this is the earliest given explanation for the Grail cup in the medieval romances, and its guardian and bearer is invariably a woman. Since the cup is one of the primary symbols of the love goddesses of the Near East, a connection between the Magdalene and the Grail should come as no surprise. As the anointer of Christ, like the chosen bride or priestess in the pagan religions, it was her role to achieve this act on his behalf, and thus she *should* have become the first Grail-bearer.

Yet this role, denied to her by the Church of Rome, fell initially upon her male counterpart John the Evangelist. Then, in medieval times, it was stolen by Joseph of Arimathea – due both to his connection with the symbol of the chalice through his ownership of the Holy Sepulchre, and to the confusion that arose between him and the Beloved Disciple through the legend of the Wandering Jew. Yet so strong did Mary's association with the Grail become by the mid-thirteenth century that she was often shown standing alongside Joseph of Arimathea, with both of them holding receptacles containing blood-relics, implying that there was not one but *two* Grails. Yet in Britain, where the cult of Joseph of Arimathea was strongest, this new idea of two Grails had to be accommodated in some way without involving the Magdalene, whose cult was mainly a French obsession. The result was a belief popularised from the mid-fourteenth century onwards that Joseph of Arimathea had come to Britain bringing not one but two cruets, or Grails, containing the blood and sweat of Christ.[387]

Joseph of Arimathea and his family have been protectors of the Grail for the past 800 years, but for the first time we can begin to discern the vessel's true guardians. Together, Mary and John reassemble all the different components of the Holy Blood and Bitter Cup tradition to create everything that the Grail represented when the first romances were written at the end of the twelfth century. It is a new vision of an ancient vessel which most scholars today envisage as either medieval in creation or the result of the Christianisation of a

Celtic cauldron of plenty, or horn of plenty. Through the androgynous world of Mary and John, the Grail in the twenty-first century is made whole again.

What exactly the relationship might be between the Holy Grail and the head of John the Baptist had still to be settled. However, I could not help but think that the two represented some kind of dual polarity – life and death, light and darkness, white and black, future and past, John the Evangelist and John the Baptist, the two Johns. Only when the physical representation of the Grail cup had been achieved, would the truth of this sacred vessel be given in full, and with the imminent visit to Headcorn just days away this could not come soon enough.

17. THE HOLLOW TOWER

Under the light of the full moon, four fugitive Templar knights carried on their shoulders a wooden bier that supported a small stone ark, or coffer, on which were strange carved forms representing their lord and master Baphomet. Inside the box was something of immense value and significance, a sacred idol venerated not only by the Order but also by those of the underground stream that had existed since the time of Christ to express the true gnosis. It was to be taken across the sea to where it would be safe from the Holy Church, which, having heard stories of its presence in this realm, would stop at nothing until it was in its possession.

The party moved swiftly along quiet paths and tracks that crossed empty fields, entered pitch-black woods, and climbed the highest hills, all to avoid the undue interest of the king's bailiffs and untrustworthy churchmen. A few years beforehand, these former Knights Templar had discarded their distinctive white-and-red livery and shaven off their long beards, and now they journeyed as merchants, travellers and nobleman, bearing false names and colours that would not arouse suspicion.

Stephen de Staplebridge, dressed in knight's dress and woollen hood, in the company of two other brothers wearing coarse brown cowls, walked briskly in front of the procession, making sure the path ahead was always clear. As they passed over one final hill crest, they gazed down at the night fires and moonlit water which raised hope that all would be fine, for they knew the port of Dover was now within easy reach. As the first light of dawn faintly illuminated the eastern sky, the brethren entered the outskirts of the town and sought out a prearranged rendezvous point, where the precious cargo was unloaded from the bier and given into the possession of trusted friends.

Sunday, 5 May. Richard broke his concentration, and sighed a note of despondency. 'Sorry, that's all I get at the moment. I just feel that the stone casket was taken out of the country via Dover, but where it went to from here, or where exactly it came from, I don't know.'

New information on the Head of God was the last thing I had expected today of all days, when we were supposed to be gearing ourselves up for the retrieval of the Grail cup at Headcorn. I looked up at the closed curtains preventing the blazing sunlight from entering the room that late spring afternoon and wondered what was going on. Richard seemed almost to be fading into the darkness, as Sue sat silently on the other side of me, hoping, like us all, that something crucial might be revealed through the process of collective meditation. On a small table were placed five small brass bowls, which, until several minutes beforehand, had contained methylated spirits that burned, when lit, with a bright blue flame. It was something we had done a few times now, following a visionary visit one day from the Sufi master,[388] who I believed had appeared to the four knights who conducted a ritual around the Mithraic altar in Stone-in-Oxney church at some time in the past. He sat cross-legged in front of me, and before him burned five flames that came from small metal bowls containing a flammable liquid, and he explained their purpose.

When all five lights burn bright, one should contemplate the first *latifa*, whose colour is yellow, but when the first light fades out the second *latifa* should be contemplated, and so on, until a single light remains. One had then to concentrate on the highest *latifa*, *Akhfa*, governed by the green ray, and when this flame had extinguished, and the mystic is in complete darkness, then he or she should contemplate their innermost consciousness, the Ultimate Unseen, *Ghayb-ul-Ghaib*, and the search for the Cup of Jamshid or, in our case, the Grail cup of the romances. Whether such knowledge stemmed from a true Sufi source, accessed somehow by my mind, or whether the whole thing was simply my imagination, seemed irrelevant as it appeared a perfect way to utilise our newfound knowledge of the *latā'if*.

A VISIT TO BROOKLAND

I had felt everything was going very much to plan in the weeks leading up to this bank-holiday weekend, but now, on the day designated for us to find the cup, I was just a little uncomfortable about the lack of positive psychic information. My edginess had begun, if I am to admit it now, on Sunday, 21 April, when Richard, in the company of his partner Pandora, accompanied Sue and me to Headcorn to pay our respects to what remained of King John's Oak. A meditation at the site produced virtually nothing of any note, unusual for Richard, and entirely unexpected as he had been picking up so strongly on the site since the previous December. We had then journeyed on to Stone-in-Oxney, where our attempts to reconstruct the ritual conducted by the four knights around the Mithraic altar were thwarted when an elderly couple entered the church just as we were burning copious amounts of pungent incense upon its already scorched stone surface! So it had been on to St Augustine's church at nearby Brookland, where we gazed in awe at the incredible circular lead font with its two tiers of arched panels showing the twelve signs of the zodiac and the corresponding twelve labours connected with each month of the year.

We carefully examined those panels relevant to us: the butcher slaying a bull, the hooded smith at his forge and Janus seated at a table, a sceptre in one hand and a cup in the other. Taking too many photographs of this single image made me wonder for the thousandth time about the nature of psychic questing, and how just three weeks beforehand the existence of this church, with its unique font, was not even known to us. Richard felt that Janus was somehow a key to finding the cup, or at least understanding the full nature of the Grail, even though my researches had failed to turn up anything whatsoever on his association with the cup, other than to confirm it was actually a wine-cup.

'I just get the feeling that he was carved that way for a reason,' Richard had mused, as all four of us stood around this wonderful art treasure in lead. 'It is something to do with the influence of the cup – connected, perhaps, with the presence locally of the Chapel of Abominations.'

According to the church guidebook, experts on medieval Christian art have concluded that the font was fashioned in c. 1150, even though the earliest church fabric only dates to c. 1250. Just one other similarly designed lead font exists, and this can be seen in the church of St Evroult-de-Montford near Orne in Normandy, suggesting that both are French in design. Yet on the example in France, double-headed Janus is replaced by a *single*-faced figure, even though he does still sit at a table and hold a cup in one hand. There is also an impressive *opus alexandrinum,* or mosaic pavement, in the retro-choir of Canterbury cathedral, which includes sculptured stone roundels showing the twelve signs of the zodiac, the twelve labours and the seven virtues triumphing over the seven vices.[389] Once again, Janus represents January's labour, although here the twin-faced deity is seen standing between two doors, one signifying the past and the other the future; he is closing one and opening the other.[390] The mosaic is positioned directly above the crypt that featured in Richard's dream.

Despite our great interest in the Brookland font, the two brief meditations we conducted in its proximity, the second after circumnavigating it seven times, produced next to nothing on a psychic level. Only a few meagre morsels of inspiration emerged at this time. Into Richard's mind had come flashes of two-faced Janus sitting beneath the arch of a ruined chapel holding the cup, while I was unexpectedly drawn to just one place – Ide Hill in Kent. The mention once more of Janus and a ruined chapel had afterwards led us to try to find the Chapel of Abominations. Yet not one of the ecclesiastical ruins scattered about Romney Marsh seemed in any way to match the description of this woodland chapel we so eagerly wanted to find.

CROWLEY'S DEAL

Ide Hill was forgotten about, until just four days later, when on Thursday, 25 April, a new psychic session at our home opened with Richard seeing himself seated opposite Crowley, who was cross-legged on the small green in front of Ide Hill's picturesque church. Before our long-dead occultist friend was a small square wooden table, over which was a black silk cloth, and after offering Richard a cup of tea, the English thing to do, the spirit of Crowley had insisted that he: 'Behold blood and the cup', and 'look to the church. See into the churchyard.' Crowley was then seen holding the silver chalice, retrieved from a secluded spot in the churchyard almost exactly thirteen years beforehand. Once again, blood trickled up over its rim and down its outside, like a tiny red snake in movement, so I asked Crowley what this signified.

'You remember, you have been here before,' was his response.

That was true, I was with Helen when she had retrieved the chalice from there in 1989, but what of it? What relevance had any of this to now?

'Then you did not drink from the cup,' he said.

That was because it was too dirty, and I didn't know where it had been, or what it had contained, or who put it there. This was my immediate reaction to his words. However, I realised that what he really meant was that at the time I had not yet tasted the wisdom and knowledge experienced through drinking from the true Grail, the Serpent Grail, borne in Christian art by the apostle John, for this is surely what the chalice with its snake-like trail of blood represented, even back in 1989.

Crowley then produced a Tarot pack, his own Thoth deck – designed by him, and painted by Lady Freda Harris, who completed the set in 1944 – and started to shuffle the cards, asking Richard to take one. He did so, and turning it over revealed the card known as 'The Tower', on which he saw was the lion-headed serpent, Ialdobaoth, the Gnostic demiurge, to which Crowley exclaimed: 'You know what this means? It's war, blood.'

I felt I knew where this was going. The previous week Richard had picked up on a previously unknown monument called the Gibraltar Tower, a neglected circular belvedere erected within the grounds of Heathfield Park, East Sussex. It was commissioned by Brigadier General George Augustus Elliot, the owner of the estate, to commemorate the fact that he had fought valiantly against the French and Spanish when Gibraltar came under siege between 1779 and 1783. A plaque, which bears the inscription *'calpes defensori'*, or 'to the defender of Gibraltar', is said to have been made from metal taken from a gun barrel removed from a floating Spanish battery.

We had been able to check out the Gibraltar Tower on the way home from Kent the previous weekend. Although only around 150 metres from the B2203 road into Heathfield, it stands behind a huge barbed wire fence and perimeter wall, on which are signs proclaiming, 'PRIVATE PROPERTY – DOGS PATROLLING', making the tower virtually inaccessible to anyone. Richard's feeling that we might have to come back here and actually go over to the monument as part of the Grail quest had filled us with dread, especially after I discovered that it fell exactly on the perimeter of the great circle of sites, thus confirming the place's apparent significance to us.

Yet Crowley answered in the negative. It was not what he had been alluding to, although he did imply that it would be necessary to return to Heathfield as part of the quest. 'Behold the tower is ruined. It has been struck,' he announced, before producing a crystal ball and placing it on the table in front of him. Reaching out, he grabbed hold of Richard's head and more or less forced him to stare into its starry depths. Instantly, Richard was sucked into a void until suddenly he was no longer at Ide Hill, but on a woodland path walking towards a ruined stone tower, which stood where four tracks converged.

I asked Richard where it was.

'Near Ide Hill,' was his response. 'We've been there. I'm sure we have.'

It sounded vaguely familiar, but I could not remember going there ever myself. Anyway, what about this place – what did it mean to us?

'I give you three sites,' Crowley then answered through Richard.

Was this tower another site, then?

The reply was 'yes', and so we knew then that in order to gain some psychic momentum before reaching Headcorn, we should visit the Gibraltar Tower at

Heathfield, as well as this other tower, which we later found was located in woods on Horns Hill, in the grounds of Squerryes Court, above the town of Westerham in Kent. Little is known about it, other than that it was erected in the late eighteenth century by the Warde family, who owned the estate. As the crow flies, it is just 4 kilometres (2.5 miles) from Ide Hill (and a similar distance from the perimeter of the great circle). Richard recalled that he had been there once before with some friends back in the early 1990s, although he could not remember why they had gone there.[391]

Crowley implied that the cup might be found at any one of the three sites, although our money was still on it being at Headcorn. In spite of this, we did need to know in which order the sites should be visited.

'I cannot tell you that. You must work that out,' he had exclaimed.

OK, but what would happen if we did achieve the Grail cup?

'It should be given to the lady,' he said, referring to Sue.

This would be done. And what would happen then?

'She will become Babalon in the Chapel of Abominations.'

Which was where?

'You do not need to know.'

What about Janus? Did we need to call him? His influence had come up so strongly in the Brookland material that it had to mean something.

His response was quick: 'He will watch you. He shall guard you in the way of travel that you have chosen. He understands the leaps of time as you. The past, present and future are one. He is the nexus.'

THE QUEST BEGINS

Overall, it had been a productive evening, but then nothing more of any direct relevance had emerged before the commencement of our quest on Saturday, 4 May. We began by going to Ide Hill, sitting on the green and focusing our attentions on 'The Tower' card from Crowley's Thoth deck, with a crystal ball placed next to it on a piece of black silk cloth. Nothing of any consequence happened, even though there had been a strong pull towards the rear of the churchyard where the chalice had been found back in 1989, and so it was on to Heathfield's Gibraltar Tower. Nobody was looking forward to going back to this place, which had been designated the first of the three main sites we would visit that day. After a few drinks to conjure a certain amount of Dutch courage, the three of us waited in the darkness for the right moment to tackle the estate's perimeter wall. One by one, we ran across the busy road and somersaulted over the wall commando style, and then crawled through the undergrowth for some distance before finding a suitable spot to slide underneath the tall, barbed-wire fence. Suddenly, we heard voices beyond the wall, indicating that our presence had been revealed, and so we remained still for several minutes before silence returned. Then we made a run for the base of the derelict tower, nervous of the possibility that guard dogs really were on the loose.

I started to lead us through a suitable meditation, but very quickly Richard opened his eyes and began looking very edgy indeed. Sue, too, was uncomfortable with what was going on here. It seemed that both of them could see wispy forms, shades, wraiths, rising out of the ground all around the tower. Worse still, they were moving towards us, our cue to get out of there now rather than later. No more could be done at the building, allowing us to journey on to the next site. Sue would afterwards recall the assault on Gibraltar Tower as one of the most terrifying experiences of her life.

Headcorn became the next site on the psychic journey, in the full knowledge that we might have to return there later that night if called to do so. En route, I kept seeing flashes of a ghostly rider galloping across a bleak landscape in negative black and white, even though as the driver I was trying to concentrate on the road ahead. His face was that of a skull, and he wore a grey capuchin hood, a pale surcoat and medieval chain mail and armour I recognised as fourteenth century in style. I got the impression that he was some kind of astral guardian associated with both Headcorn and the entire matrix of sites contained inside the great circle. He seemed to be racing ahead of us, almost as if he wanted to reach Headcorn before our arrival. I mentioned this fact to Sue and Richard, although they seemed oblivious to his presence on that fateful journey.

Once in Headcorn we approached the site of King John's Oak, before moving off to find a suitable place for an in-depth meditation. We came to a halt on a footbridge over a nearby river, a few hundred metres south of the church. In meditation, Richard saw a faceless individual approaching on a boat along the river, although this non-human intelligence said nothing. In my mind's eye, I saw a globe suspended over the water, out of which came an arm with a large golden torque in its hand. It was the royal *farr*, which conferred divinity on the Persian *shahinshah*, the 'king of kings'. I felt we should symbolically accept the ring, which we did. To me, this symbol represented the twelfth degree in the cult of Mithras and its unwritten association with Headcorn's past as the 'chief' or 'head-crown' of the land, something perhaps that the spade of the archaeologist would one day throw better light upon.

No more came to anyone that evening at Headcorn, and so we ventured on to the third site, the belvedere tower deep within the woods at Horns Hill, near Ide Hill. It was a very strange place, looking more like a leaf-covered hollow tree than a manufactured structure. It stood alone in the middle of four converging pathways – a crossroads of the type so important to fate and destiny in many ancient religions, and some contemporary ones too. Pentagrams crudely painted on the tower's interior walls made it clear that this was a site frequented by local pagans, or would-be pagans at least, for no true pagan would ever do such a thing.

Following a brief meditation, we waited for something to happen. Nothing did, and eventually we left, but as we walked away from the site Richard was unexpectedly 'hit' by some kind of invisible force, like a tiny arrow shot from the top of the tower. It felt as if something was trying to draw him back to the site, and although he tried to ignore it, the same thing happened as we turned to walk away a second time.

'Something wants us to go back into that tower,' he insisted, perplexed by the whole thing. 'But I really think it would be a bad idea to do so. I don't know why, I just do.'

Sue and I could only but go along with his gut feeling over the matter, even though we all gained the distinct feeling that there was unfinished business here. Therefore, with the time now well past one o'clock in the morning, we stopped for the night, knowing that unless anything happened to suggest otherwise we would return to the tower later that day.

KLINGSOR

Sunday, 5 May. Having dropped Richard off at his home in southeast London, Sue and I drove back to Leigh-on-Sea, and slept soundly for the remainder of the morning. Richard arrived in the early afternoon and, after blacking out the windows, the five brass bowls containing the methylated spirits were lit and the meditation began. Unexpectedly, Richard had locked into the extraordinary vision of fugitive Templars carrying a stone casket containing the Templar relic known as the Head of God. Exactly why he should have been granted a visionary glimpse of this great treasure being taken to Dover for transportation overseas, when our minds were focused firmly on the retrieval of the Grail cup, was unclear.

Following a short break, the meditation resumed, and into Richard's mind came the same pale rider I had glimpsed on the journey between Heathfield and Headcorn the previous evening. He, too, now felt that this deathly figure was some kind of astral guardian set up in the past to protect the great circle, yet Richard went further by identifying him as 'Klingsor'.

This was not a good omen, as Klingsor is a character that features in German medieval Grail romances as the evil sorcerer Clinschor. His character is fully developed in Richard Wagner's great opera *Parsifal*, first performed in 1882, where Klingsor is introduced as a failed knight in the Order of the Holy Grail. Rejected by its brethren due to his impurity, he turns to black magic, which he uses to obtain the Holy Spear, after which he creates a fairy castle peopled by beautiful women. Klingsor imprisons their souls, and will only return them if they succeed in beguiling Grail knights so that they might forget the nature of their quest. One such woman is the seductive Kundry, whose actions result in the misconduct of Amfortas, the Fisher King and grandson of Titurel, the original guardian of the Holy Grail in the German romances. His wound, inflicted by Klingsor, cannot heal so long as the spear that caused it remains in the hands of the sorcerer. When finally Parsifal arrives at the fairy castle, Klingsor realises his identity and mission, and so appoints Kundry to do whatever it takes to seduce the Grail knight. Although reluctant to take part in this dangerous venture, she finally agrees, but ultimately fails. So angered is Klingsor by this that he hurls the spear at Parsifal, which miraculously comes to a halt directly above the Grail knight's head. Reaching out, he takes possession of the weapon, which on touching Amfortas's wound immediately heals it.[392] Previously, Amfortas's grandfather had read on the rim of the Holy

Grail that his grandson's wound would one day be healed by 'a guileless fool who would accidentally climb the mountains and moved by sympathy ask the cause of his suffering'.[393] That 'guileless fool' was, of course, Parsifal, the finder of the Grail.

What kind of warning was this? Did it suggest that we too could face failure because of impurity or self-indulgence, which might impede our vision of what the Sufis would call the Ultimate Unseen, *Ghayb-ul-Ghaib*? Should we reconsider what we were doing, and how we intended to achieve our goals?

'We shall meet soon,' were Klingsor's only words, as flashing into Richard's mind came images of the belvedere at Horns Hill, where it now seemed certain the fate of the quest would be decided.

CONFRONTATION AT THE HOLLOW TOWER

Two and a half hours later, we were back at the Horns Hill tower, this time ready for anything that could be thrown at us. Around dusk I constructed a circle of protection on the earthen floor and took us through a creative visualisation exercise known as the raising of the 'cone of power' in order to build up some kind of barrier between us and what lay in wait outside. Yet, according to Richard, we were not alone *inside* the hollow tower. Clairvoyantly he perceived the presence, among the gnarled branches of the trees that strangled its interior walls, of elemental forms, like tiny anthropomorphic beings, who answered collectively to the name 'Crog'. We were not alarmed by their presence, since the existence of anciently created thought-forms of this nature was widespread, and over the years I had worked with various good psychics who could see such beings. Was it the Crog who had fired the tiny arrows at Richard's head the previous night in an attempt to draw us back to the tower? It certainly seemed possible, but if so, then why exactly?

The elementals watched silently from their elevated positions, but could not help us directly with our predicament. Then, all of a sudden, they became highly agitated, like a pack of monkeys sensing the approach of danger, and very soon we understood why. Having waited some fifteen minutes inside the tower, Richard could now hear the sound of horses' hooves moving steadily closer.

'It is him. It is him. He is coming,' the Crog said to Richard, before they scurried, frightened, into the shadows.

From along the path to the west, the direction of the underworld in many religions of the ancient world, came the pale rider, Klingsor. It was the same figure I had seen the night before, and now it was manifesting on a subtle level that Richard could clearly perceive, and Sue and I could sense, feel and glimpse in our mind's eye. Once again, he came as a ghostly knight in chain mail, his skull face visible inside his pointed woollen hood. The figure rode a gigantic grey mare that reared up and whinnied aggressively as it reached our position. For a moment, I was not sure what to do or say, and tried as best I could to prevent this deathly force from entering within the tower, protected by the cone of power and the circle on the ground.

'Who calls me here?' was Klingsor's opening address to Richard. 'What manner do you intend to serve me?' I proclaimed our quest for the Grail cup in truth, purity and righteousness, but the ghostly rider was having none of it as he continued to ride around and around the hollow tower. Suddenly, my head began to swirl as images of Templars and Grail quests entered my mind. For some reason, I just kept getting the same words going around in my head: 'To whom serves the Grail?' It is the simple, but crucial, question that Perceval should have asked after witnessing the Grail procession in the Castle of the Fisher King, but failed to do so. Because of his silence, Perceval's host – the Fisher King – cannot be healed, and the kingdom remains in a state of darkness and decay (see Chapter 2 for further clarification). On learning that he is responsible for prolonging Britain's great malady, he dedicates his life to understanding the nature of the Grail.

I could only recall the words spoken in John Boorman's film *Excalibur* where Perceval is asked, 'What is the secret of the Grail?' and 'Whom does the Grail serve?' Here the secret of the Grail is that the king and the land are one – a symbiotic relationship exists between the two, in that so long as the chosen king remains healthy the land will prosper. However, should for any reason he falter in his duties through health, madness or negligence then the land would fall prey to maladies, such as famine, plagues, wars or natural catastrophes, exactly what happened in the Grail romances. So-called divine kingship is something dealt with in books by the noted Egyptologist Margaret Murray, who cited classic examples in English history of kings which she saw as being murdered on ancient pagan festival days because they have faltered in their duties.[394] They are then replaced by a stronger and more able successor who restores the kingdom to its former glory.

Thus there seemed little doubt that the answer to the question, 'To whom serves the Grail?' could only be the king and the land. The response at this moment from Klingsor was not encouraging, for according to Richard, the pale knight merely taunted us with thoughts of death and failure, before becoming more and more restless, until a further request for the cup was met with a dismissive: 'It is yours to take.' At this, he swung his horse around and departed back from whence he came. I had no idea where we stood now, but suggested that we return immediately to Headcorn.

THE ROAD BACK TO HEADCORN

For some while we sat in the car, parked alongside Headcorn churchyard. It was now close to midnight on the day we expected to gain the Grail cup, and I was hoping for a miracle, for it was a miracle that was clearly needed. I started to feel desperate, so insisted that we were going nowhere until *something* happened. The three of us sat slumped in our seats, our eyes half open, trying to grasp on to anything that would tell us what to do next, when suddenly Richard jolted upwards with the words: 'What the hell was that?'

What was what?

'Over there, by the tree,' he revealed, nodding in the direction of the remains. 'There was a bright flash of light, and in it was the form of the cup. I only saw it for a second, and it's gone now.'

In psychic questing, flashes of light are known to highlight the whereabouts of concealed artefacts or, more often, mark the sudden appearance of out-of-place artefacts called apports, or *termas* in Tibetan Buddhist tradition. I had seen objects found in this way on many occasions over the years.

'It's funny, because I thought I saw Crowley standing by the tree just before it happened,' he added.

This was promising. Crowley had not appeared so far on this quest, even at Ide Hill the previous day, which I had expected him to do as a matter of course. It was certainly our cue to leave the car and go over there, for it was now or never as far as finding the cup was concerned. So, in the darkness we walked briskly across to the overgrown area where the large crater left by the burned-out trunk of King John's Oak was now filled with brambles and weeds, and started to search the vicinity, trying to use the torch as little as possible.

As precious minutes ticked by, despondency began to set in, and I knew that we were losing our chance of success, so finally I suggested that we stop and go back to the car. Long moments were spent in contemplation before we decided that enough was enough and that we should admit defeat. The drive away from Headcorn was initially sombre until Sue, seated in the back, mentioned that, while searching, she had heard a clanging sound, as if her boot had made contact with something metallic.

'Yeah, I heard that as well,' Richard confirmed. 'I wondered what it was at the time.'

What! This was the first I knew about it, and here we were driving *away* from Headcorn, without anything to show for our efforts.

After making them describe exactly what they had heard again and again, I was ready to turn around and go back to take another look. Yet I was talked out of it by Sue with the simple argument that we could return in daylight to make sure that nothing had been missed.

Thus we decided to take one final look at the tree, even though I knew that the place would be crawling with visitors, since it was the Headcorn Fayre later that day. However, I needed to be certain that we had not left behind a sacred vessel that was now accessible to anyone who just happened to walk past the tree.

The return to Headcorn for the third time in three days was a very strange experience. Richard had commitments at home, and so could not join us on our final search for the Grail cup. Keeping one eye on passers-by, we entered into the circular area marked out by the trunk's burned-out crater and made a thorough search of where Sue had distinctly heard the metallic-sounding clang the previous night. There was nothing there, but we could not help but feel that it *had* been there, if only for a few brief moments in time. Perhaps unduly, Sue kicked herself for not having brought the matter to my attention when it happened. Then again, maybe the cup was not ours in the first place, or, worse still, it never existed at all, or perhaps we had simply got it wrong and it was elsewhere awaiting discovery. It was a difficult situation and one that, for the moment at least, we could do nothing else but walk away from.

Had the whole thing been a waste of time? What would happen when we reconvened for another psychic session? What sort of excuses would be given by Crowley, or whoever, as to why we had not been able to find a measly representation of the Grail cup? Why had we been led to Brookland to view the lead font that showed Janus holding a cup, and why was he seen sitting beneath the arch of the wooded ruin named by Crowley as the Chapel of Abominations? Was all this information now obsolete, and the psychic quest over? Somehow it all seemed such a shame, especially as I remained convinced that Headcorn, at least, had so much to offer as a major sacred centre of southeast England, something which ought to be studied in its own right.

LIFE OR DEATH?

There was no time even to contemplate our unexpected failure, since for Sue and me our lives were now preoccupied with the preparations for our marriage the following weekend, and Grails played no part in this world. The wedding was a beautiful occasion, and immediately following the reception at a pub function suite in our home town of Leigh-on-Sea, we travelled out to Las Vegas for the honeymoon. No better contrast can there have been from the rolling green landscape of southeast England to this grotesque and highly fabricated neon-world in the middle of the Nevada Desert. Initially I hated it, but as the days rolled by, it took on its own surreal appeal, which for some reason I grew to enjoy immensely. Yet still I needed to break free from this mad world of 24-hour gambling and gross cabaret entertainment, summed up by the popularity of Las Vegas residents Siegfried and Roy, who gaze down at you from gigantic video billboards wherever you go.[1]

We made plans to hire a vehicle and journey the 145 kilometres (90 miles) to Tikaboo Peak, the last remaining spot where one can gaze out across the rocky desert towards the highly secretive Area 51 'Dreamland' airbase at Groom Lake, some 42 kilometres (26 miles) away. This zone is so intimately connected with UFO lore, and Black Operation projects, it simply had to be done, or so we thought. However, some 27 kilometres (17 miles) from the nearest road or human being, we took a wrong turning and the front-wheel drive Dodge truck we were driving became stuck in a dry riverbed, and quickly began to sink into the soft sand. Without a cell phone, a spade or any food, just a few bottles of juice and one of water, we were forced to abandon the vehicle and walk nonstop for eight hours through the soaring heat, along unfamiliar paths, towards safety. Attempts at doing a Jim Morrison and calling the spirits of Native Americans to guide us met with no response whatsoever as the supplies ran out.

---

[1] The Siegfried and Roy spectaculars have since ceased due to Roy being badly mauled by one of his animals on stage.

We had to keep on walking, for the alternative was almost certain death through dehydration or encounters with one or other of the deadly spiders or snakes that frequent the rocky desert wastes. As we trudged along, never stopping, I could not help thinking about the climax to our quest for the Holy Grail just eleven days beforehand. It all seemed so meaningless now and here, where no one would ever hear your screams, and personal survival was the only thing that consumed your every moment. I came to realise one important thing on that torturous journey, and this was the sheer power of nexus points where a split decision can quite literally mean the difference between life and death. One fork on the track led back to civilization, while the other took you even deeper into the desert, towards almost certain oblivion. They looked identical, and in the fading light I could no longer pick out the truck's tyre tracks, so which one were we to choose? That was the magical potency behind double-headed Janus, god of all beginnings, who presided over every moment of nexus and the infinite possibilities which might result from that decision. Through our own actions, he had the power to offer us the Grail in one hand and take it away with the other. Somehow, our choices had been wrong, but here in the middle of the Nevada Desert, as darkness drew ever nearer, there was only one right choice, and that was always going to be life.

And so it was that after reaching the outside world, and making the possibly dangerous decision to hitch-hike to the nearest motel, Sue and I attracted the attentions of an enormous inter-state juggernaut that came to a halt hundreds of metres further along the desert highway. Despite the agony caused by the intolerable walk back to civilisation, we found the effort to run and run until we caught up with the monster truck, its engine still idling and no sign of life behind its cab's mirror-tinted windows. Following what seemed like an eternity, the driver's door flew open and the smiling face of an English Sikh with turban and noble beard and moustache invited us inside. The journey was short, but as he began to relate stories about his family in West London, his belief in the one true God, and Guru Nanak, the founder 500 years ago of Sikhism – which combines aspects of the Hindu faith with the Islamic Sufi tradition – I knew we were in safe hands. The strange synchronicity of being picked up – illegally as it is in Nevada State – by a clearly genuine person from our own neck of the woods, told me that we were being watched over, and that despite the outcome of the Grail quest we had to carry on and that somehow it would all come right in the end.

18. THE LIFE OF MARY

Entering a rocky valley through a mountain pass one bright sunny morning, I saw crowds of people starting to gather in front of a large cave mouth. Here, some while back, children had reported experiencing visions of the Virgin Mary, and ever since that time hundreds of people, mostly Catholics, had gathered here on the anniversary of that first event, as well as on other Marian feast days, in the hope of witnessing another miracle. It brought comfort to their souls and strengthened their faith in the Holy Trinity.

I felt I should remain just in case the Virgin Mary did put in an appearance to her dedicated followers. Yet as the minutes ticked by, the crowds increased so much that I could scarcely catch a view of the grotto's interior, which meant I might miss out if something was to appear. Desperate now, I tried to lift my head above the people in front of me, when all of a sudden a bright light began to illuminate the darkened cave mouth to gasps of delight and awe that gave way to uncontrollable displays of devotional love. I feared the onset of mass panic and hysteria, but before this could happen something even more unexpected began to take place. As the dazzling light started to form into a beautiful woman, it became obvious that she was *not* the Virgin Mary, who could be expected to appear in blue and white apparel, her head lolled gently to one side, and with signs of sorrow still plainly visible on her saddened face.

The woman manifesting here and now was altogether different, with a proud, serene face, long flowing hair and seductive figure enhanced by her blue medieval-style dress and red overgarment. She was not the Mother of God at all, but Mary Magdalene, in her guise as the bride of Christ, the personification of feminine spirituality, and Sophia, female wisdom. Her power had increased with such strength in recent times that she was usurping even the popularity of her great orthodox rival, the Blessed Virgin Mary.

Her appearance was just too much for those at this unnamed mountain location, since it was something that they were unwilling to accept or even understand. The great joy and bliss they had begun to experience in the presence of what they believed was the Mother of Jesus instantly changed to screams of utter horror and disgust, sending them scurrying in every direction, many holding their heads in despair. I knew, too, that the same thing was happening at religious sites associated with the Virgin Mary across the world. Everywhere, the popularity and importance of the Magdalene was rising to become a collective force that was changing the face of Christianity forever.

Tuesday, 11 June. It was a dream I woke up from that changed everything. Although purely symbolic in nature, it emphasised a special significance in Mary Magdalene that I had scarcely realised. It had been a potential first hinted at in the symbolism of the Cat Monument at Shugborough Park, and its associations with the Magdalene's cause at Rennes-le-Château, but thereafter nothing had occurred to take us further down that road. I had even begun dismissing the importance of the Magdalene, especially when I came to realise the fragility of medieval legends recalling how she spent her final years in southern France. Such stories dated back no earlier than the mid-eleventh century, when the monastery of St Marie-Madeleine at Vézelay, in France's Burgundy region, first announced that it held the saint's relics in a holy shrine within its abbey church. [395]

It is unlikely that any authentic account of the Magdalene or her remains reaching France existed before this time. What is more, her earliest and most popular shrine of veneration prior to this age was at Ephesus in Asia Minor. From there her relics were supposedly translated to Constantinople in 886, and following the sack of that city by the Crusaders in 1204, her head and certain other bones are said to have been brought back to Lower Saxony, a province in northern Germany, by Conrad de Krosik, Bishop of Halberstadt, although how and where he got hold of them is unclear. [396] Meanwhile, the church of S. Giovanni Laterano in Rome also claimed to possess her headless body, [397] while, from around 750 through until the mid-twelfth century, the most popular view of her life was that she had retired after the Crucifixion into the desert wilderness where she became a repentant hermit. [398]

THE MAGDALENE IN FRANCE

The problem with Vézelay's claim to possess the bones of Mary Magdalene is that no one ever saw them, and there was no explanation initially as to how they might have got there. Its only offered explanation was that the Magdalene herself had appeared before the monastery's Abbot Geoffrey whilst at the tomb one day, insisting: 'It is me, whom many people believe to be here.' [399] Realising they needed to better attest their fantastic claims, the abbey began professing that the Magdalene's remains had been miraculously carried across the sea from the Holy Land. [400] However, in the first half of the twelfth century the abbey seized on the growing belief that the Magdalene had sailed to France in the company of Maximinus, one of the 72 disciples of Christ, and Martha, the sister of Mary of Bethany, their rudderless boat having made landfall at Les Saintes-Maries-de-la-Mer in the Camargue region of southeastern France.

One of the first works to feature the story of Mary's later life is the *Vita Beatae Mariae Magdalenae* ('Life of the Blessed Mary Magdalene'), [401] attributed to the French Carolingian churchman Rabanus Maurus (d. 856), although almost certainly of mid-twelfth-century construction. [402] It speaks of how the saint spent the final thirty years of her life repentant in a mountainous grotto at St Baume high up in the massif of Provence, east of Marseilles. In contrast, her companion Maximinus became the first Bishop of Aix-en-Provence; while Martha settled in Tarascon, Provence, where she overcame the fearful Dragon of Rhone before dying of old age (her relics were 'discovered' there in 1187 [403]). Such passionate stories developed dramatically in a very short time, and Jacobus de Voragine included them in his famous book of saints' lives entitled the *Golden Legend*, which first appeared around 1267.[404] One variation of the story tells of how Martha and Mary were joined in France by their brother Lazarus, who became the first Bishop of Marseilles, while still later versions have Joseph of Arimathea accompanying the Magdalene to France before continuing his journey to Britain.[405]

At the end of her life, Mary was miraculously transported by angels to the hermitage of Bishop Maximinus, who gave her the last rites before laying her body to rest in an oratory constructed by him at Villa Lata, which afterwards became the town of St Maximin, located some 35 kilometres (22 miles) from Aix-en-Provence. Here, too, at the Basilique de Sainte Marie Madeleine was the alabaster flask of Holy Blood, which liquefied every Good Friday and was said to have been collected by the Magdalene at the time of the Crucifixion.[406] Yet none of this made sense of Vézelay's own claim to possess the saint's body. Therefore, they began circulating various stories, each one contradicting the other, of how the bones had been translated from wherever they had been in Provence to Vézelay, generally during the mid-eighth century.[407]

In 1265, following increasing concerns over the abbey's failure to exhibit any kind of evidence to account for their possession of the saint's relics, the Pope sent a legate to Vézelay to establish what was going on. Yet before he arrived, the abbot, Jean, summoned two delegates of the Holy See who were shown a bronze metal coffer containing relics wrapped in silk material, as well as 'an extraordinary abundance of female hair', which they identified as those of the Magdalene.[408] A previously unknown charter was also produced supporting the abbey's claim to have the relics, enabling the delegates to confirm to the legate what they had seen. As might be expected, the charter was later proved to be false, while the delegates were, in fact, in league with the abbot, and as Magdalene scholar Susan Haskins observes in this respect: 'It seems that the monks, fearing the visit of the legate from the Holy See, decided to take matters into their own hands, and organised the "invention".'[409] Two years later Abbot Jean was able to entice the King of France, Louis IX, to visit Vézelay and witness the relics for himself, causing them to be officially recognised as the real thing. However, Vézelay's days as a popular shrine to the Magdalene were numbered.

ST MAXIMIN'S COUNTERCLAIM

On 9 December 1279, during an official visit by Charles II, King of Naples, the monks of St Maximin are said to have miraculously 'discovered' the saint's remains inside a marble sarcophagus located in the basilica's crypt. When opened, it exuded a sweet balm, while a plant, identified as either fennel or palm, was said to have been growing out of the skeleton's mouth. More importantly, a piece of parchment purportedly found in the sarcophagus told how the body of Mary Magdalene had been transferred from an alabaster tomb to its present position on 6 December 710.[410] This was 35 years before the earliest of Vézelay's claims to have removed the relics from Provence, rendering them now useless. Conveniently, the parchment disintegrated into dust the moment it was removed from the tomb.

This remarkable hoax, a coup d'état for the monks and abbot of St Maximin, created the desired effect. The cult of the Magdalene spread rapidly throughout Provence, whilst Vézelay's popularity waned so much that the abbey was virtually forgotten. As Susan Haskins points out: 'It seems that the Benedictine monks, resentful of the capital Vézelay had made out of relics supposedly taken from their church, may have been seeking to turn the legend to their own profit.'[411]

St Maximin remains the official site of the Magdalene's relics, and every year on 22 July, her official feast day, a tobacco-coloured skull – believed to be that of the saint and encased in a peculiar reliquary resembling a space-helmet – is paraded through the streets during a weeklong series of celebrations that attract thousands of people to the town. Locals in costume sing songs of the Magdalene in the native Provençal language, as a huge procession enters the Basilique de Sainte Marie Madeleine decorated with gilded statues of the saint carried through the air. Meanwhile, 60 kilometres (38 miles) away at the elevated mountain shrine of St Baume, where Mary is supposed to have lived the final thirty years of her life, Midnight Mass is celebrated from 21–28 July.

VENUS AND THE GREAT PENTAGRAM

Exactly how the Magdalene came to be venerated so strongly in southern France is explained by Dr Arnold Lebeuf, an expert on astronomical mythology. He has pointed out that the Magdalene cult, particularly at Ste Baume, developed from a pre-existing cult of Venus, the Roman goddess of sex and love, which, he ably demonstrates, flourished in Provence and other parts of southern France prior to this age.[412] As was the case with pagan deities across Europe, Venus's sacred places and personal attributes were appropriated by a suitable Christian saint, in this case Mary Magdalene. Even more interesting is that Lebeuf shows that the Magdalene's cult absorbed certain elements of Venus's star lore, which focuses on the risings and settings of the planet Venus over its eight-year cycle as viewed from the earth.[413]

Such a discovery will be of some interest to followers of the Rennes-le-Château mystery, for one of the earliest theories put forward to explain the great secret preserved by the Knights Templar and certain local families in the Aude Valley is that five prominent local peaks make a gigantic landscape pentagram. Broadcaster and writer Henry Lincoln felt this geomantic design reflected the celestial loops the planet Venus is seen to make during one complete revolution of its cycle, which if mapped form a perfect five-pointed star.[414] Perhaps this goes some way to explaining why the Magdalene features so prominently in the story of Rennes-le-Château, she having absorbed a much earlier landscape mystery surrounding the goddess Venus.

HOLY BLOOD, HOLY GRAIL

The medieval legends implying that the Magdalene ended her days in France appear to have been the fabrications of medieval churchmen, wishing to earn capital out of the thousands of pilgrims who flocked to see her holy relics. It is a story that parallels exactly the growth of the cult of Joseph of Arimathea in Britain in the thirteenth and fourteenth centuries, and thus any legends suggesting that she might have brought the Holy Grail to France have to be treated with extreme caution.

This includes the sensational claims made in *The Holy Blood and the Holy Grail*, the 1982 blockbuster by Michael Baigent, Richard Leigh and Henry Lincoln. They proposed that Jesus survived his ordeal on the Cross, and went on to marry Mary Magdalene. Yet she was forced to flee Palestine from those, like Peter, who were not in on the plot, and so sailed to France in the company of her brother Lazarus, taking with her a child, or children, the fruits of her marriage to Jesus. They settled among the Jewish communities of Provence, and centuries later their descendants married into the French royal dynasty known as the Merovingian Franks. They reigned as kings by virtue of their divine birthright, but were eventually deposed, forcing the bloodline, and any trace of it, to go underground through until the present day. According to the authors, the continued existence of this sacred bloodline was behind the concept of the *san graal*, or 'Holy Grail', a French term which in reality should read *sang real*, 'blood royal'. Therefore the true Grail was either a knowledge of the divine bloodline or the womb of the woman who carried it to France, i.e. the Magdalene.

Although I greatly respect the research and findings of the authors of *The Holy Blood and the Holy Grail*, which is one of my favourite books of all time, I have come to realise that there are certain flaws in some of their arguments. I accept the possibility that Jesus *might* have survived the Crucifixion, and *could* have been married to Mary Magdalene, a marriage that just *may* have produced children. Yet countering this evidence is the basic knowledge, derived mostly from the Gnostic gospels, showing that she played a major role in keeping alive the faith in Christ after the Crucifixion, inspiring the other disciples, who knew she was beloved of their Lord. However, if the legends can be believed, she eventually departed Palestine, not for France, but for Ephesus, where John was establishing the Johannine community. If Jesus had survived the Crucifixion, then he certainly was not with her.

Obscure references do exist which suggest that the Magdalene either married or was 'betrothed'[415] to Jesus. For instance, a nineteenth-century copy of what is purported to be a lost Jewish Christian text of unknown origin claims that she gave birth to Jesus's child, was the priestess of a 'female cult' and ended her days in Roman Gaul.[416] However, such sources all post-date the emergence of the cult of the Magdalene in France, and even if she *was* 'married' to him then it must have been before the Crucifixion, and not afterwards. As previously determined, the Cathars of France secretly portrayed the Magdalene as Jesus's companion, and wife even, a unique teaching which, although not inherited from their Bogomil ancestors in Eastern Europe,[417] probably inspired the Templars to deny that Jesus was God incarnate, causing them to spit and trample on the Cross. However, such views need not be seen as firm evidence of Jesus and Mary's 'marriage', for the Cathars and Templars could quite easily have been influenced by the rise in the cult of the Magdalene in France.

Moreover, such stories were probably just distorted variations of her role as Sophia, the spiritual bride to the ascended Christ in Gnostic tradition.

Then we come to the theory proposed by *The Holy Blood and the Holy Grail* team that the term *san graal* derives from the expression *sang real*, 'blood royal'. The earliest reference to the *san graal*, or 'Holy Grail', as opposed to the singular *graal*, is found in the romance entitled *Perlesvaus*, also known as *The High History of the Grail*, written c.1205.[418] However, the term was only popularised in another, slightly later, romance entitled *l'estoire del saint graal* ('The History of the Holy Grail'), written c. 1220. This is a full 15 to 25 years after the word *graal* (which most probably derives from the *langue d'Oc* term *grasal, grazal, grezal, grasal*, etc.) came to mean the vessel of light carried in the procession witnessed by Perceval in the castle of the Fisher King, as well as the cup used to collect drops of the Holy Blood. The term *sang real* is certainly attractive from the point of view of the Grail being a container of the 'royal blood' of Christ. Yet it is its role as the Bitter Cup, used as a simile to describe the sacrifice Jesus made to bring salvation to the world, which better embodies the magical potency it exemplified to medieval sects such as the Cathars, Bogomils and Manicheans, who, I feel, inspired the creation of this vessel in the romances.

WISDOM OF THE SERPENT

Even though I did not believe that the Holy Grail was a royal bloodline or the womb of the Magdalene, I had come to accept that she was a true successor of Jesus, plausibly working in concert with John the Evangelist. Yet any real knowledge of her leadership was whitewashed by Peter's Roman Church, just as Catholic scholar Ramon Jusino has proposed. The Gnostic Gospels suggest that she was to have continued the secret teachings of Jesus, which plausibly derived from John the Baptist and included a deeper understanding of the Christ. Tiny glimpses of this hidden teaching are found in St Irenaeus of Lyon's *Against Heresies*, completed c. 180. Speaking out against Cerinthus, the founder of Cerinthianism, an unorthodox form of Johannine Christianity verging on Gnosticism, Irenaeus reports on his beliefs, which include the fact that:

> After Jesus' baptism the Christ, coming down from that Power which is above all, descended upon him in the form of a dove . . . In the end, however, the Christ withdrew again from Jesus . . . the Christ, being spiritual, remained unable to suffer.'[419]

Here the dove represents the Christ, the divine, which entered into Jesus when he was baptised by John the Baptist, and subsequently left him at the time of the Crucifixion. Since it is this same Holy Spirit that makes holy the wine of the communion meal practised by the early Christians during the Paschal vigil, then the vessel itself must represent the holder of the Holy Blood which, as the wine of the communion meal or Eucharist, will now bring every would-be Christian closer to the divine. The unguent jar, or *alabastron*, from which came the spikenard that Mary used to anoint Jesus as the Christ, or the Anointed

One, must have been imbued with the same power to contain the divine, especially when it is remembered that this, too, was seen as a receptacle of the Holy Blood. In Gnostic tradition the wisdom of such knowledge was represented by the serpent, which is seen emerging from the Poison Chalice that became the sign of John the Evangelist. Such hidden teachings eventually came to be symbolised by one vessel alone, the Grail. Yet the question remains, is the Grail purely metaphysical, or are there any physical artefacts that truly embody the original concept of this holy vessel?

Various claimants for the title Holy Grail exist across Europe. There is the *Sancto Caliz* in Spain's Valencia cathedral, the only Holy Grail officially recognised by the Vatican.[420] It is thought by some to be the drinking vessel passed around at the Last Supper and afterwards taken by St Peter to Rome. It was used during mass by the earliest popes until in 258 the Emperor ordered the death of the existing Pope and the distribution of the Church's wealth. The Pope's deputy, St Lawrence, refused to hand over the cup, and tradition asserts that, before he was roasted on a gridiron for his disobedience, the precious vessel was given into the safe keeping of a legionnaire who took it to Spain, where it has remained ever since.

Then there is the *Sacro Catino*, the hexagonal dish of green-coloured glass, found in Caesarea in 1101 and thought to have been the *catinus*, or dish, of the Last Supper used later to catch drops of the Holy Blood. At Glastonbury there is the so-called Sapphire Blue Bowl, a Florentine glass dish of beautiful quality, found in a holy well locally at the beginning of the twentieth century and revered today as the authentic Holy Grail. Finally, we have the Nanteos Cup, a wooden drinking vessel housed until recently at Nanteos House, near Aberystwyth in West Wales, and which is thought to have been kept originally at nearby Strata Florida Abbey. It, too, is said to have been used at the Last Supper, although this claim goes back no earlier than the nineteenth century.

In addition to these sacred relics, there are the various examples of blood-relics and their receptacles, which have also been seen as the Holy Grail at some time or another. Yet do any of these Grails truly mean anything? Was there a true physical Grail out there somewhere?

I write these words nearly two years after our own Grail quest, when so much more knowledge is at my disposal, but at the time it was another dream that helped focus my attentions on the role played in this story by Mary Magdalene.[421]

MARY OF THE TOWER

In slumber, I found myself in a hot dusty desert somewhere in the Middle East. Going around my head was the name 'Arish', and before me was a ruined church, founded in the year 'AD 316'. More peculiarly, I felt that this building resonated the same frequency as the so-called Chapel of Abominations, the Grail chapel we felt existed somewhere in southeast England. Furthermore, just in the same way that the Grail was associated with the Chapel of Abominations, I sensed that the *original* cup had once been associated with this desert location, causing some kind of dual polarity between the two sites. The only clue as to the whereabouts of 'Arish' was the lingering impression that not far away was a prominent watering hole, a well or spring of some sort, which might help us to find it.

I checked online and discovered that el-Arish is a village in the Negev region of North Sinai, between Egypt and Palestine. It is situated on the coastal highway, known in Pharaonic times as the 'Ways of Horus', or the 'Horus Road', which has connected these two countries since Old Testament days. In Egypt, the town was known as Tharu, which formed the kingdom's easternmost outpost. In the Old Testament, it is named as 'nahal Misraim', the 'stream of Egypt', modern Wadi el-Arish, which marked the southwestern limit of God's Promised Land.[422] In the village of Ein el-Qudeirat, within the Wadi el-Arish, is the spring of Ein Qadis, traditionally thought to be the site of ancient Kadesh. Here the book of Numbers tells us Moses brought forth the waters of Meribah,[423] after tapping a rock during the Israelites' forty years in the wilderness (even though it is more likely that Kadesh was the fabled rock city of Petra in neighbouring Jordan[424]).

In Greek times, the town of el-Arish was called Rhinocoloura, the name it retained until the tenth century. Roman remains discovered there show that it was occupied at the time of Christ, and from a very early date was the seat of a Christian bishopric, with the earliest attested bishop being St Melas, martyred in 385. Yet there are known to have been churches in el-Arish by the early fourth century, and a Coptic manuscript says that one of its bishops attended the Council of Nicea in 325, although this is dismissed as erroneous, while a Salomon is cited as bishop in 338.

Some 37 km (23 miles) west of el-Arish is the Flousseya church at el-Zaraniq, which came under the bishopric of Rhinocoloura. Here Egyptian Coptic tradition asserts that the Holy Family (Joseph, Mary and the infant Jesus) rested on their flight from Bethlehem to Egypt. Holy confirmation that the church of Flousseya was one of the stations of the Holy Family's flight into Egypt was granted by Theophilus, patriarch of Alexandria (385–412), who was said to have received visions concerning the route taken. This must mean that the church, now just low foundations gradually being reclaimed by the desert sand, or some earlier structure on the site, existed prior to this time.

I was happy with how everything in my dream had checked out. Yet why this ruin in the Negev desert should have resonated the same frequency as the still-undiscovered Chapel of Abominations was a complete mystery. My only thought was that since Crowley linked the latter with Babalon and the Grail, the church at el-Zaraniq was connected with her Christian counterpart Mary Magdalene, a personification of Sophia in Gnostic literature.

The matter was forgotten until a short while later when, reading Lynn Picknett and Clive Prince's The Templar Revelation, I realised something important. They explain how the epithet 'Magdalene' derives from the Hebrew root mgdl, 'tower', and means 'of the tower'. Some language scholars interpret this as implying that she was 'elevated, great, magnificent',[425] while most others associate the name Magdalene with Magdala, or Magadan,[426] an ancient fishing village known today as el-Mejdel, situated on the northwest coast of Lake Tiberius (the Sea of Galilee of the Gospels). This, it is assumed, was the town of her nativity.

Picknett and Prince point out that there is no evidence whatsoever to show that Mary Magdalene had any connection with the town of Magdala in Galilee,[427] only that she and the other women followed Jesus out of Galilee and ministered to him when he was there.[428] Instead, they note that a town named Magdolum existed 'in the northeast of Egypt, near the border with Judaea – probably the Migdol the prophet Ezekiel describes as Egypt's northern frontier'.[429] This fortified town is situated close to Farma (ancient Pelusium), and was probably synonymous with the Migdol of the Old Testament (Magdolum in the Latin Vulgate Bible[430]), one of the stations of the Israelites during their flight from Egypt into the wilderness of Sinai.[431] Might Mary Magdalene have been connected with this Magdolum as opposed to the Magdala on Lake Tiberius? Both places derive their names from the Hebrew root *mgdl*, 'tower', and in the knowledge that Picknett and Prince argue that the Magdalene expressed a form of Gentile religion blatantly Egyptian in origin, could the Northern Sinai have been her true ancestral home?[432]

Strangely, the German artist Albrecht Dürer (1471–1528) produced a mystifying image of the Holy Family's flight into Egypt around 1512 (see Plate 24). Here, the Virgin Mary sits with the infant child in her hands, while an elderly Joseph crouches beside her. Immediately behind is John the Evangelist with his left arm around Mary Magdalene, both of whom look compassionately at the infant, as a hook-nosed old man, identified by Dürer as Nicodemus, stands at the rear, looking away from the group.[433] What kind of symbolism Dürer might have been implying by this picture is open to speculation, although, like the art of his contemporary Leonardo da Vinci, nothing ever appears without good reason.

In the knowledge that there are firm legends to suppose that Jesus spent his early life in Egypt learning its 'wonderful arts',[434] was it possible that the Magdalene came to know him at this time? Perhaps her family helped the Holy Family to reach Egypt or, alternately, she met him in later life. If Mary did come from Magdolum, was she familiar with the nearby village of el-Zaraniq, where the church in my dream would eventually be built?

They were thoughts I played around with for some while, leading me to conclude that her unguent jar, the so-called *alabastron*, had more of a relevance to the Grail story than I had previously imagined. Yet it was the nocturnal vision that showed the Magdalene manifesting as Sophia in front of thousands of devotees of the Blessed Virgin Mary which finally convinced me that, cup or no cup, the ritual at the Chapel of Abominations had to go ahead. What is more, I somehow knew that it was to take place on 22 July, the Magdalene's feast-day in both Eastern Orthodox and Catholic tradition, which was now just six weeks away.

19. THE CUP WILL COME

Seven Templar fugitives, their floppy brown hoods withdrawn, stood in a circle around the small stone chapel located in the middle of a woodland clearing. Like the Tyler who guards the entrance to a Masonic lodge, their drawn swords were pointed to the ground as they kept watch for any intruders that might approach the temporary resting place of the Head of God.

Inside the small nave, the precious holy item had been concealed beneath the chapel's altar, where it would remain for exactly seven days before being transferred to the port of Dover. This solemn duty was overseen by Stephen de Staplebridge, who had supervised the transfer of the silver reliquary from Garway in the diocese of Hereford via the oratory of St Clement in the town of Hastings to this ancient place of sovereignty. As the 'head of Bran' had protected Britain against plagues and invasion so long as it remained buried beneath the White Mound – on which the Tower of London was constructed – the buried head would act as its own talisman.

The setting then shifted to the same woodland several centuries later. The ground was covered in snow, like a scene from a Christmas card, and Aleister Crowley, wearing a thick tweed coat with a scarf around his neck, was walking briskly towards the now-ruined Chapel of Abominations, the chapel of the Grail. Here, in 1952, just five years after his death, occultists perhaps linked with the OTO had conducted their own rite of passage. 'I answer your call to arms,' was all he would say, referring rather sarcastically to the seven knights who had guarded the head reliquary all those years ago.

The scene then changed once more; it was the present day, around dusk on a warm July evening. Three people were at the small chapel; one, a tall, slim woman with long flowing hair, lay spread-eagled on the ground, a Grail cup upon her stomach, illuminated by five small bowls of burning liquid positioned around her to form the points of a pentagram, a symbol of Venus. 'Five become one,' Crowley's voice was heard to say, referring to the attainment in Sufi mysticism of the highest *latifa*, *Akhfa*, and the Ultimate Unseen, *Ghayb-ul-Ghaib*. At that moment, she lifted the holy vessel over and behind her as her legs closed like scissors to form a perfect arrow that pointed at two men standing back-to-back just a few metres away. Their heads formed the dual nature of Janus, past and future combined as one.

'Now all is aligned,' Crowley asserted, boldly. 'As the lance and the cup become one, *pierce the veil*.'[435]

After Richard had described his extraordinary visionary glimpses of the Chapel of Abominations, and what Sue, he and I would have to do when we reached there in just six days' time, I asked him to tell me more about the seven fugitive knights who had guarded the head at the chapel for exactly seven days. When did he feel this took place?

'Just a few years after the arrest of the Templars,' he responded. 'I'd say around 1311–12. That's when the head left England for good.'

Stephen de Staplebridge was still at large in 1311, and so it made sense of what we knew already, and implied that he had been in charge of ensuring the Templar relic's safe passage from Garway in Herefordshire to Dover in Kent, via Hastings Caves and this tiny woodland chapel.

Richard was seated in the half-light of the room, following what was turning out to be another extraordinary psychic session, the final one before our long-anticipated ritual at the Chapel of Abominations, which we hoped would become our stepping stone into France where the search for the Head of God would begin in earnest.

Ever since we had returned from Headcorn in early May, the quality of the psychic information had not abated. Initially, there had been an emphasis, without due explanation, on the importance of The Fool card of the Tarot pack, which usually shows a youthful figure with a pack tied to a staff walking blindly towards the edge of a cliff as a small dog tries to bite his legs. It can be interpreted as one who passes through life naively, not realising the dangers ahead or the consequences of their actions, and if he or she were to do so then this alone would inhibit their progress. No better example of the fool in this context is the manner in which psychic questers blindly accept what they are doing and worry about the consequences or implications when it is all over. Were these references to the fool – a character linked with the Jungian archetype known as the trickster – some indication of how we were to continue our quest? Perhaps we were acting like fools, and should reconsider what we were doing.

Then, on another occasion during a psychic session, Richard had told me that he had seen a masked jester in medieval costume burst forth unexpectedly into the lounge of our Leigh-on-Sea home.[436] With a big smile, he had turned his head to reveal a second face at the back of his headdress, associating him with the god Janus. Laughing, he then showed us the Grail cup, before placing a finger to his lips and tutting.

I told him through Richard that I did not understand.

'I gave you the cup,' he had responded, cryptically.

But we did not find it.

'Because you want the cup, you shall have it.' He then laughed again, before adding: 'Follow me into the veil. Behold your Grail. I am a *true* knight of the Grail.'

Not taking in what he was saying, I had asked for his name.

'I am Per-ce-val'. The syllables were drawn out for some reason.

Perceval was the supreme 'guileless fool' of the Grail romances, who initially brought darkness and despair to the kingdom by failing to ask the correct question on witnessing the Grail procession, but who then redeemed himself by becoming the best knight in the land as well as the guardian, or keeper, of the Grail. In some romances, it is Sir Gawain, Sir Lancelot or the pure and holy knight Sir Galahad who embraces this same role.

I asked him if this meant that we should become more like Perceval, if we were *still* to achieve the Grail cup.

'Do as I. Pierce the veil.'

Pierce the veil? I needed some explanation.

In response, Richard had seen flashes of a verdant green landscape, before ending up in a cold, dark cellar. Crowley was there and on one wall was a crude drawing of Thoth, the Egyptian god of writing and the moon.

Where was this, I had asked.

'Netherwood,' came the reply from Crowley.

At the time none of us recognised the name, even though it sounded familiar, and only afterwards did we realise that 'Netherwood' was the Victorian guesthouse, situated just outside the town of Hastings, where Crowley had spent the final two years of his life. Although no longer standing, it was located in four acres of ground where today there is a modern housing estate. Richard felt that we needed to go there as Crowley had something to give us, not a physical artefact but knowledge, perhaps, that we required for some reason.

At a later session, Crowley suggested that we do something that we had been told to do some nine months beforehand (although had failed to do so for various reasons), and this was go to Hastings Caves. Here we should receive the 'Baptism of Fire' by linking our minds with the 'Baphomet' statue using creative visualisation.[437] It would help put us back on track, and afterwards we should visit Netherwood and attempt to make contact with Crowley's spirit.

It was at this point that Richard suddenly found himself looking at a farmhouse in open countryside. It was all he felt was left of a former monastic building called 'Langdon Abbey', which was somewhere of immense importance to our story, for it was near here, it seemed, that the Head of God had rested before being moved overseas via the port of Dover. Yet then, somewhat unexpectedly, Richard said: 'I think the chapel is near here.'

What chapel?

'The Chapel of Abominations,' he had confirmed. 'I think it could be Sussex, or Kent, not too far from the coast.'

A break followed, allowing me to establish that there was an East and West Langdon in Kent, several kilometres north of Dover. Moreover, there was an abbey at West Langdon, a few remaining fragments of which had been incorporated into a modern farm building. Locating the relevant Ordnance Survey map, I found the two Langdons, and began scanning the surrounding woodland for any ruined chapels.

Almost immediately, my eyes locked on to an ecclesiastical ruin located in woodland belonging to Bisley Manor, not far from the Langdons, next to which were the words 'chapel (remains of)'.[438] Had we at last found the Chapel of Abominations, our Grail chapel, where Crowley insisted that Templar-linked occultists had performed their own rite involving the Holy Grail some fifty years beforehand? Everyone was dumbfounded, but jubilant at the same time. Yet Richard almost wished that we had not found it so soon, as there was now a huge temptation to go there before 22 July. In our terms, there was a 'big hit' to be had from this site, and it could be expended without the necessary result if we were not careful.

THE WHITE CANONS OF LANGDON

The following day, I slid off to Southend Central Library to see what I could find out about Langdon Abbey, and the ruined chapel at Bisley. The lands and money to build the abbey were donated to the Premonstratensian order, known also as the Norbertines, the White Canons, or White Friars, in c. 1189 by William de Aubervilla, who owned Bisley Manor. In addition to this, he granted the canons possession of various local churches, as well as the Bisley chapel. Further notes indicated that it had been constructed shortly after the Norman Conquest, and was used by the residents of Bisley Manor for private services. As a possession of Langdon Abbey, its canons celebrated mass there each day, although after the abbey was abandoned following the Dissolution in 1536, the chapel became redundant, and was certainly in ruins by the end of the eighteenth century. From what I could find out about the place, the tiny building, consisting of a single roofless nave, was more or less intact. However, as late as the 1960s part of the south wall had collapsed, destabilising the remaining stonework, and making it structurally unsafe (it is now no longer accessible to the public).

Strange facts emerged concerning the abbot of Langdon Abbey during the very time frame that the Head of God is supposed to have left England for France. It would seem that in 1331 royal protection was granted to the abbot, William, 'while going beyond the seas on the king's service'.[439] What is more, in 1316, 1325 and 1329 he was given licence 'to cross at Dover' to attend the chapter general at Prémontré, the mother house of the White Canons in France's Aisne district, near Laon, taking 20 marks with him for his expenses.[440] Abbot William would also seem to have been an important figure at Prémontré itself, as in 1310 he was asked to act as the principal intermediary in a dispute between the abbot of Prémontré and the English houses of the Order.[441] Then in 1345 'Abbot W.' of Langdon, plausibly the same William, acted as the abbot of Prémontré's vicegerent, or deputy.[442] Could he have been responsible for ensuring that the Head of God reached France safely?

I checked out the origins of the Premonstratensians' mother house at Prémontré, and discovered that it was founded in 1120 by St Norbert of Xanten (1080–1134). According to the story, whilst staying at the city of Laon in eastern France, he came upon a valley in the Forest of Coucy, which was cruciform in shape. That night he prayed in a ruined chapel of St John the Baptist and received a vision of the Virgin Mary, who instructed him to found an abbey on the spot. Thereafter, he gathered together thirteen companions and under his leadership they lived in huts of wood and clay positioned in a circle around the ruined chapel, which had long been abandoned by the hermits who formerly inhabited the place. A more permanent church was then built on the site, and from these humble beginnings the abbey of Prémontré arose.

The Order received papal recognition in 1126, two years before the Templars received theirs. One tentative link between the White Canons and the Templars is that St Norbert was a close friend of St Bernard of Clairvaux, who developed the rule for the Knights Templar based on that of the Cistercian Order. Norbert admired the Cistercian ideals, but decided to adopt for his Order a more austere form of Augustinian rule, like that practised at Merton Priory in Kent and Christchurch Priory in Dorset, where Stephen de Staplebridge did penance following his discharge from prison. As canons, the work of the Order would have included preaching and other lay duties, such as tending the sick, missionary work, etc.

On being given official recognition by the Holy See in 1126, the Order possessed nine houses, yet by the middle of the fourteenth century they are said to have had over 1,300 monasteries of men and 400 of women in several countries. The Premonstratensians shared the same patron as the Knights Templar, for it would seem that by virtue of his austere lifestyle St Norbert saw fit to adopt John the Baptist as the Order's role model. The White Canons have always paid special devotion to him, and a large number of their religious houses are dedicated to this saint. If the Head of God really was a twin-faced reliquary containing fragments of a skull of John the Baptist, then it starts to make sense why fugitive Templars might have been in league with an abbot of the White Canons. Langdon Abbey was just five kilometres (three miles) away from Temple Ewell, the Kent preceptory of the Templars, meaning that Abbot William's predecessors would have dealt with members of the Order on a regular basis. Knowing that Abbot William regularly crossed the English Channel, on either the king's service or official ecclesiastical business, makes him a likely candidate to have carried the Templar relic out of the country, for who would have suspected a devout holy man such as him of dealing with known fugitives?

A DAY IN HASTINGS

On Sunday, 7 July, Sue, Richard and I finally visited St Clement's Caves, Hastings, eight months after they had first been brought to our attention through dreams. Deep inside the network of tunnels, where bizarre sound and light displays involving smugglers and seamen befuddle the brain, we examined the life-sized statue of the seated horned figure identified as Baphomet, the idol of the Knights Templar. With no way that we could conduct a meditation there, the three of us retired to a small quiet pub called The Angel Inn, situated within sight of the entrance to the 'Smugglers' Caves', as they are now known. Here we visualised ourselves back in the caves, and after calling on Bartzabel, the angel of Mars, for his protection, we linked in mind with the statue in order that he might bestow on us the Baptism of Fire, seen as a raging fire that engulfed our souls. Everything seemed to go OK, even though at the very end of the meditation Frank Sinatra's 'My Way' rather incongruously blasted out of the jukebox.

Thereafter we journeyed on to the site of Netherwood, the guesthouse where Crowley had died on 1 December 1947. Next door to where it had once been is the Robert de Mortain pub, and so we sat down at the end of its beer garden and attempted to reach out to Crowley's departed spirit. Richard saw him around the age of 45 putting the final touches on a well-known painting of Leah Hirzig (1883–1975), a young woman he met in late 1918 when living in Greenwich Village, New York City. On 11 January the following year she had come to his apartment and, after making love for the first time, he decided to draw her. She agreed and, on being asked how she would like to be portrayed, replied, 'Paint me as a dead soul.' That night Crowley could not sleep, and so he got up and painted a picture of her, which went on to form part of a triptych and was given the title 'Queen of Dead Souls'. The next day she called again, and he asked her to be his Scarlet Woman, his incarnation of Lady Babalon, and help him spread the doctrine of the new aeon which he felt had begun in 1904 when he received the channelled work *Liber Al*, also known as 'The Book of the Law'. She agreed, taking the magical name Alostrael, meaning 'the womb (or *grail*) of God', a fact unknown to us at that time.

It was the 'Queen of Dead Souls' that Crowley was painting, and having finished her somewhat abstract body, he now added rather oversized lips. As if in the room there with him, he asked Richard to 'come closer', which he did, only to have his mind flit about all over the place.

I urged Crowley to speak to us in the wake of our reception of the Baptism of Fire in the pub next door to St Clement's Caves.

'You have done well,' he responded, patronisingly. 'I was beginning to doubt your faith to understand my words.'

And what, in his opinion, would happen now?

'You already have the key,' he sighed, somewhat reservedly. 'The Chapel of Abominations. I would not have told you yet, but I have been overruled.'

He had been *overruled*? This seemed a strange statement and implied that he was subservient to some greater ruling intelligence. If so, what was its identity?

Yet he remained silent.

As we sat at a wooden bench, pints of beer before us on that sunny afternoon, Richard now saw Leah Hirzig lying on her back, conducting a ritual with a cup full of liquid as Crowley watched on. It was placed on her bare navel, but was then lifted into the air with both hands and brought over her head until her arms were straight out behind her, which was what Sue would need to emulate when we reached the chapel.

Richard now saw Crowley standing before him as a very old man indeed, thin-faced and with a goatee beard; perhaps only months or even weeks before his death.

Why see him like this?

Crowley's response was emphatic: 'The cup will come.'

Those were his final words, said with a stern voice that was difficult not to believe. There was no more. Crowley had left the building.

I felt what he had said was a little too optimistic, and was willing to let the whole matter ride and presume that when it came down to it, we could use a substitute chalice of our own. In many ways, which cup we used no longer mattered, for simply by doing what we needed to do at the Chapel of Abominations would, I firmly believed, surpass all expectations, and any thoughts of finding a Grail cup would finally give way to the much greater quest for the Head of God. It was this possibility that I looked forward to now.

20. THE FEAST OF FOOLS

Saturday, 20 July. We were on a mission to help a friend. Sue and I had travelled from Essex to the Midlands city of Coventry to see Graham Phillips, someone I had known for 24 years, following his emergence into my life back in 1978. Together, Graham and I kick-started the subject of psychic questing one night in October 1979 when we uncovered a nineteenth-century short sword by a lake called Knights Hill Pool in Worcestershire. Graham had gone on to write a series of books on ancient history including *King Arthur – the True Story*, which identifies Arthur as Owain Ddantgwyn, a Dark Age chieftain who ruled the kingdom of Powys from the Roman city of Viroconium at Wroxeter in the Welsh Marches of Shropshire.[443]

Yet so many years later Graham was in a quandary. Despite his success as a popular writer, he had recently been experiencing growing disenchantment, and so appealed to Sue and me to help him out. Having not seen Graham for several months, we had made the decision to go up to visit him at his Coventry home, and see what we could do.

Sue and I sat inside his first-floor flat, and listened to his predicament.

'You know, I honestly feel that sometimes fate is working against me, and that I am not being allowed to fulfil my potential in life,' he reasoned, offering us a can of lager. 'It's as if something is holding me back.'

I understood what he meant, and sympathised.

'I think the only way I'm going to find out what's going on is a fool sketch,' he offered, in all seriousness.

THE FOOL SKETCH

A fool sketch is something you do when your whole life appears to be falling apart. The principle is that you place your entire self in the hands of fate, and initiate a ritual whereby everything done is decided by the roll of a dice, the pick of a card, or the interpretation of chance events in the world around you. You provide a number of possible outcomes which are either sensible or progressively more outrageous, depending on how far you want to go. These are then put to the dice or the cards, and whatever comes up decides what you do next, or where exactly you go from there.

The reason for calling it a fool sketch is that it echoes the madness attained at times of misrule, which in the past took place during the period between one year and the next, a moment perceived as occurring outside of real time when chaos rules (our New Year celebrations are a watered-down vestige of this practice). For instance, in the Roman festival of Saturnalia, held in honour of the god Janus at the end of each year, whatever happened was seen as a microcosm of what could occur in the coming year. It was an indication of a nexus of activity that had the potential to direct, alter or influence your path in life.

Are such beliefs based on scientific reality? No, is the answer; however, reality is not as fixed as the scientific world would have us believe, and there are ways of bucking space-time and shifting our lives onto alternative possibilities, or parallel existences, which can be created and collapsed through infinite amounts of split decisions that occur all the time. In other words, all of us have the opportunity to switch or change our lives onto more favourable paths, where we are doing better than we are now, provided that we can completely let go of everything we value or hold dear in life, if only for a few brief hours. This, then, is where the fool sketch comes in useful, for it creates a temporary existence where you are no longer in control of your own decisions, and can easily be thrown into alternative possibilities. Some of them will be more favourable than the one that you were on; others could be worse, while still others might even be disastrous.

If you want to throw in your cards and be dealt a new hand, then a fool sketch is the perfect way to do it, and this is what Graham wished us to embark upon that evening. I wanted to try and talk him out of it, in order that we might explore other possibilities available to us, but he seemed adamant.

'I need to find out what it is that's holding me back,' he insisted, 'and a fool sketch seems the best possible option at this time.'

So it began in a local pub, where we attempted to find answers by using divination through the use of cards and dice as the bar got busier and busier. For example, a pair of dice determined a table for us to concentrate on (all pub tables seem to be numbered these days), while the actions of the people sitting there either confirmed or denied propositions and suggestions. If someone got up to go to the toilet, or buy another round of drinks, or leave completely, it had a specific meaning based on the questions we had voiced beforehand.

Through such answers, Graham became convinced that there was something important he had to do in order to ascend to the next level, provided that he understood what, if anything, was preventing him from moving on in life. Eventually it became clear from the dice that we should continue the fool sketch at his flat, where we would conduct a psychic session.

THE PENTACLE

Two of Graham's friends from Coventry, Lisa and Paul, accompanied us back from the pub, intrigued by what we were doing that night. After a while, Graham attempted to channel what he refers to as 'Mr Punch'. This is not simply the character from the 'Punch and Judy Show', or the Mr Punchinello found in Italian pantomime. No, what Graham wanted to try and communicate with was an aspect of the cosmic trickster, the Lord of Misrule, who presided over the medieval Feast of Fools (derived from the Roman festival of Saturnalia),[444] personified as the medieval jester. In mythological traditions from around the world, shamans acting out the role of the fool use a kind of psychobabble to induce true genius and enlightenment within either themselves or those in their presence.[445] In Graham's case, Mr Punch represented some aspect of his higher self, his creative genius, which could be accessed and externalised by inducing an altered state of consciousness.

Lisa and Paul watched on in tense anticipation as suddenly Graham screamed out the number 'five', which he did twice, and was asked not to do so any more! It took him next to the significance of the pentagram, known also as the pentacle, which as a disc or platter, generally inscribed with a five-pointed star, features as one of the four suits of the Tarot.

It was at this point that I began to sit up and listen, for Graham knew nothing of our search to find the Grail cup, or about the much greater quest for the Head of God, which we felt might contain a fragment of the skull of John the Baptist. His severed head had, of course, been presented to King Herod on a plate, or platter, by his stepdaughter Salome. The number five had become important to us with respect to the five *latā'if* of Sufi tradition, in which the highest one, *Akhfa*, signified the Fifth Element. Moreover, in less than 48 hours, on the feast of Mary Magdalene, we were to ignite five small bowls of methylated spirit to form the shape of a pentagram around Sue as we began our rite of passage at the Chapel of Abominations.

Graham continued with this new line of thought, which now included the question: 'Who was the *last* saint worshipped by the Templars? Wasn't it St Andrew?'

No, it was presumably John the Baptist, I said, but no more.

'I feel there's some connection between this saint and certain events which occurred around the time of the fall of the Templars,' he offered, feeling that this was leading somewhere.

It seemed no coincidence that Sue, Richard and I were working on exactly the same period in history with respect to the quest for the Head of God.

'Wasn't the head of John the Baptist offered on a plate?' Graham now recalled, continuing to make new links. 'Perhaps that's got something to do with both the pentacle and the story of Sir Gawain and the Green Knight.'

SIR GAWAIN AND THE GREEN KNIGHT

Sir Gawain and the Green Knight is a late Arthurian romance written in England c. 1375–1400, and is considered by scholars to be one of the finest examples of medieval literature still extant. Sir Gawain, the greatest knight of Arthur's court, agrees to accept a challenge made by a giant of a man known as the Green Knight, who rides into Camelot one Christmas Day. Gawain is first requested to cut off the man's head with his own great axe. On doing so, the Green Knight simply replaces his head back on his shoulders and tells the knight that he must meet him one year's hence to fulfil the bargain by offering his own head in return. Yet after tracking down the Green Knight to the mysterious Green Chapel at the appointed time, and resigning himself to certain death, Gawain's life is spared because he has three times resisted the temptation of a beautiful young woman at the castle in which he was invited to spend Christmas. She is the wife of Bercilak de Hautdesert, the owner of the castle, who turns out to be the Green Knight in disguise – the whole thing having been a trial to test Gawain's chivalry and knighthood.[446]

Sir Gawain and the Green Knight describes Gawain's shield as bearing a gold pentacle on a red field, and the reader is told that the five-pointed star is a token of truth, with each point linked and locked together to form the 'endless knot', a sign of King Solomon. In addition to this, the pentacle signifies truth, applicable to Gawain since in this story he is the faultless knight, true in all his five senses. It also represents the five wounds that Christ received on the Cross and the five joys that the Virgin Mary experienced because of Jesus (i.e. the Annunciation, Nativity, Resurrection, Ascension, and Assumption). Why exactly this work focuses on the pentacle is unclear. However, in medieval grimoires, or books of magic, such as the *Clavicle of Solomon* ('Key of Solomon'), the pentagram becomes a protective symbol to be inscribed on a ring to control demonic forces.

It seemed reasonable to surmise that the beheading of the Green Knight, who appears at Arthur's court holding an axe in one hand and a holly bough in the other, was linked in some way with the story of the beheading of John the Baptist. In European folklore, two mythical figures guard the changing of the seasons. The Holly King, identified as Jesus Christ, presides over midwinter, while the Oak King, seen as John the Baptist, guards midsummer. Although the Holly King, as the Green Knight, should more correctly be associated with John the Evangelist, through his role as guardian of midwinter, the connection between the beheading of both the Green Knight and John the Baptist is apparent.

22 YEARS OF NOTHING

As the clock ticked through into the early hours, Graham's friends went home, leaving us to continue our attempts to find a solution to his dilemmas.

'I'll play you that track about the fool that Graham Russell has done for his Robin Hood rock opera,' Graham said, getting up and going across to the CD player. 'It's called "22 Years of Nothing", and it's about my life, really. When he wrote it last year it was exactly 22 years since we discovered the sword in the bridge at the Knights Hill Pool, which started everything. And there I was, 22 years later, with very little to show for everything that has happened, and all the books I have written.'

Graham Russell is a singer, songwriter and music producer, as well as a founding member of Anglo-Australian rock band Air Supply, whose first hit 'All Out of Love' was a worldwide success. The band went on to have five top-five hits in the United States, and many more hits worldwide, and were described at the time by *Billboard* magazine as one of the most successful groups of the 1980s.[447] Air Supply have continued to tour and make records, but in 1994 Graham Russell turned his attentions to writing a rock opera on the subject of Robin Hood, and was introduced, with his wife Jodi, to Graham Phillips, who was in the process of finishing a book on the true history of Robin Hood.[448] The three of them became firm friends, embarking on various psychic quests and creating new ideas for both the rock opera and other future projects. Eventually, Graham Russell started writing tracks for the opera, to be entitled *The Heart of the Rose*, named after a mythical location thought to mark the geomythic centre of England. Although the album consists mainly of rock ballads, one particular track is unlike any of the others: '22 Years of Nothing'.

Its creation was inspired by Graham Phillips' devotion to Mr Punch and the concept of the Fool current ('The Fool' card of the Tarot being seen in this instance as the 22nd, or final, card of the so-called Major Arcana), and now Sue and I were listening to the track for the first time.

With Graham Russell's opening rant followed by haunting vocals, accompanied only by a simple keyboard arrangement and female vocal choir on the choruses and middle eight, it is a brilliant piece of work, far removed from the soft-rock ballads of Air Supply. The purpose for describing this elegy to the fool is that once it had finished, Graham Phillips felt the urge to play it again, and again, until it became a strange mantra meant to trigger altered states of consciousness and answers out of the chaos of the night. He felt that the key lay in the lyrics and, after a while, he got up and said he knew what to do next.

Graham then left the room, as I put the CD on for the umpteenth time.

> Welcome to the forest, won't you be my guest,
> Let's burn an abbot on a great big fire.
> All that money taken from the poor,
> They've all disappeared because they've all gone mad.
> From richer for poorer this fool is the one,
> From richer for poorer, where's Robin and John.
> If you don't solve the riddle, you're in my domain . . .[449]

THE MARIAN CHALICE

Graham returned with something I had not expected to see – a small green stone cup known as the Marian Chalice, which I never knew he kept in his Coventry flat. Back in 1995 Graham had written his own book about the Grail entitled *The Search for the Grail*, which provided new theories concerning the earliest sources of the Grail romances. It also included a historical quest he undertook to find an artefact that he proposed was associated with the story of the Holy Grail. Its existence had been suggested by references in certain old romances, which led him to believe that a cup of some kind was concealed local to the Shropshire town of Whittington – meaning 'white town' or 'white castle' – which in the reign of King John was home to Fulk Fitz Warine, an outlawed baron whose life eerily parallels that of Robin Hood. Indeed, there is good reason to suggest that some elements of the ballad of Robin Hood are derived from a work of late thirteenth-century composition entitled *The History of Fulk Fitz Warine*.[450] Also, certain mythological quests contained in this book echo stories found in *Perlesvaus*, the Grail romance written c. 1205, implying to American Grail historian Robert Loomis that there was an earlier common source that provided core material for both works.[451] Beyond this is an incident in *The History of Fulk Fitz Warine* where a blinding light appears in Fulk Fitz Warine's bedchamber towards the end of his life, which Graham argues is a manifestation of the light of the Grail.[452]

The White Castle, i.e. Whittington, also known as the *Blaucheville* or *Blaucheland*,[453] appears in some Grail romances, such as the *Didot Perceval*, written c. 1190–1215.[454] Here a major tournament takes place to win the hand of the daughter of 'the lady of the White Castle', who is of unsurpassed beauty, after which Perceval rides off to the Castle of the Fisher King, which he reaches the same day.[455] Strangely, a great jousting tournament in the presence of the king also takes place at the White Castle in *The History of Fulk Fitz Warine*. Its purpose is to attract knights from all over the realm to try and win the affections of the beautiful Mellette of the *Blaunche Tour* ('White Tower'). She is the daughter of William Peverall, whose father, Payn Peveral, came to England with William the Conqueror at the time of the Norman Conquest (and whom Graham sees as the role model for the Perceval of the Grail romances). Her hand, along with all the inheritance of Whittington, is finally won by Sir Guarin de Meez, the grandfather of Fulk Fitz Warine. So similar are the two stories concerning the tournament at the White Castle that one must have influenced the other, or else they have a common origin.

Loomis believed that the idea of the Grail was based on a Celtic cauldron of rebirth or horn of plenty belonging to the folk god Bran, and that a prominent fortification called Castell Dinas Bran, the 'castle of Bran', just over the Shropshire border in Denbighshire, North Wales, was Corbenic, the original castle of the Grail in the romances.[456] Similar thoughts led Graham to speculate that the Holy Grail found its way to Whittington, his preferred Grail castle, and so he searched for clues as to the vessel's final resting place. His efforts led him to Hawkstone Park, a large country estate lying some 20 kilometres (13 miles) away.

Here is to be found an old ruin known as the Red Castle, which local legend asserts was formerly the home of two gigantic knights, Tarquin and Tarquinus, while another tells the story of 'two perilous knights, Sir Edward of the reed Castle and Sir Hue of the reed Castle', two brothers who had 'disinherited the Lady of the Rock of lands by their extortion'. The maiden, whose residence was a nearby rocky eminence, known as the White Rock (plausibly Hawkstone's Grotto Hill – see below), called upon the assistance of Sir Ewaine, a knight of the Round Table, who promptly ejected the guileful brothers and went on to stay 'nigh halfe a yeare' in order that his wounds might be tended by the obviously grateful Lady of the Rock.[457]

Further clues led Graham to nearby Hodnet Hall, once the home of the Vernon family. Inside Hodnet's parish church of St Luke, Graham was drawn to a Victorian stained-glass window of four lights, each showing one of the four Evangelists. The last of these, St John, drew Graham's attention since this strangely effeminate figure held a chalice, reminiscent of Mary Magdalene carrying her *alabastron*. Above him was the eagle, John's evangelical symbol, and this sparked something off in Graham's head, for he knew that in caves inside Hawkstone Park's Grotto Hill there stood statues of the four evangelical symbols, the so-called Tetramorphs – the lion, bull, eagle and man. He thus wondered whether the cup, symbolised by the chalice in the hand of St John, might have been concealed behind the eagle statue.

It was a wild hunch, but when he came to investigate the part of the caves known as the Grotto he discovered that the statues had been removed and broken up around the time of the First World War (it was actually 1917 – see Chapter 22). So any mystery they might have concealed would have been lost long ago. However, he then turned up the name of the local builder responsible for removing the statues from the caves. He was Walter Langham, and it seemed that a small stone cup was indeed found by him inside the eagle as it was being broken up. Graham went on to trace a female descendant of Walter Langham, who checked through a box of heirlooms left by her ancestor and came across a small green stone cup, which she took to be the one found at Hawkstone Park.

In his book, Graham proposed that the Magdalene's *alabastron* was found in Jerusalem by the Empress Helena, St Helen, the Christian mother of Constantine the Great, around AD 326. She returned with it to Rome where it remained until the capital of the Western Empire came under threat from the Visigoths in 410. Before they sacked Rome, the sacred vessel was taken to the city of Viroconium in Shropshire, then under the control of the rulers of the kingdom of Powys, who remained loyal to Rome. These were the ancestors of Owain Ddantgwyn, Graham's candidate for Arthur, who eventually became its guardian, hence the Grail's association with Arthurian tradition. Thereafter it was passed on from generation to generation until it came into the hands of Fulk Fitz Warine of Whittington, and much later Sir Robert Vernon (1577– 1625) of Hodnet Hall. Sometime afterwards it was concealed in the caves at Hawkstone Park, where the cup remained hidden until its rediscovery some seventy years beforehand.

Unfortunately, the evidence presented in Graham's book to back up his belief that the Magdalene's *alabastron* was found by St Helen and eventually reached Britain was not accepted by the academic community. The whole matter was eventually forgotten, and certainly it was not a matter that I ever contemplated being linked with our own quest to find some representation of the Grail cup. Moreover, I did not buy into the idea that Arthur, the warrior chieftain of the Britons, who lived c. 500, had anything whatsoever to do with the Holy Grail, since the vessel's long association with Britain only began after the appearance of the first Grail romances, written in France during the last quarter of the twelfth century.

'Here you are, drink from the Grail,' Graham now suggested as he placed down the cup in front of us and filled its tiny bowl with beer, urging us to sip from it. Since we were in the middle of a fool sketch, we did as he insisted with a somewhat blasé attitude, and when no lightning bolts struck us down, we did it again.

From richer for poorer,
This joker is one.
From richer for poorer,
With Robin and John.
Ha, ha, ha, ha, hah, they've all gone mad,
Polly dolly. Ha, ha, ha, hah. Ha, ha, ha, hah.

Amid crumpled beer cans, empty bottles and overflowing ashtrays, the Marian Chalice was left on a round plastic table, and neglected for a while.

Twenty-two years, twenty-two years, twenty-two years of nothing.

The CD burst out the same track again and again, until finally, exhausted, Sue fell asleep as the light of day began curtailing the hours of darkness. Yet still Graham and I attempted to understand the mechanics of fate, and what exactly it was that held him back from progressing on to the next level. Was it some kind of creation of nature which prevented certain people with specific jobs earning pots of money, for fear that they might lose sight of their true goals in life? Perhaps Graham was under attack from some psychic force, or maybe it was just the flat he was in; perhaps he needed to move out and find somewhere more conducive to a healthier state of being.

Was he searching so long for a miracle,
When only the mirror could see.
Did his life lose its meaning,
Like the point of a sword.
Was he moving, was he free . . .

It was in the words of the song, Graham kept emphasising. Yet then, quite suddenly, he sighed in relief and said: 'OK, I've got it. I think I know the answer.' He then disappeared out of sight, leaving me with the still-sleeping Sue.

Yes, I'm just the fool.
And no one ever listens to me.
Am I madness and laughter disguised as the truth,
But truth is a hard place to see.
Truth is a hard place to see . . .

He returned wielding a large claw hammer, insisting, 'I've got to smash the Marian Chalice. It's what's holding me back.'

No, Graham, I shouted as I rushed towards him and grabbed his raised arm as the hammer swung in readiness to destroy an object that was possibly a very ancient relic indeed, whatever its origin.

'No, I've got to do it.'

Graham, there had to be another way.

He did stop, eventually, and calmed down enough to explain to me how he believed that, since he saw the cup in terms of the Grail, certain custodial duties came with its ownership. If one became its guardian, then that person would be made to focus on this single function in life, and nothing else. Thus in his opinion some supernatural force attached to the cup might be preventing him from moving on, and, if this was the case, then he could break free of its influence by ridding himself of this burden.

I told him that he could always pass it on to somebody else, if he felt it would help free up his life. If not, then there were other ways around this problem.

He agreed that he had acted foolishly, but would keep the cup, for the time being at least. Since it was now almost eight o'clock in the morning and light outside, and we had probably heard '22 Years of Nothing' around eighty times by now, we called it a day and slept.

> But I can show love just like anyone can,
> And I am the one with the key,
> Yes, I am the gateway, and I'm in no rush.
> For you all must enter through me.

THE SEARCH FOR JOHN'S HEAD

Over lunch that afternoon, Graham explained how he felt he should start a search for the head of John the Baptist, which he equated with the head of the Green Knight and the golden pentacle on Gawain's red shield, even though I had said nothing to him about our own quest to seek the Head of God

Graham felt sure clues regarding the head of John the Baptist would be found if we drove out to the medieval parish church dedicated to this saint in the village of Brinklow, located on the Fosse Way, just outside Coventry. Beyond the churchyard is a great earthen mound that was here even before the Romans built their famous road, which curves around its base.

Inside the church the three of us searched for possible clues as to why we had been drawn here. After discovering nothing of apparent significance, I suggested that what we needed to do was to act out the part of Gawain in the story of *Sir Gawain and the Green Knight*, and kneel down as if about to be beheaded by the Green Knight. Symbolically, Graham then 'cut off' my head. Nothing happened as a result, but then, on staring at the large brass crucifix on the altar, I unexpectedly saw flashes of the fall of the Templars, and of their brethren trampling on the Cross. I knew somehow that the only reason they did this was to tread over and *beyond* it, since they believed the Cross to be worthless. To them it did not represent an understanding of the true Christ, which came originally from those disciples, such as John and Andrew, who had been followers of John the Baptist before deciding to become devotees of Jesus.

More than this, I suddenly realised that the word Baphomet – the so-called idol of the Templars, plausibly a skull kissed during reception into the *Templi Secretum* – was indeed the Greek *bapho metis*, 'baptiser of wisdom', as von Hammer had suggested in the early nineteenth century. However, it related not to some demon, or devil in the form of a cat or goat, but to John the Baptist, who bestowed the Holy Spirit, the Christ, on Jesus through *baptism*, as the writings of Cerinthus recorded. This formed part of the *wisdom* of God known to the Gnostics and Templars, and adopted by the underground stream, explaining why the Templecombe panel almost certainly showed John the Baptist and not Jesus.

Once again, I was reminded of the question going around my mind at Horns Hill Tower: 'To whom serves the Grail?'

Was it John the Baptist, the Baptiser of Wisdom? No, it wasn't – it was the Christ, the divine light, symbolised by the dove, and not Jesus, that it originally served. Jesus's role as the incarnation of the Christ was confirmed by Mary Magdalene, who in the Gnostic literature understood fully the light and whose symbol was the dove, while John the Evangelist, and not Peter, was the founder of the Christian priesthood of the Eucharist. This is why together, as the Beloved Disciple, Mary and John bear the Cup of Christ. There was a connection, too, between all this and the original answer to the question I gave when at the tower on Horns Hill. The Grail does serve the king and the land, but how exactly was beyond me at that moment.

Suddenly, I clicked out of the daydream and looked around for the others. I felt strangely satisfied that something significant had happened, an important connection had been made, from which there was now no going back.

You all must enter through me.
You all must enter through me.

Back at the flat, Sue and I readied ourselves to leave as the evening drew to a close, knowing that we had a long journey ahead of us. Graham was feeling much better now, realising that the only person who could ultimately put him on to the next level was himself, and that there were no demons or powers of nature holding him back. The fool sketch had hopefully been successful, and good fortune now awaited us all.

Before leaving I went to the bathroom, and on my return I saw Sue smiling as Graham stood by, a look of contentment on his face. She held in her hand the Marian Chalice. When I asked for an explanation, Graham merely said: 'I just felt you should have it.'

What! Was he sure?

'Oh yes, totally,' he confirmed, vigorously nodding his head. 'It's better off with you, anyway, than here in this flat.'

This was an incredible honour, even if uncertainty did surround the origin of the tiny stone cup. Both Sue and I assured Graham of its safety, before departing into the night, our hearts racing uncontrollably. We had just become guardians of what is arguably one of the few candidates for the title 'Holy Grail' in the world, and knowing Graham's ability to come up with inspired conclusions regarding mysteries of the past, there was no way that this cup was a meaningless mistake.

Never did I anticipate that the Grail cup that we had been searching for might be the Marian Chalice, since I had no idea of its final fate. What the cup really represented would have to wait for another day, but going through my mind was the fact that we had been fooling ourselves into believing that the vessel had to be *found,* when the romances state quite clearly that the Grail is achieved, along with its 'secrets', only by a chosen guardian who has proved themselves worthy in the quest of life.

More bizarre than any of this was the simple fact that inside 24 hours, on the feast of Mary Magdalene, we were to conduct our rite of passage at the Chapel of Abominations, the Grail chapel, which we had been told months beforehand would require the presence of a Grail cup. Yet over the past few weeks we had resigned ourselves to using a suitable substitute chalice. Never in a million years did I expect that we might be able to use a *real* Grail cup; moreover, one which was already linked with Mary Magdalene's *alabastron*. This was sheer absurdity carried to the extreme.

Over and above this, Richard had felt – and the spirit of Crowley had stated – that the Grail cup would be handed directly to Sue, since she embodied some semblance of the female current expressed in myth by goddesses such as Venus, Sophia and Babalon, Crowley's own modern-day role model for unbridled female spirituality. The Grail itself was a symbol of corporeal existence encapsulating the divine light of the Christ, and conveyed to others through moving vehicles such as sacred blood (symbolised by the wine of the sacrament) and the anointing unguent of divine kings. So perhaps the Magdalene really was meant to have carried it in the name of Christianity, and for a short while she did. However, very quickly it became clear that in a male-dominated Christian Jewish environment, the Grail would have to be the possession of a man, and the only person who could absorb that feminine role was the Beloved Disciple. Despite attempts in medieval times to express the female guardianship of the Grail through the creation of the Grail maiden, or the female Grail-keeper, this sacred vessel remained a wholly masculine symbol through to the present age. Now, once more, what was *a* 'Grail', at least, had been given into the hands of a woman, and from my research into the subject this was certainly no bad thing.

21. THE FACELESS ONES

It might have been a scene out of Victor Hugo's *Les Misérables*, walking through the busy streets of a French medieval town, church bells ringing and everywhere high gothic architecture. In front of me was an enormous cathedral church, its entrance arch festooned with carved figures in niches and relief. Passing beneath it, I entered the building's chasm-like interior, lit only by the flickering candles on individual altars and the blazing sunlight pouring in through the stained-glass windows set high in the walls. Out of sight, a choir practised in Latin as I made my way towards a side chapel, off to the right of the great nave.

I was here to take possession of a holy relic of incredible Christian significance, something that was present at the Passion, an object found by St Helen. It was kept inside an ornate oblong casket in gold, about 30 centimetres (12 inches) in length and half that in width, which had rested here for hundreds of years. Amazingly, after intense negotiation with the local mayor, he had agreed to give it into my possession so that I might translate it back to England, where it would be placed at a corresponding holy site of great spiritual potency sacred to St Helen, located somewhere in the county of Oxfordshire.

Monday, 22 July. It was the feast of Mary Magdalene, and as I awoke odd words and thoughts still accompanied the residue of the curious dream. There was a strong connection between the French cathedral church and a saint or person called 'chac', which I quickly realised was probably Jacques, the French form of James. No name was given for the town, although a gut feeling said it was located at the very centre of France. All of this was linked somehow with a fleeting flash of inspiration I had received in meditation just a few days before, suggesting that somewhere in Oxfordshire was a site of ancient power that once constituted the sacred centre of England, and that it would be important for us to find. Both places exuded the same energies and seemed to be linked in some way with St Helen. Moreover, the movement of the holy relic symbolised the transfer of some kind of spiritual power base from France to England.

As for the holy relic I acquired, it felt linked with the Passion, and was probably brought back to Europe by the Empress Helena – the mother of the Roman Emperor Constantine the Great – who started life as an innkeeper's daughter, and according to some sources might even have been a reformed harlot. Before Constantine embraced Christianity on behalf of the Roman Empire in AD 312, legend asserts that his mother was already a devout Christian, and in 326 St Helen, as she was to become known, embarked on a pilgrimage to the Holy Land. Whilst in Jerusalem she is said to have rediscovered the site of Golgotha, the place of the skull, known also as Calvary Mount, and here she uncovered various items connected with the Passion. The list varies from source to source, but generally she is said to have found the three nails removed from Jesus's wounds, the plaque placed above Jesus's head (the so-called *Titulus*), the nail that affixed it to the Cross, along with the True Cross itself.[458] All of these items were allegedly retrieved from beneath the ruins of a Temple of Venus built on the site of the Holy Sepulchre and dedicated in AD 319. Whether any of these objects were actually what she assumed them to be is quite another matter, but then it is the belief in their historical reality that gives them power and not necessarily their genuineness.

Why exactly I should have experienced such a specific dream just hours after Graham had handed the Marian Chalice to us at his Coventry home, and so soon before our planned visit to the Chapel of Abominations in just a few hours' time, remained unclear. Yet as the car sped along the M20 towards Folkestone, Dover and the Eurotunnel that sunny afternoon in late July, I recounted what I could remember to Sue and Richard and left it at that.

THE KEY OF THE ART

Richard's own slumber had also been disturbed one night beforehand when a shadowy figure, whom he recognised as Aleister Crowley, showed him a series of mystical drawings from a manuscript thought to have been compiled around the year 1800. Known only as *Aleph*, the first character of the Hebrew alphabet, the diagrams, he was told, were a key to joining together the four elements – earth, air, fire and water – to make the Fifth Element, named in the dream as 'the One', a term used in Gnosticism and alchemy to denote God. One picture he recalled seeing showed a Janus-style double-head, enveloped in light, which he felt expressed the culmination of everything that we stood to achieve that day.

A little research before our departure that lunchtime had revealed the existence of just such a manuscript, housed in Vienna's Austrian National Library. With a catalogue date of 1802, it is described as a German Rosicrucian work composed by a mysterious individual who went under the name Archarion.[459] The Rosicrucians were those of the underground stream who united themselves under the sign of the rose upon the cross. From the time of their emergence in the seventeenth century, they expressed a teaching and philosophy based on Christian and Jewish mysticism, as well as medieval alchemy and Graeco-Roman Hermetica – the teachings of Hermes, god of writing.

I was able later to track down the illustration from *Aleph* seen by Richard. It shows a head with two faces, both bearded males, amid a blaze of light. Between them is an angel with outstretched wings, beneath which are the letters YHVH in Hebrew, constituting the so-called Tetragrammaton, the ineffable name of God. The head is enclosed in a circle from which emanate rays of light containing the names of the ten spheres of influence, or *sephiroth*, of the Cabbala, complete with their individual God names. In addition to signifying some kind of celebration of what we intended to achieve when Richard and I would stand back-to-back at the chapel, the double-head was also a nod towards the supposed Templar reliquary known as the Head of God.

Another drawing from *Aleph*, certainly alluded to by Richard, although not described, shows an eagle-headed Gnostic serpent with a key in its mouth. It rises up from the keyhole of a strongbox shaped like a double cube that bears characters from an unknown magical cipher. On the key are the numbers 1, 2, 3 and 4, seen by one Rosicrucian historian as representative of the four elements, which he says 'unlock the secrets of matter',[460] a sentiment supported by the Yiddish–Hebrew script beneath the box, which speaks of 'the key of the art'. If related to what we were doing, then it was probably connected in some way with the creation of the Fifth Element, something which had come through strongly ever since I had dreamed about the concept of the five *latā'if* in Sufi tradition.

ENTERING THE MIRROR WORLD

Thinking about everything that had happened in the past 48 hours made me realise that over the months, especially since our ill-fated journey to Headcorn in May, there had been a number of signs suggesting that the Grail cup would come to us in the fashion it did. There was the incredible Brookland font, showing Janus holding a cup, and the visions experienced by Richard of the twin-faced Roman god seated beneath an archway at the Chapel of Abominations, once again, with a cup in his hand. No better antecedent can there be for Mr Punch, or Punchinello, Graham's perceived higher self, who began as a strange fool-like figure in Italian pantomime in the seventeenth century, but whose origins are infinitely older.

Janus is thought to have been the inspiration behind an original Tarot card found in some of the earliest packs, which first began appearing in Italy during the mid-fifteenth century. Entitled 'Prudence', or 'The Female Joker', it shows a woman – sometimes with two faces – who gazes into a mirror, in which is a reflection of herself in the otherworld, what might be described as the mirror world.[461] Clearly, the mirror replaces Janus's wine-cup, which can equally be seen as an access point into the mirror world, as is the case with Jam's Cup, or the Cup of Jamshid, in Sufi tradition. Here the surface of the wine it contains creates a mirror-like surface in which the whole world can be seen, both past and future. Mirror symbolism was very much associated with fools in general, who were often shown holding mirrors in which their grinning reflections can be seen. Such ideas also helped inspire the development of the bauble, the grinning face of the fool or jester on the end of a stick,[462] which perhaps started life as Janus's rod, or wand.

Only after this time did I discover a rather revealing reference to Janus and his associations with Prudence in a work entitled *Etruscan Roman Remains* (1892), by the noted nineteenth-century journalist and Romany Tuscan folklore expert Charles Godfrey Leland (1824–1903). Here it speaks of a form of Janus known as Jano, who has two heads – one Christian (i.e. human) and the other animal (i.e. pagan) – and whose favour can be gained by binding two Tarot cards – The Wheel of Fortune and The Devil – to an iron bed-frame and then reciting an ancient incantation.[463] Leland admits that 'there were few gods with whom there were so many occult, strange, and forbidden mysteries connected, as with Janus, and there are marked traces of this in the modern tradition'. He goes on to say:

> As having two heads, or being all-seeing, he [Janus] became the symbol of Prudence – the *Prudentia* of *Gothic* sculpture, which is also the mystic Baphomet, or two-headed figure girt with a serpent, of the Knights Templars . . . The Baphomet signified secrecy and 'illumination'. . . Janus was *the god of the door*, i.e., the entrance or admission to the mysteries. By him the chief devil (or evil) is conquered, and fortune or fate mastered. The incantation to Jano is therefore of great interest and value as possibly indicating a very curious tradition handed down from the old initiation. He is the weird, i.e., prophetic spirit.[464]

Janus was thus linked by Leland not only with Prudence, who is shown with the serpent of wisdom about her legs, but also with 'mystic Baphomet', identified here with the twin-faced head reliquaries of the Knights Templar. If nothing more, his observations indicate a special relationship between our future quest to find the Head of God, representing the duality of the two Johns in occult tradition, and the lingering influence of two-faced Janus.

The Prudence, or Female Joker, card was removed from the Tarot deck at an early stage in its development. However, originally it was designated card number twelve,[465] while The Fool was the twenty-first card (even though in modern packs it is generally numberless, or simply bears a zero). Since the reflected face in the mirror held by Prudence represents her higher genius in the mirror world, then the transposition of the numbers twelve and twenty-one, i.e. 12/21, indicates that The Fool card was taken to be the mirror reflection of Prudence, a realisation that has since inspired Richard to write elsewhere on this fascinating subject.[466]

As I knew, there had been an emphasis on The Fool card of the Tarot in the psychic sessions leading up to gaining the Marian Chalice, while the occasion on which a jester figure with a Janus-like second face on the back of his headdress had appeared holding the Grail cup must also have held some significance. He gave his name as 'Perceval', the 'guileless fool', who eventually becomes the best knight in the land and achieves guardianship of the Grail.

Somehow, all of these psychic clues should have told us that the Grail would appear under unlikely circumstances, and that the key was the cosmic joker, chaotic ruler of the mirror world. Place two mirrors opposite each other and stand between them and you will see an infinite number of reflections of yourself. Each one represents a version of you gradually diverging from this reality, and thus the reflections signify alternative linear possibilities of your life that have independent parallel existences. Thus the mirror shows a world of illusion, governed by the cosmic trickster, someone whom you might be able to bargain with using magical processes in the hope that you can switch your life on to a better course (which is precisely why fool sketches seem to work).

It would be this same otherworldly knowledge of parallel existences, moments of nexus and linear possibilities, that we intended to utilise at the Chapel of Abominations in order to catapult some part of ourselves into the future so that we might more easily see the path forward.

All of this suggested that we had not been meant to find the Grail at Headcorn. In a sense we did fail, although not so much with respect to achieving the Grail, but in failing to comprehend the vessel's true nature. It had been brought home to us by the appearance on the quest of Klingsor, the sorcerer of the German romances who attempted to beguile the Grail knights into losing sight of their true quest. We should have realised then that something was going drastically wrong, and we were unlikely to attain the Grail at that time. To start with, we were supposed to have traversed seven different sites around the perimeter of the great circle making up the landscape Star of Babalon, but had forgotten to do so. Furthermore, it is now clear that I did not properly understand the question, 'to whom serves the Grail?' It was not so much the king and the land, but a true understanding of the Christ, the Holy Spirit, the divine light, symbolised by the dove. It was this divine power that Jesus received through his own baptismal initiation and used like a magician to perform miracles, heal the sick and instil visions of the kingdom of heaven within his disciples, and caused to be passed on to all celebrants through the communion meal of the Paschal vigil. It was a simple answer, but one which could only be known and thus said at the correct time, otherwise it would have been meaningless.

PSYCHOMETRY

We had called Richard on our way home from Coventry the previous night to tell him the good news about our possession of the Marian Chalice. He was obviously delighted by this revelation so late on in the day, and just said, 'I told you we would get it, and that it would be given directly to Sue. I knew my feelings couldn't be totally wrong.' Richard felt vindicated, and now I was hoping that he would find time to psychometrise the small stone cup to see what he could ascertain about its history. Psychometry, or the art of attuning to the vibrations of an object in order to obtain some knowledge of its past, was an important tool in psychic questing, and so I expected some interesting results, particularly if the cup was as important as Graham believed it to be.

The chance came when Richard, Sue and I were relaxing in our hotel room before the journey out to the Chapel of Abominations. With the curtains drawn, and a single candle burning, he sat on the edge of a bed and simply touched the chalice with his fingers as it stood on the carpet before him.

After a minute or so of silence, Richard opened his eyes and sighed. 'I don't get a lot, I'm afraid.'

What did he get, then?

'I think it once had a lid made of the same type of stone,' he revealed, 'perhaps with a small knob which enabled you to lift it away from the cup itself.'

This really did suggest it was an unguent jar once used to hold scent or oil. As to its age, or provenance, I did not wish to speculate as I had an archaeologist friend that I wanted to show it to at the earliest opportunity.

'On either side I saw a lion rearing up, as if they were protecting it,' he added, before shrugging his shoulders. 'That's it, really.'

His words made me recall certain Jewish mosaics from Roman and Byzantium times that show a pair of lions protecting holy objects such as the seven-branched Menorah candleholder, the Tablets of the Law and the Tabernacle of the Ark. All of these sacred relics were once to be found in the Holy of Holies of the Jerusalem Temple. The lions also reminded me of the twin griffins that flank the rococo-style vase on the plaque attached to the Cat Monument at Shugborough Park, which we had already identified as a representation of the Magdalene's *alabastron*.

Very little else occurred as we waited patiently in the hotel room, and then afterwards in the restaurant bar, before we gathered together what we would need for the evening ahead and, as the sun slowly set, moved off towards the remotely placed chapel. We were now pretty well psyched up, and a little anxious of exactly what might happen in the middle of a wood as dusk turned to darkness, for we were unlikely to be alone out there.

Half an hour later we were staring at the tiny religious house, which is just as it is described in the archaeological reports – roofless, but with all four walls intact, one being slightly damaged. Moreover, at its western end is a prominent gable arch which has to be the one beneath which Richard saw Janus with the Grail cup. Encroaching the structure from all sides are overhanging trees and dense undergrowth, making it impossible to fully examine its exterior, or take good pictures. Tiny lancet windows date its earliest masonry to the Norman period, although a larger window in the English medieval style was inserted into the existing south wall during the fourteenth century. Inside, a line of cobbled stones leads up to the position of the altar, while either side of this are a scattering of fallen headstones, showing that the chapel remained consecrated until fairly recent times. The rest of the structure, devoid of anything that might denote its former sanctity, is lined with a layer of earth, rubble and broken masonry.

After examining the building's empty interior, Richard tried to find the position where he believed Templar-inspired individuals, possibly linked with the OTO, had conducted their own rite of passage here almost exactly fifty years beforehand. It turned out to be a sparse clearing around fifty metres from the ruined chapel, which we quickly deemed ideal for our own purposes. So, in the diminishing twilight, the five small bowls were placed in the shape of a pentagram and filled with a small amount of methylated spirits, which was then ignited to represent the five *latifa*.

Sue, adopting the role of Babalon, or Venus, reclined within the pentagram, her arms and legs outstretched in mimicry of Leonardo da Vinci's drawing of the 'ideal man' seen in his picture 'Proportions of a Human Figure'. Upon her bare navel she placed the small green stone cup, containing a little green absinthe, this being our own chosen sacrament to Lady Babalon.

At the same time, Richard and I stood back-to-back at right angles to the line of Sue's body. Thereafter we readied ourselves for the moment of coming together of everything past – towards which I would look – and everything future, the direction in which Richard now stared in anticipation.

As the five blue flames continued to burn, Sue began to visualise concentric rings of green energy radiating out from the tiny cup, which passed beyond the woods into the surrounding countryside. Long minutes passed as one by one each bowl emptied of its bubbling contents, plunging us into darkness and creating the necessary environment to herald the coming moment of nexus.

It was now or never as the final flame extinguished, and Sue closed her legs at the same moment that she lifted the cold stone cup and its contents over her head until her arms were horizontal behind her. Using the length of her body as a lance or arrow, directed at the point between our heads, she visualised a ray of golden energy that struck its desired target in order to pierce the veil between this world and the next.

As I saw before me fleeting glimpses of everything that had brought us to this point in time – Bartzabel, Crowley, Canterbury, Stockbury, Shugborough, Headcorn, the Brookland font, Janus, the Fool, Hastings Caves, Netherwood, Graham Phillips and the Marian Chalice – Richard received a huge download of images and impressions of people and places concerned with the future. Some of it seemed familiar, but much of it was entirely alien to him. These thoughts, he hoped, would filter back into his conscious mind in the coming days, weeks and months.

Opening his eyes, Richard saw Crowley standing in the clearing, dressed in a pharaoh-like headdress and leopard-skin garment, like that worn by the *sem*-priest in ancient Egypt. With his forearms crossed over his chest, he appeared contented, even a little amused at the situation. Yet accompanying this vision was the feeling that he would no longer be around, for a while at least. His duty had been done, and now he would bow out in favour of God knows what. Moments later, Sue rose up from the damp earth and in the semi-darkness walked slowly towards Richard and me holding before her the Marian Chalice, and each of us drank of its contents, enlivening our souls once more.

Yet there was no time to stay around, for something else lurked in the darkness of the woods – an ancient guardian associated with the site that appeared as a giant cowled figure with only a shadow where its face should have been. Both Richard and Sue independently glimpsed its presence, and knew it did not take too kindly to us being there. We were treading in its world, and too many loud cracks in the undergrowth nearby indicated that it was getting stronger by the minute. Not helping matters was Richard's sudden feeling that this guardian was enticing him to go back to the chapel. Why exactly he could not be sure, and only after Richard and I had left Sue alone in the clearing did it occur to us that this supernatural figure was attempting to split us up for some reason. More disconcerting was Richard's sudden image of a monk's limp body hanging by a rope from a nearby tree branch, a consequence of the chapel's importance at the time of the fall of the Templars. This, along with Richard's overwhelming sense that we were standing in the middle of a charnel area reserved for the dead (and disturbing them was not an option), prompted us to withdraw back to the comfort and security of our hotel.

Lighting the five bowls of methylated spirits once more, we waited as one by one each flame flickered before extinguishing completely. In the darkness, I suggested that we concentrate our minds to see where we went from here, now that the Grail quest was presumably over.

'I don't think it is,' Richard said unexpectedly, lying down on the carpet, as Sue rested on a bed and I sat cross-legged on the floor. 'There's something else that we need to do, or find out. Something about the final secrets of the Grail which still elude us for some reason.'

I was listening, and wanted to know more. Was this the result of what we had just done at the Chapel of Abominations?

There was a period of quiet, before he said, somewhat cryptically: 'No, I can't make out any of this yet.'

I asked him to explain.

'I know this might sound mad,' he replied, still hesitating, 'but the only thing I can see is a group of black cowled figures wearing white masks – like those worn at a masked ball. They are standing in a great circle around an enormous twelve-pointed star design in red and black upon a polished marble floor, located in a huge oak-panelled room with a balustrade that opens out on to a second floor level.'

It sounded like a scene from Stanley Kubrick's cinematic epic *Eyes Wide Shut*. I tried to imagine the situation.

'There seems to be twelve of them. They are all quite tall, and the setting is a big house somewhere, and it's upstairs, on the first floor.'

Who were these masked figures, and what relevance were they to us?

Richard remained silent for a while, before saying: 'No, this can't be real. This house has to be symbolic, or something.'

I asked again: who exactly were they? We needed to know.

One of the twelve answered directly: 'It is like my face. If you see it, you still will not know.'

Who was saying this? I asked the same question twice. Was it *they* who had overruled Crowley and provided us with enough information to locate Langdon Abbey and the Chapel of Abominations?

'All I keep getting is "the council",' Richard cut in.

What council? This was not enough. We needed to know who they *really* were.

'They are now calling for someone,' he said, having not received any answers to my questions. 'One of the twelve figures has produced a large metal key on which are inscribed some numbers and magical sigils.'

I wondered whether this imagery was linked with the key held in the mouth of the eagle-headed serpent in the picture by Archarion in the Rosicrucian manuscript. That had numbers written along the length of its shaft.

Richard stopped to take in what happened next. 'It's being given to a dwarf who's entered the room. He's running out through two big oak doors and into a hallway. Now he's descending a flight of stairs, and moving out into a courtyard, where there's a rider waiting. He's dressed like a court jester.' There was a moment's pause, before: 'The dwarf's given him the key, and now he's riding off.'

A court jester? He could be seen as a form of the cosmic trickster. Curiously, Janus was often portrayed in Roman art with a baton in his left hand and a key, not a cup, in his right hand. Did the key and the cup signify the same thing? Were they both symbols of access into the mirror world? These were thoughts going around my head as I asked Richard to follow him and see where he went.

After long moments of silence, he said: 'The château of Arques.'

This, of course, was close to Les Pontils, the site of Poussin's Tomb in the Aude Valley, close to Rennes-le-Château, but did these masked figures come from this region?

'I'm not sure. Possibly, although it could just exist in my mind.'

Any more?

Before he could answer, the scene faded, and once more Richard saw the twelve faceless individuals standing in a circle around the great star inlaid within the beautiful mosaic floor.

Who overruled Crowley? Did this council now guide us?

'They're trying to pull you there,' Richard said next.

What? They wanted *me* to join them in the astral vision?

'Yes.'

All right, I would try and visualise myself going to them now.

Richard described what he could see. 'I see you approaching a drawbridge into a large castle, which is like something out of a Walt Disney film. It's set in a mountainous countryside. Beyond its entrance gates there's a big brick building inside a courtyard.'

So, it was a castle, then?

'It looks like it.'

I passed through doors, and up a staircase which led into a first-floor hallway. Beyond this were the two large oak doors that opened into the wood-panelled room where the council of twelve stood awaiting my presence. Two of them stepped aside to allow me to enter their circle.

Who, or what, were they?

'I am you,' was their collective response. 'We are legion.'

I did not understand.

One by one, the black-cowled figures began removing their masks to reveal their faces, but every one of them was me.

Thinking fast, I asked them whether they were the product of everything that would be in the future.

They just laughed, and replaced the masks over their faces.

OK, so they were not going to reveal their identities. We would just have to accept their presence and go with it for now. But if they did guide us, had we passed the test out there at the chapel earlier that evening?

'There was no test,' one of them responded, in a low, deliberate tone through Richard. 'You just follow in the footsteps of those who have failed before you.'

Then we had not ourselves failed.

'Not yet.'

What exactly were we to do now?

'You seek the key to unlock the truth of the Grail, and the head of the true messiah.'

So what exactly was the 'truth of the Grail'? Had we not already completed our quest to find the Grail cup? And how was this linked with the quest to trace the whereabouts of the Head of God? Was the head of John the Baptist really linked with the concept of the Grail? Although a Welsh Grail romance of late thirteenth-century composition entitled *Peredur* describes the Grail as a head on a platter, this can easily be seen to relate, not to the head of John the Baptist, but to that of the folk hero Bran the Blessed. According to legend, this was buried beneath the White Mound, where the Tower of London was built in Norman times.

THE COUNCIL OF TWELVE

No more came from the council of twelve before Richard's mind went blank, and the psychic session came to an end. The identity of the Faceless Ones, as they quickly became known to us, occupied our minds for weeks afterwards. Further communications with the black-cowled figures gradually revealed the names of individuals, groups and organisations who they claimed had been in contact with them over the millennia. However, it became obvious that they were not historical characters at all, but the collective memory and embodiment of those groups of twelve who had come together to celebrate or preserve the secrets of the Grail since the beginning. The Faceless Ones existed as the echo of the twelve disciples of Jesus Christ who sat around the table of the Last Supper; the twelve followers of Joseph of Arimathea who gathered around the table of the Grail; the twelve sons of Bron, one of whom, Alain, was destined to become the father of Sir Perceval, the Grail knight; the twelve knights of the Round Table, fashioned by Merlin for Uther Pendragon, Arthur's father; the twelve ancient knights who sat at the table with Gawain in the Castle of the 'King Fisherman' in *Perlesvaus*; the twelve knights of the twelve chapels encountered in the same story by Perceval on the island where rested twelve dead knights, all brothers, and the twelve knights who in a holy place encircle the Grail, seen as a cup of pure gold and crystal, in Richard Wagner's opera *Lohengrin* (1850).

In addition to this the Faceless Ones embody the memory of the twelve peers of Charlemagne, crowned Emperor of the West by the Pope on 25 December 800, who met around a copy of the table of Solomon;[467] the twelve Teutonic knights who in medieval times convened each year at the request of the Grand Master at the Order's headquarters in Marienburg, Germany;[468] the convent of twelve councillors who met during the rule of German king and Holy Roman Emperor Frederick II (1194–1250); and the twelve knights appointed to guard the *Sacro Catino* Grail cup at Genoa.[469]

THE ORDER OF MELCHIZEDEK

Yet who were they, really? Aside from the obvious association with the twelve divisions of the night sky we know as the astrological zodiac – which probably influenced the creation of Arthur's Round Table, with its twelve knights – they are to be associated with the celestial 'order of Melchizedek'. Its existence is alluded to in Psalm 110,[470] and then again in the New Testament where Jesus Christ is named as 'a high priest after the order of Melchizedek'.[471] Melchizedek is the mysterious 'priest of God Most High' and King of Salem, or Jerusalem, who in the book of Genesis met Abraham on the road and brought forth 'bread and wine'.[472] He was thus considered to have instituted the first priesthood, the reason why he is so often shown in Christian art bearing a Grail-like cup of the sacrament.

In Early Christian and Gnostic tradition, Melchizedek became a powerful prince of heaven, and in a religious text attributed to him, he is equated directly with Christ himself.[473] The followers of Melchizedek, known as Melchizedekians, have always believed in the existence of an order of Melchizedek, which, since it was led by Jesus Christ, who was seen to have instituted the Christian priesthood during the Last Supper, had to consist of a council of either twelve or thirteen. This heavenly order might be compared with the 'twelve saviours to the Treasury of Light', which the Gnostic text known as the Pistis Sophia tells us Jesus cast into Elisabeth, the mother of John the Baptist, and also into his own mother Mary, and all the disciples.[474] Yet at the end of the day, the Faceless Ones are the collective personification of every conceivable communication with what might be seen as the twelve heavenly guardians of the Grail, explaining why they chose to reveal their existence on the feast of Mary Magdalene, just 24 hours after we had been given the Marian Chalice.

The rite of passage at the Chapel of Abominations had been on the cards since December the previous year, and although no artefact or dramatic climax had resulted at the time, there was no disappointment afterwards. Planning something so far in advance causes a future moment of nexus that you then have to work towards, and you can start reaping the benefits of this even before the ritual takes place. A dream had suggested that we should visit the ruined chapel on the feast of Mary Magdalene, 22 July 2002, and just one day beforehand we were unexpectedly given a vessel, plausibly an ancient unguent jar, already linked with the Magdalene's *alabastron*. Not only did this make the whole trip that much more heightened for all of us, but that very night we had found ourselves in psychic communication for the first time with what was seemingly the collective intelligence behind the whole concept of the Holy Grail since the very beginning. In our opinion, none of this was simply chance alone. Behind it somewhere was a strange interplay between our minds and what might be described as pre-destiny, however dimly we might have realised it at the time.

I needed to know much more about the Faceless Ones, the whereabouts of their castle (if it existed), and what kind of influence they might have on our lives and on the world as a whole. Yet more pressingly, I needed to know more about the Marian Chalice – its history, its past owners and its purpose, for it seemed obvious that there was an entire untold story surrounding how it came to be at Hawkstone Park and why it was concealed inside a carved statue of an eagle representing John the Evangelist.

22. THE MARIAN CHALICE

Thursday, 1 August. The door opened and standing there, saying hello and ushering me through into her home, was Dr Mary Keeble,[475] an archaeologist who had worked extensively on excavations across southern England, and today teaches classes on archaeology. As she tried in vain to keep control of her many cats, almost all of them black and indistinguishable from each other, I followed her into the front room, stacked high with books, reports and trays full of ancient potshards. Mary looked and spoke like a stereotypical teacher, yet her knowledge of all periods of history was impeccable, and I regularly had cause to ask her opinion on artefacts found at sites local to me.

I was here to show her the Marian Chalice in the hope that she might be able to throw some light on its true age and function. Without saying anything about the vessel's known history, I just asked her what she would think if it was found during one of her archaeological digs.

Taking hold of the small stone cup – which is 49mm (1.9 inches) in height, 44mm (1.7 inches) in diameter with a tulip-shaped bowl and stemless circular base – she brought it up close to her eyes and examined it carefully.

I waited in silence for a few brief moments, before asking her verdict.

'Well, I would say it's a Roman scent jar,' she stated, with some conviction, 'and high status. I would say it was fashioned in either Egypt or the Near East, somewhere like that. Yes, I'd say the former, most probably.'

This was remarkable, but I let her continue without trying to show any obvious signs of excitement. What might it have contained?

'Rich, extremely expensive perfumes or scented oils,' she responded, as she continued to turn it in her hands. 'It would have been an object of value in a high-class Roman household, its possession denoting real wealth.'

Was it complete?

'No, there would have been a small lid made of the same stone, which looks like a variety of green onyx. Is it onyx?'

It certainly seemed to be, yes, although it also bore a striking resemblance to green alabaster, which can seem identical in appearance and is confusingly referred to occasionally as onyx marble (see below).

'I feel it would also have had a small lip running around the top edge of the bowl, although this seems to have been ground away to give it more the appearance of a small cup.'

This was something I had not noticed. So, was it handmade?

'Well, certainly hand finished, yes. It's a very beautiful object,' she continued, holding it against the natural light coming in through the window. 'The colour banding in the stone combines with the variable thickness of the bowl to give the impression of alternating sequences of light and darkness. This cannot be coincidence.'

Light and darkness in the same vessel – I wondered whether its makers deliberately achieved this effect for a specific reason.

If Mary was right, then it placed the manufacture of this precious vessel in Egypt or the Near East during the very era that Christianity was still under the yoke of the Roman Empire. Moreover, the fact that it was a scent or perfume jar used to contain what she described as 'rich, extremely expensive perfumes or scented oils' could not help me from thinking about the Gospel scene in which Mary anoints Christ's feet and head.

A VISIT TO THE BRITISH MUSEUM

Despite the incredible things that Mary had said about the green stone vessel, I knew I would have to gain a second opinion from other experts in the field of ancient history. To this end, Sue and I visited London's British Museum in the hope of finding a sympathetic ear in one of the departments responsible for Roman antiquities.[476] The first person we were directed to see was Thorsen Opper, of the Department of Graeco-Egyptian Studies. He took minutes out of his valuable time to give the Marian Chalice the once-over. What he said was not good, for the vessel's shape was totally unfamiliar to him. He admitted that he had never seen anything quite like it before, although this unfortunately suggested to him that it might not be old at all.

Dr Opper advised that we show it to Dr James Robinson, of the Department of Prehistory and Europe. His comments were slightly more encouraging, for in his opinion the vessel was probably a perfume jar, although it was incomplete since part of its circular lip was missing (confirming what Mary had said). Yet to him it was unquestionably *not* of medieval manufacture, his own specialist field of study. Initially, he suggested that it might come from the Renaissance period, c. 1400–1500s, even though it was not in the usual 'high-art style' of the time. Yet this realisation made him suddenly revise his opinions and admit that the cup could well be part of what he termed a 'folkloric tradition', in that it was made to a pattern and style kept alive by indigenous societies across hundreds if not thousands of years. This meant that the vessel could have been manufactured anywhere, and be of any age.

These assessments of the Marian Chalice were useful, though quite naturally disappointing. They blatantly contradicted what Dr Keeble had emphatically stated with regards to the antiquity of the tiny vessel. So who was right? Was it fashioned for use as a scent or perfume jar in Egypt or the Near East in Roman times, or, alternatively, was it of more recent manufacture, perhaps part of a 'folkloric tradition' of unknown origin?

In the knowledge that Graham had himself taken the Marian Chalice to the British Museum and been told by an unnamed expert that it was a Roman scent jar, I tended to favour Mary's analysis, especially as she had known nothing about the vessel when it was presented to her for the first time. However, I was obviously biased in this respect, since I wanted to explore the cup's possible links with the Magdalene's *alabastron*, used in the anointing of Jesus. Yet setting aside the uncertainty surrounding the cup's age, other hurdles needed first to be overcome, starting with the fact that the Gospels refer to the vessel Mary used as an *alabastron*, which in the King James Bible is translated as 'alabaster cruse'.[477] Such a description implies that the vase or jar in question was fashioned out of alabaster, a calcite-based stone used extensively in ancient Egypt to manufacture jars and vases, hence the name *alabastron* given to such vessels. If the Marian Chalice is made of onyx, could this enormous discrepancy be overcome in some way?

The answer to this question was quite definitely yes, for just as all carpet cleaners became known as Hoovers, after the name of the company that patented the original design, the term *alabastron* came to apply to any scent jar, whether stoneware, glass, metal or faïence. Furthermore, in Roman times there was great confusion between onyx and alabaster, for, as Pliny the Younger, the first-century naturalist, wrote with respect to 'onyx marble':[478]

> This stone is sometimes called 'alabastrites', for it is hollowed out to be used also as unguent jars because it is said to be the best means of keeping unguents fresh.[479]

This might initially suggest that *alabastrites* was a form of quartz-based onyx as opposed to a calcite-based alabaster. However, the term *alabastrites* generally applies to a substance known as Oriental alabaster, which is a translucent marble (calcium carbonate) that comes from stalagmites and other layered calcite deposits forming in caves, and is also known as travertine. Like onyx, it has distinctive colour banding, usually white, green and honey-brown, hence the fact that it is also referred to as onyx marble, alabaster onyx and, quite erroneously, just onyx. Pliny records that in the ancient world it was mined in the neighbourhood of Thebes in Upper Egypt, Damascus in Syria, Carmania in Persia, Cappadocia in Asia Minor as well as in India.[480] Most of these sources produce the white or honey-coloured forms, and not the green variety, which is infinitely rarer and today is mined only in Pakistan, South Africa and on the Sinai–Jordan border area.[481]

The *Vita Beatae Mariae Magdalenae* ('Life of the Blessed Mary Magdalene'), written in France c. 1150, says that the Magdalene's unguent jar was fashioned from 'Indian alabaster, which is a kind of white marble streaked with various colours'.[482] Why the author of this work should have believed it to be made of this particular stone, surely a reference to Oriental alabaster, i.e. onyx marble, is unclear, unless he had some specific knowledge about a holy relic thought to be Mary's *alabastron*. Perhaps there was a connection here with the alabaster flask of Holy Blood – said to have been collected by the Magdalene and seen to liquefy every Good Friday – housed in the Basilique de Sainte Marie Madeleine at St Maximin, Provence. Was this thought to be the vessel that Mary had earlier used when anointing the head and/or feet of Jesus with spikenard? The church of St Victor at Marseilles in southern France did actually claim to possess the true *alabastron*, yet I was unable to establish what it was made from.[483]

Although there was nothing in the Gospels to say exactly what Mary's *alabastron* might have been made from, there is every indication that, by medieval times at least, it was thought to have been manufactured from a type of alabaster, possibly onyx marble, and not genuine onyx. It was an awkward realisation, yet one which convinced me that at some point in the future I would need some expert advice in order to finally determine the type of stone used to fashion the Marian Chalice.

Another problem with drawing comparisons between the Marian Chalice and Mary's *alabastron* is that John's Gospel tells us that she 'took a pound of ointment of spikenard, very precious, and anointed the feet of Jesus, and wiped his feet with her hair: and the house was filled with the odour of the ointment.'[484] If this quote is factually accurate, it means that the Marian Chalice cannot be the same *alabastron*, since it could never hold 'a pound of ointment', with a pound being a Roman 'pound' of twelve ounces. This is a problem; yet there is no mention in any of the three Synoptic Gospels of exactly how much spikenard was used to anoint Jesus. Since John's Gospel was not formulated in its present form until at least the last decade of the first century AD, twenty or so years after Mark, it is possible that the story had become exaggerated among the Johannine community who saw the Beloved Disciple/John the Evangelist as their founder. As I had already determined, spikenard is a very expensive oriental spice likely to have been sold in small vases or jars, quite plausibly no larger than the Marian Chalice.

ORIENTAL EMPORIUM

In spite of the doubts cast on the antiquity of the Marian Chalice by experts from the British Museum, the thought that it could have been manufactured in Egypt or the Near East during Roman times made me recall the dream in which I found myself at the site of a fourth-century church in the Egyptian Sinai. I had identified it as the Flousseya church at el-Zaraniq, 37 kilometres (23 miles) west of el-Arish, close to the town of Magdolum, which I now felt was the ancestral home of Mary Magdalene. What is more, I connected the site with the Magdalene's *alabastron*, and so Dr Keeble's comments on the origins of the green stone cup made me wonder whether it might have been manufactured locally. To this end, I rechecked the history of el-Arish, which in Roman times was known as Rhinocoloura, and found that according to the Greek geographer Strabo (60 BC–AD 20) this fortified town was a major emporium for merchandise arriving from India and Arabia via Leuce Come on the eastern shore of the Red Sea and Petra in nearby Jordan.[485]

It was tantalising to contemplate the possibility that the spikenard used by Mary Magdalene was imported into Rhinocoloura from India. Could it have been transferred to an *alabastron* of local manufacture for sale on the open market, or was there a possibility that the unguent jar came from India, along with the spikenard? Such thoughts would have to be put aside until better evidence emerged to support the view that Mary Magdalene had indeed come originally from Egypt, and not from the village called Magdala on Lake Tiberius in what was formerly the Roman province of Galilee.

THOMAS WRIGHT OF LUDLOW

Little more could be said about the Marian Chalice's apparent antiquity, and so I next concentrated my efforts on the story surrounding its rediscovery at Hawkstone Park. According to Roger Whitehouse, the park's spokesman on the estate's history, this occurred during the First World War when the house was being used as a prisoner-of-war camp. One day in 1917, some prisoners were helping local builder Walter Langham to carry out restoration work inside the caves. On moving the statue of the eagle from its position in a room known as the Grotto, the cup came into view and, without realising its possible significance, Langham decided to keep it for himself.

Since Graham believed that the Grail romances alluded to events in British Dark Age history, and thus implied that the Holy Grail had reached the Welsh Marches, the existence of the Marian Chalice led him to establish a genealogical solution to explain how it came to be hidden at Hawkstone Park. In his book *The Search for the Grail*, published in 1995, Graham cited familial successions that stretched from the age of King Arthur through to the medieval folk hero Fulk Fitz Warine of Whittington and Robert Vernon, the owner in Elizabethan times of nearby Hodnet Hall. Graham proposed that the cup had remained in Vernon's family until the nineteenth century when it passed into the hands of Thomas Wright of Ludlow (1810–77), whom he put forward as the person responsible for concealing it at Hawkstone Park.

Wright was a well-known Shropshire antiquarian and writer on historical and literary topics, who is said to have taken a keen interest in Hawkstone Park.[486] He attended Trinity College, Cambridge, and after graduating became a writer for *The Gentleman's Magazine*. He went on to found the British Archaeological Association, and was a prominent member of many other learned societies both in Great Britain and abroad, including the Druid-influenced Society of Antiquaries. In 1859 he became superintendent of excavations at the Romano-British city of Viroconium at Wroxeter, near Shrewsbury, and then moved to London where, after a prolific life writing dozens of books, he died in his sixty-seventh year.

For reasons outlined in this book, I do not believe that any physical artefact which might have come to be termed the Holy Grail was ever connected with the King Arthur of history, and to me there had to be another means to explain how the Marian Chalice came to be deposited where it was. Thomas Wright's suggested involvement in this affair was extremely tempting, especially as I knew he possessed a keen interest in the history of witchcraft and the occult, and in 1865 wrote and published a major work on sexual rites and symbolism in ancient worship, which included a lengthy discourse on the religious beliefs of the Knights Templar. Yet even if Wright did possess the Marian Chalice, how exactly might he have come to conceal it in a cave complex situated on private property?

The caves of Grotto Hill, as it is known, are thought to have been created when the Romans began extracting a copper ore known as malachite from the rocky outcrop's soft white sandstone. Thereafter the caves were abandoned, but under Sir Rowland Hill (1705–1783) the tunnels were enlarged and converted into a series of rooms divided by pillars and arches and decorated with shells and crystal work. They were given names such as the 'Labyrinth' and the 'Grotto', with a new stairway being cut up to the cave's entrance. This great engineering feat was certainly completed by 1774, for it was then that Dr Samuel Johnson records a visit up the steep flight of steps to see the newly opened Grotto.[487]

Between 1824 and 1875 Hawkstone Park was in the hands of Sir Rowland Hill (1800–75), 2nd Viscount Hill, who inherited the estate from his grandfather Sir John Hill (whose son and heir had died in 1814). He must have been in on whatever was happening in the caves, otherwise the whole connection with Thomas Wright makes no sense whatsoever.

MASONIC HERALDRY

Next, there is the problem of the statues of the four Tetramorphs, or Evangelical symbols – when and how they reached the caves at Hawkstone Park is not recorded. Since the publication of Graham Phillip's book in 1995, the owners of Hawkstone Park have identified fragments of two out of four of the statues, the eagle and the lion. They are to be found in the caves, although neither are currently on display. So finely worked are they that some experts now believe that they are medieval in origin and were brought to the park from a nearby ecclesiastical ruin, where they might have served as corner stones on a tomb.[488] If so, then somebody must have decided that they would look good inside the Grotto, yet was this the only reason for this immense amount of effort?

In my opinion, placing statues of the Tetramorphs within a darkened cave grotto in the middle of a remotely placed rocky outcrop smacked of unorthodox religious activity. I thus set about researching the usage of the evangelical symbols in a religious context, and was intrigued to discover that the Evangelists feature in the symbolism of nineteenth-century Rosicrucian (or Rose-Croix) lodges, where banners bearing one each of the four symbols were hung in the corners of the room.[489] The four evangelical symbols also play an important role in Masonic heraldry. They feature in the coat of arms for the Grand Lodge of England (known as 'the Ancients') unveiled in 1764, as well as in those of other Grand Lodges, such as the Grand Lodge of Ireland.[490] In the case of the Ancients, they retained the use of these arms until 1813 when the Grand Lodge of England merged with its rival the Grand Lodge of London ('the Moderns') to form the United Grand Lodge. Thereafter the two separate coats of arms were squeezed together to form one single emblem which remains in use today. Although the lion, bull, eagle and man in this context do represent the Evangelists, they also signify the four elements as well as four of the twelve tribes of Israel: Judah, Ephraim, Dan and Reuben.[491]

ST JOHN'S EAGLE

In addition to these facts, the eagle itself is particularly important to certain branches of Freemasonry. For instance, one of the jewels of the Rose-Croix

(Rose Cross) degree shows an eagle with outstretched wings at the foot of the Cross, the position at which St John remained during the Crucifixion.[492] Furthermore, the eagle of St John is also an important symbol for a subsidiary order of Masonry known as the Order of the Holy Sepulchre and of St John the Evangelist. Although only instituted at the beginning of the nineteenth century, tradition asserts that it was founded by St Helen following her discovery of the True Cross in 326.[493]

Beyond any of this was the sheer fact that John the Evangelist was revered as the founder of neo-Templarism and Freemasonry. Moreover, through his identity as the Beloved Disciple, St John was associated with the Magdalene whose *alabastron*, I believe, merged with the memory of the Bitter Cup, the communion cup of the Paschal vigils used by the earliest Christians, to become St John's Gnostic Grail. Thus to find a green stone cup linked with the Magdalene's *alabastron* within the statue of an eagle symbolising John the Evangelist was almost certainly no coincidence. It had to have been knowledge understood by those responsible for concealing the vessel in the first place, strongly suggesting therefore that they were part of the underground stream, and were very likely neo-Templars, Rosicrucians or Freemasons with unorthodox religious views.

NEO-PAGAN CELEBRATIONS

Much has been written on the mystery of Hawkstone Park – its links with King Arthur, the Holy Grail, the Knights Templar, Freemasons, and even Rennes-le-Château. Almost all of this material post-dates the publication of Graham Phillips' book. However, there are certain connections that do seem to make sense, and one is the relationship between the Hill family of Hawkstone Park and the Anson family of Shugborough Hall in neighbouring Staffordshire. Most significantly, Sir Rowland Hill, 2nd Viscount Hill (1800-75), MP for Shropshire North, was a friend and colleague of Sir George Anson, (1769–1849), MP for Lichfield.

The Anson family, as I knew, were linked with both the mystery of Rennes-le-Château and Templarism through the presence at Shugborough of the Shepherd's Monument and the Cat Monument, both of which were designed by Thomas Wright of Durham, the namesake of the much later Thomas Wright of Ludlow. Could there have been some bond of friendship between Thomas Anson, the owner of Shugborough at the time these two monuments were commissioned, and the Hill family of Hawkstone Park?

Nothing is certain. Yet as with St Clement's Caves, Hastings, rumours abound concerning the strange activities which allegedly took place inside the caves at Hawkstone Park. In my opinion, the Grotto could once have been used for neo-pagan celebrations of a type very common to high society in the eighteenth century (and exemplified by Francis Dashwood's Hellfire Club). However, it seems unlikely that any more serious unorthodox religious activity could have taken place there until the estate came into the possession of either John Hill in 1808 or, more likely, Sir Rowland Hill, 2nd Viscount Hill, who inherited Hawkstone in 1824. Prior to this time the estate had been the possession of Sir

Richard Hill, 2nd Baronet (1732–1808), who was an enthusiastic promoter and defender of Calvinistic Methodism.

THE STORY SO FAR

Yet if this was so, what exactly was going on at Hawkstone Park? How did a small green stone cup, which just might be a Roman scent jar fashioned in Egypt or the Near East, come to be concealed behind a statue representing John the Evangelist located inside one of its caves? To me, the most likely explanation is that it was purchased by a wealthy European whilst on a Grand Tour of the Holy Land. Perhaps it was sold to him as a religious relic, leading to its perceived significance drawing the interest of those who held unorthodox religious ideals, most probably neo-Templars or Rosicrucians on the Continent.[494] They then procured it for their own purposes, and for a brief time it came to symbolise an object of mystical significance. Then internal politics may have caused some kind of schism within the organisation, whereby two rival factions emerged, both claiming it as their own. In the end it was spirited away to Hawkstone Park, and deposited there for safekeeping.

It seems unlikely that the Marian Chalice was in circulation prior to the eighteenth century, simply because if it *was* revered as a holy relic, then there would be some notice of its existence, and this does not appear to have been the case. The argument against this supposition is the repeated references in medieval legend to the so-called Emerald Cup, fashioned from a stone that fell from Lucifer's crown during his struggle with the archangel Michael at the time of the war in heaven. It was this story that inspired the story of the *Lapsit exillis*, the small stone Grail alluded to in the German romances, said to have been guarded by Templars in the Castle of the Grail. Was this same vessel being alluded to by Jacobus de Voragine when recording in his *Chronicon Januense,* c. 1277, that a 'certain vessel of emerald (*vase emeraldino*)' present at the Last Supper was taken by Nicodemus and used by him to collect 'the sacred gore which was still moist, and which had been ignominiously spilled about'?[495] Even though there is a good chance that this story was influenced by the existence of the *Sacro Catino* at Genoa, long held to be fashioned from a single emerald, it might also preserve the opinion that the Grail cup was originally emerald-like in colour and appearance.

Even though the Marian Chalice was definitely not fashioned from emerald, there remained the possibility that it was linked in some way with the legend of the Emerald Cup of Lucifer. This assumption makes sense in the knowledge that by medieval times the Magdalene's *alabastron* was thought to have been fashioned from Oriental alabaster, or onyx marble, plausibly a variety with green banding. On the other hand, maybe Graham was right, and the vessel had been in circulation in and around Shropshire since the age of King Arthur, and did indeed contribute to the belief that the Holy Grail was once to be found in the Welsh Marches.

Whatever the real answer, and perhaps it is none of these possibilities, there seems no escaping the fact that those who finally concealed the Marian Chalice were associated with some kind of unorthodox religious group or organisation. Nobody else would have been interested in preserving the spiritual potency of such a simple-looking object. So why place it behind a statue of an eagle representing John the Evangelist? Firstly, if these individuals did associate the cup with the Magdalene's *alabastron*, then perhaps they were privy to the knowledge that some part of her life merged with that of St John to form the more-or-less androgynous figure of Christian art based on the Beloved Disciple. Thus to bring the holy vessel under the protection of the eagle of St John would have made total sense.

As to who concealed it, the only name on the table is Thomas Wright of Ludlow, who, I discovered, was a friend of Baron Edward George Earl Bulwer-Lytton (1803–73),[496] the well-known Victorian novelist, poet, mystic, Freemason, and suspected Rosicrucian and ritual magician. Lord Lytton was also a long-time friend of French occultist Eliphas Levi, who famously conjured the spirit of Apollonius of Tyana, a wizard of antiquity, on his initial visit to London to see Lytton in 1854.[497] Levi returned to London again in 1861, this time staying for a while at Lytton's country seat at Knebworth House in Hertfordshire.

Despite his friendship with Lord Lytton, there is evidence only of Wright's interest in the *history* of the occult, witchcraft, sexual worship and Templarism, and of his visits to Hawkstone Park, not that he practised what he wrote about, or that he ever shared a conversation with Eliphas Levi, despite the Frenchman's great interest in Baphomet and the mystery of the Knights Templar. On the other hand, in Wright's two-volume *Narratives of Sorcery and Magic*, published in 1851, he had this to say about the belief in spirit realms beyond that of our own:

'It was founded on the . . . creed, that, besides our own visible existence, we live in an invisible world of spiritual beings, by which our actions and even our thoughts are often guided, and which have a certain degree of power over the elements and over the ordinary course of organic life.'[498]

Such words might well sum up the views of a modern-day psychic quester. And on the question of controlling that supernatural power, Wright wrote in the same book:

'The magician differed from the witch in this, that, while the latter was an ignorant instrument in the hands of the demons, the former had become their master by the powerful intermediation of a science which was only within reach of the few, and which these beings were unable to disobey.'[499]

Although considered a sceptic of such idle practices, did Thomas Wright himself practice the occult, or spiritualism at least? If he did, then it would make better sense of why he might have been responsible for concealing the Marian Chalice at Hawkstone Park.

One more question remained: why Hawkstone Park? The answer is probably quite simple. Firstly, there was a strong tradition linking the Welsh Marches with stories taken from the Arthurian romances and, secondly, Sir Rowland Hill, 2nd Viscount Hill, was perhaps a soft touch. In this era of Enlightenment and outré societies, it is quite conceivable that he allowed trusted friends and acquaintances to conduct religious celebrations in the caves of Grotto Hill, without realising the full seriousness of these activities.

It is my opinion that sometime during the mid-nineteenth century those who possessed the Marian Chalice brought it to Hawkstone Park and conducted an empowering ritual with the intention that it would forever remain concealed under the protection of John the Evangelist. However, they could never have anticipated that less than a century later a builder would find the cup by chance. Certainly, this is the way it would seem to have happened, and until such time as further evidence emerges concerning how exactly the Marian Chalice came to be where it was when it was found, then its very existence is enough to make it an enigma of our time.

23. THE THREE CROWNS

It was another quest, this time in Oxfordshire, and Sue, Richard and I were in a small town next to the River Thames. Having already examined some sites locally, we stopped off at the medieval parish church, which seemed important somehow. There were minor items of interest inside, but finding nothing that might help us further, we journeyed on to one final site. Taking the road out of town, the car travelled a short distance towards the base of the Chiltern Hills, before coming to a halt once more.

Leaving the vehicle, our party of three ascended a bare, exposed hill that overlooked the Thames Valley, right across to the White Horse Hills in neighbouring Berkshire. As dusk fell, we reached our destination – an ancient earthwork, something like an encampment or ditch, on the edge of a wooded environment. Here we encountered the spirit form of a man dressed in dark-grey sackcloth, with a cowl that covered his face and sleeves that hung loose from his arms. He was awaiting our presence, and although a guardian of this open and exposed landscape, he was also a king deposed, beaten in battle, doomed to forever wander the woods and forests. Only from him could we gain knowledge of a matter that still eluded us – the key to unlock the final secrets of the Grail.

THE CENTRE OF FRANCE
I awoke from the brief but specific dream with the name 'Benson' going around in my head.[500] Reaching for the map, I quickly found it was a small town, situated on the River Thames about 19 kilometres (12 miles) from Oxford, with a 900-year-old church dedicated to St Helen. Realising this made me recall the earlier dream in which I had carried a holy relic associated with the Passion from a large cathedral church located in the centre of France to a corresponding sacred centre linked with St Helen in Oxfordshire.

Although this particular dream made no sense at the time, I afterwards discovered that the cathedral church in question was almost certainly that of Saint Etienne (Stephen) in Bourges, Roman *Avaricum*, a royal city and capital of Aquitaine, located at the confluence of the Auron and the Yèvre rivers, some 200 kilometres (125 miles) south of Paris. Here, between the banks of the two rivers, an extensive Bronze Age barrow cemetery had been unearthed, showing that the city started its life as a sanctuary or enclosure of the dead. Not only does it stand at the geographical centre of France, but Bourges is also equidistant from three other French cathedrals, which form a perfect triangle around it. They are Gisors to the north, Jarnac to the southwest and Montrevel to the east, all of them with supposed links to the Knights Templar.[501]

Whether such landscape geometry was coincidence or not, certain other facts about Bourges made me research this place further. For instance, the cathedral's celebrated west entrance is exactly as I saw it, dripping with carvings of a deeply symbolic nature, while the city's most famous inhabitant was Jacques Coeur (c. 1395–1456). He was an alchemist and mystic, as well as the finance minister to Charles VII, King of France (1422–61), who ruled his kingdom from Bourges and died there on 21 July 1461, the eve of the feast of the Magdalene. Coeur left his mark on the town by commissioning literally dozens of mystically inspired carvings and reliefs that adorn various buildings.[502] He was almost certainly the 'chac', i.e. 'Jacques', alluded to in my original dream, which took place during the early hours of 22 July, the feast of Mary Magdalene 2002. That was 515 years to the day after Bourges suffered a terrible fire in 1487, which destroyed one-third of the entire city and started its economic decline. Because it occurred on 22 July, this monumental event in Bourges' history is remembered locally as *le feu de la Madeleine*, 'the fire of the Magdalene'.

What is more, the city's late-twelfth, early-thirteenth-century cathedral of Saint Etienne once boasted a number of religious relics from the time of Christ. They included, I was surprised but pleased to learn, one of the holy nails of the Passion brought back from the Holy Land by St Helen.[503] How it got there is unclear, although I was sure that this was the holy relic I had translated in my dream from Bourges to a similar sacred centre in Oxfordshire. I learned too that the city stands exactly on the Paris Meridian, which was created in the late seventeenth century by the French as a rival to Greenwich Observatory's own meridian. Although the latter was finally recognised as the International Zero Meridian, its rival is still marked on French-produced maps.

Trace the Paris Meridian northwards from Bourges and eventually it hits the church and seminary of St Sulpice, south of Paris, which have been much linked with the mystery of Rennes-le-Château. Here the priest Berenger Saunière is said to have sought assistance in order that he might decipher parchments found in the village's church of Mary Magdalene. By strange coincidence, the founder of the seminary, St Sulpice (d. 647), was originally Bishop of Bourges. Follow the Paris Meridian southwards and eventually it hits Les Pontils, the site of the Tomb of Arques, where Nicholas Poussin may well have painted his *Les Bergers d'Arcadie* in 1640. What is more, at both Bourges and St Sulpice the meridian is marked on the floor by a red copper line. Termed the russet-red line or rose line, it is phonetically reminiscent of Roseline, the name of a little-known late-thirteenth, early-fourteenth-century saint who came from the Château des Arcs in Les Arcs sur Argens, Provence, and shares her feast day of 17 January with St Sulpice.[504] As any aficionado of the Rennes-le-Château mystery will know, this single date crops up far more than it should ever do by chance alone.

Over and beyond this knowledge, I discovered that although Bourges was known in Roman times as *Avaricum*, its original Gallic name was *Biturix*, from which the modern Bourges derives. *Biturix* was the legendary ancestor of the *Bituriges*, a Celtic tribe that inhabited this area of Aquitaine, and saw the city of the same name as their capital. *Biturix* derives from *bitu*, meaning 'world' and 'time', and *rix* or *ri*, meaning 'king', thus *Biturix* was quite literally the 'king of

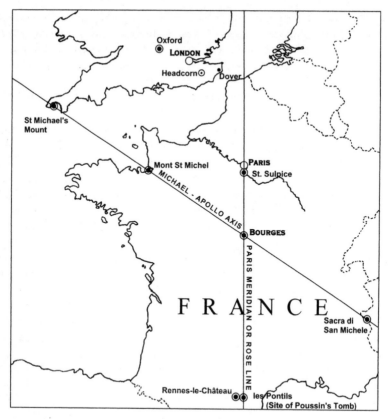

Fig. 9. Bourges, the centre of France, and its relationship to the St Michael-Apollo Axis and Paris Meridian, also known as the Rose Line.

the world' (or even the 'ruler of time'). These are all key etymological elements that one might expect to find attached to a sacred centre of a country, seen by its indigenous Celtic peoples as the dead centre not just of France, but of the whole world. In this role, Bourges would have been venerated as a pivot or cosmic axis, symbolised by the royal seat of the 'king of the world', around which revolved the starry firmament, its rhythmic movement regulating the passage of time.[505]

Bourges was once seen as crucial to the cosmic harmony of France's spiritual dimension, of this there can be no doubt. Yet its influence extended far beyond the boundaries of one country alone, for it falls precisely on the so-called St Michael-Apollo axis provisionally discovered by French scholar Jean Richer during the 1950s. This long-distance corridor of sacred places begins at Skellig Michael in Ireland and extends at an angle of virtually 120° East of North to strike St Michael's Mount, Cornwall; Mont St Michel, Brittany; the city of Bourges; and the mountaintop monastery of Sagra dei Michele at Piedmont in northwest Italy. It then aligns with various key sanctuaries and oracle sites in

Greece, including Delphi, Athens, Delos and Lindos, before continuing on to Mount Carmel in northern Israel.[506] Curiously, it was as a direct result of a dream that Jean Richer discovered the axis of the St Michael-Apollo line, and so I felt privileged that Bourges was first introduced to my psyche by exactly the same means.

CYNEWULF'S GRIEF

I had thought no more about the Bourges dream until this latest nocturnal manifestation, which highlighted the significance of St Helen's church, Benson, and led me to more closely research the town's history. According to *The Anglo-Saxon Chronicle*, battles have twice taken place at Benson due to its strategic importance as a crossing point on the River Thames, as well as the fact that it was the royal seat of a West Saxon tribe known as the Gewassae. They were kings of Wessex from the sixth century through until the end of the eighth century. The first battle of Benson occurred in 571,[507] while the second took place in 777/779 between two great opponents – Cynewulf, King of Wessex, and Offa, King of Mercia, with Mercia being an enormous Saxon kingdom that embraced the whole of the Midlands and stretched from the borders of Wales to the Home Counties.[508] In the ensuing Battle of Bensington, as Benson was anciently known, Cynewulf was defeated, losing his seat of power to Offa, who went on to conquer the whole of Berkshire, even pushing his way as far south as London. *The Anglo-Saxon Chronicle* relates how Cynewulf lived on for another six years, desperately trying to keep control of his kingdom, until, finally, he was ambushed and killed by Cyneheard, the brother of Sigeberht, a king he had deposed in 755/757.[509]

Cynewulf was the wandering king I had glimpsed in my dream, I felt sure of it. Yet where exactly was he to be found? I knew the hill and earthworks I had seen were southeast of Benson, so I grabbed a map and followed the roads out of the town. I soon came across the small village of Nuffield, marked with a spot height of 666 feet (203 metres). Its tiny church is Norman in origin with an older Saxon font still in place. More significantly, I saw that just to its south was the termination of a local section of Grim's Ditch, a linear earthwork of Iron Age origin found in various parts of the county. When the Anglo-Saxons overran the region they encountered these mysterious earthworks, and decided to name them after Grim, from *grimr*, 'devil', which was a nickname for Woden, a Saxon god of fury, war and death, who also governed poetry, wisdom and speech. Grim was the 'hooded' or 'masked' one, a reference to the fact that in this guise he would wander the woods and forests dressed as a lowly traveller, rewarding those who gave him food and shelter and punishing those who did not. No better archetypal form could there be for a deposed Saxon king, seen to be forever wandering the woods and forests.

GRIM'S DITCH

Unable to hold ourselves back any longer, Sue and I made the decision to visit the church of St Helen at Benson on the way home from a trip to

Glastonbury.[510] As in the dream, too much had changed both with respect to its situation on a busy road and its architectural features for there to be any obvious clues regarding its past significance. Therefore, as the light slowly faded, we moved on to Nuffield church. Here just two things drew our attention – an east window showing a pelican feeding its young with blood from its own breast (a symbol of the Rose-Croix degree in the Ancient and Accepted Rite of Freemasonry), and the beautiful Saxon font, which was found to bear a cryptic inscription, which read: 'Go and wash in a sacred place. Either *grace* cleanses the whole or washing by the font is not complete [author's emphasis]'. In early Christian Gnostic tradition, 'grace' (*charis*) was an epithet of Sophia, female wisdom. It also signified the Mercy of God, which was seen to descend upon a follower of Christ, like the dove of the Holy Spirit. The font's strange quotation so baffled me that I quickly became convinced that it alluded to the presence locally of a sacred spring or holy well, which, for some reason, we would now have to find. The thought was so strong that it would not leave me.

To the south of Nuffield's little church are woods that conceal Grim's Ditch, which we reached along a muddy footpath that skirted a ploughed field. As darkness fell, we sat beneath a tree and waited for something to happen. Very quickly, images of the Saxon king flashed into my mind. He stood around thirty metres away and was as I had seen him previously, dressed in a charcoal-grey sackcloth robe and cowl. Yet this time he held a tall wooden staff in one hand, confirming his personification as Grim. He actually said nothing, and instead there was just a sequence of strange thoughts. I saw an image of the letter Y, which suddenly started spinning to become a triskelion, like the national emblem of the Isle of Man. It then transformed into three female heads contained in a circle located at the centre of a huge landscape design. They signified some kind of three-fold personification of St Helen; why exactly, I could not be sure, although somehow I knew they represented the holy well I felt existed locally, and which Cynewulf and the Saxon font had been here to guide us towards.

THREE HEADS IN THE WELL

Back in Leigh-on-Sea, the striking image of the three female heads lingered. What possible connection might they have either to holy wells, St Helen or, indeed, the truth of the Grail? I mentioned the fact to Richard on a brief visit to the flat, and he provided a crucial answer.[511]

'What about the legend concerning the three heads in the well,' he offered, as I made some tea in the kitchen. 'That features St Helen, and even though I think it's recorded in Essex folklore, I'm not sure that it actually relates to Essex itself. It could be Oxfordshire.'

I needed to know more. Were they female heads?

'No, they were the heads of three kings,' he responded, 'but the symbolism could be what's important here. I'll dig out a book I've got with it in. See what that says.'

A few days later Richard presented me with photocopies of the legend extracted from *Tales of Old Essex*, by Adrian Gray.[512] Helen, the future saint, it says, was the daughter of King Coel, a legendary ruler of Colchester, which was an ancient seat of kingship in north Essex. Having watched his queen die, and finding that he had no more money to fight wars, Coel decided to marry a rich – though very ugly – widow who had an equally unsightly daughter with a club foot. Before long the old woman poisoned Coel against his daughter, since she knew that with Helen out of the way her own daughter would be heir to the throne.

Consequently, the young princess was forced to leave her father's castle and seek her fortune elsewhere. After a while, she came across an old hermit by the roadside, with whom she decided to share her packed lunch. By way of a reward, he offered her some wisdom. He told her that she would soon come across a hedge, which if she tried to pass through would rip her clothes and skin. To go beyond it she would require a wand – which he promptly produced and gave to her. With this, she was to tap the hedge three times, and then ask for her safety to be ensured. On the other side, she would find a well. Here she should sit on the edge and watch as, one by one, three heads of three kings would emerge into view.

Thanking the hermit, she continued on her journey and very shortly encountered the hedge, which she tapped three times with the wand, and passed beyond unharmed, only to find the aforementioned well on the other side. One by one, the heads emerged, each king asking her if she would wash and comb them, and then place them down on the bank to dry. She complies with their wishes, and afterwards they consulted each other to agree on how best to reward the princess. The first head announced that it would increase her beauty, the second said it would make her body and breath smell even sweeter, while the third ensured her good fortune and predicted that she would marry the noblest prince in the land. They then asked her if she would be so kind as to replace them in the water.

The story continues with what happens after King Coel finds out that his daughter is to marry, and how his rich wife responds by sending her own daughter off to seek her fortune. This unfortunate girl fails to give the hermit any of her food when she meets him, and so rips her skin and clothes when she tries to pass through the hedge, after which she abuses the heads in the well by hitting them with a bottle of sherry! Consequently, she is made even more hideous than before, despite a cobbler taking pity on the girl and curing some of her ailments in exchange for her hand in marriage.

Richard waited for me to finish reading the piece before delivering his own verdict. 'Although the heads in the story were those of kings and not women, their connection with the well suggests you are right, and that the sacred centre in Oxfordshire really is a holy well. Perhaps it's the well of the story.'

The legend spoke clearly of the well with the three heads being an oracle site where the fate of the princess and thus the kingdom were decided, and to me this indicated that the story related to the concept of kingship, and its inextricable link to the harmony of the land through the king and his heir's right to rule. It was also worth recalling that according to Christian legend, on her trip to the Holy Land, St Helen discovered not only the True Cross and the nails of the Passion, but also the crowned heads of the three Magi. These she carried back to Europe and presented to the cathedral at Cologne in Germany. Because the Magi are said to have seen the coming of Jesus Christ in the stars, Helen – plausibly an ancient British deity associated with the divine light and the fecundity of the land – thus became associated with not just the symbol of the Three Crowns but also the concept of divine kingship.

Once again, we were now touching on a subject integral to the story of the Holy Grail, especially the idea that by understanding the nature of this vessel, i.e. asking the right questions, the Fisher King would be healed of his wound and the spell holding the country in a state of enchantment would be lifted. Did we have to do something with the Marian Chalice – like take it to this holy well for some reason?

Once more, my mind found itself returning to the question: 'Whom serves the Grail?' Initially, I had thought the answer to be the king and the land, but after failing to gain the Grail cup at Headcorn I had discarded this solution as at best inadequate. Perhaps it had not been so wrong after all, and there was some clue here linking places of ancient sovereignty, such as Headcorn, Bourges and this holy site in Oxfordshire, with the seat not just of kings, but also of the Grail itself.

Richard listened to my musings, but wanted to add something: 'The symbol of the Three Crowns in Britain definitely signified kingship, as well as divine sovereignty. Also, don't forget, it was through the de Vere family that Oxford University adopted the Three Crowns as part of its arms, linking the symbol with that area of the country.'

Richard, I knew, had done a considerable amount of research into the mystery of the Three Crowns. I also felt it worth pointing out that someone in medieval times deemed that King Arthur's own heraldic device should be the Three Crowns, probably because he was seen as an idealistic king, following his defeat of the Saxons on various occasions. Yet none of this helped us locate the holy well suspected of being a sacred centre of England, so later that evening Sue, Richard and I attempted to pick up more information on the subject.[513] Various images, some not particularly helpful to the immediate situation, invaded our thoughts, until finally I saw a chasm opening in the ground, and something dark and black oozing forth, almost like crude oil. I felt I was seeing the holy well, although I could not be sure.

'I can see the well, now,' Richard confirmed, his voice emerging out of the darkness of the room. 'There's a dragon link, somehow. I think I've been here before, when I was researching the Three Crowns stuff with Yuri.'

Yuri was Yuri Leitch, our friend from Glastonbury, who had made the remarkable observations about the Grail in connection with the Franks Casket.

'It's St Margaret's Well, Binsey,' he said, as if relieved by this sudden realisation.

Binsey's holy well had been on my mind for some days, although I assumed this was because it was the only one I could think of in Oxfordshire. I had never been there before, and certainly knew no details about it.

Excited now, I reached for a copy of Robert Charles Hope's classic work *The Legendary Lore of the Holy Wells of England*, published in 1893, and read its entry for Binsey. It said that its well, dedicated to St Margaret, lay three yards from the edge of St Margaret's church, situated just two miles (three kilometres) outside of Oxford.

'It's at the end of a long lane, which is near Oxford train station,' Richard interrupted. 'There's a good pub before you reach the church called The Perch Inn, if I remember correctly. But the whole place is strangely out in the wilds – a mile or so from anywhere, even though it is so close to the city.'

BINSEY'S HOLY WELL

The book said that the spring was enclosed in stone. Five steps led down to an arched vault within which was a round basin containing the holy water. Apparently, a relief in stone showing St Margaret was to be found there until 1639, when it was destroyed by Puritans who thought it somewhat unfashionable to venerate holy wells.[514] Despite this, people would still come here to pray for cures or 'to ease their burdened soules and obtain resolutions of their doubts, as they would to an oracle'.[515]

This last statement reminded me of the story of St Helen and the three heads in the well, and how they were seen to be oracular. It occurred to me that there were other stories of heads emerging from wells in an oracular fashion in other parts of the country, while still others were associated with triple-aspected female guardian spirits. Indeed, a mezzotint plate in Hope's book shows a stone panel found close to Coventina's Well at Carrawbrough, at the base of Hadrian's Wall in Scotland. It depicts three 'naiads' (water-dwelling nymphs), possibly representing different forms of Coventina, the Roman deity to whom the well was dedicated.[516] Each naiad raises in one hand a wine-goblet, and in the other a flagon, from which water is being poured. Perhaps the guardian of Binsey's holy well was originally a triple-aspected goddess. Indeed, it might be argued that it was Helen herself, for there are various St Helen's Well's in England (indeed, more than any divinity other than 'Our Lady'[517]). Moreover, many of these springs – particularly those in the Celtic regions – were formally just Elen's Well, an allusion to Elen of the Hosts, or Elen of the Legions, a beautiful woman featured in 'The Dream of Maxen Wledig', found in the collection of medieval Welsh texts known as *The Mabinogion*.[518]

In the story, the Roman Emperor Maxen Wledig – thought to be based on Magnus Maximus, a Roman general serving in Britain who was proclaimed Emperor by his legionaries in 383 – dreams about Elen, and makes every effort to find her. She is said to have ordered the building of roads from one end of Britain to the other, the reason why there exist various 'Sarn Elen' roads in Wales. As a goddess symbolising the waters of life and the fecundity of the land, Elen has her own representation local to Binsey in the form of a so-called

Sheela-na-gig statue, a crude carving of a naked woman pulling open her genitalia, located in St Michael's church, Oxford. Such carvings are perhaps an archaic form of the goddess of sex and love, the precursor of Venus, Babalon and, of course, the Magdalene. Another example of a Sheela-na-gig statue is to be seen in Colchester Museum in Essex, the legendary home of Old King Coel and his daughter Helen. Running up the carving's right leg is the word 'Elui', coming from the root *el*, as in *elf*, which means 'light', 'god' or 'angel' in various Indo-European languages, and from which the name Elen almost certainly derives.

Yet Hope's book makes it clear that the well at Binsey is dedicated not to St Helen, but to St Margaret of Antioch, whose cult reached England following the Norman Conquest of 1066. In legend, she was the daughter of a pagan priest who lived during the reign of Diocletian, Emperor of Rome (284–313), one of the last persecutors of the Christians. According to her legend, Margaret was forced to flee after she received advances from the prefect Olybrius, who afterwards denounced her as a Christian. Consequently, she underwent various tortures, including being swallowed by Satan in the form of a dragon, before she was finally beheaded – sacred heads and beheadings being a common feature in British well lore.

The only explanation Hope provides as to how St Margaret might have become patroness of the well is that the church itself was already dedicated to St Margaret. However, this has to be a chicken-and-egg situation. Which came first – the well or the church, and if it was the well then surely this would have decided the dedication of the church. Complicating matters still further is the fact that St Margaret, as guardian of the holy well, has competition in the form of a Saxon saint named Frideswide (680–735), the patroness of Oxford, whose story is indelibly linked with that of Binsey.

24. ANGEL OF THE PIT

St Frideswide was a princess, the daughter of King Didan, or Dydda, who ruled Wessex from his seat in Oxford sometime during the mid-seventh century. He was thus most probably a leader of the Gawassae tribe, and an ancestor of Cynewulf. Didan would also have been a sub-king of the kingdom of Mercia, which lost and gained possession of this region on various occasions. It is said that Frideswide was asked to become the wife of a Mercian prince named Aelfgar, most probably to seal an alliance between Wessex and Mercia. However, because she had already taken the vows of a nun, and lived in a nunnery founded by her father in Oxford, she refused his advances. Aelfgar was obviously not amused, and tried his hardest to convince her that they should marry. Knowing that she might now be forced to submit to her suitor, Frideswide and two companions escaped by boat, and came eventually to a place called *Bentona* (not to be confused with Benson), or *Thornbury,* accepted by Oxfordians to be Binsey, although contested by others. Here Frideswide founded a chapel, and begged God to send her water. He obliged by making a spring gush forth from the ground. For three years, the three women lived off the land, drinking the well water, and dedicating their lives to the scriptures. Eventually, however, Aelfgar learned where she had retreated to and went after her, but as he approached her encampment the Mercian prince was struck blind. However, Frideswide took pity on him and said she would cure his blindness, if he left her alone. Aelfgar accepted her offer, and so she then took some holy water into her hands and placed it on his eyes, curing him on the spot. Frideswide later returned to the nunnery at Oxford, which eventually became St Frideswide's Priory. Today it no longer exists, although built on the site is Christchurch cathedral, where the saint's remains rest beneath a floor slab that marks her grave, close to which, in a side chapel, is a reconstructed stone shrine in her honour.

ALICE AND THE TREACLE WELL

How St Frideswide might fit into our story remained unclear. Despite this, I did manage to pick up some rather unusual information regarding St Margaret's Well, Binsey. Firstly, and somewhat tangentially, it was the model for the 'Treacle Well' in Lewis Carroll's *Alice's Adventures in Wonderland*, first published in 1865. He chose the name because in medieval times the word 'treacle' meant an antidote to poison, thus it might be said that a treacle well was indeed a healing well. Carroll, or to give him his real name, the Rev. Charles Lutwidge Dodgson (1832–98) – who lived and studied at Oxford – featured the Treacle Well in a conversation between Alice and the Dormouse during the Mad Hatter's Tea Party:

'Once upon a time there were three little sisters,' the Dormouse began . . . 'their names were Elsie, Lacie, and Tillie; and they lived at the bottom of a well.'

'What did they live on?' said Alice, who always took a great interest in questions of eating and drinking.

'They lived on treacle,' said the Dormouse, after thinking a moment or two.

'They couldn't have done that, you know,' Alice gently remarked; 'they'd have been ill.'

'So they were,' said the Dormouse; '*very ill*.'[519]

Were the 'three little sisters' synonymous with the three female heads I saw in association with the well? Probably; however, the chances are that the Rev. Dodgson, being familiar with both the Rev. T.J. Prout, who restored the well in Victorian times, and the legend of St Frideswide, created the 'three little sisters' from the story of the Wessex princess and her two companions. Yet was his concept of the Treacle Well responsible for my own vision of the oil-like substance seen oozing out of the ground? It was possible, although there was now even better evidence to suggest that we had found the correct place . . .

THE FIGHTING DRAGONS

The Mabinogion, the collection of Welsh medieval texts, based on much earlier British stories, includes a tale called 'Lludd and Llevelys'.[520] It concerns two brothers who are said to have been the sons of Beli the Great, a legendary King of Britain. The first one, Lludd, succeeds to the throne following the death of his father, while his brother, Llevelys, becomes King of France after marrying the princess who has inherited the throne following the death of her father. Yet during Lludd's reign of Britain, the country suffers a series of plagues, or maladies, one of which is that on May-eve each year a terrible scream is heard to emit from every hearth in the land.

Not knowing what to do, Lludd sets sail for France to consult his brother about these problems. After listening to his brother's plight, the French king tells him that the piercing scream is caused by a dragon that is being attacked by a foreign dragon (representing the recent invasion of the country by a 'demon' race known as the Coranians). In order to overcome this plague Llevelys must 'cause the Island to be measured in its length and breadth, and in the place where thou dost find the exact central point, there cause a pit to be dug'.[521] Within the hole, a cauldron should be placed, and then filled with the best mead. Once this has been done, the face of the vessel is to be covered in satin. Then, on May-eve, he will see the two dragons come together overhead and fight fiercely before they fall as pigs into the cauldron, where they will drink up the mead and fall asleep. When this happens, the beasts are to be tied up in the sheet and taken away to the strongest place in his dominions, and there buried below the earth in a *kistvaen*, which is a stone-lined chamber. 'And as long as they shall bide in that strong place no plague shall come to the Island of Britain from elsewhere.'

Returning to Britain, Lludd measures the length and breadth of his realm and discovers that the 'exact central point' is *Oxford*. Here he digs a pit and fills it, as instructed, with a cauldron full of the best mead, before covering the face of the vessel with satin. On May-eve, the dragons appear overhead and fight fiercely until, finally, they grow weary and fall exhausted into the cauldron placed within the pit. As expected, they drink the mead, and fall asleep. They are then tied up in the sheet and taken away to be buried in a *kistvaen* located on a rocky hill-fort in West Wales named Dinas Emrys (which has its own legend of two dragons, one red and one white, that constantly fight against each other in a cavern beneath it). At the same time, the Coranians, the demon race that have overrun the country, are banished using a 'charmed water' prescribed by Llevelys. The tale concluded: 'And thus the fierce outcry ceased in his dominions.'

Everything seemed important about this legend, particularly the connections between the king and his sovereignty over the land, and the relationship between countrywide plagues and what went on at the sacred centre of a kingdom, in this case Oxford. The idea of two dragons coming together above an 'exact central point' of a country is echoed in the Greek myth which speaks of how, in order to find the *omphalos* (Greek for 'navel') of the world, Zeus lets fly two eagles at each end of the earth and waits to see where they meet. It turns out to be Delphi, the location of the famous oracle. Another similar story, this time featuring doves to find the dead centre of a kingdom, is told in Egyptian myth.

Above all this is the simple fact that scholars of the earth mysteries have pointed out that the pit full of mead mentioned in the story of Lludd and Llevelys could easily be a metaphor for a prominent spring, which might once have been an important Celtic religious shrine.[522] Like Bourges, Oxford lies at the confluence of two rivers, in this case the Cherwell and the Thames, where a number of Bronze Age barrows have been found, demonstrating that it was once an ancient sanctuary of the dead. According to one article consulted, Binsey was very likely a pre-Roman religious shrine located in a kind of no-man's land between the territories of three Iron Age tribes – the Dubunni, the Atrebates and the Catuvellauni.[523] Even the Christianisation of the well is attributed to a pre-existing local religious tradition concerning female 'chthonic powers' symbolised by the two dragons in 'Lludd and Llevelys',[524] as well as St Margaret's triumph over Satan in the form of a dragon. Support for such a theory comes from the recent discovery of an Iron Age or early Saxon enclosure that once surrounded Binsey's churchyard.

Over and above this is a very curious tradition concerning the ill omen that was once thought to accompany the appearance of dragons. It is found in Jacobus de Voragine's the *Golden Legend,* written in Genoa during the second half of the thirteenth century, which tells us: 'When they [the dragons] flew through the air they became impassioned and dropped their seed into the wells and the coursing waters, which brought about a year of plague.'[525] In order to combat this problem, fires constructed from animal bones were to be lit on the feast of the nativity of St John the Baptist, the smoke from which would drive away the dragons.[526] This ancient folk custom suggests that there existed in Europe in the distant past some kind of perceived inter-relationship between holy wells, the power of dragons and plagues of the land, which was so strong that midsummer fires were lit in order to prevent such supernatural-linked maladies from taking place.

For me, St Margaret's Well, Binsey, was the most likely location of the mead-filled pit at the sacred centre of Britain featured in the tale of 'Lludd and Llevelys' as found in *The Mabinogion*. This fact seemed to be confirmed by the knowledge that Oxford mimics in every respect the original foundation of Bourges, its French counterpart, which was the royal seat of the *Biturix*, the 'king of the world', or 'ruler of time'. Therefore, my dream of transferring some kind of divine power, imbued in a nail from the Passion, from one sacred place to another had to mean something, and was almost certainly related to St Helen, the Three Crowns and the seat or source of the Grail king, whatever that meant. Would we now have to take the Marian Chalice to Binsey's holy well for a ritual act reflecting divine kingship and sovereignty of the land? If so, when should this take place, and what might happen when we did? Would it provide some final clue regarding the secrets of the Grail?

KNIGHTS OF THE APOCALYPSE

More disconcerting, however, were fresh visions experienced by Richard which highlighted certain neo-Templar organisations who had, like us, found themselves in contact with the council of twelve Faceless Ones. One was the Order of the Apocalypse,[527] founded in Italy in 1693 by Agostino Gabrino, who styled himself Prince of the Septenary Number, referring to sequences of the number seven in St John's Revelations (seven hills, seven cups, seven seals, etc.).[528] It was the precursor of certain rites of Masonic Templarism, and its emblems were a blazing star and a naked sword, which its members carried around even when at work.[529] The Order aimed to defend the Church against the coming of the Antichrist, although those they chose to protect turned against them when the Order was denounced by the Inquisition as heretical in nature. It lasted, probably, through until the middle of the eighteenth century, when it seems to have vanished without trace. Its founder, Gabrino, is described as a 'religious maniac', who eventually died in a madhouse.[530]

Connected to them was another French organisation founded in Paris in 1758 called the Emperors of the East and West,[531] who worked the Templar degrees, formulated originally by Andrew Michael Ramsay when in Rome during the mid-1720s. The Emperors of the East and West are thought to have evolved from the so-called Chapter of Clermont, founded some four years earlier.[532] Apparently, the Emperors survived through until 1780, when they were last heard of issuing a circular inveighing against those degrees that were not included in their own system. The French revolution is thought to have put an end to them, although they were soon succeeded by their Americanised offspring, the Ancient and Accepted Rite 33°, founded in 1802. This spread quickly back to the mother continent, and is still practised today by Freemasons worldwide.

The seventeenth degree of the Ancient and Accepted Rite, or Scottish Rite, is Knight of the East and West, which probably encapsulates some part of the beliefs and aspirations of the Emperors of the East and West. During a candidate's investiture, he must provide, at the appropriate moment, a secret password, which enables him to become a full member of the lodge. That password is 'Abaddon' (the Greek Apollyon), the name given in Revelations to the angel who guards the bottomless pit in which Satan, in his guise as the dragon, is bound for a thousand years.[533] The degree's philosophical lecture, which is apocalyptic and Gnostic in nature, teaches an importance in the recurrence of the number seven, as well as the mystical significance of the holy Lamb of God and book of seven seals in Revelations.[534] The degree's legendary history tells of how it was first instituted in 1118, traditionally the same year as the Knights Templar, by eleven knights who – in line with the literature of the *Ordre du Temple* concerning its alleged medieval origins – entered a vow of secrecy with the patriarch of Jerusalem. Lodges where candidates are initiated into the degree are heptagonal in shape and known as 'preceptories', the English term used to describe Templar houses. Confirming their Templar affiliation is the knowledge that the degree's master is styled 'John the Baptist'.[535]

The disturbing factor about this new information was the psychic suggestion that members of an organisation connected to a Templar-oriented Gnostic Church had resurrected certain apocalyptic rituals practiced by the Emperors of the East and West, and had for a very long time been taking an unhealthy interest in St Margaret's Well, Binsey. They saw it as a nerve centre into the British energy matrix, as well as some symbolic representation of the bottomless pit of Revelations, and had gone there to conduct a ritual in order to bind an ancient power which they saw in terms of a dragon, or serpent, of ill omen. Their actions had involved the invocation of Abaddon, the angel of the pit, which they had set up to preside over the well, along with the use of a physical key inscribed with magical sigils.

Richard believed that this group had strong French links and that the key either came from, or was connected to, the château at Arques, near Rennes-le-Château, and was immensely important for some reason. The existence of this key, and its purported association with Arques, was something first hinted at on the occasion that we had made contact with the Faceless Ones on the feast of Mary Magdalene, the day after we were given the Marian Chalice.

Whether the key was retrievable today was still unclear. Yet what *was* becoming clear, however, is that the Faceless Ones' acolytes on earth have frequently been Gnostic or Templar-orientated churches and organisations with Johannine and apocalyptic leanings, whose latter-day followers have taken a special interest in Binsey's holy well, one of the reasons why we had been led to discover its significance. What was in store for us when finally we got there remained a complete mystery. Yet the fact that we had identified the Faceless

Ones as spiritual guardians of the Grail implied that none of this was unconnected with our present situation. Furthermore, we realised that only by taking the Marian Chalice to the well, however risky that might seem, did we stand a chance of achieving the true knowledge of the Grail.

25. LIGHT AND DARKNESS

Thursday, 26 September. We wanted somewhere more atmospheric to conduct a psychic session on Saxon matters, and so drove out a short distance to the sprawling woodland at Thundersley in southeast Essex. The name itself belies its Saxon roots as the clearing or settlement of Thunnor (or Thor), the god of thunder, and here more than anywhere else locally the presence of the ancient gods can still be felt among the gently swaying trees, especially at night. What better place to come in order to further our knowledge of Binsey's holy well in its role as a sacred centre of Britain.

Sue, Richard and I had taken with us a cast-iron cauldron, within which now blazed a small fire, illuminating the small clearing where we had settled and providing the focus for the meditation that began as darkness fell. With the tape recorder running, Richard, sitting on the other side of the flames, opened the proceedings by describing a woman he could see somewhere in the woods, her arms outstretched in the form of a cross, the ancient manner in which Christians prayed. She was quite petite, with a white but ruddied face and long fair hair, plaited into a ponytail. Her dress was a simple blue robe, with crisscrossed stitch work running down the front. She seemed to be distant, as if standing some way away, and her only words at this time were: 'Seek me at the well on my day.'

I went to say who I thought it might be, but then held back to wait and see what might happen next. Competing with her presence here at Thundersley were heavier images that now filled Richard's mind. He could see the key to the pit, used in the ritual at Binsey by members of some Templar-orientated Gnostic Church. Yet what about the lady – was she still present? Did she have a name?

'She just says again that she's the lady of the well,' he replied, his seated form silhouetted by the crackling fire.

I thought it might be St Frideswide, but still said nothing.

'She's saying she will lead us to the key.'

What more could she tell us?

'She says: "Only on my day".'

It was a reference to her feast day, convincing me that it really was Frideswide.

'Soon will be the time of my calling,' were her next words, even though she still appeared to be distant. Her presence was constantly being interrupted by other thoughts, flashing through our minds. I saw St Clement's Caves, Hastings, and the Baphomet figure with a physical key placed in its cupped hands, and one of us reaching out and taking hold of it. Suddenly, I was plunged through a vortex into a tunnel-like corridor, emerging at a spot in the darkness where a bright star fell from the sky and hit the ground before me. Slowly, it transformed itself into an androgynous being of light. Moments later, the figure vanished to leave a residue, an orange glow, as very gradually the earth split asunder and a chasm opened to reveal a cavern-like realm underneath. Out of this rose a thick cloud of grey smoke. It was the bottomless pit of the book of Revelation, and the being of light was the Fifth Angel, who fell as a star and held the key to the pit. It was standard apocalyptic imagery, although necessary to help us understand what was going on, and explain why my mind had seen Binsey holy well as a chasm opening up in the ground with a black oil-like substance issuing forth from its depths.

'She wants me to go over to her at some point,' Richard now said, trying desperately to switch back to what was going on in the woods. 'She's still on the periphery of things.'

What did he mean, 'go over to her'?

'I can see us going for a walk, off into the woods, downhill, and coming across a small clearing, where there's a kind of crossroads, like four paths coming together,' he explained. 'She wants us to go there, although something else wants me to remain here and find out more about the angel of the pit, and what the Grail has to do with all this.'

I suggested staying put for the moment, and if the pulling became too strong then we would do as she wished.

So Richard attempted to concentrate further, but gave up after a while as he could not get her image out of his head. 'OK, let's do it, then,' he finally decided.

Leaving the fire still burning in the cauldron, we went for a walk, being guided through the darkness by the light of a single torch and Richard's pure instinct, which was not rational. I certainly did not recall any crossways in the woods matching the description he had given, even though I knew this place quite well.

'Frideswide,' he suddenly announced, as if it was a revelation. 'That's who it is, and she's waiting for us at this crossroads, and there's a tree there, right in the middle.'

So, at last, a positive identification. It really was her.

Eventually, after much stumbling about in the dark for what seemed like ages, we did come across a meeting of four paths, and, sure enough, there was a tall, slim tree at the very centre. Instinctively, Richard hugged its trunk, and just waited and listened.

'Frees-wid, that's how it's pronounced,' he insisted, in order that we might correctly address her.

I asked her to speak to us.

Her response came soon enough: 'Come on my day bringing offerings and gifts to the well.' Images came to Richard with this last statement – the three of us were now at Binsey, and it was nearing dusk. Something would have to be done there both before and after dark, involving a dual polarity, light and darkness together. 'I see her standing against a wall of the church,' he added. 'She's indicating a spot on the ground, and now she's pulling away a tuft of grass, making a little hole, and it's just down there . . . the key. We need that key.'

Any more?

'No, she's going,' he said, sighing in confusion. 'There was something about the sun, and numbers, that sort of thing. There are sigils on this key, although I can only see one side of it, and not the other, which seems shrouded in darkness, for some reason.'

We still needed to know more. Could she tell us what we had to do when we got to Binsey?

'Set them free,' was Frideswide's somewhat cryptic answer.

Could she tell us anything else – why she had pulled us here, to this spot, for instance?

'Something to do with a link between the legend of the True Cross, the Three Crowns and the three female heads,' was all Richard could offer on her behalf.

This was sounding very interesting indeed, so what was the importance of the three female heads? Yet before Richard could answer, I accidentally knocked his arm, causing him to jolt out of the vision.

Back at Leigh-on-Sea, I got online immediately and checked out the feast of St Frideswide, as Sue and Richard stood behind me. It was 19 October, just over three weeks away! It could not have been timed better, unless it happened to fall on a Saturday. So I looked at the computer calendar and saw that the nineteenth was indeed a Saturday, which suited us fine; there was no way that we would not be going to Binsey on that day. I went on to check out St Frideswide's life a little deeper, and discovered a few facts of direct relevance to our quest. Firstly, on her arrival at Binsey, she and her two companions came across a pigsty and decided to make it into a chapel. So the Saxon princess tempted out the animals by scattering a path of acorns. The animals were unable to resist them, and so they lost their home, which afterwards became a house of God. This was obviously what Frideswide had been alluding to when she said 'set them free' – we would have to bring acorns as 'offerings' and act out her role of enticing the swine from the church, which was supposedly built on the site of the original pigsty.

All of us were quite astounded by the level of accuracy of the psychic information that evening, especially as St Frideswide had said 'soon will be the time of my calling'. Everything seemed to be going right, and hopefully we were now in with a chance of finding a physical key to unlock the truth of the Grail when finally we reached Binsey on her feast day.

Saturday, 19 October. Delays on the road meant that we did not reach Oxford until around 3.30 p.m. Before going out to Binsey, we first paid our respects to St Frideswide's thirteenth-century stone shrine in Christchurch cathedral, which we entered shortly before the building closed. It was when I saw this magnificent monument – destroyed at the time of the Reformation in the mid-sixteenth century and then repaired, jigsaw style, in Victorian times – that something struck me as greatly significant. Between the arches supporting the roof of the tomb were three faces peering out between the foliage, with vines emerging from their mouths. Normally such carvings would be termed Green Men, but these, if they had a name, were Green Ladies, for they were undoubtedly female heads! The guidebook said they probably represent St Frideswide and her two companions, although once again I was reminded of the three female heads I saw in association with the well. It was a unique discovery, especially as they might originally have represented a triple-aspected fertility goddess, plausibly even the beautiful Elen of the Hosts.

A meditation next to the shrine, as the choir raised the energy of the mighty edifice with its powerful harmonies, produced some worrying results. Richard saw St Frideswide, once again in blue, standing next to the low stone wall that enclosed the well, around which were the pigs ejected from their pigsty. She seemed annoyed, for breaking through to this same astral level was the presence of Aleister Crowley, who had put in another appearance at a psychic session conducted just before we embarked on this journey.[536] He had said much, although the gist of it was that he would be around on the day and could provide us with the key. Presumably, he was here on behalf of the Faceless Ones, whom we saw as presiding over the whole show. Now Frideswide appeared to be getting upset because Crowley was treading on her turf, so to speak, and threatening her guardianship of the site. More disconcerting was Richard's feeling that, sooner or later, we would be forced to make a choice as to whether we went with St Frideswide or Crowley.

Leaving behind the decorated shrine, we stopped to pay our respects to the stone floor slab in the chancel that covers St Frideswide's earthly remains. A red nightlight had been placed at each of the four corners, and all but one of them had now burned out, while placed on the gravestone's carved inscription was a bunch of yellow flowers, all this indicating that someone, at least, knew it was her feast day.

From Christchurch, Oxford, we continued on to Binsey church, which held a few surprises of its own.[537] On the wooden pulpit is a representation of St Margaret emerging from the mouth of Satan in the form of a dragon, as well as another heraldic shield on which are three female heads above an ox crossing a ford, the symbol for Oxford. No explanation is given, although I presumed that this was Frideswide's own coat of arms, especially as she is patroness of Oxford. The presence here of the shield was final confirmation not only that we were at the right place, but also, I felt, that we were doing the right thing searching for the key.

Having gained our composure inside the church, the three of us stepped outside into the diminishing light and sat beneath a large tree in the middle of the churchyard. After visualising the building as a simple pigsty in wattle and clay, Sue got up and took on the role of the saint, laying a path of acorns from the church's south entrance across to the holy well. At the same time we pictured the swine being drawn out by her actions, exactly as St Frideswide had done during her lifetime.

It was time now to make contact with the saint herself, so I called out her name.

Richard said she seemed displeased: 'I cannot help you,' she began, standing by the well, again with the pigs around her. 'You have given yourself over to the darkness. The Faceless Ones control you. Do you want to step into the light?'

We wished only to find the key.

'The key is not with me.'

We were told we could have it.

'The key is damnation,' she broke in. 'The opening of the pit. They want you to release him. The thing they call Abaddon.'

We needed the key to help us better understand the Holy Grail, and not to bring about some apocalypse.

'The key is not with me. It is with him.'

She meant Crowley.

'It's been taken from me.'

But if she was willing to give it to us in the first place, then it must be all right for us to pursue the key, meaning that its removal could not be all doom and gloom.

Richard then said: 'This is very odd. It's like the key has now changed. It's hard to explain it. It's like two keys in one, although they are on split levels – we can have either one, although one form represents light and the other darkness. It relates in some way to two possible paths into the future – one Christian and the other not, as well as the light and darkness contained in the Marian Chalice itself. Yet the final decision is ours.'

Richard had implied that there might be two keys during the last session, although what he was implying now was that there were in fact two forms of the same key. Was that right?

'It's all going to be down to an interpretation of the symbols on the key,' he explained, having now come out of the meditational state. 'The key which she would have given us has different symbols to the one Crowley will present to us. It's all to do with split decisions and linear possibilities, which we can still jump between at this stage, although everything will become certain, fixed, once the choice is made and the path taken.'

We would have to go with what our hearts said, and just complete the course. I asked Sue what she thought, and she said go with Crowley, as he had been our guide all along. Richard was unsure, although I suggested that what Sue had said was correct, for if Frideswide had been willing to give us the key originally, and it was now under Crowley's jurisdiction, then we would have to go with him.

'Well, Crowley's been the overshadowing presence to me for a long time,' Richard admitted. 'Yet I feel we are being pushed towards making a decision.'

At the end of the day, if we got lucky and found the key then surely it would be up to us how we used it. Were we in agreement on this one?

All of us finally agreed.

Thus we had now to bid farewell to St Frideswide, for a while at least, and welcome back the spirit of Aleister Crowley, Frater Perdurabo, although a break was in order before trying to make contact with him.

It gave us a chance to chat about things. Here we were on a psychic quest to better understand both the Holy Grail and a Templar reliquary with two faces that symbolised the head of John the Baptist and, quite possibly, that of John the Evangelist, the writer of Revelations. These were the two figureheads, along with the Magdalene, of the Gnostic doctrine practised by the first Christians of Ephesus, as well as the Cathars, the Templars and all those of the underground stream through to the present day. It constituted the true wisdom, the true Gnosis of Christianity, cut off in its prime, before it even had a chance to prove itself. Whichever way one might look at it, rediscovering the secret teachings of Christ, as the Grail seemed to represent, was certainly not the road to oblivion. Frideswide, on the other hand, signified the face of orthodox Christianity, created, controlled and manipulated by the Church of Rome. Furthermore, it was important to remember that the Frideswide present here at Binsey was the sum total of the veneration and worship she had received from visitors to the church and the well over the past 1,300 years, and so her views did not necessarily reflect those of the mortal woman who lived all that time ago.

Richard admitted at this point that it was almost as if she had known we were going to make the choice we did, even before the matter had cropped up. He felt there were forces working with Crowley, and forces working with her – each of them trying to steer us on to a different path, which would ultimately lead to the same destination – truth and enlightenment.

When we were ready again, the three of us, still seated beneath the shelter of the big tree, focused our concentration on Aleister Crowley. Almost immediately, Richard felt his powerful presence standing behind him, virtually breathing down his neck.

I called out Crowley's name, saying we were ready to receive him. We sought only the key to unlock the inner knowledge of the Grail, and needed to know what to do next.

The presence behind Richard began to speak: 'You are on the threshold of my realm. You will return to the well when it is black.'

What should we do?

'Stare into the well,' came the reply. 'See the dark waters – become at one with them. You must walk through the abyss to understand the true Grail.'

And then what?

'I shall give you the key,' he said next. 'The key of the pit, which you must use. You must take it with you whenever I tell you. It's your link. Your symbol. The symbol of your intent.'

And he would tell us where it was placed?

'You will see me, and it will be given to you.'

But he was in spirit, and we were in the physical world. We would need energy to manifest its presence.

'This I can provide with your help.'

Suddenly, Richard burped and came round, complaining now of feeling sick. Everything around us was 'fizzy' he said, as if reality had begun subtly to shift, even beyond the swift onset of dusk.

As we drove back down the deserted Binsey Lane towards the Oxford Road, something strange occurred. Before us in the road was a localised bank of mist which suddenly engulfed the whole car, so much so that nothing could be seen beyond it. Getting out, I looked around and saw that the curtain of fog did not extend into the fields beyond the hedges on either side. Like some ethereal blanket, it just lingered in the road blotting out the surrounding landscape. If nothing more, it was strangely coincidental, especially as I had earlier said that we would encounter Abaddon in the form of an intelligent mist, a throwaway line I had not even thought to record. Concentrating my mind, I saw within the fog an orange glowing ball, like an eye, representing some kind of window on to our world, suggesting that, when later we returned, it might not only be Crowley waiting for us out there.

26. DESCENT OF THE DIVINE

After driving around in the dark for half an hour or so, attempting in vain to find an Indian restaurant, we went back to The Perch Inn in Binsey Lane, and ordered drinks and an evening meal there. It was lucky we arrived when we did, for only fifteen minutes later the bar staff were rushed off their feet when a group of around twenty to thirty people unexpectedly descended on the place. The barmaid said they were residents from barges moored on the local canal who came here to play and listen to folk music. Arriving after them would have meant waiting an awful lot longer for our meals, a crucial point to remember, for timing was everything that night.

Walking out of the pub into the pitch black somehow felt significant on this of all nights, particularly as we seemed to be so far away from the city of Oxford, even though it was just three kilometres (two miles) as the crow flies. We made the decision to leave the car parked at a suitable spot halfway down the track leading to the church, and walk the rest of the way, so as not to alert the residents of the two small farmhouses located just behind the churchyard of our presence. Over and above this consideration was Richard's growing anxiety, caused by his belief that everything might not go the way we had planned it. He was not sure why, but had a sneaky suspicion that the Faceless Ones would put in an appearance, since they wanted to prove something to us.

We reached the churchyard around 9.15 p.m. and, resisting the temptation to see whether the church was open, we made straight for the holy well. After a brief few minutes to gain our composure and focus on the matter at hand, the meditation got under way with Sue seated on the lowest step, me on another step halfway up, and Richard sitting on the uppermost one. As Crowley had suggested, we visualised ourselves sinking down into the round cauldron-like basin of dark water beneath the miniature arch, which now became our gateway into another realm. Each person visualised themselves standing on the edge of a precipice, calling out to their own spiritual guardians for guidance and protection. Thereafter we saw ourselves jumping together into the abyss of our unconscious minds, embracing the void, wishing only to learn the truth that lay on the other side, where light would once more be restored.

We found ourselves perpetually falling through the blackness as occasionally weird creatures manifested before us and strange scenes formed momentarily, before evaporating away into nothing. The whole process continued for around ten minutes as we pushed ever onwards until finally we glimpsed the light of the Grail.

I saw the three-spoked triskelion once more, spinning faster and faster until it transformed into three female heads, symbols of Elen, enshrouded by a dazzling brilliance. They grew to become three beautiful women, Grail maidens, dressed in white, who each held a chalice made of a different metal – one in gold, one in silver and the other in copper. From different directions, they gracefully came together to form one single female being who held the Marian Chalice, which transformed into pure light, reaching out like the rays of a cross. Into this brilliance now descended a dove, the feminine symbol of the descent of the divine into corporeal existence, symbolised by the Bitter Cup, as well as Mary's *alabastron,* the cup of the Last Supper, the Holy Grail and, most importantly, the communion cup of the Paschal vigil, where the Holy Spirit was experienced by those who drank from its contents after undergoing the rite of baptism.

This is what the well signified – it was not just a place of ritual cleansing, like the church font at Nuffield; its curious inscription being a clue to this end. Similar to other sacred centres, such as Headcorn and Bourges, the well existed as an access point to the divine light through an imaginary cosmic axis linking heaven, earth and underworld (seen at Binsey by some as the pit of Revelations), where kings of the world, rulers of time, once sat in majesty controlling their dominions, so long as they remained pure conduits of the divine. This, then, was the other aspect of that perennial question, 'to whom serves the Grail?' – when the king, the land and the light come together as one the world axis turns and life thrives in that realm. When they are not in harmony and the king falters, then the country becomes susceptible to plagues, invasion and other maladies symbolised by the fighting dragons in the story of 'Lludd and Llevelys', and the wasteland and lame king of the Grail romances.

In the case of the Grail, contact with the divine is generally twelve-fold, sometimes seven-fold or even three-fold. It is like the spokes of an enormous wheel controlling the passage of time, with the axle existing beyond time itself. Whether Christian, Gnostic, Cathar, Templar, Johannine or anyone else, the source of the Grail relates to the containment in physical or bodily form of the divine, the One, the All, expressed as the Light of God. In Christianity, the divine light is seen as *grace*, the Holy Spirit, and the tongues of fire which descended on to the apostles at Pentecost, their 'baptism of fire', yet in Jewish mysticism it is the feminine and sexually oriented *shekinah*, or 'presence of God', that best expresses the divine light. Like Babalon, Elen, Sophia and Venus, the *shekinah* is the earthly gateway to the divine, and through her all must pass to reach heaven. In Hindu Tantric beliefs, she is Shakti, the Primordial Female Energy whose union with Shiva enables human kind to ascend and find oneness with the divine. Yet in reality, it is a universal cosmic power source, invariably connected with female sexual energy, and exalted by humanity since the goddess cults of Palaeolithic and Neolithic times. Once, chosen women, priestesses, would sit at the *dead centre* of their realms on stone 'thrones' and channel this divine light outwards to bring fecundity to the land, as well as divine revelation in the individual and contact with the One, the All. The *sri ma*, 'divine mothers', of India, still bear some knowledge of channelling this divine light, even today. Moreover, it is an intelligent force still expressed in western culture through the continued presence of the Faceless Ones, the order of Melchizedek, and the Grail maidens, personifications of Elen as the light of the land, which exist as part of the necessary apparatus preserving the truth of the Grail.

THE HOODED FIGURES

Unexpectedly, everything began to shift in the churchyard, as a wind squall made the trees hiss loudly, and Richard broke out of the meditation, complaining that he felt sick and dizzy. Each of us then clearly heard the sound of someone lifting the metal latch on the gate into the churchyard, breaking our train of thought. I told Sue and Richard to ignore it, as it was probably just someone out walking their dog. We fell silent for a moment or two, before we saw a very disturbing sight indeed. Out of the darkness emerged a long line of cowled figures, quite human on this occasion, who moved at a steady pace along the path towards the church's south entrance. They were at right angles to our line of vision as they came within six metres (twenty feet) of where we were staring in disbelief. More than this, I could hear their voices in the breeze, *and realised that they were chanting in Latin!*

There seemed to be around twelve of them, and from the manner of their walk I quickly concluded that they were probably all male. Where the hell had they come from? They had not been in the pub, and had arrived on foot in the total darkness, without a torch between them. Fright and a strange rationalisation of the situation now overwhelmed me. For the moment, who exactly they were did not matter. However, as they appeared to be directing their attentions towards the church, which we presumed was still open, they could not have spotted us yet. Once they had disappeared inside the building, then hopefully they would be occupied in there long enough for us to complete what we were here to do.

'I started to feel something happening, just before their arrival,' Richard now revealed, as the last of the cowled figures disappeared from view inside the church, 'and I can sense Crowley, right behind me, now.'

'I think we should get out of here,' Sue said, fearing for our safety. 'I really don't think we should stay here. We don't know who they are, and they might not take too kindly to us messing up their evening.'

As slow minutes ticked by, and we could now hear Latin chanting coming from inside the darkened interior of the church, I tried to convince her that we were safe. There was nothing to worry about, and everything was under control.

By now Richard was focusing his mind on the presence standing behind him: 'Crowley's using this energy to manifest the key.'

Suddenly, everything changed. 'I just saw a flash,' Richard exclaimed, excitedly.

Where exactly?

'Over by that wall.' He turned his head around, and nodded towards the west end of the church.

'I thought I saw a flash as well,' Sue broke in, looking in the same direction. 'It was definitely over by the wall.'

'*It's the key*', Richard hesitatingly announced. 'He's standing, pointing down.'

Go there, now. Go!

The three of us then moved stealthily across to the base of the wall and, as I began to illuminate the spot with a small torch, Richard searched beneath the thick mat of green chickweed that encroached the concrete runoff at the base of the wall.

Still the sound of Latin chanting could be heard emanating from the window above our heads.

We had to move fast, as they might re-enter the churchyard at any time.

'The torch is reflecting off the window,' Sue suddenly exclaimed. '*They can see it.*'

Perhaps we had already given away our presence. Perhaps it was too late, but there was no way that we were going to give up now.

'Might be further across to the right,' Richard suggested, not too certain himself. Knowing the failure rate of our artefact retrieval, I was not banking on anything. Still, I sat down on the wet grass and shielded the light from the torch to allow a bright orange glow to hit the area in question.

Richard tugged hard at another clump of chickweed, releasing its fine white roots from the earth, as I unexpectedly saw something metallic come into view.

Oh my God. *Oh my God . . .*

It was an ornate metal key with a heavily oxidised patina, indicating both its age and the fact that it had been out in the open for some while.

Get it!

Richard picked it up as we instantly rose to our feet.

Go now! Run!

Without a further word, we ran as fast as we could out past the south entrance, and then across the churchyard towards the exit gate.

I never looked back, but Richard did, noting that there was no light whatsoever coming from the interior of the church, making the presence of these people seem almost ethereal in nature, and causing Sue to later question whether or not the figures were physically real.

As we came within a few metres of the gate, Sue stumbled over a jutting piece of kerbstone and fell awkwardly, spraining her ankle.

'Sue, get up,' I yelled in frustration, as both Richard and I lifted her to her feet and carried her out of the churchyard. Despite the pain, she now began to laugh uncontrollably at what had just happened. 'This is just unbelievable,' she cried, shaking her head. 'What the hell is happening to us?'

Richard slowly came to a halt, allowing us all to catch our breath. 'D'you think we should go back there?' he suggested, in all seriousness. 'It's the only way we're going to find out what's going on. I mean, who exactly are they?'

His suggestion was not greeted too kindly. We just needed to get away from here as quickly as possible.

Sue felt they were representative of the Faceless Ones.

'Well, I did tell you that I thought they wanted to try and prove something to us here tonight,' he responded, in a 'told you so' voice, 'and I am now convinced that this did not just mean finding the key.'

Once more, each of us questioned where the men in the church had come from, or what they were doing chanting Latin in the darkness. OK, they might just have been students from Christchurch coming here for a little choir practice, and if this was the case then their timing was impeccable, and probably resulted in us finding the key. However, there was a definite sense that something was not right, and that they would not have taken too kindly to our presence here. As it turned out, we were right to act the way we did, for when a week or so later I spoke to the rector of the church, the Rev. Robert Sweeney, he admitted having no knowledge whatsoever of any service, choir practice or function that had gone on in St Margaret's church on the feast of St Frideswide. Indeed, when I told him what had been seen, he was initially lost for words and said that it was 'not official', somewhat of an understatement in my opinion.

These views were shared by a deacon I spoke to from Christchurch, which owns Binsey church and whose choir *does* occasionally practise there. He confirmed that no official choir practice had taken place that day, and even when there was, the rector would usually be notified and those involved would certainly not wear cowled robes and conduct the whole thing in the dark. He sensibly suggested that the individuals responsible probably belonged to one of the 'many unorthodox religious groups' known to exist in Oxford. Maybe they really were some quasi-Templar Gnostic Church with monastic overtones, and either they or someone associated with them had come to Binsey to deposit the metal key now in our possession. Yet in the end, there was no clear indication as to who exactly the twelve or so individuals actually were, and we could never discount the possibility that they *were* simply members of Christchurch's choir who gained pleasure out of dressing in cowled robes and *unofficially* practising their Latin chanting in the darkened interior of an atmospheric medieval church.

Still we half-ran, half-walked back to where the car had been left, helping Sue where necessary. We jumped inside and sped off into the night, glancing behind us at a large four-wheel-drive vehicle that seemed to appear out of nowhere. We did not feel totally safe until we were back on the Oxford Road, heading into the city once more. My brain was so fried that I got completely lost trying to navigate the awkward one-way system and ended up going round and round in circles for half an hour or more.

We did eventually settle down in a pub, The Plasterers Arms, which was full of local men watching the Saturday night football on television, and here we examined the key for the first time. It is around 95mm (3.75 inches) in length with a large kidney-shaped bow, a ribbed shaft and an ornate box of wards incorporating what might be described as an anchor design. It is made of cast iron, well worn, and from my meagre knowledge of keys it is of a style popular in Britain during both the Georgian and Victorian eras, and probably fitted the lock to an interior door.

The matter of the key's symbols was most intriguing. Those on one side had been completely erased, chiselled out even, some while back, echoing what

Richard had said about there being two forms of the same key. If we had gone with St Frideswide and taken the orthodox path, then the symbols on the other side would have been erased, but because we made the decision to side with Crowley, the sigils were as they are now; at least that was the implication. Reading from left to right was, firstly, a small circle with a point in its centre, which is the symbol for the sun. After that is the sign for Taurus, which has a line trailing from its right-hand corner to an inverted triangle, representing the element of water, probably the well itself. In addition to this, where the oxidised patina had peeled away from the area around the end of the barrel, a triangular shape had been added to the wavy line formed by its removal to signify what appeared to be a dragon or serpent, perhaps Satan in the form of a dragon or the Gnostic serpent.

From these clues, I concluded that the key had been inscribed to fix its placement at the well when the sun was in Taurus (i.e. between 21 April and 21 May), and that those who left it there were attempting to bind the dragon or serpent depicted on its shaft. One symbol remained – halfway along the shaft was a ringlike line that embraced its entire circumference and ended in an oval shape reminiscent of an eye. This I took to be the sigil representing the binding of Abaddon, leading me to recall the strange bank of mist encountered in Binsey Lane earlier that evening. As to the erased symbols on the other side, I tried to figure out what they might have been. The first one was probably another triangle, the second and third ones were totally erased, while the fourth symbol was possibly another circle representing the sun.

Although the symbols on the key were inscribed long ago, there was some indication that they had been scored lightly again in the recent past. What this meant was simple: the key had only been in the ground for a limited period, plausibly since May, when the sun was last in Taurus and our own hunt to find Crowley's Cup of Babalon at Headcorn climaxed in the way it did. No one could rightly say how or when it got where it was, and there the matter would have to rest until such times as we were able to take it to the château of Arques and see whether it unlocked a door into the mystery of Rennes-le-Château.

I looked up from studying the key at the very moment that the television screen showed the first-ever Premiership goal by England wonder kid Wayne Rooney, as he put Everton ahead with a blinding kick which sailed past stunned Arsenal goalkeeper David Seaman, who was at the time still in the England squad.

A moment more contradictory in atmosphere there could not have been.

All I knew was that the build-up of activity that had preceded the events of that day was quite extraordinary. I was not just talking about the discovery of the key, or the profound vision revealing the truth of the Grail, but the combined effort that had led us to find Binsey in the first place. What was there about this place that was so important? OK, it was an *omphalos* site of Britain, and was probably the focus of some kind of national landscape geometry, but why lead us here? Was it really somewhere that the human mind could access and channel the divine light and thus affect the wellbeing of the outside world?

Perhaps we would never know, for in questing you just do it and see what happens. It is that simple.

Leaving the pub at closing time, we found a grotty bed and breakfast, of the kind sadly reserved for students and foreign tourists, and spent a few hours just holding the key and using psychometry in an attempt to learn something about its history. Only flashes of the future and the past came – seven churches in Rome, underground catacombs, the Order of the Apocalypse, a castle aligned to the sun, the château of Arques, and a horse and cart departing from a large fortified medieval citadel in the heart of the French Languedoc. In the front seat were two monks dressed in simple brown hoods. Once they were out of range of prying eyes and the king's guard, one of them reached behind and pulled away a sackcloth covering to reveal the presence of the Head of God, the two-faced head reliquary previously in the hands of the Knights Templar, and smuggled out of England with the help of the White Canons. Realising that their dangerous mission was almost over, and that the priceless relic was now safe, the two men turned to each other and smiled knowingly, as they continued the journey unhindered towards their final destination.[538]

EPILOGUE

There was just one more thing I needed to do in order to better understand the provenance of the Marian Chalice, and this was to verify its composition. For some time, I had been experiencing nagging doubts about it being onyx, which has a certain feel to it – when polished its surface is smooth, and it is invariably cold to the touch. Yet the Marian Chalice has a matt lustre, and generally it is warm to the touch, tending to suggest that it might just be Oriental alabaster, also known as onyx marble, which, in similar with true onyx, bears characteristic green, white and honey-brown colour banding. The only real difference between the two types of stone is that onyx is a hard silicate, or quartz-based rock, while Oriental alabaster is a slightly softer sulphate-based, or calcareous, substance – a calcite in fact.

Was the cup made from onyx, or green alabaster? It was a simple question, even though I seemed unable to answer it myself. I knew therefore that before the publication of the book, it made sense to take the cup along to the geological department of the Natural History Museum in London to see what they might have to say about it.

The chance came on Friday, 5 March 2004, when Sue and I spent a day in the capital. Having failed in advance to secure the name of a person who might be able to help us with our query, we stepped blindly into the busy museum foyer, crowded with spring tourists there to see the stunning mineral exhibition before venturing through to the somewhat more child-friendly dinosaur hall. The receptionist made telephone calls before pointing us towards the Earth Lab, where members of the public are able to bring fossils, rocks and crystals for identification.

On duty that afternoon was Dr Adrian Rundle, a palaeontologist, who would have been able to tell me about any fossil in my collection, but admitted to not being an expert in the subject of mineralogy. He called on the assistance of Dr Mark Welch, a research mineralogist, and as we waited for his arrival Dr Rundle took time to examine the Marian Chalice under an extremely powerful microscope. It revealed a world of small scratches left on the bowl's exterior when it was polished using some kind of abrasive material. These lines were mostly vertical or horizontal in direction, although occasionally they were diagonal. Yet what was most striking about them was how they invariably ended abruptly in a deeper groove, implying that the movement from the hand that finished the vessel had abruptly halted or changed direction.

It was an interesting observation, but failed to help us identity the type of stone used in the manufacture of the cup, so I asked Dr Rundle whether there was any definitive way to achieve this information. At first he suggested waiting for his colleague to arrive, but then the palaeontologist stopped suddenly, and realised the answer: 'Of course – the acid test,' he announced, going across to the safe, unlocking it and taking out a small bottle of clear liquid. 'If it's calcareous, then when you place a small amount of acid on its surface the whole thing will effloresce – bubble, I mean – and this won't happen if it's a silica-based stone.'

The mere thought of such an apparently destructive process stunned us for a moment or two, but in order to determine the vessel's true composition, it seemed like the only quick solution. What is more, Dr Rundle did promise that it would not damage the vessel, and so we agreed to the test.

Moving back across to the microscope, he placed the Marian Chalice so that it was visible on the video screen, before allowing a minute drop of acid to fall from a glass pipette onto the underside of the cup's circular base.

I had been waiting for this moment for a very long time, and finally we would know whether or not the vessel really was carved from the same substance thought to have been used to fashion Mary Magdalene's *alabastron*.

We watched with bated breath as the tiny drop of acid hit the fibrous surface of the cup and exploded outwards like a mini nuclear blast. Yet then, very gradually, all eyes saw the liquid momentarily bubble like water boiling in a pan, before evaporating away to nothing. The test confirmed once and for all that the stone was calcareous, meaning that the Marian Chalice was fashioned from Oriental alabaster, or *alabastrites*. It was this rock that Pliny the Younger in the first century AD said was used more than any other to make unguent jars because 'it is said to be the best means of keeping unguents fresh'.

The realisation that the stone cup was fashioned from green alabaster was a shock and a revelation, which we were hardly able to take in. It now took the matter on to a whole new level, for not only did it increase the chances that the vessel was manufactured in either Egypt or the Near East during Roman times, but just maybe the Marian Chalice really was the Magdalene's *alabastron*, and thus by virtue of this the best candidate in the world for the title Holy Grail.

BIBLIOGRAPHY

Abbreviations: $AC = Arch\alpha ologia$ Cantiana, Kent Archaeological Society, Maidstone, Kent; $EN = Earthquest$ News, Leigh-on-Sea, Essex; $JHA = Journal$ for the History of Astronomy, Cambridge; $JSS = The$ Journal of Semitic Studies, University of Manchester, Manchester; $nd = no$ date of publication printed; $OUP = Oxford$ University Press, New York & Oxford; $SPCK = Society$ for Promoting Christian Knowledge, London.

NB: The initial date cited in entries is the first date of publication – the second date, if given, denotes the imprint/edition consulted.

Allegro, John M., *The Sacred Mushroom and the Cross*, Hodder and Stoughton, London, 1970.

Anglo-Saxon Chronicle, trans and ed. by G.N. Garmonsway, 1953, J.M. Dent/Everyman Library, London and Melbourne, 1986.

Baigent, Michael, Richard Leigh and Henry Lincoln, *The Holy Blood and the Holy Grail*, Jonathan Cape, London, 1982.

Baigent, Michael, Richard Leigh and Henry Lincoln, *The Holy Blood and the Holy Grail*, revised edition, Arrow, London, 1996.

Barber, Malcolm, *The Trial of the Templars*, Cambridge University Press, Cambridge, 1978.

Baring-Gould, S., *Curious Myths of the Middle Ages*, Longmans, Green and Co, London, New York and Bombay, 1901.

Baring-Gould, Rev. S., *The Lost and Hostile Gospels: An Essay of the Toledoth Jeschu, and the Petrine and Pauline Gospels of the First Three Centuries of Which Fragments Remain*, Williams and Norgate, London and Edinburgh, 1874.

Bashiri, Iraj, *Hafiz' Shirazi Turk: A Structuralist's Point of View*, posted at www.iles.umn.edu/faculty/bashiri/Hafiz%20folder/Hafiz.html.

Begg, Ean, and Deike Begg, *In Search of the Holy Grail and the Precious Blood*, Thorsons, London, 1995.

Bible, The Holy, 1611, Revised Edition, OUP, 1905.

Booth, Martin, *A Magick Life: A Biography of Aleister Crowley*, 2000, Coronet/Hodder and Stoughton, London, 2001.

Boumendil, Claude, ed., *Les Cahiers de Rennes-le-Château: Archives, Documents, Études 2*, Belisane, Monaco-Ville, France, June 1984.

Branston, Brian, *The Lost Gods of England*, Thames and Hudson, London, 1974.

Broadhurst, Paul, and Hamish Miller with Vivienne Shanley and Ba Russell, *The Dance of the Dragon*, Pendragon Press, Launceston, Cornwall, 2000.

Brown, Allen R., ed., *Anglo-Norman Studies IX: Proceedings of the Battle Conference*, The Boydell Press, Woodbridge, Suffolk, 1986.

Brown, Raymond E., *The Community of the Beloved Disciple*, Paulist Press, New York, NY, 1979.

Bryant, Nigel, trans, *Merlin and the Grail: Joseph of Arimathea, Merlin, Perceval: The Trilogy of Prose Romances Attributed to Robert de Boron*, D.S. Brewer, Woodbridge, Suffolk, 2001.

Buechner, Col. Howard, *Emerald Cup – Ark of Gold: The Quest of SS Lt Otto Rahn of the Third Reich*, Thunderbird Press, Metairie, LA, 1994.

Cabaniss, Allen, 'Joseph of Arimathea and a Chalice', *Mississippi Studies in English* 4 (1963), pp. 61–7.

Carley, James, trans David Thompson, *The Chronicle of Glastonbury Abbey: Cronica SIVE Antiquitates Glastoniensis Ecclesie,* 1978, The Boydell Press, Woodbridge, Suffolk, 2001.

Carley, James P., *Glastonbury Abbey: The Holy House at the Head of the Moors Adventurous,* The Boydell Press, Woodbridge, Suffolk, 1988.

Carroll, Lewis, *Alice's Adventures in Wonderland,* 1865, Macmillan, London, 1907.

Collins, Andrew, *From the Ashes of Angels,* Penguin, London, 1996.

Collins, Andrew, *Helen and the Beast: The account of a woman who claimed Aleister Crowley as her spirit guide,* ABC Books, Leigh-on-Sea, Essex, 1988.

Collins, Andrew, *The Black Alchemist,* ABC Books, Leigh-on-Sea, Essex, 1988.

Collins, Andrew, *The Second Coming,* Century, London, 1993.

Collins, Andrew, and Chris Ogilvie-Herald, *Tutankhamun: The Exodus Conspiracy,* Virgin Books, London, 2002.

Colquhoun, Ithell, *Sword of Wisdom: MacGregor Mathers and the Golden Dawn,* Neville Spearman, London, 1975.

Constantine, Storm, 'Of a Cat, But Her Skin', in Taplow, ed. *Twists in the Tale.*

Crowley, Aleister, 'Energized Enthusiasm: A Note on Theurgy', in Crowley, *Gems From the Equinox.*

Crowley, Aleister, *Gems From the Equinox,* 1972, New Falcon Publications, Scottsdale, AZ, 1992.

Crowley, Aleister, *Moonchild,* Mandrake Press, London, 1929.

Crowley, Aleister, *The Holy Books of Thelema, Equinox vol. 3 No. 9,* 1983, Samuel Weiser, York Beach, ME, 1990.

Crowley, Aleister, 'Liber CLVI', in Crowley, *The Holy Books of Thelema, Equinox vol 3 No 9.*

Cumont, Franz, *The Mysteries of Mithra,* 1902, Dover Publications, New York, NY, 1956.

Daraul, Arkon, *Secret Societies,* 1961, Tandem, London, 1965.

Dunlop, John Colin, *History of Prose Fiction,* vol. I, Geo Bell, London, 1888.

Ekwall, Eilert, *The Concise Oxford Dictionary of English Place-names,* 1936, OUP, 1980.

Elliott, Ralph W.V., 1959, *Runes: An Introduction,* Manchester University Press, Manchester, 1963.

Evans, Sebastian, intro and trans, *The High History of the Grail,* 1910, J.M. Dent, London; E P Dutton, New York, 1921.

Furneaux, Rupert, *The Roman Siege of Jerusalem,* Hart-Davis MacGibbon, London, 1973.

Gould's History of Freemasonry Throughout the World, 6 vols, ed. Dudley Wright, Charles Scribner's Sons, New York, NY, 1936.

Grant, Kenneth, *The Magical Revival,* Fredk Muller, London, 1972.

Grant, Kenneth, *The Ninth Arch,* Starfire Publishing, London, 2002.

Gray, Adrian, *Tales of Old Essex,* 1987, Countryside Books, Newbury, Berkshire, 1992.

Green-Armytage, A.H.N., *John Who Saw,* Faber and Faber, London, 1952.

Guest, Lady Charlotte, trans, *The Mabinogion,* 1902, J.M. Dent/Everyman Library, London, 1932.

Guillot, R.P., *Léonard de Vinci: le mythe de l'androgyne,* J. Grancher, Paris, 1996.

Harris, Bro Reginald V., 'The Heraldry of Freemasonry', *The Builder* 15:8 (1929).

Haskins, Susan, *Mary Magdalen: Myth and Metaphor,* HarperCollins, London, 1993.

Hawkstone: A Short History and Guide, Hawkstone Park Leisure, Hawkstone Park, Shropshire, 1993.

Hippolytus, *Philosophumena or the Refutation of All Heresies, etc*, trans F. Legge, SPCK, 1921.

Hone, William, *Ancient Mysteries Described, Especially the English Miracle Plays, Founded on Apocryphal New Testament Story, etc*, privately printed, London, 1823.

Hope, Robert Charles, *The Legendary Lore of the Holy Wells of England: Including Rivers, Lakes, Fountains, and Springs*, Elliot Stock, London, 1893.

Horner, George, trans, *Pistis Sophia*, intro F. Legge, SPCK, 1924.

Hoskin, Michael, 'The Cosmology of Thomas Wright of Durham', *JHA* 1 (1970), pp. 44–52.

Hoskin, Michael A. – see Wright, *An Original Theory of the Universe*.

Jackson, Keith B., *Beyond the Craft*, 1980, Lewis Masonic, London, 1982.

James, Montague Rhodes, *The Apocryphal New Testament being the Apocryphal Gospels, Acts, Epistles, and Apocalypses with Other Narratives and Fragments*, 1924, Clarendon Press, Oxford, 1985.

Jameson, Mrs, *Sacred and Legendary Art*, in 2 vols, vol 1, Longmans, Green and Co, London, New York and Bombay, 1905.

Jarnac, Pierre, *Les Archives du Trésor de Rennes-le-Château*, Belisane, Nice, France, 1987.

Jerome's Latin Vulgate Bible (AD 405), posted at http://speedbible.com/vulgate/index.htm.

Josephus, Flavius, trans Wm Whiston, *The Works of Flavius Josephus*, Wm P. Nimmo, Edinburgh, nd (c. 1870).

Jusino, Ramon K., *Mary Magdalene: Author of the Fourth Gospel?* 1998, posted at http://members.tripod.com/~ Ramon_K_Jusino/magdalene.html#brown1.

Kahane, Henry, and Renée Kahane, written in collaboration with Angelina Pietrangeli, *The Krater and the Grail*, Illinois Studies in Language and Literature 56, University of Illinois, Urbana, IL, 1965.

Keen, Maurice, *The Outlaws of Medieval Legend*, 1961, Routledge & Kegan Paul, London and New York, 1987.

Lebeuf, A., 'Maria Magdalena: The Morning Star', *Vistas in Astronomy* 39:4 (1995), pp. 591–603.

Leitch, Yuri, 'Franks Casket: Genesis of the Grail Myth', *The Temple* 2 (February 2003), pp. 41–2.

Leitch, Yuri, 'The Franks Casket: Sabine Baring-Gould and the Sangreal', *The Temple* 1 (August 2002), pp. 5–11.

Leland, Charles G., *Etruscan Roman Remains*, 1892, Phoenix Publishing, Blaine, WA, nd (c. 1992).

Lincoln, Henry, *Key to the Sacred Pattern: the Untold Story of Rennes-le-Château*, The Windrush Press, Moreton-in-Marsh, Gloucestershire, 1997.

Lincoln, Henry, *The Holy Place*, Jonathan Cape, London, 1991.

Loiseleur, Jules, *La Doctrine Secrète des Templiers*,1873, Belisane, Cazilhac, France, 1999.

Loomis, Roger Sherman, *The Grail: From Celtic Myth to Christian Symbol*, University of Wales Press, Cardiff; Columbia University Press, New York, 1963.

Lord, Evelyn, *The Knights Templar in Britain,* Longman, Harlow, Essex, 2002.

Macgregor, G.H.C., *The Gospel of John*, 1928, Hodder and Stoughton, London, 1949.

Mackenzie, Kenneth, *The Royal Masonic Cyclopaedia*, 1877, intro by John Hamill and R.A. Gilbert, The Aquarian Press, Wellingborough, Northants, 1987.

Macoy, Robert, *A Dictionary of Freemasonry*, Bell, New York, NY, 1989.

Mainwaring Baines, John, *Historic Hastings*, F.J. Parsons, Hastings, Sussex, 1963.

Malory, Sir Thomas, *Le Morte Darthur*, 2 vols, Macmillan, London, 1900.

Malvern, Marjorie M., *Venus in Sackcloth: The Magdalen's Origins and Metamorphoses*, Southern Illinois Press, Carbondale, IL, 1975.

Mazières, Abbé Maurice-René, *Les templiers du Bézu: Haute Vallée d'Aude,* Société des Arts and Sciences de Carcassonne, Carcassonne, France, 1984.

McBride, Denis, *A History of Hawkstone,* 1987, Trustees of Hawkstone Park, Shropshire, 1993.

McCash, June Hall Martin, 'Marie of Champagne and Eleanor of Aquatine', *Speculum* 54:4 (October 1979), pp. 698–711.

McIntosh, Christopher, *The Rosicrucians: The History and Mythology of an Occult Order,* 1987, Crucible, Wellingborough, Northants, 1987.

Mee, Arthur, *The King's England: Kent,* 1936, Hodder and Stoughton, London, 1947.

Meeks, Wayne A., 'The Image of the Androgyne: Some Uses of a Symbol in Earliest Christianity', *History of Religions* 13:3 (February 1974), pp. 165–208.

Michell, John, *At the Centre of the World: Polar Symbolism Discovered in Celtic, Norse and Other Ritualized Landscapes,* Thames and Hudson, London, 1994.

Michell, John, and Christine Rhone, *Twelve-Tribe Nations and the Science of Enchanting the Landscape,* Thames and Hudson, London, 1991.

Milton, John, *Milton's Paradise Lost,* illustrated by Gustave Doré, ed. with notes and a life of Milton by Robert Vaughan, Collier, New York, NY, nd (c. 1880s).

Murray, Margaret A., *The Divine King in England,* Faber & Faber, London, 1954.

Murray, Margaret A., *The God of the Witches,* 1931, OUP, 1974.

Mycoff, David, trans and intro, *The Life of Saint Mary Magdalene and of her Sister Saint Martha,* Cistercian Publications, Kalamazoo, MI, 1989.

Nitze, William A., trans, *Le Roman de l'estoire dou Graal,* Librairie Ancienne Honoré Champion Éditeur, Paris, 1927.

Oldenbourg, Zoé, *Massacre at Montségur,* 1961, Weidenfeld and Nicolson, London, 1997.

Olschki, Leonardo, *The Grail Castle and Its Mysteries,* trans J.A. Scott, Manchester University Press, Manchester, 1965.

Olsen, Oddvar, 'St Michael's Church, Garway', *The Temple* 3 (September 2003), pp. 24–5.

Owen, D.D.R., intro, bib, and trans *Arthurian Romances,* revised intro and bibliography, Everyman, London, 1993.

O'Gorman, Richard, 'Ecclesiastical Tradition and the Holy Grail', *Australian Journal of French Studies* 6 (1969), pp. 3–8.

Page, William, ed., *Victoria County History Kent,* II, Boydell and Brewer, Woodbridge, Suffolk, 1926.

Pagels, Elaine, *The Gnostic Gospels,* Weidenfeld and Nicolson, London, 1980.

Patton, Guy, and Robin Mackness, *Sacred Treasure, Secret Power: The True History of the Web of Gold,* 2000, Pan, London, 2001.

Payne Knight, Richard, *A Discourse on the Worship of Priapus and Its Connection with the Mystic Theology of the Ancients,* with Thomas Wright, *An Essay on the Worship of the Regenerative Powers During the Middle Ages of Western Europe,* privately printed, London, 1865.

Phillips, Graham, *The Search for the Grail,* Century, London, 1995.

Phillips, Graham, and Martin Keatman, *King Arthur: The True Story,* Century, London, 1992.

Phillips, Graham, and Martin Keatman, *Robin Hood: The Man Behind the Myth,* Michael O'Mara Books, London, 1995.

Picknett, Lynn, *Mary Magdalene: Christianity's Hidden Goddess,* Robinson, London, 2003.

Picknett, Lynn, and Clive Prince, *The Templar Revelation; Secret Guardians of the True Identity of Christ,* Bantam Press, London, 1997.

Pike, Albert, *Morals and Dogma of the Ancient and Accepted Scottish Rite of Freemasonry,* L.H. Jenkins, Richmond, VA, 1921.

Pliny, *Natural History*, English, in 10 volumes, vol. ii, trans H. Rackman, 1947, Harvard University Press, Cambridge, MA; Wm Heinemann, London, 1989; vol. x, trans D.E. Eichholz, Harvard University Press, Cambridge, MA, Wm Heinemann, London, 1962.

Rappoport, A.S., *Medieval Legends of Christ*, Ivor Nicholson and Watson, London, 1934.

Read, Piers Paul, *The Templars,* Weidenfeld and Nicolson, London, 1999.

Robinson, James M., general ed., *The Nag Hammadi Library*, 1978, Harper and Row, San Francisco, CA, 1988.

Robinson, John J., *Born in Blood: The Lost Secrets of Freemasonry*, Century, London, 1989.

Robinson, John Martin, *Shugborough*, 1989, The National Trust, London, 1998.

St Irenaeus of Lyons, *Against Heresies, Book 1*, Paulist Press, New York, NY/Mahwah, NJ, 1992.

Schaberg, Jane, *The Resurrection of Mary Magdalene: Legends, Apocrypha, and the Christian Testament,* Continuum, New York, NY, and London, 2002.

Schaff, Philip, *History of the Christian Church: The Swiss Reformation*, 2 vols, T&T Clark, London, 1893.

Schonfield, Hugh J., *The Essene Odyssey*, Element Books, Longmead, Shaftesbury, Dorset, 1985.

'Secret Statutes of the Weather Order, from The Book of the Baptism of Fire', trans from French, Dr Carlos Raitzen, from the Ordnances proceeding from Count Menno van Limburg-Stirum library, posted at http://templarchronicle.homestead.com/templarsecstat2.html.

Sède, Gérard de, *The Accursed Treasure of Rennes-le-Château*, 1967, DEK Publishing, Worcester Park, Surrey, 2001.

Selander, Dr Maxwell, intro, *The Secret Book of Judas of Kerioth*, trans from Coptic by Mohammed al-Murtada and Francis Bendik, American Gnostic Church, Corpus Christi, TX, 1989.

Shah, Idris, *The Sufis*, Jonathan Cape, London, 1964.

Sinclair, Andrew, *The Discovery of the Grail,* Century, London, 1998.

Sinclair, Andrew, *The Secret Scroll*, Sinclair-Stevenson, London, 2001.

Skeels, Dell, intro and trans, *The Romance of Perceval in Prose: A Translation of the E Manuscript of the Didot Perceval*, University of Washington Press, Seattle and London, 1966.

Skinner, Matthew, letter to editor, *Gentleman's Magazine*, Part II, August 1786, pp. 649–51.

Smith, Morton, *The Secret Gospel: The Discovery and Interpretation of the Secret Gospel According to Mark*, Victor Gollancz, London, 1974.

Smyth, Frederick, *Brethren in Chivalry 1791–1991*, Lewis Masonic, Shepperton, Middx, 1991.

Souers, Philip Webster, 'The Wayland Scene on the Franks Casket', *Speculum* 18 (1943), pp. 104–11.

Southall's Pocket Guide to St Leonards and Hastings, Hastings, Sussex, c. 1837.

Springett, Bernard H., *The Secret Sects of Syria and the Lebanon*, Geo Allen & Unwin, London, nd (c. 1922).

Stein, W.J., *The Ninth Century and the Holy Grail*, trans Irene Wood, 1988, Temple Lodge, London, 2001.

Stoyanov, Yuri, *The Hidden Tradition in Europe*, Arkana, London, 1994.

Strabo, *The Geography of Strabo*, in 8 vols, viii, ed. by H.L. Jones, Loeb, London, 1932.

Subhan, John A., *Sufism: Its Saints and Shrines,* Samuel Weiser, New York, NY, 1970.

Taplow, Ellen, ed., *Twists of the Tale*, Bantam Dell, New York, NY, 1996.

The Mystery of Hawkstone Park, Hawkstone Park Leisure, Hawkstone, Shropshire, 1996.

Thiede, Carsten Peter, and Matthew d'Ancona, *The Quest for the True Cross,* Phoenix, London, 2000.

Thune, Nils, *The Behmenists and the Philadelphians: A Contribution to the Study of English Mysticism in the 17th and 18th Centuries*, Almqvist & Wiksells Boktryckeri, Uppsala, Sweden, 1948.

Toke, N.E., 'The Opus Alexandrinum and Sculptured Stone Roundels in the Retro-choir of Canterbury Cathedral', *AC* 42 (1930), pp. 189–221.

Tolkien, J.R.R., E.V. Gordon and Norman Davis, eds., *Sir Gawain and the Green Knight*, OUP, 1979.

Trubshaw, Bob, 'Oxford', *Mercian Mysteries* 13 (November 1992), pp. 8–10.

Tull, George F., *Traces of the Templars*, The King's England Press, Goldthorpe, Rotherham, 2000.

Tullett, Ken, and Ray Lax, *Stephen de Stapelbrigge*, private notes, Christchurch, Dorset, 1997.

Ulansey, David, *The Origins of the Mithraic Mysteries*, OUP, 1989.

Van Buren, Elizabeth, *The Secret of the Illuminati,* Neville Spearman, Sudbury, Suffolk, 1982.

Vaux, Roland de, *The Bible and the Ancient Near East*, Darton, Longman and Todd, London, 1972.

Vinas, Robert, *L'Ordre du Temple en Roussillon*, Editions Trabucaire, Perpignan, France, 2001.

von Eschenbach, Wolfram, *Parzival*, trans A.T. Hatto, Penguin Books, London, 1980.

Voragine, Jacobus de, *The Golden Legend,* English trans Granger Ryan and Helmut Ripperger, 1941, Ayer Company, Salem, NH, 1991.

Waite, Arthur Edward, *A New Encyclopaedia of Freemasonry*, 2 vols bound as one, Weathervane Books, New York, NY, 1970.

Wake, Archbishop, *The First Gospel of the Infancy of Jesus Christ*, The Project Gutenberg E Book Forbidden Gospels and Epistles, 2001, posted at www.gutenberg.net/etext04/fb03w10.txt

Wallenberg, J.K., *The Place-names of Kent*, Appelbergs Boktryckeriaktiebolag, Uppsala, Sweden, 1934.

Walsh, William S., *Heroes and Heroines of Fiction: Classical, Mediæval, Legendary etc.*, J.B. Lippincott, Philadelphia, PA, and London, 1915.

Ward, Richard, 'The Magic of Folly: A Brief Study of the Fool in Certain Religio-magical Traditions', *Starfire* 2:3 (April 2004), BCM Starfire, London WC1N 3XX.

Wartburgkriege, MS. c. 1250, Strophe 143.

Wasson, R. Gordon, Albert Hofman and Carl A.P. Ruck, *The Road to Eleusis: Unveiling the Secret of the Mysteries,* Ethno-mycological Studies 4, Helen and Kurt Wolff/Harcourt Brace Jovanovich, New York and London, 1978.

Webb, Diana M., 'The Holy Face of Lucca', in Brown, Allen R., pp. 227–37.

Webster, Nester, *Secret Societies and Subversive Movements*, Boswell, London, 1924.

Weston, Jessie, *The Quest of the Grail*, Bell, London, 1913.

Wilkins, David, *Concilia Magnae Britanniae et Hiberniae,* 4 vols, 1737, privately published, Brussels, 1964.

Willeford, William, *The Fool and His Sceptre,* Edward Arnold, London, 1969.

Williams, Frank, *The Panarion of Epiphanius of Salamis, Book 1, Sects 1–46*, E.J. Brill, Leiden, 1987.

Wood, David, *Genisis: The First Book of Revelations*, The Baton Press, Tunbridge Wells, Kent, 1985.

Wooll's Stranger's Guide to Hastings and St Leonards, Hastings, Sussex, c. 1833.

Wright (1), Thomas, *An Original Theory of the Universe*, intro Michael A. Hoskin, Macdonald, London; American Elsevier, New York, NY, 1971.

Wright (1), Thomas, *A Theory of the Universe* – see Wright, *An Original Theory of the Universe*.

Wright (2), Thomas, *An Essay on the Worship of the Regenerative Powers During the Middle Ages of Western Europe*, privately printed, London, 1865 – see Payne Knight.

Wright (2), Thomas, *The History of Fulk Fitz Warine, An Outlawed Baron in the Reign of King John*, Warton Club, London, 1855.

Wright (2), Thomas, *Narratives of Sorcery and Magic from the Most Authentic Sources*, 2 vols., Richard Bentley, London, 1851.

PRIMARY CHRISTIAN AND GNOSTIC TEXTS IN OTHER WORKS

Melchizedek, see Robinson, *The Nag Hammadi Library*.

Acts of John – see James.

Dialogue of the Saviour – see Robinson, *The Nag Hammadi Library*.

Evangelium Nicodemi ('Gospel of Nicodemus')/Acts of Pilate – see James.

First Gospel of the Infancy of Jesus Christ – see Wake.

Gospel of Mary – see Robinson, *The Nag Hammadi Library*.

Gospel of Philip – see Robinson, *The Nag Hammadi Library*.

Gospel of Thomas – see Robinson, *The Nag Hammadi Library*.

Pistis Sophia – see Horner.

EARLY MANUSCRIPTS IN SECONDARY SOURCES

Chrétien de Troyes, *Perceval: The Story of the Grail* – see Owen, *Arthurian Romances*.

Epiphanius of Salamis, *The Panarion* – see Williams.

John of Glastonbury, *Cronica sive Antiquitates Glastoniensis Ecclesie* – see Carley, *The Chronicle of Glastonbury Abbey*.

Josephus, Flavius, *Antiquities of the Jews* – see Flavius Josephus.

Josephus, Flavius, *Wars of the Jews* – see Flavius Josephus.

'Lludd and Llevelys' – see Guest.

Perlesvaus – see Evans.

Rabanus Maurus, *Vita Beatae Mariae Magdalenae* – see Mycoff.

Robert de Boron, *Joseph d'Arimathea* – see Bryant and Nitze.

Sir Gawain and the Green Knight – see Tolkien.

Strabo, *Geographia* – see Strabo, *The Geography of Strabo*.

The Didot Perceval – see Skeels.

'The Dream of Maxim Wledig' – see Guest.

ILLUMINATED MANUSCRIPTS AND ILLUSTRATIONS

'Archarion', MS Austrian National Library, Vienna, 1802.

Badische Landesbibliothek, Karlsruhe: Cod.Aug. perg. 161 fol. 55v.

Dürer, Albrecht, 'The Holy Family with Saint John, the Magdalene, and Nicodemus', c. 1512, drypoint, Fletcher Fund, 1919 (19.73.51).

The Stuttgart Psalter, Württembergische Landesbibliothek Stuttgart: MS. Biblia 2° 23 fol. 27.
Württembergische Landesbibliothek Stuttgart: Biblia 2° 56 fol. 131v.

DOCUMENTARIES

'Legend Hunters: The Holy Grail', directed by Chris Triffo, produced by Partners in Motion, Regina, Canada, in association with the Travel Channel and Discovery Canada, 2003. For further information go to www.partnersinmotion.com.

NOTES AND REFERENCES

1. PERDURABO CALLS

1. Wright, *Narratives of Sorcery and Magic,* i, pp. 56, 60–1.
2. Ibid., i, p. 56.
3. Booth, *A Magick Life: A Biography of Aleister Crowley,* pp. 305–6.
4. Letter from Matthew Skinner to the editor, *Gentleman's Magazine,* Pt. II, August 1786, pp. 649–51.
5. *Southall's Pocket Guide to St Leonards and Hastings,* p. 57; *Wooll's Stranger's Guide to Hastings and St Leonards,* p. 24.
6. Mainwaring Baines, *Historic Hastings,* p. 311.
7. *Wooll's Stranger's Guide to Hastings and St Leonards,* p. 24.
8. Ibid.

2. THE CUP OF BABALON

9. See Collins, *Helen and the Beast.*
10. See Collins, *The Second Coming.*
11. The following précised account of the Grail story is based on Robert de Boron's *Joseph d'Arimathie,* taken from the French text of *Le Roman de l'estoire dou Graal,* trans. Nitze (from which the verse numbers derive), as well as Bryant, *Merlin and the Grail: Joseph of Arimathea, Merlin, Perceval: The Trilogy of Prose Romances Attributed to Robert de Boron.*
12. Mark 14:22–25. All quotes from the Bible are taken from the King James Revised Edition, 1611.
13. Boron, vs. 3332.
14. Ibid, vs. 909.

3. THE HEAD OF GOD

15. Ekwall, *The Concise Oxford Dictionary of English Place-names, s.v.* 'Stalbridge', p. 436.
16. Personal information supplied by Geoff Wilson, the present owner of The Manor, Templecombe, Somerset.
17. Lord, *The Knights Templar in Britain,* pp. 118–9.
18. Luke 1:5.
19. Matthew 3:11, 12; Luke 3:16.
20. John 1:29.
21. Pliny, *Natural History,* v, 15.
22. Josephus, *The Antiquities of the Jews,* XVIII, 5, 2.
23. Matt. 14:17–8.
24. Matt. 14:1–2.
25. Matt. 14:19–21.
26. Matt. 11:11, Mark 6:15, 8:28, Luke 1:17, 9:8, 19, John 1:21.
27. Matt. 14:9–12.
28. Voragine, *The Golden Legend of Jacobus de Voragine, s.v.* 'August 29, the Decollation of Saint John the Baptist', p. 504.

29. Ibid., pp. 505–7.
30. Ibid., p. 507.
31. Ibid., p. 509.
32. Sinclair, *The Discovery of the Grail*, p. 142.
33. This seal belonged to Simon, Commander of the Paris Temple, 1242.
34. Sinclair, *The Secret Scroll*, p. 53.

4. THE FRENCH CONNECTION

35. Barber, *The Trial of the Templars*, p. 202.
36. Ibid.
37. Ibid.
38. Olsen, 'St Michael's Church, Garway', *The Temple* 3 (September 2003), pp. 24–5.
39. Wright, *The Worship of the Generative Powers*, p. 138, cf. Wilkins, *Concil.*, ii, p. 363.
40. Wright, *Narratives of Sorcery and Magic*, i, p. 56.
41. Ibid., i, p. 59, for the two-faced head with beard at the Paris temple; Wright, *The Worship of the Generative Powers*, p. 136, for the account of Guillaume de Arrablay.
42. Wright, *The Worship of the Generative Powers*, p. 135.
43. Picknett and Prince, *The Templar Revelation*, pp. 213–4.
44. The Baroness of Arques, Henrietta-Catherine de Joyeuse, the wife of Charles de Lorraine, Duc de Guise, was banished with her husband to Italy in 1631, when Poussin was also in residence in Rome. It seems highly probable that they would have met whilst there since they shared a dislike of Louis XIII, King of France, and Cardinal Richelieu, the French Prime Minister. See emails from Guy Patton to the author dated 31 March and 1 April 2004.
45. Mazières, *Les templiers du Bézu*, p. 11.
46. Patton and Mackness, *Sacred Treasure, Secret Power*, pp. 44–5.
47. See for example *Wartburgkriege*, MS. c. 1250, Strophe 143.
48. Dunlop, vol. 1, pp. 463–65. See also Stein, *The Ninth Century and the Holy Grail*, pp. 80, 80 n. 4, cf. Sopranis in his biography of Guglielmo Embriaco.
49. See Buechner, *Emerald Cup – Ark of Gold: The Quest of SS Lt Otto Rahn of the Third Reich*.

5. LIGHT OF THE GRAIL

50. See Chrétien de Troyes, *Perceval: Le Conte de Graal*, in Owen, *Chrétien de Troyes, Arthurian Romances*, pp. 374–495.
51. First Continuation, trans. Loomis, in Loomis, *The Grail: From Celtic Myth to Christian Symbol*, pp. 67–73, 225–7.
52. Ibid., p. 225.
53. Ibid.
54. See Wolfram von Eschenbach, *Parzival*, trans. Hatto.
55. Kahane, Kahane and Pietrangeli, *The Krater and the Grail*, pp. 152–4. The authors cite several examples of *langue d'Oc*, Aragonese and Gascony words preserved in *Parzival*.
56. Ibid., p. 154.
57. Skeat, *Joseph of Arimathie*, p. xxxvi.
58. In an early thirteenth-century work, Rigaut de Barbezieux, a troubadour of southern France and contemporary of Chrétien de Troyes, compares himself to Perceval in a poem and speaks of failing to ask the question when the Holy Lance

and Grail came into view. His spelling of Grail is not the *graal* of Chrétien but *grazaus*, a variation of the *langue d'Oc grazal*. See McCash, 'Marie of Champagne and Eleanor of Aquatine', *Speculum* 54:4 (October 1979), p. 703. Moreover, by the mid-fourteenth century the authors of the Troubadour-inspired *Leys d'Amor* and the *Flors del Guy Saber,* both written in the *langue d'Oc*, allude to the prose version of the 'Sant Grazal', emphasising the southern usage of the word *grazal* instead of the French *graal*.

59. Wolfram von Eschenbach, *Parzival*, trans. as quoted in Stein, *The Ninth Century and the Holy Grail*, p. 102.
60. Olschki, *The Grail Castle and Its Mysteries*, p. 6.
61. Ibid., p. 40.
62. John 1:4–5.
63. 1 Epist. 1:5–7.
64. Webster, *Secret Societies and Subversive Movements*, p. 31.
65. See Matthew 3:11; Acts 2:1–4.
66. See Oldenbourg, *Massacre at Montségur*, pp. 46–7.

6. THE POISON CHALICE

67. Blair, *The World Illustrated Bible Handbook*, p. 254.
68. Mark 1:16–20; Luke 5:1–10.
69. John 13:23, 19:26, 20:2, 21:7, 21:20.
70. John 18:16.
71. John 18:15.
72. John 13:23, 19:26, 20:2, 21:7, 21:20.
73. See Green-Armytage, *John Who Saw,* for a full argument in favour of John the Evangelist being the Beloved Disciple, as well as the author of the Fourth Gospel, the Epistles of John and the book of Revelation.
74. John 13:23, 13:25.
75. John 21:20.
76. John 18:15.
77. John 18:15–6.
78. Green-Armytage, p. 69.
79. John 19:26–7.
80. John 19:25.
81. John 19:38–40.
82. John 19:34.
83. John 19:35.
84. John 20:2.
85. John 20:4–5.
86. Schonfield, *The Essene Odyssey*, p. 52.
87. John 21:7.
88. Gal. 2:9.
89. Rev. 1:11.
90. See James, *The Apocryphal New Testament*, p. 229.
91. Probable reconstruction of chapters 1–17 of the Acts of John in James, *The Apocryphal New Testament*, pp. 228–9.
92. Ibid., p. 229.
93. Jameson, *Sacred and Legendary Art*, i, pp. 158–9.

94. Ibid., i, p. 159. See also Acts of John, appended Greek text entitled the Death or Assumption of John, ch. xx.
95. Ibid.
96. Matt. 20:20–3.
97. Mark 10:38.
98. Mark 10:39–40.
99. Jameson, i, p. 159.
100. Ibid., i, p. 164.
101. Brown, *The Community of the Beloved Disciple*, p. 184.
102. John 21:20.
103. Rappoport, *Medieval Legends of Christ*, p. 291.
104. The Toledoth Jeschu of Huldrich, as quoted in Baring-Gould, *The Lost and Hostile Gospels*, p. 109.
105. Epiphanius *The Panarion*, 3, 37, 5.6–5.7.
106. Selander, *The Secret Book of Judas of Kerioth*, pp. 6–7. See also Wasson, Hofman and Ruck, *The Road to Eleusis: Unveiling the Secret of the Mysteries*.
107. Selander, p. 6. See also Allegro, *The Sacred Mushroom and the Cross*.
108. Sinclair, *The Secret Scroll*, p. 151.
109. Ibid., p. 66.
110. John 21:22.
111. John 21:23.
112. Acts of John, 115.
113. Green-Armytage, pp. 125–7.
114. Macgregor, *The Gospel of John*, p. 376, commentary on John 21:21.
115. Baring-Gould, *Curious Myths of the Middle Ages*, p. 6.
116. Schonfield, p. 110; Baring-Gould, *Curious Myths of the Middle Ages*, p. 13.
117. Rappoport, pp. 235–6.
118. Ibid., p. 241.
119. Ibid., pp. 241–2.
120. Baring-Gould, *Curious Myths of the Middle Ages*, p. 35, after Matthew 2:11.
121. Wolfram von Eschenbach, *Parzival*, p. 408.

7. THE TWO JOHNS

122. John 1:36.
123. Picknett and Prince, *The Templar Revelation*, p. 316.
124. Ibid., p. 315.
125. Jameson, *Sacred and Legendary Art*, i, p. 163.
126. Mackenzie, *The Royal Masonic Cyclopaedia, s.v.* 'Dedication', pp. 148–9.
127. Waite, *A New Encyclopaedia of Freemasonry*, i, p. 178.
128. Waite, i, pp. 178–9.
129. Macoy, *A Dictionary of Freemasonry, s.v.* 'Dedication', pp. 482–3.
130. Ibid., i, p. 179.
131. Webster, *Secret Societies and Subversive Movements*, p. 65.
132. *Manuel des Chevaliers de l'Ordre du Temple*, 1811, in Ibid., p. 65.
133. The *Levitikon*, in Ibid., p. 65.
134. Smyth, *Brethren in Chivalry 1791–1991*, pp. 40–1.
135. Webster, p. 66.
136. Ibid.

137. Barber, *The Trial of the Templars*, p. 202.
138. Webster, p. 69.
139. Sinclair, *The Secret Scroll*, p. 33.
140. Yarker, John, *The Kneph*, v, 4. as quoted in Springett, *The Secret Sects of Syria and the Lebanon*, p. 288.
141. Springett, pp. 290–1.
142. Ibid., p. 292.
143. Charter No. 206 of 14 February 1148 as quoted in Boumendil, *Les Cahiers de Rennes-le-Château: Archives, Documents, Etude* 2 (June 1984), pp. 9–10.
144. Boumendil, *Les Cahiers de Rennes-le-Château: Archives, Documents, Etude* 2 (June 1984), p. 9.
145. Ibid., p. 10.
146. Ibid.
147. Ibid.
148. Sède, *The Accursed Treasure of Rennes-le-Château*, p. 83.
149. There was also a church of St Pierre (St Peter) in Rennes-le-Château, the location of which is still preserved.

8. THE WORLD TREE

150. The dream in which Aleister Crowley crowned Richard King Mithras took place overnight Friday/Saturday, 28/29 December 2001. His first glimpse of the gnarled old tree at the centre of the great circle of sites known as the Star of Babalon occurred on Sunday, 23 December 2001. I have conflated the two events for continuity purposes.
151. This psychic session took place on Tuesday, 11 December 2001.
152. Mee, *The King's England: Kent*, s.v. 'Stockbury', p. 425.
153. Cumont, *The Mysteries of Mithra*, p. 156.
154. Michell, *At the Centre of the World*, pp. 117–8, 122–5.

9. THE CALL OF ARCADIA

155. This meditation took place on Sunday, 23 December 2001.
156. Robinson, *Shugborough*, p. 25.
157. Ibid., p. 31.
158. Wright, *An Original Theory of the Universe*, pp. 62–3. See also Hoskin, 'The Cosmology of Thomas Wright of Durham', *JHA* 1 (1970), pp. 44–52.
159. Wright's *The Elements of Existence or A Theory of the Universe* is included alongside his *An Original Theory or New Hypothesis of the Universe* found in Ibid.
160. Ibid., p. 5.
161. Hoskin, intro. to Wright, p. xxiii n. 28.
162. Ibid., p. xxiii n. 28. See also Thune, *The Behmenists and the Philadelphians,* for a full history and account of the philosophy of the society.
163. See Mackenzie, *The Royal Masonic Cyclopaedia*, s.v. 'Ramsay, Andrew Michael', pp. 592–3; s.v. 'Ramsay's Rite', p. 594.
164. See Lincoln, *Key to the Sacred Pattern: the Untold Story of Rennes-le-Château*, pp. 78–80.
165. Thanks to Andrew Baker for this information, and other facts on the life of Thomas Wright of Durham.

166. This same explanation was given in a letter to Rennes-le-Château researcher Paul Smith from Margaret, Countess of Lichfield, dated 18 May 1987. However, she claimed that the words simply came to her when showing some friends around the garden one day.

167. Thanks to Rosemary Arscott for pointing this out to me.

10. SECRET LAST SUPPER

168. See Carley, *Glastonbury Abbey*, p. 98.

169. See, for instance, Picknett, *Mary Magdalene: Christianity's Hidden Goddess,* pp. 218–9, 224.

170. For a full account of the pagan Saxon symbolism of the Frank's Casket see Branston, *The Lost Gods of England*, pp. 9–14, 62, 126; Elliott, *Runes: An Introduction*, pp. 106–9; Souers, 'The Wayland Scene on the Franks Casket', *Speculum* 18 (1943), pp. 104–11.

171. Among those taken hostage following the siege were the sons and brothers of Isates, King of Adiabene, a Jewish kingdom of Mesopotamia. See Furneaux, *The Roman Siege of Jerusalem*, p. 171.

172. Josephus, *Wars of the Jews*, VI, ix, 3.

173. Elliott, pp. 100–1.

174. Leitch, 'The Franks Casket: Sabine Baring-Gould and the Sangreal', *The Temple* 1 (August 2002), pp. 5–11. See also Leitch, Yuri, 'Franks Casket: Genesis of the Grail Myth', *The Temple* 2 (February 2003), pp. 41–2.

175. John 3:1–21.

176. Voragine, *Chronicon Januense*, as quoted in Dunlop, *History of Prose Fiction*, i, p. 465.

177. Weston, *The Quest of the Holy Grail*, p. 57.

178. Begg and Begg, *In Search of the Holy Grail and the Precious Blood*, s.v. 'Fécamp', pp. 43–9.

179. Account taken from Webb, 'The Holy Face of Lucca', in Brown, *Anglo-Norman Studies IX: Proceedings of the Battle Conference*, pp. 227–37.

180. Begg and Begg, s.v. 'Lucca', pp. 141–3.

181. John 3:1

182. John 7:50–52.

183. John 19:39–40.

184. Matt. 27:57, Luke 23:50.

185. See, for example, the miniature from a manuscript created c. 1165 in the Benedictine abbey of Zwiefalten, Germany. Württembergische Landesbibliothek Stuttgart: Biblia 2° 56 fol. 131v. See also the Crucifixion scene from a Latin manuscript of the late eleventh century, probably Bavarian in origin. Badische Landesbibliothek, Karlsruhe, Germany: Cod.Aug. perg. 161 fol. 55v.

186. This assumption is confirmed in the knowledge that elsewhere in Egbert's Psalter is an illustration showing Joseph and Nicodemus placing Jesus's body in the sepulchre, and here Joseph is also depicted as an elderly man with a beard.

187. Rappaport, *Medieval Legends of Christ*, p. 291.

188. See Stein, *The Ninth Century and the Holy Grail*, pp. 9–28, for the legend and history of Reichenau's blood-relic.

189. The Stuttgart Psalter. Württembergische Landesbibliothek Stuttgart: MS. Biblia 2° 23 fol. 27.

190. Cabaniss, 'Joseph of Arimathea and a Chalice,' *Mississippi Studies in English* 4 (1963), pp. 61–7. For some arguments against Cabaniss's theories see O'Gorman, 'Ecclesiastical Tradition and the Holy Grail', *Australian Journal of French Studies* 6 (1969), pp. 3–8.
191. Luke 22:50, John 18:10.
192. Matt. 26:51, Mark 14:47.
193. Mark 14:48–9.
194. Epistle or Report of Pilate, Acts of Pilate, Pt. II, XIII (XXIX), trans and notes James, *The Apocryphal New Testament*, p. 146.
195. See Malachi, 2 & 3.
196. John 18:11.
197. Matt. 26:37, Mark 14:33–4.
198. Mark 14:36.
199. Matt. 22:43–4; Luke 22:44.
200. Luke 22:15.
201. Smith, *The Secret Gospel*, p. 64.
202. Ibid.
203. Ibid., p. 43.
204. Ibid., p. 64.

11. THE APOSTATE

205. Compiled from the notes made by Ken Tullett and Ray Lax of Christchurch between 1994 and 1997, and drawn from a plethora of sources including Wilkins, *Concilia Magnae Britanniae et Hiberniae*, London, 1737, and the diocesan records of Hereford and Worcester, catalogued as Tullett and Lax, *Stephen de Stapelbrigge*.
206. Barber, *The Trial of the Templars*, p. 200.
207. Ibid.
208. Lord, *The Knights Templar in Britain*, p. 146.
209. Barber, p. 200.
210. Ibid.
211. Ibid.
212. Ibid.
213. See 'The Secret Statutes of the Weather Order, from The Book of the Baptism of Fire', translated from the French by Dr Carlos Raitzen, from the Ordnances proceeding from Count Menno van Limburg-Stirum library.
214. See Matt. 3:11; Acts 2:1–4.
215. See Vinas, *L'Ordre du Temple en Roussillon*.
216. Schonfield, *The Essene Odyssey*, p. 164.
217. Loiseleur, *La Doctrine Secrète des Templiers*, pp. 146–55.
218. Ibid., p. 149.
219. Barber, p. 200.
220. Lord, p. 116.
221. See Robinson, *Born in Blood*.
222. Ibid., p. 237.
223. Ibid.

12. THE CROWN OF MITHRAS

224. Ekwall, *The Concise Dictionary of English Place-names, s.v.* 'Headcorn', p. 229.
225. I have found nothing subsequently to connect Queen Elizabeth with Headcorn.

226. Mee, *The King's England: Kent, s.v.* 'Headcorn', pp. 231–3.
227. Tull, *Traces of the Templars,* p. 51, cf. Walter Map.
228. Ibid.
229. Read, *The Templars,* p. 184; Lord, p. 163.
230. Lord, p. 163.
231. Several websites on pit-bulls mention this fact, including 'The Online Pitbull Source' at www.bluepitstop.com/history.html.
232. See Ulansey, *The Origins of the Mithraic Mysteries,* for a full account of the relationship between the Mithraic *tauroctony* and the dawn of the astrological age of Aries, which began around 2200–2000 BC.
233. Ekwall, *The Concise Oxford Dictionary of English Place-names, s.v.* 'Headcorn', p. 229.
234. Ibid.
235. Wallenberg, *The Place-names of Kent, s.v.* 'Headcorn', pp. 220–4.
236. Ibid.
237. Ibid.
238. Ibid.
239. Ekwall, *s.v.* 'Penge', p. 361.

13. THE CUP OF JANUS

240. Mee, *The King's England: Kent, s.v.* 'Stone-in-Oxney', p. 428.
241. This dream took place overnight on Saturday, 30 March/Sunday, 31 March 2002.
242. Subhan, *Sufism: Its Saints and Shrines,* pp. 8–11.
243. Ibid., pp. 25–6.
244. Ibid., p. 58.
245. Ibid., pp. 61–2. Cross-checked with Shah, *The Sufis,* p. 430.
246. Subhan, pp. 62–3.
247. Ibid., p. 63.
248. Ibid., p. 64.
249. The seven spheres are in order of appearance *khatt-i jawr, baghdad, basrah, siyah* (or *azraq), ashk, kasigar,* and *farudina* (or *muzawar*). See Iraj Bashiri, *Hafiz' Shirazi Turk: A Structuralist's Point of View,* posted at www.iles.umn.edu/faculty/bashiri/Hafiz%20folder/Hafiz.html.
250. Subhan, p. 64.
251. Daraul (Idris Shah), *Secret Societies,* p. 72.
252. See Collins, *From the Ashes of Angels,* pp. 118–22, 143, for more on the Persian concept of the royal *farr.*
253. This was *Tutankhamun: The Exodus Conspiracy,* co-authored with Chris Ogilvie-Herald.
254. Mee, *s.v.* 'Brookland', p. 76.
255. Ibid.
256. This psychic session took place on Tuesday, 11 December 2001.
257. Grant, *The Ninth Arch,* pp. 80–2, 84.
258. See Grant, *The Magical Revival.*
259. Crowley, 'Liber CLVI', in Crowley, *The Holy Books of Thelema, Equinox* vol. 3 No. 9, pp. 101–3.
260. Crowley, *Moonchild,* p. 100.
261. Ibid., pp. 92–3.

14. PUZZLES IN STONE

262. See Constantine, 'Of a Cat, But Her Skin', in Taplow, ed., *Twists in the Tale*.

263. For a full account of the Cat Monument see Robinson, *Shugborough*, pp. 82–3.

264. Picknett and Prince, *The Templar Revelation*, pp. 48–9.

265. Ibid., p. 194. Thanks to Clive Prince for providing details of the finger bone of John the Baptist at St Anne's church, Arques.

266. I think the first reference to this alignment is found in Wood's *Genisis: The First Book of Revelations*, pp. 53–4.

267. Milton, *Paradise Lost*, II, 943–7.

268. Picknett and Prince, p. 214.

269. Jarnac, *Les Archives du Trésor de Rennes-le-Château*, pp. 384–5.

270. See the Manichaean Psalm Book II, 187, as quoted in Schaberg, *The Resurrection of Mary Magdalene*, pp. 142–3.

15. THE MAGDALENE

271. See Lynn Picknett's *Mary Magdalene: Christianity's Hidden Goddess* for her latest opinions on the Magdalene.

272. Luke 8:2.

273. Ibid.

274. John 11:18.

275. Luke 24:50.

276. Luke 10:39.

277. Luke 10:42.

278. Matt 26:26.

279. Matt. 26:7.

280. Matt. 26:8–11.

281. Matt. 26:20–13.

282. Mark 14:3.

283. Mark 14:4–5. It says 'pence' in the Revised Edition, although it was originally denarii and makes for better reading.

284. Mark 14:7–8.

285. Luke 7:36–7.

286. Luke 7:37.

287. Luke 7:38.

288. Luke 7:39.

289. Luke 7:44–6.

290. Luke 7:47.

291. John 12:1.

292. John 12:2.

293. John 12:3.

294. John 12:4–5.

295. John 12:7.

296. Vaux, *The Bible and the Ancient Near East*, p. 152.

297. Mark 15:1–2.

298. Isaiah 61:1.

299. Daniel 9:24–26.

300. Zechariah 12:3–10.

301. Cant. 1:12.

302. See Smith, *The Secret Gospel.*
303. Luke 10:39.
304. Matt. 27:55.
305. Matt. 27:55–6.
306. Mark 15:40.
307. John 19:25.
308. John 19:39.
309. Matt. 27:61.
310. Mark 15:47.
311. Luke 23:55
312. Luke 23:56.
313. Matt. 28:5–7.
314. Matt. 28:8–10.
315. Mark 16:1–2.
316. Luke 24:1.
317. Mark 16:9.
318. Luke 24:24–5, 50–1.
319. John 20:1.
320. John 20:2.
321. John 20:3–8.
322. John 20:9.
323. John 20:10–12.
324. John 20:13.
325. John 20:14–15.
326. John 20:16.
327. John 20:17–18.
328. Haskins, *Mary Magdalen: Myth and Metaphor*, p. 63.
329. Ibid., p. 65.
330. Schaberg, *The Resurrection of Mary Magdalene,* p. 82, cf. Clement, *Excerpta* 50, 1 and Origen, *Joh. Comm.*, fr. 78, pp. 544–5.
331. See Rom. 16:1–16.
332. For a fuller account of the discovery of the Nag Hammadi library and Mary Magdalene's role in the Gnostic gospels see Pagels, *The Gnostic Gospels*; Malvern, *Venus in Sackcloth: The Magdalen's Origins and Metamorphoses*; Haskins, *op. cit.*, and Schaberg, *op. cit.*
333. Gospel of Philip, 59.
334. Haskins, p. 40.
335. Gospel of Philip, 63.
336. Schaberg, p. 168.
337. Gospel of Mary, 10.
338. Ibid., 17.
339. Ibid., 19.
340. Gospel of Thomas, 114.
341. Ibid.
342. Dialogue of the Saviour, 12–13.
343. Ibid.
344. Schaberg, pp. 136, 155.
345. Pistis Sophia, p. xviii n. 1.
346. Ibid., 27b.

347. Ibid., 54b.
348. Ibid., 149b–150a.

16. THE BELOVED DISCIPLE

349. Hippolytus, *Philosophumena or the Refutation of All Heresies*, v, 7; x, 9.
350. Pistis Sophia, 96 cf. Schaberg, *The Resurrection of Mary Magdalene*, p. 150.
351. Haskins, *Mary Magdalen: Myth and Metaphor*, pp. 136, 158.
352. Ibid., p. 158.
353. Ibid., p. 107, cf. Modestus of Jerusalem, J.-P. Migne, *Patrologiae cursus completus. Series graeca*, LXXXVI, cols 3273–6.
354. Ibid., pp. 106–7.
355. Ibid., p. 106.
356. Picknett and Prince, *The Templar Revelation*, p. 243.
357. Jusino, *Mary Magdalene: Author of the Fourth Gospel?* Much of his core ideas about the Johannine community derive from the work of eminent Catholic scripture scholar Raymond E. Brown, particularly his *The Community of the Beloved Disciple*, published in 1979.
357. John 21:7.
358. 2 Cor. xii. 2–5.
360. See Green-Armytage, *John Who Saw*, pp. 68–9.
361. Picknett and Prince, pp. 19–24.
362. Ibid., p. 20.
363. Ibid., p. 21.
364. Ibid., p. 53.
365. See, for instance, Guillot, *Léonard de Vinci: le mythe de l'androgyne*.
366. Meeks, 'The Image of the Androgyne: Some Uses of a Symbol in Earliest Christianity', *History of Religions* 13:3 (February 1974), p. 189.
367. Ibid., p. 186 n. 94, 189.
368. Ibid., p. 191.
369. Ibid., p. 189.
370. Ibid., pp. 189, 191.
371. See Collins, *From the Ashes of Angels*, pp. 224–7, for a full account of the sacred marriage in the religious practices of ancient Mesopotamia.
372. Meeks, p. 189.
373. A ciborium is the covered chalice-like vessel in which the wafers of the sacrament are kept.
374. Lebeuf, 'Maria Magdalena: The Morning Star', *Vistas in Astronomy* 39:4 (1995), pp. 96–99.
375. First Gospel of the Infancy of Jesus Christ, II, 2.
376. Haskins, p. 278.
377. Haskins, p. 104.
378. Boron, *Joseph d'Arimathie*, ll. 319, 375–7, see Nitze, *Le Roman de l'Estoire dou Graal* and Bryant, *Merlin and the Grail: Joseph of Arimathea, Merlin, Perceval*.
379. Boron, ll. 434, 495–520. See also Rappoport, *Medieval Legends of Christ*, pp. 290–1.
380. Rappoport, p. 291.
381. Voragine, *Chronicon Januense*, as quoted in Dunlop, *History of Prose Fiction*, i, p. 465.
382. See Sinclair, *The Discovery of the Grail*, pp. 117, 120.

383. Haskins, p. 196.

384. Sinclair, p. 42, regarding the Aachen Passion Altar of 1520.

385. Ibid., p. 114.

386. Ibid., p. 115. See also Begg and Begg, *In Search of the Holy Grail and the Precious Blood, s.v.* 'Saint-Maximin', pp. 75–6. Apparently, the Holy Blood was seen to liquefy and bubble as late as 1876, although today the flask is no longer displayed.

387. See John of Glastonbury, *Cronica sive Antiquitates Glastoniensis Ecclesie,* 14.

17. THE HOLLOW TOWER

388. This vision occurred on Monday, 8 April 2002.

389. See Toke, 'The Opus Alexandrinum and Sculptured Stone Roundels in the Retro-choir of Canterbury Cathedral', *AC* 42 (1930), pp. 189–221.

390. Ibid., p. 199 & pl. 1.

391. Richard visited the belvedere at Horns Hill after reading about occult activities that had supposedly happened at nearby Ide Hill in 1986. See Collins, *The Black Alchemist.*

392. Summary of the story of Klingsor taken from Walsh, *Heroes and Heroines of Fiction etc., s.v.* 'Klingsor', pp. 167–8.

393. Ibid., *s.v.* 'Amfortas', p. 20.

394. See Margaret Murray's books *The God of the Witches* (1931) and *The Divine King in England* (1954).

18. THE LIFE OF MARY

395. Haskins, *Mary Magdalen: Myth and Metaphor*, p. 114.

396. Ibid., p. 120.

397. Ibid., p. 108.

398. Ibid., pp. 119–20.

399. Ibid., p. 117.

400. Ibid., pp. 120–1.

401. For the *Vita Beatae Mariae Magdalenae* of Rabanus Maurus see Mycoff, *The Life of Saint Mary Magdalene and of her Sister Saint Martha.*

402. See Mycoff, Introduction to Ibid., and also email communication from David Mycoff to the author on 30 April 2003.

403. Haskins, p. 121.

404. Voragine, *The Golden Legend of Jacobus de Voragine, s.v.* 'July 22, Saint Mary Magdalene', pp. 355–64.

405. Sinclair, *The Discovery of the Grail*, p. 114.

406. Ibid., p. 115.

407. Ibid.

408. Ibid., p. 124.

409. Ibid., p. 125.

410. Ibid., p. 130.

411. Ibid., p. 127.

412. Lebeuf, 'Maria Magdalena: The Morning Star', *Vistas in Astronomy* 39:4 (1995), pp. 591–603.

413. Ibid., pp. 599–602.

414. Lincoln, *The Holy Place*, pp. 68–72, etc.

415. The Secret Book of Judas of Kerioth, 1:6.

416. See Baigent, Leigh and Lincoln, *The Holy Blood and the Holy Grail*, 1996 edition, pp. 486–8, and also Picknett and Prince, *The Templar Revelation*, pp. 50–51.

417. Stoyanov, *The Hidden Tradition in Europe*, pp. 222–3.

418. See Evans, intro and trans., *The High History of the Grail*.

419. St Irenaeus of Lyons, *Against Heresies*, I, xxvi, 1. As quoted in Brown, *The Community of the Beloved Disciple*, p. 112.

420. Sinclair, p. 115.

421. This dream occurred overnight on Thursday, 2 May 2002.

422. See Gen. 15:18, Isa. 27:20.

423. Num. 20:12–3.

424. See Collins and Ogilvie-Herald, *Tutankhamun: The Exodus Conspiracy*, pp. 209–12, 238.

425. Starbird, *The Woman with the Alabaster Jar*, p. 50.

426. Matt. 15:39.

427. Picknett and Prince, *The Templar Revelation*, p. 248.

428. Mark 15:40, Matt. 27:55, Luke 23:55.

429. Picknett and Prince, p. 248. See also Ezek. 29:10, 30:6.

430. Num. 33:7 in *Jerome's Latin Vulgate Bible* (AD 405), posted at http://speedbible.com/vulgate/B04C033.htm.

431. Ex. 14:2, Num. 33:7–8.

432. Picknett and Prince see the Magdalene as having been a priestess of the cult of Isis, the wife of Orsis..

433. See Albrecht Dürer, 'The Holy Family with Saint John, the Magdalene, and Nicodemus', c. 1512, drypoint, Fletcher Fund, 1919 (19.73.51).

434. See the Gospel of the Hebrews, which includes the passage 'Out of Egypt have I called my Son', in Baring-Gould, *The Lost and Hostile Gospels etc.*, p. 121. See also Origen answering Celsus, who thrived in the mid-second century. He speaks of Jesus's residence in Egypt having some 'spiritual meaning', and says that Celsus claimed that following a bad education Jesus 'passed into service there, and there learnt some wonderful arts. When he came back to his fatherland, on account of these arts, he gave himself out to be a God.' See Ibid., cf. Origen, *Contra Celsus*, lib. i.

19. THE CUP WILL COME

435. This psychic session took place on Tuesday, 16 July 2002.

436. This psychic session took place on Tuesday, 21 May 2002.

437. This psychic session took place on Thursday, 27 June 2002.

438. I have deliberately provided a pseudonym for the location of the chapel in order to ensure its privacy.

439. Page, ed., *Victoria County History Kent*, II, p. 169.

440. Ibid.

441. Ibid., II, p. 170.

442. Ibid.

20. THE FEAST OF FOOLS

443. See Phillips and Keatman, *King Arthur – the True Story*.

444. For a full account of the medieval Feast of Fools see Hone, *Ancient Mysteries Described*, pp. 148–92.

445. For a full account of this process see Willeford, *The Fool and His Sceptre*.

446. Tolkien, Gordon and Davis, eds., *Sir Gawain and the Green Knight*.

447. Information supplied from the Air Supply official website found at airsupplymusic.com.

448. Phillips and Keatman, *Robin Hood: The Man Behind the Myth*.

449. I thank Graham Russell for permission to quote lyrics from '22 Years of Nothing'.

450. Wright, *The History of Fulk Fitz Warine, An Outlawed Baron in the Reign of King John*. See also Keen, *The Outlaws of Medieval Legend*, pp. 44–52 for the full relationship between Robin Hood and Fulk Fitz Warine.

451. Loomis, *The Grail from Celtic Myth to Christian Symbol*, pp. 132–4.

452. See Phillips, *The Search for the Grail*.

453. Keen, p. 41.

454. Skeels, *The Romance of Perceval in Prose: A Translation of the E Manuscript of the Didot Perceval*, p. vii.

455. Ibid., p. 66, even though on the same page the distance between the White Castle and the Castle of the Fisher King is cited as 'one year pass'.

456. Loomis, pp. 132–4.

457. See *Hawkstone: A Short History and Guide*, p. 36, cf. Miss Jane Hill, *The Antiquities of Hawkstone*, 1834. The story of Sir Ewaine/Uwaine and the Lady of the Rock is found in *Le Morte Darthur* by Thomas Malory, IV, xxvi–xxvii.

21. THE FACELESS ONES

458. For a full account of these discoveries, and their plausible historical authenticity, see Thiede and d'Ancona, *The Quest for the True Cross*.

459. 'Archarion', MS, Austrian National Library Vienna, 1802. See McIntosh, *The Rosicrucians: The History and Mythology of an Occult Order*, pls. 11 & 12.

460. See McIntosh, pl. 11.

461. See Willeford, *The Fool and His Sceptre*, pl. 12 on p. 39.

462. Again, see Ibid., particularly pl. 8 on p. 35, pl. 9 on p. 36, pl. 10 on p. 37.

463. Leland, *Etruscan Roman Remains*, p. 130: '*Diavolo che sei capo, di tutti i diavoli! La testa ti voglio stiacciare fino che o spirito di Jano, per me non vai a pregare!*' ('Thou devil who art chief of all the fiends! I will crush thy head until the spirit of Jano thou callest for me!').

464. Ibid., pp. 130–1.

465. Occasionally, Prudence was card number seventeen in the Tarot pack.

466. Ward, 'The Magic of Folly: A Brief Study of the Fool in Certain Religio-magical Traditions', *Starfire* 2:3 (April 2004).

467. Sinclair, *The Discovery of the Grail*, p. 78.

468. Ibid., p. 141.

469. Begg and Begg, *In Search of the Holy Grail and the Precious Blood*, s.v. 'Genoa', p. 140.

470. Ps. 110:4.

471. Heb. 5:10.

472. Gen. 14:18.

473. Melchizedek, in Robinson, *The Nag Hammadi Library*, pp. 438–44.

474. Pistis Sophia, 12a–13b.

22. THE MARIAN CHALICE

475. Dr Mary Keeble is a pseudonym at the request of the archaeologist in question. She features under her real name in a documentary produced in 2003 by Partners

in Motion of Regina, Canada, in association with the Travel Channel and Discovery Canada, called 'Legend Hunters: The Holy Grail'. Here she confirms her views on the Marian Chalice during an interview with Graham Phillips and the author.

476. This visit to the British Museum took place on Tuesday, 8 April 2003.

477. Matt. 26:7, Mark 14:3, Luke 7:37.

478. Pliny, *Natural History*, XXXVI, xii, 59–61.

479. Ibid., XXXVI, xii, 60.

480. Ibid., XXXVI, xii, 61.

481. This information was supplied by a number of alabaster traders I consulted in Cairo, Egypt, in April 2004.

482. *Vita Beatae Mariae Magdalenae*, lls. 194–6.

483. Haskins, *Mary Magdalene: Myth and Metaphor*, p. 137.

484. John 12:3.

485. Strabo, *Geographia*, XVI, 781.

486. Personal communication with Roger Whitehouse, the spokesman on history at Hawkstone Park, on 12 February 2003.

487. McBride, *A History of Hawkstone*, p. 6.

488. *The Mystery of Hawkstone Park*, p. 3. This contains a full account of the discovery of the Marian Chalice and other Templar-based mysteries associated with the park.

489. Crowley, 'Energized Enthusiasm: A Note on Theurgy', *Gems From the Equinox*, p. 635.

490. Harris, 'The Heraldry of Freemasonry', *The Builder* 15:8 (1929).

491. Macoy, *A Dictionary of Freemasonry, s.v.* 'Arms of Freemasonry', pp. 92–3.

492. Mackenzie, *The Royal Masonic Cyclopaedia, s.v.* 'Eagle', pp. 168–9.

493. See Jackson, *Beyond the Craft*, pp. 42–7.

494. Perhaps showing the Hill family's continental connections is the fact that Richard Hill (1654–1727), as well as being Lord of the Admiralty and a wealthy diplomat, was Envoy Extraordinary to Maximilian II Emanuel, Elector of Bavaria (1680–1726), at Brussels between 1696–99.

495. Voragine, *Chronicon Januense,* as quoted in Dunlop, *History of Prose Fiction*, i, p. 465.

496. I discovered this connection when a series of five letters from Thomas Wright to Sir Emerson Tennant at the Board of Trade between April and October 1872 were offered for sale in February 2003 by Julian Browning of London, a dealer in autograph letters, manuscripts and historical documents. They included references to several of Mr Wright's friends including Edward George Earl Bulwer-Lytton, J.A. Froude, Charles Kingsley and J.O. Halliwell.

497. See, for instance, Colquhoun, *Sword of Wisdom: MacGregor Mathers and the Golden Dawn*, pp. 62–3.

498. Wright, *Narratives of Sorcery and Magic from the Most Authentic Sources*, i, p. 1.

499. Ibid., i, p. 2.

23. THE THREE CROWNS

500. This dream took place overnight Wednesday/Thursday, 14/15 August 2002 while Sue and I were in Virginia Beach, VA, USA.

501. Van Buren, *The Secret of the Illuminati*, p. 99.

502. See Ibid., pp. 98–116 for a full pictorial account of the carvings and reliefs in Bourges commissioned by Jacques Coeur.

503. Schaff, *History of the Christian Church: The Swiss Reformation*, vol. ii, p. 608.

504. The feast of St Roseline is also celebrated on 11 June and 16 October in some Catholic *Acta SS* ('Lives of Saints').

505. See Michell, *At the Centre of the World*, p. 40, for an account of Bourges as the centre of France. A Roman pillar said to mark the absolute centre of the country can be seen in the town of Bruère-Allichamps, some 19 kilometres (12 miles) from Bourges.

506. Ibid., pp. 105–27. See also Broadhurst and Miller, *The Dance of the Dragon*, for a brilliant narrative on the St Michael-Apollo axis.

507. *The Anglo-Saxon Chronicle*, trans. G. N. Garmonsway, A & E 571.

508. Ibid., A & E 777 [779].

509. Ibid., A & E 755 [757].

510. This first visit to Benson and Nuffield took place on Wednesday, 28 August 2002, although the account is combined with a second visit made with Richard on Saturday, 7 September 2002.

511. This conversation between Richard and me took place on Monday, 9 September 2002.

512. Gray, *Tales of Old Essex*, pp. 27–31.

513. This psychic session took place on Tuesday, 3 September 2002.

514. Robert Charles Hope, *The Legendary Lore of the Holy Wells of England*, s.v. 'Binsey', pp. 124–6.

515. Ibid.

516. Ibid., p. 113 pl. 8.

517. See the index of saints given in Ibid., pp. 214–5.

518. 'The Dream of Maxen Wledig', in Guest, *The Mabinogion*.

24. ANGEL OF THE PIT

519. Carroll, *Alice's Adventures in Wonderland*, pp. 108–9.

520. I was first introduced to this story by Caroline Wise on Monday, 9 September 2002.

521. 'Lludd and Llevelys' in Guest.

522. Trubshaw, *Mercian Mysteries* 13 (November 1992), pp. 8–10.

523. Ibid.

524. Ibid.

525. Voragine, *The Golden Legend of Jacobus de Voragine*, s.v. 'June 24, the Nativity of John the Baptist', p. 326.

526. Ibid.

527. Following earlier images and impressions about the Order of the Apocalypse, I was able to check them out after another psychic session on Thursday, 8 August 2002.

528. Waite, *An Encyclopaedia of Freemasonry*, ii, s.v. 'Apocalypse, Order of the', p. 141.

529. Mackenzie, *The Royal Masonic Cyclopaedia*, s.v. 'Apocalypse, Order of the', p. 46.

530. Waite, s.v., 'Apocalypse, Order of the', p. 141.

531. The first information about the Emperors of the East and West emerged during a psychic session on Thursday, 3 October 2002.

532. *Gould's History of Freemasonry Throughout the World*, iv, pp. 303, 357.

533. Rev. 9:11, 20:1–3.

534. See Macoy, *A Dictionary of Freemasonry*, s.v. 'Knights of the East and West', pp. 200–1. For the philosophic readings of the degree see Pike, *Morals and Dogma of the Ancient and Accepted Scottish Rite of Freemasonry*, pp. 246–75.

535. Macoy, s.v. 'Knights of the East and West', pp. 200–1.

25. LIGHT AND DARKNESS

536. This psychic session took place on Thursday, 3 October 2002.
537. This was not the first occasion we went to St Margaret's church, Binsey. Sue, Richard and I paid it a cursory visit during a perambulation of Oxfordshire sites on Saturday, 7 September 2002. It was then that we introduced it to the Marian Chalice. We did not take it with us when we returned on Saturday, 19 October, even though I now realise that this had been intended all along. However, luckily this did not spoil the purpose or outcome of the quest, since we were able to visualise it instead.

26. DESCENT OF THE DIVINE

538. Although there was some indication of this castle scene from Richard's mind on the night in question, it did not fully develop until Sunday/Monday, 29/30 December 2002. However, it was worth putting in at this point in the story, just to let you know that the Head of God did eventually reach its final destination! As to what happened after that, you'll have to wait, I'm afraid!

INDEX